Out of School

WILEY SERIES ON STUDIES IN CHILD PSYCHIATRY

Series Editor
Michael Rutter
Institute of Psychiatry
London

The First Year of Life
Psychological and Medical Implication of Early Experience
Edited by
David Shaffer and Judy Dunn

Out of School
Modern Perspectives in Truancy and School Refusal
Edited by
Lionel Hersov and Ian Berg

Further titles in preparation

Out of School

Modern Perspectives in Truancy and School Refusal

Edited by
Lionel Hersov, M.D., F.R.C.P., F.R.C.Psych., D.P.M.
Consultant Psychiatrist
Children's and Adolescent's Department
The Bethlem Royal and the Maudsley Hospital
London

Senior Lecturer and Honorary Consultant in Psychological Medicine
The Royal Postgraduate Medical School and Hammersmith Hospital
London

and

Ian Berg, M.D., F.R.C.P.E., F.R.C.Psych., D.P.M.
Consultant in Child and Adolescent Psychiatry
Leeds Area Health Authority (Teaching) and
Yorkshire Regional Health Authority

Senior Clinical Lecturer, Department of Psychiatry
University of Leeds
Leeds

JOHN WILEY & SONS
Chichester · New York · Brisbane · Toronto

British Library Cataloguing in Publication Data:

Out of school.—(Wiley series on studies in
  child psychiatry).
  1. School attendance—Psychological aspects
  I. Hersov, Lionel Abraham
  II. Berg, Ian
  371.5   LB3081   79–41725

ISBN 0 471 27743 6

Phototypeset by Dobbie Typesetting Service, Plymouth, Devon, England
and printed in the United States of America.

Contributors

DAVID BAUER, Ph.D.,

Associate Professor, California State University, Chico, California 95929

IAN BERG, M.D., F.R.C.P.(Edin)., F.R.C.Psych., D.P.M.,

Consultant in Child and Adolescent Psychiatry, Leeds Area Health Authority (Teaching), and Yorkshire Regional Health Authority.

Senior Clinical Lecturer, University of Leeds, Department of Psychiatry, 15 Hyde Terrace, Leeds LS2 9ET

RONALD CLARKE, M.A., Ph.D.,

Senior Principal Research Officer, The Home Office Research Unit, Romney House, Marsham Street, London SW1P 3DY

LEON EISENBERG, M.D.,

Maude and Lilian Presley Professor of Psychiatry, Harvard Medical School, Boston, Massachusetts 02115

DAVID FARRINGTON, M.A., Ph.D.,

Lecturer in Criminology, University of Cambridge, Institute of Criminology, 7 West Road, Cambridge CB3 9DT

KEN FOGELMAN, B.A.,

Principal Research Officer, National Children's Bureau, 8 Wakley Street, London EC1

DAVID GALLOWAY, M.A., M.Sc.,

Director, Sheffield School and Home Project, 9 Newbould Lane, Sheffield S10 2PJ

RACHEL GITTELMAN-KLEIN,   *Psychologist, Research Department, Hillside*
   Ph.D.,   *Hospital, 75–59 263rd Street, Glen Oaks,*
                                 New York 11004

GRACE GRAY, B.A.,   *Research Worker, Department of Child and*
                                 Adolescent Psychiatry, Institute of Psychiatry,
                                 University of London, Denmark Hill, London
                                 SE5 8AF

LIONEL HERSOV, M.D.,   *Consultant Psychiatrist, Children's and*
   F.R.C.P.(Lond)., F.R.C.Psych., *Adolescents' Department, The Bethlem Royal*
   D.P.M.   *and The Maudsley Hospital, Denmark Hill,*
                                 London SE5 8AZ

                                 Honorary Consultant in Psychological
                                 Medicine, Royal Post Graduate Medical
                                 School and Hammersmith Hospital, Du Cane
                                 Road, London W12 0HS

ANNE JONES, B.A.,   *Headmistress, Vauxhall Manor School,*
                                 Stannary Street, London SE11 4PT

DEE JONES, B.A.,   *Scientific Staff, Medical Research Council*
                                 Epidemiology Unit, Cardiff

DONALD KLEIN, M.D.,   *Director of Research, New York State Psy-*
                                 chiatry Institute, 722 West 168th Street, New
                                 York 10032

LYDIA LAMBERT, B.D.,   *Senior Research Officer, National Children's*
                                 Bureau, 8 Wakley Street, London EC1

MELVIN LEWIS, M.B., B.S.,   *Professor of Paediatrics and Psychiatry, and*
   F.R.C.Psych., D.C.H.,   *Director of Medical Studies, Yale University*
                                 Child Study Center, 333 Cedar Street, New
                                 Haven, Connecticut 06510

SHEILA MITCHELL, B.Sc., Ph.D.,   *Senior Lecturer, Department of Sociology,*
                                 University of Stirling, Stirling FK9 4LA

STEVEN MURGATROYD, B.A., *Senior Counsellor, Open University in Wales, Cardiff*

KATHRYN RATCLIFFE, Ph.D., *Assistant Professor of Sociology in Psychiatry, Department of Psychiatry, Washington University School of Medicine, 4940 Audubon Avenue, St. Louis, Missouri 63110*

DAVID REYNOLDS, B.A., *Lecturer in Social Administration, University College, Cardiff*

LEE ROBINS, Ph.D., *Professor of Sociology in Psychiatry, Department of Psychiatry, Washington University School of Medicine, 4940 Audubon Avenue, St. Louis, Missouri 63110*

MICHAEL RUTTER, M.D., F.R.C.P.(Lond)., F.R.C.Psych., D.P.M., *Professor of Child Psychiatry, Department of Child and Adolescent Psychiatry, Institute of Psychiatry, University of London, Denmark Hill, London SE5 8AF*

SELWYN ST. LEGER, M.B., M.Sc., F.S.F., *Scientific Staff, Medical Research Council Epidemiology Unit, Cardiff*

MICHAEL SHEPHERD, D.M., F.R.C.P.(Lond), F.R.C.Psych., *Professor of Epidemiological Psychiatry, Institute of Psychiatry, University of London, Denmark Hill, London SE5 8AF*

ALAN SMITH, M.Sc., *Lecturer, Biometrics Unit, Institute of Psychiatry, University of London, Denmark Hill, London SE5 8AF*

ALAN TIBBENHAM, B.A., Ph.D., *Research Officer, National Children's Bureau, 8 Wakley Street, London EC1*

JUDY TRESEDER, M.A., *Principal Social Worker, Children and Adolescent's Department, The Bethlem Royal and Maudsley Hospitals, Denmark Hill, London SE5 8AZ*

DAVID WALLER, M.D., *Instructor in Psychiatry, Harvard Medical School.*

Assistant in Psychiatry, The Children's Hospital Medical Center, 300 Longwood Avenue, Boston, Massachusetts 02115

WILLIAM YULE, Ph.D., M.A., Dip.Psych., *Senior Lecturer in the Psychology of Childhood and Adolescence, Institute of Psychiatry, University of London, Denmark Hill, London, SE5 8AF*

Principal Psychologist, The Bethlem Royal and Maudsley Hospitals, Denmark Hill, London SE5 8AZ

Series Preface

During recent years there has been a tremendous growth of research in both child development and child psychiatry. Research findings are beginning to modify clinical practice but to a considerable extent the fields of child development and of child psychiatry have remained surprisingly separate, with regrettably little cross fertilization. Much developmental research has not concerned itself with clinical issues, and studies of clinical syndromes have all too often been made within the narrow confines of a pathological condition approach with scant regard to developmental matters. The situation is rapidly changing but the results of clinical-developmental studies are often reported only by means of scattered papers in scientific journals. This series aims to bridge the gap between child development and clinical psychiatry by presenting reports of new findings, new ideas and new approaches in a book form which may be available to a wider readership.

The series includes reviews of specific topics, multi-authored volumes on a common theme, and accounts of specific pieces of research. However, in all cases the aim is to provide a clear, readable and interesting account of scientific findings in a way which makes explicit their relevance to clinical practice or social policy. It is hoped that the series will be of interest to both clinicians and researchers in the fields of child psychiatry, child psychology, psychiatric social work, social paediatrics and education — in short all concerned with the growing child and his problems.

Contents

Introduction

The Editors

Absence from school is a common problem encountered by teachers and others who work in the field of education, by doctors whether general practitioners, school medical officers, paediatricians or child and adolescent psychiatrists, by social workers who deal with young people and their families in a variety of circumstances, by psychologists who study and treat children and by magistrates, concerned with upholding the law requiring regular school attendance.

This book includes a number of contributions with different perspectives on the problem presented by failure to attend school. A broad epidemiological approach has been adopted by several contributors. Fogelman, Tibbenham, and Lambert report the features of absentees from school who were included in a longitudinal study of all children born in England, Scotland, and Wales in one week in 1958. Mitchell and Shepherd concentrate on the phenomenon of reluctance to go to school in a random sample of all children attending normal state schools in the county of Buckinghamshire in one year. Farrington describes the characteristics of truants in a prospective longitudinal survey of 411 youths who were first contacted when they were in the second forms of half a dozen junior schools in a working-class area of London and were followed-up until age 25. Robins and Ratcliffe outline the findings of a retro- spective longitudinal study of a sample of black schoolboys from schools in St Louis in the United States of America. Gray, Smith, and Rutter describe the employment records, in the first year after leaving school, of a sample of youngsters from an inner London borough who had been studied both at primary and secondary school.

Other writers adopt a more clinical point of view, Waller and Eisenberg look at the problem of school refusal and similar difficulties masquerading as physical illness. Berg deals with school refusal affecting children of secondary school age. Gittelman-Klein and Klein devote about half of their contribution to an account of separation anxiety as seen by the clinician. Galloway includes a description of the features of persistent absentees identified in a number of Sheffield schools.

1

A psychological or sociological point of view characterizes other chapters. Bauer discusses children's fears in developmental terms in so far as they affect school attendance. Reynolds confines his attention to the way in which schools contribute to the occurrence of absenteeism. Clarke discusses the analogous problem of absconding from boarding schools for children In Care and provides evidence for a particular behavioural hypothesis to explain it.

The remaining chapters are concerned with how school attendance problems can be managed. In respect of school refusal as a clinical problem, Lewis describes the approach of a psychoanalytically-oriented child psychiatrist, Yule, Hersov, and Treseder cover the use of behaviour therapy techniques, Gittelman-Klein and Klein present some evidence that tricyclic anti-depressent drugs may help and Hersov writes about the role of hospital day and inpatient units in treatment. The management of school attendance problems in a wider context is discussed by Galloway who outlines the way in which community based services can help to cope with these difficulties. Berg indicates the legal aspects of unjustified absence from school and how they might be used to assist in reducing absenteeism. Jones looks at truancy in its widest sense as a challenge to a large secondary school.

Some chapters are based on original work carried out by the writers. A few contributions describe studies not previously published elsewhere. This applies to Farrington's chapter, that of Fogelman, Tibbenham, and Lambert, the contribution of Robins and Ratcliffe and to the chapter by Gray, Smith, and Rutter. Others give authors an opportunity to review their previous reports and discuss them in the light of how they are currently reviewing the problem. Yule, Hersov, and Treseder provide a review of literature on the behavioural treatment of school refusal which has not been previously attempted.

The contents raise several issues which will be briefly mentioned.

DEFINITIONS

The term *truancy*, when narrowly defined, applies to unjustifiable absence from school without the parent's knowledge or approval. Absence is of course justified when there is a physical illness which makes it unwise for a child to be at school. Occasional family holidays are also a legitimate excuse for absence. As Fogelman and his colleagues point out in their chapter, and as Robins and Ratcliffe's contribution illustrates, *truancy* is in fact sometimes used more loosely to refer to absence from school without an acceptable reason, whether or not the parents know and approve.

The clinical view of *truancy* is that of staying off school as one of several kinds of antisocial behaviour such as stealing, lying, destructiveness, and excessive fighting. Associated educational difficulties, often present as well, make the tendency to stay away from school comprehensible. The fact of the parents not being aware of their child's absence, focusses the problem squarely on the child's deviant conduct. It is of interest that the studies showing this deal exclusively or predominantly with boys. The association between truancy, broadly defined, and antisocial conduct in girls is less well-established; yet the problem of truancy is almost as frequent in girls as boys. Whether girls express their antisocial tendencies predominantly by staying off school or whether truancy, especially in girls, may reflect a combination of factors including parental irresponsibility, conduct disorders, social pathology, and even neurotic tendencies are questions raised in this book especially in Galloway's chapter. The fact that absenteeism other than typical school refusal is associated with evidence of neurotic symptoms emerges from the contributions of Farrington, of Berg, and of Mitchell and Shepherd.

School refusal and the closely-related diagnostic label, *school phobia*, refer to a syndrome the main features of which are: unwillingness to attend school, staying home when not at school, parents who know about and disapprove of their child's absence, and severe emotional upset at the prospect of having to attend. Although many of the children who show this syndrome have additional symptoms of emotional disturbance and problems of adjustment, some have no other signs of psychiatric disorder. The chapters of this book devoted to the school refusal syndrome indicate some other criteria, in addition to those given above, that have been used to define it. The finding that children who refuse to go to school tend not to be antisocial in their behaviour is made one of the defining characteristics by Berg in the chapter on school refusal in early adolescence.

It will, however, be appreciated that a much more limited conception of this disorder is put forward by Waller and Eisenberg and by Gittelman-Klein and Klein. The central importance of so-called separation anxiety, that is fears of being away from mother, is emphasized by these authors. Although parents may, on the surface, seem to be insisting on normal school attendance, the child with severe separation anxiety may surreptitiously be encouraged to remain in the security of home by an overprotective mother. A different view emerges from the chapter devoted to behavioural methods used in the management of school refusal by Yule and his colleagues. They emphasize the importance of the parents' inability to provide firm support, which would help a neurotic child to overcome his aversion to school. In either case some lack of parental guidance is seen as a defining characteristic of school refusal.

AGE, SEX, AND SOCIAL CLASS

The epidemiological contributions to this book clearly demonstrate the importance of age, sex, and social background in determining the prevalence of unjustifiable absence from school. The problem is particularly common in the last year or two of compulsory schooling and predominantly affects children from poor homes. The possibility that boys and girls who stay off school without adequate reason may differ in some respects has already been mentioned, in so far as truancy is closely associated with antisocial behaviour in boys.

That the increased independence and self-reliance which come about as the child gets older are, in themselves, relevant, is suggested by the findings of Mitchell and Shepherd that reluctance to attend school is only reflected in actual absence over the age of ten. Fogelman, Tibbenham, and Lambert, who present the results of the National Child Development Study at age 16 for the first time in relation to truancy, argue that the problem may often be a social phenomenon linked to a particular situation of young men from disadvantaged home backgrounds whose interests are more directed towards work than school.

SCHOOL

It is still uncertain to what extent factors within the school contribute to the problem of truancy. On the one hand, Reynolds describes an investigation which indicates that school variables are important determinants of absenteeism. However, Farrington, although his study showed similar findings in this respect to those of Reynolds, is able to explain differences between schools in truancy rates by the effect of selective intake of previously antisocial youngsters into certain schools. Likewise, Fogelman and his colleagues do not consider that the variables measuring features of schools, recorded in the National Child Development Study, to be important in the production of truancy. Evidence just coming out, only recently available for contributors to this book to comment on, and which concerns a detailed investigation of secondary schools in London, indicates that the characteristics of schools do make an important contribution to children's problems including truancy. (*15000 HOURS — Secondary Schools and Their Effects on Children*, 1979, by Michael Rutter, Barbara Maughan, Peter Mortimore, and Janet Ouston.)

Clarke's chapter also makes a strong case for the importance of factors within schools in determining truancy, in so far as the analogous problem of absconding from boarding schools catering for children in Care is shown to be produced by environmental factors rather than the attributes of individuals.

However, some attributes of children may still contribute to the production of truancy. Fogelman and his colleagues in their chapter report the relationship between absence from school and educational backwardness that emerged in the National Child Development Study. Mitchell and Shepherd also report an association between poor attainment and reluctance to go to school. It is not clear whether the lack of attainment usually causes absenteeism or the other way round.

A similar difficulty arises in connection with disruptive behaviour in class which is commonly associated with truancy. Farrington says that disruptiveness appeared to precede truancy in the prospective investigation he describes, whereas Robins and Ratcliffe found that truancy is an early predictor of later disruptive conduct in school.

PSYCHIATRIC DISTURBANCE

The chapters devoted to school refusal make it evident that the majority of the children who are identified as suffering from this condition have neurotic disorders. It is also clear from the contributions concerned with the much larger problem of truancy, that conduct disorders are frequently associated with this problem, especially in boys. To a considerable extent the links between school refusal and emotional problems of a neurotic kind and between truancy and antisocial difficulties are reinforced by the definitions of school attendance problems that are employed.

Several contributions to this book suggest that neurotic disturbances are more often found in association with truancy than would be expected. Thus psychiatric problems of a neurotic type may be important in truancy as well as in school refusal. It will be seen that Mitchell and Shepherd found that children in the normal school population, who disliked going to school, were more likely to have symptoms suggestive of a neurotic disorder. Similarly, in the longitudinal survey by Farrington, the boys who truanted showed an excessive tendency to have neurotic symptoms such as anxiety, misery, neurasthenia, and social isolation. In the chapter on Truancy and the Law it will be seen that children brought to court for failure to attend school tend to have an excess of neurotic features. Galloway's findings suggest that neurotic problems may make a significant contribution to persistent absenteeism without the affected youngsters necessarily being identified and treated as school refusers. In addition, the chapter by Waller and Eisenberg indicates the extent to which neurotically disturbed children are kept off school by over-protective parents who allow them to masquerade as physically ill to a greater extent than the limitations imposed by any actual disease.

It would therefore appear that neurotic disorders may be factors in a whole variety of school attendance problems that are not considered to be instances of school refusal as well as in those that are.

OUTCOME

A connection between school attendance problems and difficulties later on in early adult life is referred to in four of the chapters. Indeed it is the main concern of Gray, Smith, and Rutter's chapter on school attendance and the first year of employment. School refusal can be followed by problems in adult life. Berg's chapter on school refusal in early adolescence indicates this and reports that neurotic disturbances, sometimes with agoraphobic symptoms, characterize the adult difficulties. Persistent truancy in boys appears to be a predictor of adult deviance. Both Robins and Ratcliffe, who write from America, and Farrington, who works in Britain, come to this conclusion. The more frequent absenteeism affecting youngsters in their last year or so in secondary school is probably less pathological. This is suggested by Fogelman, Tibbenham and Lambert who report on the National Child Development Study. Similar findings emerge from the longitudinal study of young people at school in inner London whose subsequent work records were investigated by Gray, Smith and Rutter. At least in the short-term, the main effect of absenteeism in the final year of compulsory schooling was the low level of scholastic attainment and the limitations this placed on the kind of employment that could be found.

MANAGEMENT

It will be apparent from reading the section of the book devoted to the treatment of school refusal that this problem is managed clinically using the full range of available facilities. It will also be evident that although a wide variety of management techniques are used, hardly any evaluative studies have been carried out to establish their relative effectiveness.

The chapters concerned with the management of truancy illustrate the important role of community-based services in handling the problem as compared with hospital clinics.

In both types of school attendance problem there is an understandable emphasis on securing an early return to normal school attendance since this should have the effect of eliminating the adverse consequences of being away.

However, particularly in school refusal, the long-term outcome may depend less on absenteeism than on associated neurotic disturbances. The contributions of Lewis, concerned with psychotherapy, of Hersov describing day-patient and inpatient treatment, and of Yule, Hersov, and Treseder, dealing with behavioural methods, indicate the efforts made to treat emotional difficulties in general rather than those only connected with going back to school.

Out of School
Edited by L. Hersov and I. Berg
© 1980, John Wiley & Sons, Ltd.

Chapter 1

Reluctance to go to School

Sheila Mitchell and Michael Shepherd

Although reluctance to go to school has been the object of public awareness since at least the end of the sixteenth century, when Shakespeare refers to 'the whining school-boy with his satchel and shining morning face creeping like a snail unwillingly to school' (*As You Like It*, Act II), surprisingly little attention has been given to more scientific study of the phenomenon. In general, studies of pupil's attitudes are relatively scarce so that in a recent comprehensive and widely defined over-view Wagner (1975) could only cite eighty relevant reports including those which related to very specific attitudes (for example, to mathematics) and those which related to college students rather than school-children. Studies which relate expressed verbal attitudes to actual behaviour such as school attendance are very rare indeed — an omission that seems peculiarly remiss when one considers the current preoccupation of British Government departments and teachers' associations with the phenomena of truancy and indiscipline in schools, each of which is presented in the media as a reflection of unfavourable pupil attitudes.

Whether such an assumption is justified is, however, a point which requires consideration. In their definition of attitude, Secord and Backman (1964) point out that the term relates to 'certain regularities of an individual's feelings, thoughts and *predispositions to act* towards some aspect of his environment' (Author's italics). In other terms the concept of attitude may be regarded as including what an individual believes himself to 'know' about something, what he feels and what he is inclined to do about it. What the individual actually does, however, will be a function not only of his own predispositions but also of other external factors which impose constraints limiting the overt expression of his attitudes. School attendance in Britain (and in most, if not all, countries of the developed world) is compulsory. Failure to attend provokes the use of penal sanctions against the pupil and/or against his parents for failing to ensure that he attends. In view of this the child who 'knows' he does not like school or some aspect of it, and whose feeling of reluctance to attend is very strong, may, nevertheless be constrained by other

7

people, particularly his parents, into making regular appearances there.

Poor attendance may reflect adverse attitudes to school and constitute the behavioural component of these attitudes (though this has not yet been empirically demonstrated). Regular attendance, by contrast, can by no means be seen as implying the converse, i.e. highly positive attitudes.

That problems of poor attendance exist has been established by recent government enquiries. Thus, all secondary and middle schools in England and Wales were asked by the Department of Education and Science to submit data for all pupils who were absent from school for all or part of the day on Thursday 17th January 1974. These showed that 9.9 per cent of pupils were absent and that the schools could find no legitimate reason for the absence of 22.7 per cent of these children (i.e., 2.2 per cent of all pupils) (Hansard, 25th July 1974). In Scotland, the investigation over a six weeks period from 12 January to 20 February 1976 of a stratified random sample of secondary schools carried out on behalf of the Scottish Education Department's committee of inquiry into Truancy and Indiscipline in Schools (the Pack Report) showed that 15 per cent of both boys and girls had absented themselves without acceptable explanation on at least one occasion; 1.6 per cent of boys and 1.1 per cent of girls had been absent without adequate explanation for at least half of the 6 week period (Scottish Education Department, 1977) (See Chapter 2).

Such studies would indicate the presence in (or rather absence from) our schools of substantial numbers of disaffected scholars who are 'voting with their feet' by their failure to attend. It would, however, be overly facile to suggest that there is a simple one-to-one relationship between unfavourable attitude to school and non-attendance. We can, however, say something about the attitudes to school of pupils in general, including those who are good attenders, from the results of an empirical study carried out some years ago (Mitchell and Shepherd, 1967). Many changes in school organization and pupil attitudes have taken place since that time — a time when truancy was relatively rare in the area studied and when 'pupil power' was not yet heard of. Nevertheless, the study has not yet been superseded and the findings may be recalled to provide a basis for discussion.

THE SURVEY

The information was obtained as part of a more extensive survey carried out in Buckinghamshire, a county situated to the north of London and chosen because it was fairly typical of Southern England. It contained a socially mixed population ranging from the inhabitants of still predominantly agricultural villages to rehoused Londoners transferred to new 'overspill' estates and privately housed commuters to London offices; industry ranged from brick-making and railway locomotive construction to furniture making, food production and light engineering. Against this background our study was designed to obtain information about the age and sex distribution of various types of behavioural and emotional problems in a random sample of 'normal' children of school age and to examine the relationship between atypical items of behaviour and other aspects of the child's environment, both at home and at school. The relevant information was obtained by questionnaires sent to the teachers and parents of a ten per cent random sample of all children aged between five and fifteen years of age who were attending local authority schools in the county in 1961. Completed questionnaires were received from the parents of 93 per cent of the children (i.e. approximately 6300) and the teachers of 97 per cent (approximately 6600). Completed forms from both teacher and parent were available for 90 per cent (6100 children).

These questionnaires are described in detail elsewhere (Shepherd, Oppenheim, and Mitchell, 1971). The parents were asked to describe their children in terms of about eighty types of behaviour, including that with which we are now concerned, i.e. a question in which parents were asked to underline the most appropriate description of their child's reaction to school from among the following three sentences:

Likes school very much

Likes school about as much as most children

Dislikes going to school.

Results showed that slighly more than one third of the children were said to 'like school very much' (30 per cent of boys, 40 per cent of girls), while only 5 per cent disliked going. The bulk of the sample (63 per cent of boys, 40 per cent of girls), as might be expected, fell into the intermediate category. This raises two related methodological points which are best dealt with before proceeding to look at the results in more detail.

First, the information was obtained at second hand, i.e. we did not ask the child how he felt about school, we asked his parents to infer his feelings in the light of their own observations of his remarks and actions. It may be asked whether such inferences are necessarily accurate. Do parents know how their children feel about school? Again, hard evidence is difficult to educe but by virtue of her role in the family the mother is in an excellent position to obtain clues directly or indirectly (e.g. through bad temper, poor appetite, disturbed sleep) if all is not well with the child's world. Her accuracy of observation is certainly accepted in clinical practice (where, particularly with pre-adolescent children, she, rather than the child, is usually the main informant) and has been shown to be well substantiated in empirical studies such as that of Lapouse and Monk (1959).

This brings us to the second, and perhaps more important, problem. Parents, in answering the relevant item in our questionnaire were not merely being asked to *describe*, they were being asked to *interpret* the child's behaviour and comments about school in the light of their view of children as a generality

and what was, or was not, a 'normal' attitude to school and teachers. Some
parents, particularly those who disliked school themselves, might feel that a
considerable amount of antipathy to educational procedures was quite
'normal' and so opt for the middle category in respect of a child whose
reactions might cause a mother with more favourable expectations to
underline 'Dislikes going to school'. There may therefore be some overlap
between categories in so far as the childrens' 'real' attitudes are concerned,
and inclusion in the unfavourable category should be taken as indicating that
the reactions of the children concerned were strong enough to be considered
atypical by their own family standards.

The second questionnaire, which was completed by the child's form-teacher,
covered attainment, attendance and behaviour in class, though a 'Yes'-'No'
format rather than a three-point system was used for the purpose.

RESEARCH FINDINGS

DISLIKE OF SCHOOL

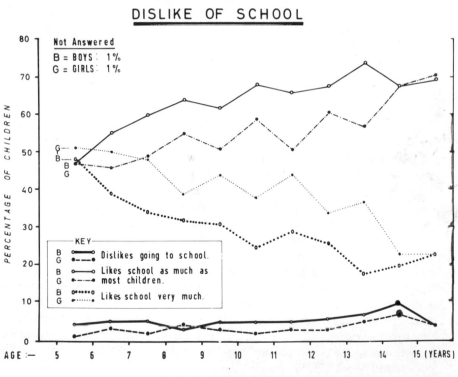

Figure 1. Dislike of school

Figure 1 presents a detailed picture of the responses analysed by age and sex
which shows that though markedly positive attitudes to school are related both

to age and sex, as has been shown by other researchers (for example, Wisenthal, 1965; Kniveton, 1969; Sharples, 1969; Berk, Rose, and Stewart, 1970, and Barker-Lunn, 1972), *dislike of school*, while slightly more prevalent among boys in all but one of the age groups, is little affected by age. As is shown clearly in Figure 1, the proportion of children who were said to dislike school remained practically constant at 5 per cent of boys and 3 per cent of girls in all age groups from five to twelve years old, before rising slightly in each sex. In view of the established positive associations between persistent unjustified absence and age (Galloway, 1976; Scottish Education Department, 1977; Mitchell, 1972) this raises some interesting issues concerning the relationship between absence and attitudes to school. In our own study we expected that the children said to dislike school might be absent more frequently than those whose attitudes were more favourable and, among the older children (i.e. those more than ten years old), this relationship did exist (see Table 1).

Table 1. Reaction to school by number of school sessions lost through absence in the previous term, among children in the 11–15 years age group

Parental assessment of child's reaction to school	Number of half-day sessions absent in previous full-term							
	Boys				Girls			
	0	1–4	5–10	11+	0	1–4	5–10	11+
Likes school very much	97	70	50	58	135	105	84	101
	(35%)	(25%)	(18%)	(21%)	(32%)	(25%)	(20%)	(24%)
Likes school as much as most	211	210	117	226	180	160	162	238
	(26%)	(25%)	(21%)	(27%)	(24%)	(22%)	(22%)	(32%)
Dislikes going to school	10	20	18	34	4	13	13	33
	(12%)	(24%)	(22%)	(41%)	(6%)	(21%)	(21%)	(52%)

For each sex separately, by χ^2 test, $p < 0.001$.

Thus, among the boys aged eleven to fifteen full attendance during the previous term occurred among only 12 per cent of those who disliked going to school compared with 35 per cent of those who liked it very much. At the other extreme 41 per cent of the disaffected boys had been absent for more than ten sessions, about twice as high a proportion as among the enthusiasts and about half as many again as occurred among boys in the middle category. Among the girls, as Table 1 shows, the relationship was even more marked, with only 6 per cent of those who disliked school having achieved a perfect attendance record.

In considering these results, it must be noted, we are referring to *all* absences not merely those which are unjustified and, in fact, all but a few of the absences appeared to be credited to illness. Among the younger children (aged five to ten), however, there was no significant association between attitude and attendance, though the little girls who disliked school were still less likely to achieve full attendance (only 7 per cent) than were those in more favourable attitude categories (19 per cent in each case). Among the boys aged less than eleven years absence remained remarkably constant regardless of attitude, with 20–22 per cent without absence and 40 per cent losing more than ten half-day sessions.

Who were these children who disliked going to school? Clearly it was feasible to set up many hypotheses concerning their personality, their family background and their school experiences and some of these could be tested using our existing data.

One obvious hypothesis was that the children who disliked school might be the least successful academically. Unfortunately, owing to the large number of schools attended by the survey children, it was not possible to obtain overall standards of comparison. Teachers had, however, provided us with an impression of the child's standard of attainment relative to others of the same age attending the same type of school and this provided an indication of how each child was coping in his or her own school setting: this is, after all, of most direct importance to the child in his everyday school experiences. On this basis a clear association between attitude and attainment was demonstrated (see Table 2). Among the children who disliked going to school, more than half the boys and more than two-fifths of the girls were placed as 'below average' by their teachers, more than twice as high a proportion as was found among those who liked school very much.

With regard to *behaviour* in school only two items discriminated between the children who disliked school and their more favourably disposed peers. The one which showed the most consistent relationship to attitude was, as perhaps might be expected, 'Not interested in school work'. Such lack of interest was reported of only 2 per cent of girls and 3 per cent of boys who liked school very much and 5 and 8 per cent respectively of those who liked school as much as most children. Among the children who disliked school, however, 21 per cent of boys, and 12 per cent of girls fell into the 'uninterested' category, a marked and statistically significant difference (χ^2 test, $p < 0.01$).

Among the boys, there was also a highly significant ($p < 0.001$) association between reaction to school and the exhibition of uncooperative behaviour while there. According to the teachers 9 per cent of the boys who disliked going to school were seen as 'Uncooperative in class' compared with only 2 per cent of the favourable, and 4 per cent of the intermediate groups. Girls over ten years of age were also more likely to be noted as 'uncooperative' if they disliked school (5 per cent compared with 1 and 2 per cent of the favourable and intermediate groups respectively) but this difference was not statistically significant. Among the younger girls there was no difference at all, with the proportion rated uncooperative remaining at a steady 2 per cent.

Table 2. Reaction to school by teachers' rating of general attainment level

Level of attainment relative to others of the same age attending the same type of school	Boys					
	Likes school very much		Likes school as much as most children		Dislikes going to school	
	No.	%	No.	%	No.	%
Above average	274	30	284	15	10	6
Average	421	47	904	48	68	40
Below average	205	23	697	37	86	54
Total	900	100%	1,885	100%	159	100%

Significance of association by χ^2 test $\qquad p < 0.001$

Level of attainment relative to others of the same age attending the same type of school	Girls					
	Likes school very much		Likes school as much as most children		Dislikes going to school	
	No.	%	No.	%	No.	%
Above average	375	32	271	17	10	10
Average	605	52	881	55	49	48
Below average	193	16	443	28	44	43
Total	1,173	100%	1,595	100%	103	100%

Significance of association by χ^2 test $\qquad p < 0.001$

No other individual items of behaviour were found to relate to feelings about school but, for the boys, there was a significant association ($p < 0.01$) with the *total number of adverse behavioural items underlined by teachers*. Thus, in the older age group (aged eleven to fifteen) 55 per cent of boys who disliked school had at least one behavioural item underlined, compared with 27 per cent of those who liked school very much and 33 per cent of those who liked it as much as most children. Among the younger boys (i.e., ten or younger) 67 per cent of those who disliked school had at least one item underlined, compared with 47 and 51 per cent respectively in the other two groups. Among the girls, there was no significant association between reported reaction to school and the number of behaviour items underlined by teachers, though the trend was still visible among those over eleven years of age. This suggests that, among girls, dislike of school does not manifest itself so obviously in actual behaviour as it does among boys, though it must also be stressed that the existence of overt lack of cooperation in class applied to only a small minority of the children of either sex who disliked school.

It might also be expected that children who did not like going to school would exhibit more signs of anxiety and stress in their home environment and, perhaps, a greater tendency to psychosomatic ailments. To some extent, this appeared to be true. Thus they were described by their parents as 'Often seems worried, worries about many things' in 14 per cent of cases — three times the proportion found among the other children (4 per cent). The group who disliked school were also more likely to complain of headaches (7 per cent suffered at least once a week compared with 3 per cent of the other children) and stomach pains (13 per cent of girls of all ages and 9 per cent of boys over ten years of age complained of pain at least once in two weeks compared with 3 per cent of other children).

So far we have only considered the child as an individual interacting with the school environment. It could be suggested, however, that this gives a false view — that the child is in fact a product of a particular type of social environment which may predetermine his attitudes to school. This obviously opens up a very wide field of enquiry and our investigation only permitted us to examine some of the more objective indices of family background: the child's position in the family, the family size, and the occupational status of the family head. None of these showed any consistent relationship to the child's reaction to school.

With regard to the family size girls who were only children were significantly *less* likely ($p < 0.05$) to dislike going to school than were those with siblings but there was no increase in the proportion disliking school as number of siblings increased. As for ordinal position, the girls again showed no variation but, among the boys with siblings, the last-born were significantly more likely to be seen as disliking school (7 per cent) than were those with younger brothers and sisters (4 per cent).

The type of job in which the child's father was employed showed some relationship to dislike of school among the boys where there was a disproportionately high representation of boys with fathers who were in manual occupations and, in particular, of those whose fathers were in semi- or unskilled occupations: these accounted for 39 per cent of boys disliking school but only 27 per cent of other boys.

Among the girls (see Table 3) the group who liked school very much tended to over-represent those whose fathers were in white collar jobs, but the girls who disliked school appeared to come from much the same socio-economic background as the intermediate category.

The results so far presented raise many issues which require further discussion. First, there is the question of the relationship between a perceived attitude towards school (dislike) and the behavioural phenomena of school refusal and truancy to which the rest of this book is devoted. Clearly the investigation so far reported could cast little light on this issue. Additional information was, however, available as the result of interviews which were carried out to consider why some children were referred to Child Guidance Clinics while others were not (Shepherd *et al.*, 1971). In this investigation, selected children from the general survey were used to form the 'non-referred' group and their parent(s) interviewed to obtain further information. Among these children were several who were said to dislike school and the parents' descriptions of their behaviour and the situation as they see it provides relevant material.

Table 3. Relationship between the child's reaction to school and the occupational status of the father

Father's occupational status (Hall-Jones' scale)	Child's reaction to school					
	Likes school very much		Likes school as much as most children		Dislikes going to school	
	Boys	Girls	Boys	Girls	Boys	Girls
1,2,3 Professional, managerial, executive, higher grade/ supervisory	214	311	371	317	21	20
4,5(a) Supervisory, lower grade and routine non-manual	140	175	277	239	16	16
Total non-manual (No.)	354	486	648	556	37	36
(%)	40%	42%	35%	35%	24%	35%
5(b) Skilled manual	296	388	711	582	58	45
6,7 Semi-skilled and routine manual	235	283	518	444	61	22
Total manual (No.)	531	671	1,229	1,026	119	67
(%)	60%	58%	65%	65%	76%	65%

Case histories

Adam (aged 9 years). When he first started school he had liked it very much and had been something of a teacher's pet. On transfer to Junior school, however, he found a changed situation in which he was no longer allowed to 'help' in class and as a result developed a great dislike of school and for the whole year used to cry silently every morning when it was time for him to go. When he moved to a different class, with a different teacher at the beginning of the following year, he seemed to become more cheerful about going.

Barbara (aged 12 years). When she started school at five she vomited daily before going to school and sometimes during the day as well (so that a bowl was placed beside her in the classroom for that purpose). After a little time this vomiting abated but it returned on transfer to secondary school when she was eleven, and once again she was sick every morning before going to school. Having attended a fairly small primary school she found it difficult to establish relationships in a large secondary school.

Colin (aged 12 years). He hated school because of teasing by his fellow pupils. When he was younger he had been decidedly plump and was taunted by his classmates because of this. Now, though he was no longer fat, he was still very self-conscious about his body and hated having showers and baths at schools because the other boys 'pushed him about'. Recently he had played truant several times, leaving and returning home at the usual times but never reaching school and just hanging about by the river. The school described him as very shy with other children, anxious and withdrawn, and as below average in attainment.

David (aged 10 years). He had always disliked going to school. Every morning he went off looking very woe-begone and tearful and sometimes looking so ill that neighbours had told his mother she should keep him at home. Sometimes he vomited in the mornings and often could not eat his breakfast, but unless he had a temperature, he was compelled to go and had only missed 7/106 possible attendances in the previous term. Once he actually arrived at school he appeared to recover. He was near the top of his teaching group which was the lowest of five streams and the school described him as crying and worrying more than most children.

Frank (aged 14 years). He had presented no troubles of adjustment at Infant School but from the time he went to Junior School at seven the picture changed. He often complained of aches and pains when it was time to go to school — one day it would be toothache, the next time a headache or abdominal pain. By the time he was eleven, such complaints were a daily occurrence. Even when he was not complaining that he was unwell he was very averse to going to school and daily had to be escorted there, crying, by his mother. If she left him before he was safely inside school, he would turn round and run home again. This ceased when he moved to secondary school and by the time he was fourteen he had lost all his pains and went off to school without any fuss; he liked his teachers and fellow pupils though he was still unenthusiastic about school as an institution. His attendance was, however, slightly irregular according to his school and he was thought, correctly, to lack interest in his school work.

Gwen (aged 15 years). She had never liked school much but had never made a fuss about going. She had obtained a grammar school place without any apparent effort and had not exerted herself much there. Because of this poor work-record and her membership of a rather disruptive 'gang', she had been 'kept down' a class the previous year. She much resented this and consequently appeared to be employing a policy of deliberate non-cooperation at school, combined with moody and difficult behaviour at home.

DISCUSSION

Various suggestions can be put forward to explain antipathy to school (See Chapter 5):
  (a)   that the fault lies in the school;
  (b)   that the fault lies in the child;
  (c)   that the fault lies in the home.

(a) The school

A system of school organization which involves 'streaming' children according to their perceived ability was prevalent at the time of our study and it could be argued that this contributed to our finding that dislike of school was associated with low attainment. Hargreaves (1967), for instance, illustrated clearly the way in which membership of a 'low ability' stream was accompanied by more generalized adverse labelling of the children concerned who were consequently deprived of status in the 'official' school hierarchy. Indeed, it has been suggested that some of the different results obtained between British and American studies of the relationship between attitude and attainment may result from the absence of streaming in the United States. Thus Berk *et al.* (1970), in their replication of Baker-Lunn's (1972) investigation, found no significant relationship, whereas the English study showed that bright primary school children had more positive attitudes to school.

One way in which streaming may be linked to dislike of school is through the status deprivation which it entails. Another possibility is boredom. Thus one of the factors considered in detail by the Pack Report (Scottish Education Department, 1977) was the relevance of the secondary school curriculum, particularly for the adolescent who had little prospect of acquiring academic 'credits'. Robinson (1975) has contributed some interesting evidence linking boredom with school to other behavioural and attitudinal expressions. Reanalysing the data quoted in Morton-Williams and Finch's (1968) study of young school leavers, he calculated a 'bore-score' based on the number of subjects, out of a total of seventeen, which the respondents had said they found boring. Comparing equal numbers of the highest and lowest scorers he found that 15 per cent of the 'bored' group had truanted occasionally or frequently, compared with 6 per cent of the control group, and that 16 per cent of the bored group were seen as aggressive by their teachers, compared with 9 per cent of controls. These differences were statistically significant — so too were the findings that showed the bored group to be more hostile towards school and more likely to express themselves as 'fed up with teachers telling you what to do'. The influence of boredom perhaps also underlies the finding of Flanders, Morrison, and Brode (1968) that in all age-groups children's expressed attitude to school-work and teachers tends to become progressively less positive as the school year progresses.

The final school-related hypothesis is one which emerges clearly from our case histories. This is that aversion to school may relate to crisis situations at school. At first glance this seems to contradict the 'boredom' hypothesis. However, this is not necessarily the case. We may once again be attempting, wrongly, to equate two types of phenomena — on the one hand generalised attitudes, on the other acute quasi-phobic behavioural manifestations. Boredom has been shown to relate to truancy and aggressiveness in school but not (as yet) to tears and vomiting. Aversion to attending school may well be induced by either circumstance, though the underlying mechanics of the aversion will differ. The argument for deleterious effects of crises is supported by Moore's (1966) study which shows, for primary school children, a subsidiary peaking effect at 8 years of age, when many children moved from the relatively informal and sheltered environment of the infant school to the more highly structured milieu of the junior school. Moore's investigations also indicate that, for some children, specific aspects of school life — for instance, dirty or very public toilets, unappetizing school meals, unfriendly or aggressive classmates, and critical teachers — may constitute critical conditions which produce avoidance behaviour and expressed aversion to going to school. In their very perceptive and detailed study of seven-year-olds, the Newsons (1977) suggest that for some young children change of teacher at the end of a school year can assume crisis proportions, particularly when the child's relationship to the 'old' teacher has been a close one. In more general terms they point out the crucial importance for the child of the way in which 'his' teacher handles her relationship with him: 'At the primary school stage, liking school depends upon liking the teacher'.

(b) The child

Can such reactions really be seen as purely the result of school-based factors, or should we also consider that the child's own personality may be an important determinant? This has been suggested in connection with the more extreme phenomenon of school refusal (Berg, Nichols, and Pritchard (1969);

Hersov (1960); Tyrer and Tyrer (1974); Kahn (1974)). Moore (1966), looking at the children who had manifested some aversion to school throughout the six years of his study, concluded that 'these were not all over-dependent children. In some of the cases cited the school atmosphere was clearly not helpful'. So far as specific difficulties were concerned, he felt that while some of these might stem from the child's personal idiosyncrasies 'there is no denying that many of the problems arise from faulty school organization, inappropriate attitudes in teachers, and underlying these a system of social pressures which makes insufferable demands on both teachers and taught'.

Jackson and Getzel (1959), however, having administered personality and social adjustment tests to adolescent pupils at an American mid-west private school as well as an opinion poll on their school concluded that 'dissatisfaction with school appears to be part of a larger picture of psychological discontent rather than a direct reflection of inefficient functioning in the classroom'. In other words, the student's dislike of school reflected 'a pervasive perceptual set that colours the students view of himself and his world'. Whether or not this is necessarily to be deprecated may be queried in the light of Reagan's (1967) finding that the ideal personality for developing a highly favourable attitude to school is characterized by self-sufficiency, perseverance, self-control, and fastidious individualism.

The relationship between intellectual ability and attitude to school has still to be established. As already mentioned, differences between the United States and Britain in studies relating attitude to attainment (by no means synonymous with ability, though employable for present purposes as a rough index) have indicated that school organization and the extent to which attainment determines status may be the crucial variables in determining attitudes. Moore (1966) found the association between IQ and reports of difficulties in school to be insignificant when the influences of social class was controlled.

(c) Family background

It seems reasonable to suppose that the interaction between child and school will not be determined solely by the characteristics of individual and institution but that the child's reaction to school will be affected by his reference groups outside school. Of these, the family is obviously the most important, particularly at the first point of entry to the school system. Socio-economic status (as measured by father's occupation) of the family (taken as correlated with their general attitudes and life style) has been shown by Baker-Lunn (1972) to be related to the attitudes toward school of English primary school children and by Robinson (1975) to relate to his 'boredom score', i.e. the lower father's occupational position, the less positive the attitude and the greater the probability of boredom. So far as boys are concerned, these results are substantiated also in our own study. Studies of younger children, however, raise some interesting points. Moore (1966) found that among his sample of London children aged from six to eight years the higher social classes were reporting *more* difficulties as being experienced by their children, while relatively few instances were being reported by mothers whose husbands were in relatively unskilled manual jobs. It is interesting to speculate on how far this may be a reflection of differing expectations in different social strata. Even so, this may not be the entire explanation as the Newsons (1977), in their study of seven-year-olds in Nottingham, found that the relationship between social class and a liking for school followed a U-shaped curve rather than a linear progression, i.e. the proportion of children said to like school 'very much' was highest at the extremes of the social class scale among those whose fathers were in professional and managerial jobs, on the one hand, and among the children of unskilled workers on the other. Similarly, children at the top and bottom of the social scale showed the lowest incidence of reported reluctance to go to school.

One of the major points of interest to arise from our own study lies in the lack of association between dislike of going to school and absence from school among the younger age groups. If the family's anti-educational bias were a prime determinant of the child's attitude, we would expect parental support and connivance for the child's intention to absent himself, particularly if he was manifesting quite severe physical symptoms. Yet below the age of eleven our children who disliked school had an attendance record as good as any others and the case histories (see, for example, those of David and Frank) show how the regular attendance could be achieved by strong parental pressure. Such pressure appears to weaken as the child becomes older and less amenable and this may account for the greater association between attitude and attendance among older children and adolescents.

It is interesting to compare our material with the findings of the two other British studies which deal with reluctance to go to school — those of Terence Moore (1966) and the Newsons (1977). Each of these authors was concerned with longitudinal investigation, from birth, of groups of children and each asked for parental reports on adjustment to school. Moore, considering a cohort of 164 London children, asked the parents at annual interviews whether, during that year, the child had shown any dislike of school or reluctance to go there. Some evidence of this was cited for approximately 70 per cent of six-year-old boys and 57 per cent of girls of the same age and, even after discounting the milder manifestations, Moore found 25 per cent of boys and 20 per cent of girls aged six were affected. Thereafter the parents reported progressively fewer cases, apart from a secondary 'peaking' at eight years of age when there was a change from infant to junior school. By the time they were eleven only 10 per cent of the boys and practically none of the girls were evincing more than minor signs of reluctance to go to school.

The Newsons (1977) asked the parents of just under seven hundred Nottingham seven-year-olds whether their child ever said that 'he doesn't want to go to school today' and found that 46 per cent had said this at least 'sometimes' since starting school. Again, however, exclusion of the more transitory cases, reduced the proportion of 10 per cent who felt this way 'often'. The main excuse adopted to avoid going to school was to 'pretend' to be unwell. (This refers to pretence which was identified as such by the parent.) Such attempts have been recognized and reported as occurring as 'often' by the mothers of 5 per cent of the children, while a further 22 per cent were said to try 'sometimes'. Only 5 per cent of the sample had refused to go to school (or run home once there) during their sixth year but a further 8 per cent had done so before their sixth birthday. These were predominantly boys (in the proportion of two boys to every girl) and their behaviour appears to have ranged from the 'one-off' flight to fairly regular refusal. The mothers' reactions to the child's avowal that he 'doesn't want to go to school today' are also interesting in that only 5 per cent of all mothers (not merely those who had encountered the problem in reality) felt that the child should be allowed to stay away in the Newsons own words:— 'This group is not mainly composed of mothers who do not value education but more typically of those who value it so much that they do not want it to be soured in any way for their child'.

According to Moore (1966), expressed dislike of school declines with age (at least among pre-teen children); our own results suggest (see Figure 1) that the number of children disliking school remains constant over time, though the proportions expressing marked enthusiasm may give way to the middling category who liked school 'as much as most children'; attitude schedules completed by children themselves, such as that of Sharples (1969), suggest that attitudes become less favourable with age even within the junior school. How can these discrepancies be resolved? Mainly by consideration of (a) the type of phenomenon being measured and (b) the source of the information on which assessment is based. Thus Moore's study, as well as our own and that of the Newsons, relied on impressions of parents which relate to clues from the behaviour of the child, either in open expression of dislike of school or through other manifestations such as sickness or tears, associated with school-going. Attitude measuring instruments, however, are directed at finding out how the children themselves *feel* about school, not necessarily how they *behave*.

With older children only very marked aversion to school is likely to lead to overt protest to parents and behavioural manifestations at home. Milder complaints are likely to be overlooked by parents as 'like most children' or, indeed, as 'like' the child under particular circumstances and probably transient. This is already apparent in many of the responses of mothers of seven-year-olds quoted by the Newsons (1977). Antipathy to school then comes to seek peer group rather than parental support, leading in some cases to the setting up of the school 'contra-cultures' described by Hargreaves (1967). Overt expression of antipathy towards, and alienation from, school, which has become so widespread as to be tolerated as part of secondary school life, has also been graphically demonstrated in recent observational studies such as that of Furlong (1976) which describe how pupils with support from their interaction group 'bunk it' (i.e. absent themselves from a lesson they dislike) and 'muck about' when they are there, as shown in this quotation:

> Debbie is playing with one of Carol's shoes; Valerie and Diane are reading comics and Carol is combing her hair and occasionally making jokes quietly to those about her. By and large no-one in the class seems very interested in the content of the lesson.
>
> (Furlong, 1976)

We cannot vouch for the typicality of such behaviour among non-academic pupils but interviews with such pupils after they have left school (Weir and Nolan (1977)) certainly indicate that many found the school curriculum in their final years at school irrelevant to the world of work which they were about to enter. Such individuals are not reluctant to attend school in the sense that they evince signs of distress as in the younger age groups. Rather they appear to demonstrate that they can carry this reluctance into action — either through asserting themselves physically (the rise in truancy and absence rates among 'non-academic' fifteen and sixteen year olds is well documented for example by the Scottish Education Department (1977)) or, as in the case of Debbie and her friends, presenting themselves at school when required to do so but opting out of the official programme (i.e. psychological truancy).

It seems that those children who attend school regularly while evincing signs of distress and antipathy and marked reluctance to do so may be seen as the casualties of a compulsory school system and, as such, are of considerable importance both from a theoretical and a practical view point. From the practical point of view they are perhaps the 'problem' of school planners (of curriculum and school organization as well as of buildings) and of those who teach them. From a theoretical viewpoint further research is clearly indicated. Existing studies have tended to deal with children whose efforts to avoid school are successful — that is the truant and the child who manifests school refusal. We must, however, ask whether studies which concentrate on the successful deviant are really exploring sufficient instances of the deviating behaviour they purport to study. The definitive interpretation of why children are reluctant to go to school has still to be undertaken.

REFERENCES

Barker-Lunn, J. C. (1972). The influence of sex, achievement level, and social class on junior school children's attitudes. *British Journal of Educational Psychology*, **42**, 70–74.

Berg, I., Nichols, K., and Pritchard, C. (1969). School phobia — its classification and relation to dependency. *Journal of Child Psychology and Psychiatry*, **10**, 123–141.

Berk, L. E., Rose, M. H., and Stewart, D. (1970). Attitudes of English and American children toward their school experience. *Journal of Educational Psychology*, **61**, 33–40.

Flanders, N. A., Morrison, B. M., and Brode, E. L. (1968). Changes in pupil attitudes during the school year. *Journal of Educational Psychology*, **50**, 334–338.

Furlong, V. (1976). 'Interaction sets in the classroom'. In Hammersley, M., and Woods, P. (Eds), *The Process of Schooling*. Routledge and Kegan Paul for the Open University; London.

Galloway, D. (1976). Size of school, socio-economic hardship, suspension rates and persistent unjustified absence from school. *British Journal of Educational Psychology*, **46**, 40–47.

Hansard (1974). Parliamentary Debates. *House of Commons Official Report (Fifth Series)*, Volume 877. London: Her Majesty's Stationery Office.

Hargreaves, D. (1967). *Social Relations in a Secondary School*. Routledge and Kegan Paul, London.

Hersov, L. A. (1960). Refusal to go to school. *Journal of Child Psychology and Psychiatry*, **1**, 137–145.

Jackson, P. W., and Getzels, J. W. (1959). Psychological health and classroom functioning: a study of dissatisfaction with school among adolescents. *Journal of Educational Psychology*, **50**, 295–300.

Kahn, J. (1974). 'School phobia or school refusal'. In Turner, B. (Ed), *Truancy*. Ward Lock International: London.

Kniveton, B. H. (1969). An investigation of the attitudes of adolescents to aspects of their schooling. *British Journal of Educational Psychology*, **39**, 78–81.

Lapouse, R., and Monk, M. A. (1959). Fears and worries in a representative sample of children. *American Journal of Orthopsychiatry*, **39**, 808–818.

Mitchell, S. (1972). The absentees. *Education in the North*, **9**, 22–28.

Mitchell, S., and Shepherd, M. (1967). The child who dislikes going to school. *British Journal of Educational Psychology*, **37**, 32–40.

Moore, T. (1966). Difficulties of the ordinary child in adjusting to primary school. *Journal of Child Psychology and Psychiatry*, **7**, 17–38.

Morton-Williams, R., and Finch, S. (1968). *Young School Leavers*. London: Her Majesty's Stationery Office.

Newson, J., and E. (1977). *Perspectives on School at Seven Years Old*. Allen and Unwin, London.

Reagan, G. (1967). Personality characteristics and attitude to school. *British Journal of Educational Psychology*, **37**, 127–129.

Robinson, W. P. (1975). Boredom at school. *British Journal of Educational Psychology*, **45**, 141–152.

Scottish Education Department (1977). *Truancy and Indiscipline in Secondary Schools* (The Pack Report). Her Majesty's Stationery Office, Edinburgh.

Secord, P. F., and Backman, C. W. (1964). *Social Psychology*. McGraw Hill, New York.

Sharples, D. (1969). Children's attitudes towards junior school activities. *British Journal of Educational Psychology*, **39**, 72–77.

Shepherd, M., Oppenheim, A. N., and Mitchell, S. (1971). *Childhood Behaviour and Mental Health*. University of London Press, London.

Tyrer, P., and S. (1974). School refusal, truancy, and adult neurotic illness. *Psychological Medicine*, **4**, 416–421.

Wagner, J. (1975). Schülereinstellungen zur Schule. *Psychologie in Erziehung und Unterricht*, **22**, 351–367.

Weir, T., and Nolan, P. (1977). *Glad to be Out*. Scottish Council for Research in Education, Edinburgh.

Wisenthal, M. (1965). Sex differences in attitude and attainment in junior schools. *British Journal of Educational Psychology*, **35**, 79–85.

Out of School
Edited by L. Hersov and I. Berg
© 1980, John Wiley & Sons, Ltd.

Chapter 2

Absence From School: Findings from the National Child Developmental Study

Ken Fogelman, Alan Tibbenham, and Lydia Lambert

INTRODUCTION

The question of enforcing compulsory attendance at school has been a live educational issue for a century or more. However, in the past decade, concern, public discussion, and research and academic attention to the topic have increased dramatically. This change seems to be mainly a function of suspicion, and some evidence, that absence has significantly increased, at least among older children in secondary schools, since the raising of the compulsory school leaving age (ROSLA) in 1973–4.

Writing in 1974, Fogelman and Richardson felt able to conclude that 'attendance rates have remained remarkably constant at around the 90% level'. Since then the pattern may have changed somewhat. In Scotland, for example, it has been reported that, in that same year, attendance in Edinburgh and Glasgow primary schools averaged above 90%, but in secondary 4 (i.e. the last compulsory year) the figure for Edinburgh was 86%, and for Glasgow 83% (Scottish Education Department, 1977). The same report claims that the amount of 'prolonged truancy' (i.e. greater than one month) among secondary pupils in Glasgow almost doubled between 1974 and 1975.

Similarly a survey of attendance in Bolton, carried out in one week of the Spring Term, 1977, found that in any one half-day session an average of 6.9% of seven-year-olds were absent, but 13.9% of fifteen-year-olds, and that this increase was mainly due to 'absence for unacceptable reasons' (Bolton Metropolitan Borough Education Committee, 1977.)

Previously unpublished figures for England, Scotland, and Wales are provided by the National Child Development Study (the sample and basis for these figures are described in detail below). For the Autumn term of 1972 the average attendance rate of this national sample (then aged fourteen) was reported by schools to have been 89.4%. A year later, the average attendance rate of these same children in the Autumn term of 1973 was 87.5%. In fact these figures are hardly dramatically low, and suggest perhaps that the overall picture is less bleak than might be inferred from more locally-based findings. Nevertheless an absence rate of at least 12.5% for fifteen-year-olds is hardly cause for complacency, and it is known that attendance rates are at their highest during the Autumn term (Sandon, 1961, ISTD, 1974; Medlicott, 1973; Tyerman, 1972.)

However, before investing resources, whether into enforcing attendance or explaining absenteeism, there is a further question which needs to be considered.

ABSENCE AND ATTAINMENT

Attempting to establish the causes and cures for absence from school implies that whether or not a child attends school does have some significance for his educational progress. On the face of it, it is natural to assume that the attainment of those children who are frequently absent is, as a result, lower than their regularly-attending peers.

Doubts about the straightforwardness of this relationship come from two sources. Firstly there is extrapolation from evidence as to the general unimportance of school variables in relation to variations in children's attainment, particularly when contrasted with social and family variables. The much-publicized American work, such as that of Coleman (1966) and Jencks (1972) (and for more recent evidence in the British context see Richardson, Ghodsian, and Gorbach, 1978) has led to some lack of confidence in the importance of schooling. However it must be emphasized that such evidence relates to variation between schools, and not to quantity of schooling as such (for a fuller consideration of this question, see Fogelman, 1978a). Thus such extrapolation is not valid.

Secondly, and more relevantly, there is direct evidence on the relationship between attendance and attainment test scores, from two national longitudinal studies. From the National Survey of Health and Development, a study of children born in 1946, Douglas and Ross (1965) related composite scores on reading, vocabulary, intelligence and arithmetic tests taken at the age of 11, to attendance records over the previous four years. In general they found the expected relationship between average scores and attendance, but not for their 'upper middle class' group. Among these, even children who had averaged about eight weeks absence per year obtained test scores no lower than the best attenders.

A similar finding was obtained by Fogelman and Richardson (1974), who examined the relationship between attendance and scores on reading comprehension, arithmetic, and general ability tests for children in the National Child Development Study, also at the age of eleven. This relationship reached statistical significance only for those children whose fathers were in manual occupations.

More recently, it has been possible to carry out a more detailed analysis of NCDS data, and to incorporate the information collected on these same children at the age of sixteen. Only a brief summary of this work will be given here, as a full account is being prepared for publication elsewhere (Fogelman, 1978b). In this paper the relationship is explored between attendance rate at seven, attendance rate at fifteen (in the Autumn term of the last compulsory year) and reading and mathematics attainment at sixteen. By means of analysis of variance it was possible to take account of the differences between children with different attendance rates, in their sex, social class, region, and housing circumstances (as indicated by overcrowding). A clear pattern emerged of a strong relationship between attendance at fifteen and attainment, and, contrary to the eleven-year results mentioned above, this appeared for each social class.

The relationship between attendance at the age of seven and attainment at sixteen was a weak one, and indeed after taking account of attendance at fifteen and the background factors it did not reach statistical significance. In part this will be due to the fairly high correlation between attendance at the two ages, but it does suggest that the attainment of children whose attendance is poor at an early age can nevertheless be as good as their peers' if their subsequent attendance is regular.

Although the relationship between attendance and attainment is not simple, it does seem that efforts to improve attendance are justified, not only because there does appear to be a clear relationship between attendance and attainment towards the end of the school years, but also because the prognosis is optimistic for children whose poor attendance improves.

THE NATIONAL CHILD DEVELOPMENT STUDY

Much of the remainder of this chapter will be based on previously un-published findings from the National Child Development Study (NCDS). It is therefore necessary to provide a brief description of the study, and in particular of the measures of attendance and truancy which it has used.

The NCDS is a longitudinal, multidisciplinary study, carried out by the National Children's Bureau, of all children in England, Scotland, and Wales born in the week 3rd–9th March, 1958. By means of parental interviews, medical examinations, questionnaires to schools, tests of attainment and — at the later ages — questionnaires completed by the children, their physical, social, and educational development has been examined at the ages of seven (e.g. Davie, Butler, and Goldstein, 1972), eleven (e.g. Wedge, 1969), and sixteen, in their last year of compulsory schooling (e.g. Fogelman, 1976).

The attendance and truancy data collected at seven and eleven have been described in detail elsewhere (Fogelman and Richardson, op. cit.), and consisted essentially of attendance rates in the current school year, and (at

eleven only) teachers' ratings of whether each child had truanted, or was
suspected of truancy.

, Earlier findings from the study relating to attendance and truancy at the
ages of seven and eleven have appeared in a number of sources. Pringle, Butler,
and Davie (1966) have reported that at the age of seven as many as 9% of the
NCDS children had an attendance rate of less than 80% in the current school
year. Davie (1972) identified a substantial increase in overall attendance rates
between seven and eleven: for example, whereas at the earlier age 66% of
children had had an attendance rate of better than 90%, the figure had
improved to 81% by the later age. However, as Fogelman and Richardson (*op.
cit.*) have pointed out, this general improvement masks considerable individual
variation: of those children identified as poor attenders at the age of eleven,
only half had been poor attenders at the age of seven.

Furthermore, behind the figures for Britain as a whole there were
considerable regional variations. At one extreme about 15% of the Welsh
children were found at eleven to be poor attenders (i.e. with an attendance rate
of less than 85% in the current school year). On the other hand the comparable
proportions of poor attenders in the Eastern, North Midlands, and South
Western regions were 8% or less.

Fogelman and Richardson paid considerable attention to the 1.2% children
indicated, at the age of eleven, by their teachers, to have truanted or to be
suspected of it. Again there was considerable variation in their characteristics:
three-quarters were boys; proportionately, there were ten times more such
children with fathers in skilled manual occupations than in professional or
managerial occupations.

In general the regional distribution of truancy was similar to that for
attendance rates, with the exception of Scotland which had the highest proportion of reported truants, even though the Scottish attendance rates were not
notably low.

Truancy at eleven was clearly related to the family's attitude to school, being
more frequent when the parents wished the child to leave school as soon as
possible and not to continue with any further education, when the parents had
not themselves made any contact with the school and where the father was
assessed by the child's teacher as not being interested in the child's education.

Although it is difficult to know to what extent a halo effect may be
operating, the 'truants' ' teachers were considerably more likely to rate them as
below average in general knowledge, number ability, oral ability, and use of
books and to regard them as 'delinquent' or 'easily led'. Such children were
eight times more likely than other children to be said to be in need of special
education.

Sixteen-year data

From the sixteen-year follow-up the following data are available for each child:

(i) Attendance record

The number of possible half-day attendances and of actual half-day absences for the Autumn terms of 1972 and 1973. From these the percentage attendance rate for each period has been calculated.

(ii) Teacher's report of truancy

An item from a school behaviour scale (Rutter, Tizard, and Whitmore, 1970), for which teachers had to indicate whether the description 'truants from school: doesn't apply: applies somewhat: certainly applies'.

(iii) Parent's report of truancy

An item from a home behaviour scale included in the parental interview, indicating whether, during the past twelve months, the child 'truants from school: never; occasionally but not as often as once per week; at least once per week'.

(iv) Pupil's own report

A question put to the sixteen-year-olds themselves — 'Have you stayed away from school at all this year when you should have been there?'

In the next section we shall consider the meaningfulness of measures such as these, before turning to a presentation of the NCDS findings on the relationship between various school, social and other factors and 'unjustified absenteeism'.

ATTENDANCE RECORDS

Much has been written of the inadequacy of school attendance records as indicators of rates of truancy. Obviously truancy constitutes only one of the many reasons for absence, and often poor school attendance acts merely as a starting point for an investigation of the reasons behind those absences (e.g. Galloway, 1976a; Medlicott, 1973; Tyerman, 1972).

School registers usually give no indication of reasons for absence even if they are known, therefore serious dangers are involved in drawing inferences about truancy from them. Hence, for example, given the suggested greater tendency for working class parents to keep children away for minor illnesses, conclusions about truancy based on high non-attendance in schools with working-class catchment areas, should be treated with caution (Williams, 1974).

A further difficulty is that a *school's* attendance rates tell very little about patterns of individual attendance. As has been pointed out by Galloway (1976), a 93% attendance rate could indicate that 7% of a school's pupils are permanent absentees or, at the other extreme, that every pupil misses one or two sessions. One widely quoted study suggested that an overall 88% attendance record at a school disguised the fact that more than a half of its pupils missed at least one session during the week (Where, 1973).

It has frequently been suggested that a further source of inaccuracy in attendance records is that a significant number of pupils register at the beginning of the session, but then skip classes (May, 1975; Where, 1973; Williams, 1974; David, 1975). However, this suggestion has tended to be based on individual anecdotes and not on any systematic evidence. The recent survey in Bolton did incorporate a 'roll-call check', and found only about 0.5% of pupils to be absent, having been present at registration. Furthermore, of these, two-thirds had an acceptable reason for their absence. Perhaps therefore this particular problem has been exaggerated.

However a question mark must remain over the use of attendance records in order to study what is really of most interest, that is absenteeism which would not be considered acceptable. For this purpose we must consider other sources.

PUPILS' OWN REPORTS

Given the extremely broad nature of the question described above put to the NCDS children, it is perhaps not so surprising that 52% of them said they had stayed away from school when they should have been there (Fogelman, 1976). Clearly such 'truancy' might range from missing one half day in the year to missing large sections of the school timetable. Does the response to the question put to children have any value or meaning?

First of all it should be stressed that the question was deliberately made a very broad one in order to elicit a clear-cut answer on a yes/no basis, so as to gain the co-operation of the children. Belson (1975), in a study of over 3000 London school boys, mainly in the 13–16 age-range, asked a similarly broad question: 'do you/did you, ever play truant from school'? A comparably high proportion of his sample (44%) also replied 'yes'. When categorized according to the amount of truanting, 11 per cent said they truanted 'once a week' and 8% 'once a month' (25% 'hardly ever'). These figures are much closer to estimates by the teachers in the NCDS that the description 'truants from school' either 'certainly applies' or 'applies somewhat' to 20% of the sample.

The figure of 52% might not then, be totally unrealistic given the generality of the question asked and the fact that there was no evidence in piloting that pupils misunderstood the question and mistakenly included absence for legitimate reasons in their response. On the other hand, pupils' reports may be of limited value if we are only concerned with the type of prolonged absenteeism likely to affect the educational performance of the individual pupil. However some educationalists argue that it could be that it is 'the sporadic rather than the extended absences which are likely to be caused by truancy' (Where, 1973). Pupils' estimates may well provide the best estimate of the numbers of *pupils* truanting sporadically (rather than the amount of time spent truanting by individual pupils) since teachers and parents probably only suspect truancy on the basis of an accumulation of absences from school. While occasional absences may not appear to affect individual's educational performance, clearly there may be, for example, a disruptive influence on the class in general, if half of the pupils miss lessons at one time or another.

We should not forget that in the first instance only the children themselves actually know whether they play truant and the extent to which they truant. Unless the child truthfully informs teachers or parents, the estimates of the latter can only be based on *suspicions*. Only the children know whether they go to school when their parents think they have, whether they deceive their parents into thinking they are ill, whether teachers' suspicions that they leave school after registration are justified, and so on.

Clearly there is a danger and probably even a likelihood of a great deal of subjectivity involved in pupils' responses. The child who says he truants may be influenced by an assessment of the prestige available from 'bragging' about missing school (although this may be diminished when it is researchers who are the audience).

As against this an *underestimate* of the truancy rate could result from the fear of children that punishment may follow an admission of truancy (although NCDS pupils were given a sealed envelope in which to put their questionnaires and given an assurance that no-one except the NCDS team would see these forms).

Such uncertainties must cast doubt on the use of pupils' estimates for our present purpose, although their value should not be dismissed entirely.

PARENTS' REPORTS

There is an immediate paradox in referring to parental reports of truancy, in that, by the strictest definition, truancy is absence without parents' knowledge or approval. It has been strongly argued that this distinction is crucial, since without knowing whether a child's absence is its parents' responsibility, 'any remedial measure undertaken is taken in the dark' (National Association of Chief Education Welfare Officers, 1974). Whilst there is considerable force to this argument as far as younger children are concerned, it is not so obviously relevant to fifteen and sixteen-year-olds such as we are mainly discussing in this chapter.

Nevertheless, it must be acknowledged that this strict definition cannot be assumed to accord with common usage. When, as in our measures, parents or teachers refer to 'truancy' it is more likely that they mean absenteeism for unacceptable reasons irrespective of whether it is known to, or approved by, the parents. It is arguable that this is the more appropriate concept for older children.

According to their parents 88% of NCDS children 'never' played truant, 10% did so 'occasionally' and 3% 'at least once per week'. Clearly, although it is a cause for concern if even 3% are missing school regularly, levels of parent-reported truancy are much lower than pupils' estimates. In looking at the relatively low level of truancy suggested by parents, some of the disadvantages of these estimates immediately suggest themselves.

Clearly parents may be genuinely unaware of their child's truancy, or at least its extent. Once the child leaves for school there will be little possibility of parents knowing about their whereabouts during the day. It may also be that parental concern for the well-being of their child may diminish their ability to detect the feigning of illness, in some instances (ISTD, 1974).

Although in such cases parents' judgements may be inaccurate because they are deceived by the child, reliance on parental estimates may also be misplaced because the parents themselves may attempt to mislead researchers or authorities. As in the case of pupils' estimates, the element of subjectivity may be large. While pupils may 'show-off' about truancy, parents may disguise their children's truancy because of embarrassment about the apparent reflection on their lack of control. Other parents may write notes of excuse because they want the child to run errands, to look after young children or sick parents or even, in the case of lonely and depressed single parents, to use them as an 'emotional prop' (Terry, 1975). Alternatively, sheer apathy about their child's education may make parents write excuses for the child's absence which cover up the unjustifiable nature of it (ISTD, 1974; David, 1975). Given that studies persistently show that the rate of absence is particularly high among working-class children (Davie et al., 1972; Fogelman and Richardson, 1974; May, 1975; Mitchell, 1972), there may also be some interest in the claim that working-class parents are more willing to keep children home with colds, a factor commonly cited as a reason for absence (Williams, 1974). There are many such reasons for absence for which, while they are not legitimate according to the terms of the Education Act, parents may feel justified in keeping the child away and not consider they are 'provoking' the child to truant. Consequently their response to the question about truancy may be misleading. Some parents might also give false information through fear that admitting their child was a truant could lead to their prosecution.

TEACHER'S ESTIMATES

We have elsewhere suggested that the figure derived from the teacher's measure of truancy probably gives the best estimate of the 'number staying away relatively frequently' (Fogelman, 1976). Similarly a recent major study of truancy in Glasgow (ISTD, 1974) argued that in defining which absences were not 'acceptable', acceptability was best measured by teachers, given their experience and intimate knowledge of pupils, which made it possible for them to estimate the amount of truancy occurring with either the connivance or tacit consent of parents. The researchers also argue the case of the considerable advantage of teachers learning things through the 'school grape-vine', as in cases where pupils were seen running errands when a medical certificate had been submitted.

The Bolton survey (1977) included a special exercise in which education welfare officers visited and interviewed parents in an attempt to determine whether schools were correctly assessing whether a child's absence was for genuine reasons. There was found to be no case in which the schools had accepted the reason for absence where this was not supported by the parents. On the other hand, of the 21 children in the study for whom the schools suspected that the proffered explanations were not genuine, six were in fact supported by the parents. From this evidence, it would seem that schools are reasonably accurate in their beliefs, although they may have a slight tendency to be over-suspicious.

Clearly teachers' reports of truancy have their limitations and an element of subjectivity. Nevertheless, the convenience of using teachers' estimates and the judgement that they are reasonably accurate, makes them the most attractive for research purposes. The ISTD study of truancy in Glasgow concluded that 'Generally it was felt that there is a judgement to be made in all irregular attendances and the teacher seemed to be the best person to estimate this to a measurable extent, (ISTD, 1974). May, too despite his reservations about teachers' estimates, adopted this instrument to measure truancy in his own study, arguing that 'Truancy is difficult to define, and even more difficult to measure with accuracy. While not wholly satisfactory, teacher assessments are generally more reliable than other measures' (May, 1975).

For such reasons we shall, in the remainder of this chapter which is concerned with the relationship of truancy with a wide range of factors, use teachers' reports as our indicator, whilst acknowledging that such reports cannot be assumed to be totally accurate.

TRUANCY IN THE PRIMARY AND SECONDARY SCHOOL

An important question which a longitudinal study such as NCDS can attempt to answer concerns the extent to which a child's unjustified absenteeism in the final years of secondary schooling might have been predicted by a similar pattern earlier in the school life.

As we have seen, absence, and in particular unjustified absence, is considerably higher in the last two years of compulsory schooling than at any earlier time. When discussing regular unjustified absence among primary school children, one is possibly concerned with, at most, one in every hundred children.

Among fourteen- to sixteen-year-olds it may be as many as one in ten. Clearly this contrast in itself limits the possibility of a very close relationship between the two. Nevertheless it is valuable to know whether those children said to be truanting at eleven are included among those said to be truanting five years later.

Of the small group of NCDS children who were reported to have truanted or to be suspected of it at the age of eleven, 60% were described by their teacher as truanting ('somewhat' or 'certainly') in the past twelve months at sixteen (compared with 20% of the total sample). On the other hand just 2.5% of those said to truant at sixteen had been thought to be truanting at eleven (compared with 1.2% of the total sample).

THE DEMOGRAPHY OF TRUANCY

Although it is well established that the actual attendance rates tend to be lower for girls than boys, the relative frequency of truancy is less well established. Fogelman and Richardson (1974) found that more boys than girls were reported by teachers to be truanting at the age of eleven. On the other hand the much criticized DES (1974) survey found virtually no difference between the sexes in the proportions unjustifiably absent on the one day to which the survey referred.

Table 1. Teacher's rating of truancy at 16 by child's social class and sex

		Doesn't Apply	Somewhat	Certainly	$N (= 100\%)$
		%	%	%	
I + II	Boys	91	7	3	1153
	Girls	94	4	1	1145
III Non-Manual	Boys	85	10	4	521
	Girls	88	9	3	457
III Manual	Boys	76	15	8	1995
	Girls	83	11	6	1900
IV	Boys	75	14	11	611
	Girls	77	15	8	582
V	Boys	59	23	18	250
	Girls	72	16	13	236
No Male Head	Boys	67	18	15	324
	Girls	74	16	11	369

Tests: For overall sex difference, χ^2 (1 d.f) = 51.23***
    For boys, social class differences, χ^2 (5 d.f.) = 234.77***
    For girls, social class differences, χ^2 (5 d.f.) = 178.34***
In all tables * indicates $p < 0.05$; ** $p < 0.01$; *** $p < 0.001$; otherwise $p > 0.05$

The relationship between social background and truancy is more firmly established (Belson, 1975; Blythman, 1975; Douglas and Ross, 1965; Mitchell and Shepherd, 1967).

Table 1 presents the relevant NCDS data for teachers' ratings of truancy at the age of sixteen in relation to sex and social class. In both cases a strong and straightforward relationship appears. For both sexes there is a clear gradient from the children whose fathers had professional or managerial occupations to those from unskilled manual backgrounds. Within each social class more boys are rated as truanting than girls, this contrast being particularly marked in social class V.

For this age group at least it would seem that, contrary to the DES figures, more boys are considered to be truanting than girls. However it is just possible that on any one day there is little difference, but that girls have longer or more frequent periods of absence, and/or that teachers tend to be less suspicious of girls.

Table 2. Type of school and teacher's rating of truancy at 16

		Doesn't apply %	Somewhat %	Certainly %	$N (= 100\%)$
Comprehensive	Boys	74	16	10	3731
	Girls	80	12	8	3554
Grammar	Boys	95	5	1	599
	Girls	97	3	0	720
Secondary	Boys	74	16	11	1348
Modern	Girls	79	13	8	1254
Technical	Boys	93	7	0	41
	Girls	86	7	7	28
Day ESN	Boys	82	10	8	60
	Girls	71	9	20	55
Residential	Boys	87	9	4	23
ESN	Girls	63	0	37	8
Day other	Boys	93	7	0	15
Special	Girls	50	50	0	8
Residential	Boys	76	14	10	21
other Special	Girls	100	0	0	6
Independent	Boys	98	2	0	254
	Girls	97	3	0	210
Direct Grant	Boys	98	1	1	147
	Girls	95	4	1	142
Approved/	Boys	67	14	19	21
Community	Girls	0	50	50	2

Table 2 shows the rating of truancy according to the type of school attended by the children concerned. As might be expected, relatively few children in grammar, direct grant or independent schools were said to be truanting (although the problem is by no means non-existent in such schools (See also Belson, 1975)).

The figures for comprehensive and secondary modern schools are very alike. However, it should be borne in mind that the schools are categorized simply according to the head teachers' designation, and no attempt has been made here to establish whether the comprehensive schools' intakes were indeed representative.

In other types of school numbers are often rather small. Nevertheless it is perhaps disappointing to find such high levels of truancy in, for example schools for the Educationally Subnormal, when we might have hoped that greater opportunities for contact between staff and pupils could produce the opposite result. On the face of it the numbers truanting in residential special and community schools are surprising. However these figures refer to current schools, and truancy in the past 12 months, so these may well include children whose truancy has been an element in a recent decision to transfer them to residential schools (and the numbers for these groups are particularly small).

Because of the different nature and timing of secondary reorganization in different parts of the country, it is wise to examine regional differences within different types of school, as is done in Table 3. Figures are presented for comprehensive and secondary modern schools only, as other types of school either contained too few pupils or too few truants to provide meaningful figures for separate regions.

Table 3. Teacher's rating of truancy at 16 by region and sex

Figures in each cell are percentages of sixteen-year-olds reported by teachers as having truanted ('somewhat' or 'certainly' see text) in past 12 months

	Comprehensive		Secondary Modern	
	Boys	Girls	Boys	Girls
North-West	25	25	30	23
North	27	22	32	14
East and West Ridings	26	17	23	23
North Midlands	25	18	19	24
East	25	17	18	19
London and South-East	27	25	32	26
South	20	15	20	16
South-West	20	15	21	15
Midlands	25	19	32	15
Wales	32	20	38($N=33$)	29($N=31$)
Scotland	29	20	26($N=27$)	55($N=11$)
χ^2 (10 d.f.)	22.4*	25.4**	23.0*	26.0*

These figures provide only moderate support for the particular concern which has been expressed about truancy in Scotland and Wales (Scottish Education Department, 1977; Carroll, 1977). In comprehensive schools (and for these two areas numbers are small in any other type of school) Scotland and Wales do have the highest proportion of boys said to be truanting, but the differences between them and some English regions are not very large. Among the girls, on the other hand, it is the North-West, London, and the South-East, and (in secondary modern schools) the North Midlands which have the highest figures.

SCHOOL VARIABLES

Several recent studies have examined the relationship between the characteristics of schools and the extent of truancy among their pupils. From these, perhaps two consistent findings can be identified: first, that truancy is weakly, if at all, related to the size of a school (Galloway, 1976b; Reynolds and Murgatroyd, 1977); secondly, that there are found to be large differences in truancy rates between schools which appear to have similar intakes and administrative characteristics (Finlayson and Loughran, 1976; May, 1975; Reynolds, 1976) (See Chapter 5).

The latter point suggests that the influence of schools resides in less easily measurable variables, concerned with 'ethos' and atmosphere. The NCDS data are not suited to pursuing such a question. Nevertheless it remains valuable to ask whether truancy is related to more straightforward administrative characteristics, not least because it is persistent folklore that it is.

Table 4 presents the association between teachers' reports of truancy and eight school variables on which the study has information. The first point to note is the general lack of statistically significant relationships: five of the variables do not reach significance for either sex or either of the types of school considered. These are:

(i) Use of corporal punishment: schools were asked to indicate whether corporal punishment was used 'regularly or occasionally', 'rarely', or 'never'.

(ii) Ability grouping policy; assessed by asking schools to describe the situation in their 12–13 year group (for discussion of this variable see Tibbenham et al., 1978).

(iii) Pupil–teacher ratio; calculated from the schools' report of its number of pupils and of full-time (and part-time equivalent) staff.

(iv) Whether the school was single sex or co-educational.

(v) The size of the school (i.e. number of pupils).

The remaining three variables, although reaching statistical significance for at least one group of children, cannot be said to show either a consistent or a very marked relationship with truancy.

Table 4. School variables and teacher's ratings of truancy at 16

Figures in each cell are percentages of sixteen-year-olds reported by teachers to have truanted ('somewhat' or 'certainly', see text) in past 12 months

(a) Whether school has a uniform		None	Yes, not Compulsory	Compulsory	χ^2 (2 d.f.)
Comprehensive	Boys	25	27	23	6.18*
Comprehensive	Girls	32	20	18	9.35**
Sec. Mod.	Boys	23	28	22	4.16
Sec. Mod.	Girls	20	21	21	< 1

(b) Use of Corporal Punishment		Regularly Occasionally	Rarely	Never	χ^2 (2 d.f.)
Comprehensive	Boys	28	25	24	4.48
Comprehensive	Girls	20	20	20	< 1
Sec. Mod.	Boys	26	27	20	1.91
Sec. Mod.	Girls	22	20	22	< 1

(c) Ability-grouping policy		Streamed	Setted	Mixed ability	χ^2 (2 d.f.)
Comprehensive	Boys	28	25	27	2.69
Comprehensive	Girls	20	19	23	3.55
Sec. Mod.	Boys	25	27	25	< 1
Sec. Mod.	Girls	22	21	16	2.36

(d) Pupil-teacher ratio		—15	—17	—19	20+	χ^2 (3 d.f.)
Comprehensive	Boys	25	22	26	30	3.12
Comprehensive	Girls	22	20	19	22	2.66
Sec. Mod.	Boys	24	25	27	26	< 1
Sec. Mod.	Girls	29	18	21	22	3.73

(e) Teacher Turnover		—5%	—10%	—15%	—20%	21+	χ^2 (4 d.f.)
Comprehensive	Boys	23	26	25	23	32	19.06***
Comprehensive	Girls	14	18	19	22	23	14.76**
Sec. Mod.	Boys	25	28	23	28	27	3.37
Sec. Mod.	Girls	24	20	23	16	24	7.90

(f) Whether school has Parent-Teacher Meetings		Regularly at least once a term	Once a year	Yes, but not regularly	χ^2 (2 d.f.)
Comprehensive	Boys	27	25	33	6.64*
Comprehensive	Girls	21	19	23	2.18
Sec. Mod.	Boys	23	26	33	2.72
Sec. Mod.	Girls	13	21	21	4.17

(g) Whether school co-educational		Single Sex	Co-educational				χ^2 (1 d.f.)
Comprehensive	Boys	26	26				< 1
Comprehensive	Girls	21	20				< 1
Sec. Mod.	Boys	29	26				< 1
Sec. Mod.	Girls	22	20				1.25
(h) Size of school		—500	—750	—1000	—1250	—1500	1500+	χ^2(5 d.f.)
Comprehensive	Boys	26	25	27	26	25	28	1.58
Comprehensive	Girls	15	16	21	22	22	20	10.03
Sec. Mod.	Boys	28	24	26	28	22	—	2.88
Sec. Mod.	Girls	19	19	26	21	24	—	5.49

(vi) Whether the school has a uniform is related to truancy only for pupils attending comprehensive schools and not for those at secondary moderns. Among the former, although, for both boys and girls, schools with a compulsory uniform report the least truancy, the difference between those schools having a non-compulsory uniform and those having none at all is inconsistent for the two sexes.

(vii) To provide an index of teacher turnover, schools were asked to give the number of teachers who left during or at the end of the previous academic year, and this has been calculated as a percentage of the total number of teachers. Again a statistically significant association with truancy is found for comprehensive school pupils and not secondary modern. For both boys and girls, those at comprehensive schools with the greater turnover tend to be more frequently reported as truanting, but the relationship is by no means absolutely regular.

(viii) The final variable in Table 4 concerns the schools' response to whether, and how regularly, they held meetings at which parents discuss child's progress with teachers' (the one per cent indicating that they held no such meetings are not included in the table). For comprehensive boys only, more truancy is reported by schools holding less regular meetings.

This overall pattern of weak and inconsistent relationships reinforces the suspicion that, where they do appear, it is likely to be the result of correlations with more important variables. It appears unlikely that such administrative variables as we are examining here are in themselves influential in affecting truancy rates.

FAMILY BACKGROUND VARIABLES

We have already seen the association between reported truancy and social class. In this section we explore the relationship with further variables which provide indices of the child's family background. Table 5 presents the data relevant to two such variables. First, the differences among children in one, two, or three child families are not very great, although there is then a considerable contrast with those from the largest families, i.e. with four or more children. Overall the association is perhaps less strong than one might have predicted, given the well-known relationship between family size and, for example, attainment (e.g. Fogelman, 1975; Fogelman et al., 1978).

We have reported elsewhere (Tibbenham, 1977) that those children said to be truanting are considerably more likely to be living in overcrowded homes. Given this, it would be expected that they were also more likely to be living in council-rented homes. The data in Table 5b confirm that this is the case.

Table 5. Teacher's rating of truancy at 16 by (a) number of children in household and (b) tenure of accommodation

Figures in each cell are percentages of sixteen-year-olds reported by teachers to have truanted ('somewhat' and 'certainly', see text) in past 12 months

(a) Number of children in household		1	2	3	4+	χ^2 (3 d.f.)
Comprehensive	Boys	20	19	25	32	23.20***
Comprehensive	Girls	13	15	18	26	46.85***
Sec. Mod.	Boys	23	19	22	35	25.48***
Sec. Mod.	Girls	15	17	18	24	8.15*
Grammar	Boys	4	3	6	9	5.15
Grammar	Girls	5	2	2	8	16.56***

(b) Tenure		Owner occupier	Council	Private rent	Tied to occupation	χ^2 (3 d.f.)
Comprehensive	Boys	16	31	27	25	80.25***
Comprehensive	Girls	9	26	23	20	216.17***
Sec. Mod.	Boys	18	34	31	20	34.10***
Sec. Mod.	Girls	12	27	25	12	37.66***
Grammar	Boys	3	12	—	—	9.73**
Grammar	Girls	2	8	—	—	8.45**

As distinct from such indications of the likely material circumstances of a child's family, many studies have demonstrated the importance of parental attitudes and in particular their interest in their child's education. Table 6 examines two measures relevant to this. First, schools were asked whether either parent had, since the beginning of the school year, met with any member of the teaching staff to discuss the child. As can be seen, this variable produced large contrasts, but only between those children both of whose parents had visited the school, and the rest, irrespective of whether one or neither parent had visited the school. This finding is very much in line with that obtained for these same children at the age of eleven (Fogelman and Richardson, 1974).

Table 6(b) offers a rather different insight into the parents' attitude, that is a rating from the children themselves of their parents' feelings about their progress at school. There are several interesting points arising from this table. First, there are very few children from non-manual backgrounds either saying that their parents 'didn't mind either way' about their schoolwork, or feeling uncertain about how their parents felt. The effect of this, since there was little difference between the other three groups (i.e. those saying their parents were 'very anxious' or 'contented if I do my best') in the reported truancy rates, is that there is no relationship between truancy and reported parental interest for the middle-class children.

Table 6. Teacher's ratings of truancy at 16 by (a) whether or not parents have visited the school in the past year and (b) child's rating of parental feelings about educational progress

Figures in each cell are percentages of sixteen-year-olds reported by teachers to have truanted ('somewhat' or 'certainly', see text)

(a) Parental visits to school

		Father only	Mother only	Both	Neither	χ^2 (3 d.f.)
Non-manual	Boys	15	19	5	14	45.11***
Non-manual	Girls	9	10	4	11	21.65***
Manual	Boys	30	31	14	28	63.34***
Manual	Girls	32	19	10	24	46.20***

(b) Parental feelings about child's progress at school (child's rating)

		Very anxious	Fairly anxious	Contented if I do my best	Don't mind either way	Uncertain	χ^2 (4 d.f.)
Non-manual	Boys	7	10	11	—	—	5.23
Non-manual	Girls	7	8	6	—	—	1.82
Manual	Boys	15	22	24	49	44	156.82***
Manual	Girls	15	16	16	36	38	32.95***

A very different pattern is found for the working-class boys and girls, because of the large numbers said by teachers to be truanting among those who were uncertain or said that their parents didn't mind either way. In particular, almost half of the boys in these groups were reported as truanting.

A question which has received some recent public attention is that of mobility and change of school (e.g. DES, 1977). It might be expected that, if changing school causes difficulties for a child, because of lack of comparability among curricula for example, this might lead to more frequent truancy. Indeed, such a relationship was found for the NCDS children at eleven (Fogelman and Richardson, 1974). However, at sixteen, this is not clearly supported by the figures in Table 7, the association between our truancy measure and number of schools attended (since eleven) reaching significance for the girls in comprehensive schools only. On the other hand, a relatively high proportion of the secondary modern girls who had been at three or more schools were also reported as truanting, although the total number of girls in this group was small. There does seem to be a suggestion that, as far as its relationship with truancy is concerned, mobility is a more important factor for girls than it is for boys.

Table 7. Number of schools attended by teachers' ratings of truancy at 16

Figures in each cell are percentages of sixteen-year-olds reported by teachers to have truanted ('somewhat' or 'certainly', see text) in past 12 months

		No. of schools attended since 11			
		1	2	3 +	χ^2 (2 d.f.)
Comprehensive	Boys	23	26	29	3.59
Comprehensive	Girls	17	20	29	8.13*
Sec. Mod.	Boys	24	34	22	5.85
Sec. Mod.	Girls	18	24	37($N=19$)	5.60

OUT OF SCHOOL ACTIVITIES

In the course of completing their questionnaire, the young people in the study were offered a list of possible leisure activities (for the full list, see Fogelman, 1976) and for each one asked to indicate whether this was something which they did 'often', 'sometimes', or 'hardly ever/never' (they were also able to respond that it was something which they would like to do but had no chance). Table 8(a) considers the number of activities (out of the eight possible) which were said to be done either often or sometimes. For the middle-class children, and the working-class boys, there is no evidence that those said to have truanted report fewer leisure activities than other children. Although there is such a relationship for the working-class girls, the differences in relation to number of leisure activities to be seen in Table 8(a) can hardly be described as very large, particularly when compared with those we have seen elsewhere in relation to other variables.

However, large differences do appear when some of the particular leisure

Table 8. Teachers' ratings of truancy at 16 and children's leisure activities

Figures in each cell are percentages of sixteen-year-olds reported by teachers to have truanted ('somewhat' or 'certainly', see text) in past 12 months)

(a) Number of activities named (see text)

		0–4	5 +	χ^2 (1 d.f.)
Non-manual	Boys	9	11	1.43
Non-manual	Girls	8	7	< 1
Manual	Boys	24	23	< 1
Manual	Girls	20	16	5.67*

(b) Reading Books

		Often	Sometimes	Hardly ever/ never	χ^2 (2 d.f.)
Non-manual	Boys	5	10	13	15.51***
Non-manual	Girls	7	6	10	6.16*
Manual	Boys	15	23	25	16.42***
Manual	Girls	12	16	24	28.39***

(c) Watching T.V.

		Often	Sometimes	Hardly ever/ never	χ^2 (2 d.f.)
Non-manual	Boys	10	9	14	2.43
Non-manual	Girls	8	5	2	7.26*
Manual	Boys	23	24	24	< 1
Manual	Girls	17	16	20	2.62

(d) Going to parties

		Often	Sometimes	Hardly ever/ never	χ^2 (2 d.f.)
Non-manual	Boys	18	11	6	35.70***
Non-manual	Girls	10	7	5	11.27*
Manual	Boys	34	24	17	298.98***
Manual	Girls	24	16	14	21.28***

activities are considered. Table 8(b) and (d), for example, show that for both sexes and social class groups, the children said to be truanting report that they read books less frequently, and that they go to parties more frequently. On the other hand, apart from the middle-class girls, who are in any case less likely to be said to truant, there is no association with how often the children said they watched television.

It might be thought that one group of children particularly likely to truant would be those who are working in their spare time: whether because such work actually interferes with the ability or energy to get to school, or because the fact that they are working is an indication that they are now more concerned with the adult world of work than with school. Table 9 offers some support for this, but the picture is not totally clear. The first part of this table enables us to consider whether the sixteen-year-olds have a spare-time job at all and if so, whether this is at weekends only, during the week only, or both. The small differences in teacher reported truancy in relation to these groups do not reach statistical significance for the middle-class girls or the working-class boys. Among the middle-class boys it is only those who have jobs both at the weekend and during the week who have a notably higher truancy rate.

In the case of the working-class girls there is little or no difference between those not working at all and those working during the week only, or both during the week and at weekends. The statistical significance stems from the contrast with those working at weekends only who are said to be truanting *less* often. It may be that what we are seeing here is a rather conscientious group of girls who tend to work primarily to contribute to the family income.

Turning to the actual number of hours worked per week, this is not associated with truancy for girls of either social class, and for boys the contrast is mainly to be found in the rather extreme groups working the largest number of hours, of whom as many as about one third are reported as truanting.

Table 9. Teachers' ratings of truancy at 16 by child's spare time work

Figures in each cell are percentages of sixteen-year-olds reported by teachers to have truanted ('somewhat' or 'certainly', see text) in the past 12 months

(a) Whether child has a spare-time job

		None	Weekends only	Weekdays only	Both	χ^2 (3 d.f.)
Non-manual	Boys	8	11	6	16	22.24***
Non-manual	Girls	5	8	9	8	5.99
Manual	Boys	23	22	23	26	3.65
Manual	Girls	19	14	21	19	8.50*

(b) Number of hours per week or work

		—3	—6	—9	—12	—15	16+	χ^2 (5 d.f.)
Non-manual	Boys	6	7	10	16	19	30	39.95***
Non-manual	Girls	5	7	8	10	16	11	2.46
Manual	Boys	23	17	21	25	28	37	31.33***
Manual	Girls	20	15	15	16	23	21	4.62

In general it seems that working outside school hours should not be seen as closely related to truancy, except perhaps for those boys with very time-consuming jobs.

TRUANCY AND CONTACT WITH SERVICES

This final section of results from the NCDS is based on the schools' responses to a question about whether or not the children in the study had had any contact, since being at secondary school, with certain services. The services concerned are listed in Table 10.

Since the reasons for such contacts and their exact nature are not known, these data should be treated with considerable caution. Nevertheless they do perhaps provide some insight into, first, whether children said to be truanting are being seen by those services which, by reason of their truancy, should be seeing them, and secondly, whether such children are possibly experiencing, or causing other types of problems which are often suggested to be concomitant with truanting.

Table 10. Teachers' rating of truancy at 16 and child's reported contact with services

Figures in each cell are percentages of sixteen-year-olds who have had contact with the service indicated, during secondary school years (school's report)

	Doesn't truant				Somewhat or certainly			
	Non-manual		Manual		Non-manual		Manual	
	Boys	Girls	Boys	Girls	Boys	Girls	Boys	Girls
Social services	1	1	3	2	9	12	17	15
Educ. welfare officer	2	1	4	3	18	21	24	25
Careers officer	69	70	78	78	80	75	75	74
Police/probation	3	0.5	5	1	23	11	31	10
Child guidance clinic	1	1	1	1	4	4	7	4
N	1490	1479	2131	2191	184	122	725	527

On the first issue, for example, it is reassuring to find that a relatively high proportion of those said to be 'certainly' truanting are also reported to have seen an education welfare officer and/or had contact with the social services department. On the other hand there remains a substantial proportion of these children who have not had such contacts. Of course this could be because the school has been able to cope without outside help, or again, because truancy has started, or been identified, too recently for a Welfare Officer yet to be involved.

It is often assumed that the child who is truanting is likely to get into trouble in other ways as well. Certainly it does appear that very high proportions of the truants (about one third in the case of working-class boys) have had some reason for contact with the police or probation service.

Perhaps particularly disturbing are the proportions not having seen a careers officer. When one takes into account that the truants are more likely to be leaving school at the minimum age, and that early-leavers are generally *more* likely to have seen a careers officer by this age (see Lambert, 1978), then one must conclude that it is the very children who are most likely to be in need of help in this area who are being missed. It is not difficult to envisage the problems which careers officers must be experiencing in attempting to see children who are truanting, but it may be the root of considerable problems in the future if they are not seen.

CONCLUSIONS

The NCDS data presented in this chapter have suggested a worryingly high level of at least occasional truancy among children in their last year of compulsory schooling. It certainly should not be assumed that truancy is restricted to one social group, but it is more likely to occur among working-class boys, living in poor housing, who spend much of their time out of school working long hours, do little reading, and whose parents show little interest in their progress at school.

Such a picture tends to suggest that the problem is social rather than educational, and is very evocative of what has been termed the 'reluctant adolescent' (Haigh, 1976); the disaffected youth no longer interested in school, and, if interested in anything at all, then only in peer-group activities and possibly in a job.

Even if the fundamental causes are, as this suggests, outside the educational system, this is not to say that schools should abandon such children as hopeless cases, or assume that they do not have any responsibility to attempt to motivate these children and involve them in school life. However this is easily said, and it is more difficult to offer positive advice to support schools in their efforts. Certainly the answer does not appear to reside in those variables which are, both within and outside the schools, traditionally interpreted as symptoms of a school's discipline and effectiveness. Of the several school variables we have examined, we have found truancy to be related only weakly to whether or not the school has a uniform (and then only in comprehensive schools and not secondary modern) and to teacher-turnover (a problem which has almost certainly considerably reduced since these data were collected); and not at all related to whether the pupils are in a school which uses corporal punishment, to the school's ability-grouping policy, to its pupil-teacher ratio, to whether it is co-educational, or to its size.

It remains possible that rather more sensitive changes to the curriculum or to pastoral structures will prove to be more effective (e.g. Hamblin, 1977). However more rigorous evidence than is presently available must be produced if we are to be confident that isolated successes are not the result simply of the charisma or enthusiasm of the individuals concerned.

ACKNOWLEDGEMENT

This work was funded by the Department of Education and Science and the Department of Health and Social Security, whose support is gratefully acknowledged. We should also like to thank our colleagues at the National Children's Bureau for their advice and comments.

REFERENCES

Belson, W. A. (1975). *Juvenile Theft: The Causal Factors*. Harper and Row, London.

Blythman, M. (1975). Truants suffer from the disadvantages of life. *Scottish Education Journal*, **58**, 80–84.

Bolton Metropolitan Borough Education Committee (1977). *Pupil Absence Survey*. Mimeo.

Carroll, H. C. M. (Ed.) (1977). *Absenteeism in South Wales*. Swansea, University College of Swansea Faculty of Education.

Coleman, J. S. *et al.* (1966). *Equality of Educational Opportunity*. U.S. Govt. Printing Office, Washington D.C.

David, P. (1975). Tracking down the truth about truants. *Municipal Review*, **46**, 549, 166–167.

Davie, R. (1972). The missing year. *The Guardian*, Sept. 12.

Davie, R., Butler, N. R., and Goldstein, H. (1972). *From Birth to Seven*. Longman in association with the National Children's Bureau, London.

DES (1977) *Educating our Children: Four Subjects for Debate*. H.M.S.O.

Douglas, J. W. B., and Ross, J. (1965). The effects of absence on primary school performance. *British Journal of Educational Psychology*, **35**, 28–40.

Finlayson, D. S., and Loughran, J. L. (1976). Pupils' perception in high and low delinquency schools. *Educational Research*, **18**, 138–145.

Fogelman, K., Goldstein, H., Essen, J., and Ghodsian, M. (1978). Patterns of attainment. *Educational Studies*, June. **4**, 121–130.

Fogelman, K. (1975). Developmental correlates of family size. *British Journal of Social Work*, **5**, 43–57.

Fogelman, K. (ed) (1976). *Britain's Sixteen-Year-Olds*. National Children's Bureau, London.

Fogelman, K., and Richardson, K. (1974). School attendance: some results from the National Child Development Study. In (Ed.) Turner, B. *Truancy*, Ward Lock, London, pp. 29–51.

Fogelman, K. (1978a). The effectiveness of schooling: some findings from the National Child Development Study. In (Eds.) Armitage, W. H. G., and Peel, J., *Perimeters of Social Repair*, Academic Press, London p. 95–103.

Fogelman, K. (1978b). School attendance, attainment, and behaviour. *British Journal of Educational Psychology*, **48**, 148–178.

Galloway, D. (1976a). Persistent unjustified absence from school. *Trends in Education*, **4**, 22–27.

Galloway, D. (1976b). Size of school, socio-economic hardship, suspension rates and persistent unjustified absence from school. *British Journal of Educational Psychology*, **46**, 40–47.

Haigh, G. (1976). *The Reluctant Adolescent*. Temple Smith, London.

Hamblin, D. H. (1977). Caring and control: the treatment of absenteeism. In (Ed.) Carroll, H. C. M. *Absenteeism in South Wales*, Faculty of Education, University College of Swansea.

ISTD. (1974). Truancy in Glasgow. *British Journal of Criminology*, **14**, 248–255.

Jencks, C. *et al.* (1972). *Inequality*. Basic Books, New York.

Lambert, L. (1978). Careers guidance and choosing a job. *Scottish Educational Studies*, **7**, 97–107.

Medlicott, P. (1973). The truancy problem. *New Society*, **25**, 768–770.

Mitchell, S. (1972). The absentees. *Education in the North*, **9**, 22–28.

Mitchell, S., and Shepherd, M. (1967). The child who dislikes going to school. *British Journal of Educational Psychology*, **37**, 32–40.

NACEWO (1975). *These We Serve*. NACEWO, Bedford.

Pringle, M. L. K., Butler, N. R., and Davie, R. (1966). *11,000 Seven-Year-Olds*. Longman, London.

Reynolds, D. (1976). Schools do make a difference, *New Society*, **37**, 223–225.

Reynolds, D., and Murgatroyd, S. (1977). The sociology of schooling and the absent pupil: the school as a factor in the generation of truancy. In (Ed.) Carroll, H. C. M. *Absenteeism in South Wales*, Faculty of Education, University College of South Wales.

Richardson, K., Ghodsian, M., and Gorback, P. (1978). The association between school variables and attainments in a national sample of sixteen-year-olds. (In preparation.)

Rutter, M., Tizard, J., and Whitmore, K. (1970). *Education, Health, and Behaviour*. Longman, London.

Sandon, F. (1961). Attendance through the school year, *Educ. Res.*, **3**, 153–156.

Scottish Education Dept. (1977). *Truancy and indiscipline in schools in Scotland*. HMSO, Edinburgh.

Terry, F. (1975). Absence from school, *Youth in Society*, **11**, 7–10.

Tibbenham, A. (1977). Housing and truancy, *New Society*, **39**, 501–502.

Tibbenham, A., Essen, J., and Fogelman, K. (1978). Ability-grouping and school characteristics, *British Journal Educational Studies*, February.

Turner, B. (Ed.) (1974). *Truancy*. Ward Lock Educational, London.

Tyerman, M. (1972). Absent from school, *Trends in Education*, 26.

Wedge, P. J. (1969). The second follow-up of the National Child Development Study, *Concern*, **3**, 34–39.

Where (1973). *Truancy:* what the official figures don't show, **83**, 228–229.

Williams, P. (1974). Collecting the figures. In (Ed.) Turner, B. *Truancy*, Ward Lock, London, pp. 20–28.

Chapter 3

Truancy, delinquency, the home, and the school

David Farrington

Using data from a longitudinal survey, this chapter investigates the kinds of home backgrounds from which truants are drawn, the kinds of people they are, and the lives they lead after leaving school. It also studies the link between truancy and delinquency, and the way in which truancy varies with the kind of school attended. Both primary and secondary school truancy have been studied, and information about secondary school truancy has been obtained both from teachers and from the children themselves.

THE PRESENT RESEARCH

This research forms part of the Cambridge Study in Delinquent Development, which is a prospective longitudinal survey of a sample of 411 males. When they were first contacted in 1961 at age 8, they included all the boys in the second forms of 6 state primary schools in a working class area of London. They have now (in 1978) been followed up for about 17 years, and are aged about 25. They were given batteries of tests in their schools when they were aged 8, 10, and 14, and were interviewed at ages 16, 18, and 21. (These ages are approximate; the tests at age 8 were actually taken at age 8–9, etc.) Their parents were interviewed in their homes by social workers about once a year from when the boys were 8 until when they were 14, and their teachers filled in questionnaires about them at ages 8, 10, 12, and 14. Information about the boys and about their parents and siblings has also been obtained from other sources, notably criminal and medical records. Further details about this research project, and about the measures described in this chapter, can be obtained in West (1969), West and Farrington (1973), and West and Farrington (1977).

MEASURES OF TRUANCY

Information about truancy was obtained from the teachers' questionnaires.

The numbers of completed questionnaires received at ages 8, 10, 12 and 14 were 404, 389, 404, 384 respectively. Different teachers completed the questionnaires at each age, and none of the later teachers had access to the questionnaires filled in by the earlier teachers. The questionnaire filled in by the primary school teachers when the boys were aged 8 and 10 was a slightly modified version of that used in the National Survey in 1955 (Douglas, 1964). Only 15 boys were said to be truants at age 8, and only 10 at age 10. The decrease in truancy from 8 to 10 is in agreement with the National Child Development Study result showing that school attendance increased from 7 to 11 (Fogelman and Richardson, 1974). However, the primary school truancy rates of the present sample are about twice as high as those found in the National Child Development Study or in the Isle of Wight survey of Rutter *et al.* (1970), possibly because our children are urban and working class. The information in the two questionnaires was combined to identify a group of 24 primary school truants (5.9% of those rated). Of the remainder, 15 were said to have been absent because of lax parental attitude, 103 absent because of illness or injury or with no explanation, and 267 were regular attenders at primary school.

The questionnaire filled in by secondary school teachers when the boys were aged 12 and 14 was based on that used in the National Survey in 1959 (Douglas *et al.*, 1968). One question required the teacher to say whether the boy had played truant frequently, occasionally or not at all in the last year. At age 12, 18 boys (4.5% of those rated) were said to be frequent truants, while the number had risen to 42 (11.2%) at age 14. Altogether, 54 boys were identified as frequent truants at one or both ages.

In a different section of the questionnaire, the teacher was asked to specify the number of attendances (half-days) which the boy could have made in the last year, and the number which he had actually made. These figures were used to calculate a percentage attendance figure for each boy. The average attendance of the sample decreased from 88.3% at age 12 to 81.2% at age 14. Nearly a quarter of the boys (22.7%) had an attendance rate of 70% or less at age 14, in comparison with only 8.9% at age 12.

Where the school attendance rate was low, the teacher was asked to give the main reason for absence. At both ages, the most common reason given was illness. For example, at age 14 the reasons were classified into illness (58 boys), truancy (37), school refusal (13), parental unconcern (12), trouble at home (11), and parents' holiday (4). Other researchers have also found that illness predominates among the reasons given for non-attendance (e.g. see Carroll, 1977). It is not clear that truancy and school refusal meant different things to the teachers. Of the boys whose poor school attendance was attributed to school refusal, 53.8% were rated frequent truants in the question about truancy. This percentage can be compared with the 59.8% of those whose poor school attendance was attributed to truancy who were also rated frequent truants. In view of the similarity between these percentages, school refusal was equated with truancy.

As might have been expected, the attendance rate at age 14 was closely related to that at age 12. The vast majority (77.7%) of those with a rate of 80% or less at age 12 were still in the same low range at age 14, in contrast to 38.9% of those with a rate of 81–90% at age 12 and only 15.9% of those with a rate of 91% or more at age 12. The truancy ratings at ages 12 and 14 were also associated. Of those who frequently truanted at age 12, 37.5% were still frequent truants at age 14, in comparison with 31.3% of those who sometimes truanted at age 12 and only 6.6% of those who never truanted at age 12.

In order to obtain a summary figure for secondary school attendance, each boy was scored according to the worst of his attendance figures at 12 and 14. Unless otherwise stated, school attendance in future will refer to this worst figure, the average of which was 79.7% over all boys. Nearly a quarter (24.1%) had a worst attendance figure of 70% or less, while 32.3% had a figure greater than 90%. In comparing the worst attendance figure with the worst reason given, it became clear that, as absence became more frequent, it was more likely to be attributed to truancy. The most frequent reason given for an attendance rate between 71% and 90% was illness (47 boys), followed by truancy (18), parents' holiday (12), and parental unconcern (9). In contrast, the most frequent reason given for an attendance rate of 70% or less was truancy (38 boys), followed by illness (28), and parental unconcern (20). This kind of result was also obtained at the secondary level in the National Child Development Study (Tibbenham, 1977).

The information in the questions about truancy and school attendance at ages 12 and 14 was combined to produce a final teachers' rating of secondary school truancy. As already mentioned, 54 boys were rated frequent truants at either 12 or 14 or both. Furthermore, a school attendance of 90% or less was attributed to truancy for 56 boys. These two groups of truants overlapped considerably, since 37 boys were members of both. The 73 boys who were identified by teachers in either or both questions comprised the final category of secondary school truants.

In addition to this measure obtained from teachers, a measure of truancy was obtained from the boy himself. At age 14, the boys were given a self-reported delinquency questionnaire consisting of 38 descriptions of deviant acts, each one set out on a separate card. They were asked to sort the cards into four piles to indicate whether they had frequently, sometimes, once or twice, or never at any time committed each act. One of the acts enquired about was playing truant from school. Of the 405 boys who were tested at age 14, 72 (17.8%) admitted frequent truancy, and these will be referred to in this chapter as the self-reported truants. These 72 self-reported truants can be compared directly with the 73 teacher-rated secondary school truants. This kind of comparison has never been made before in this country, although Rutter *et al.* (1970) compared ratings of truancy by teachers and parents. It seems that until recently only one other British researcher (Belson, 1975) has studied self-reported truancy (See Chapter 2).

The present self-reported delinquency questionnaire was completed again at age 16, and at this age less than one-fifth of those who were interviewed (19.1%) said that they had never played truant. It seems, therefore, that occasional truancy was the rule rather than the exception in this sample. This later measure of self-reported truancy will not be referred to again in this chapter, because it was taken some time after the majority of boys had left school. The contemporaneous measure at age 14 is likely to be more valid, and can be more easily compared with the teachers' ratings of secondary school truancy.

The secondary school teachers' ratings of truancy were more closely linked to school attendance than were the self-reports. Of the 97 boys with attendance rates of 70% or less, 50 were teacher-rated truants, and 32 self-reported truants. Conversely, of 130 boys with an attendance rate of 91% or more, only one was a teacher-rated truant and 8 were self-reported truants. It may be that teachers are not always aware of the true reasons for non-attendance. For example, of 51 boys whose poor attendance (80% or less) was said by the teachers to be attributable to illness, nearly a quarter (23.5%) said on the self-report questionnaire that they were frequent truants. The teachers' opinion that most absences were due to illness contrasts starkly with the opinion of Reynolds and Murgatroyd (1974), based on participant observation, that three-quarters of absences were illegitimate.

Only 11 boys in the sample were taken to court for failing to attend school, mostly between ages 13 and 15, but there was every indication that they were an extreme group. Their average school attendance was only 49.9%. Seven were rated frequent truants by the secondary school teachers, 7 were frequent truants according to self-reports, and 9 were identified either by teachers or by self-reports or both.

RELATIONSHIPS BETWEEN TRUANCY MEASURES

There was a considerable overlap between the primary school and secondary school truants. Half of the primary school truants became teacher-rated truants at the secondary school, in comparison with 16.4% of the remainder. This difference is based on small numbers (only 24 primary school truants), but it suggests that habits of truancy acquired in the primary school tended to persist in the secondary school.

There was a significant overlap between self-reported and teacher-rated truancy at the secondary school. (40.3% of self-reported truants were also teacher-rated truants, in comparison with 12.9% of the remainder; $\chi^2 = 28.5$ with 1 d.f., $p < 0.001$. Throughout this chapter, significance levels are based on comparisons of percentages in 2 × 2 tables, using the χ^2 test.) It might be thought surprising that the overlap was not even greater, but it must be remembered that teachers' ratings and self-reports are subject to different biases. The most valid conclusions about truancy are likely to be those which hold for both measures.

TEACHERS' OPINIONS OF TRUANTS

In addition to reporting about truancy, the primary and secondary school teachers were asked to answer questions about other aspects of school behaviour. The questionnaires filled in at ages 8 and 10 were combined to produce measures of primary school behaviour, and those completed at ages 12 and 14 were combined to produce measures of secondary school behaviour. For example, the 184 boys who were said to be lazy in the primary school were those rated lazy at either 8 or 10 or both.

The primary school teachers said that the primary school truants were lazy, lacked concentration, were restless, were difficult to discipline, did not care about being a credit to their parents, and were not clean and tidy on arrival at school. They said the same about those who subsequently became secondary (teacher-rated) or self-reported truants. In all cases, these statements applied especially to the primary school truants, somewhat less to the secondary school truants and less again to the self-reported truants. For example, 75.0% of the primary school truants, 65.8% of the secondary school truants, and 58.3% of the self-reported truants were said to be lazy at their primary schools. All these percentages were significantly high.

The close relationship between primary school ratings and primary school truancy could have been at least partly caused by the fact that the same teachers made all the ratings. Teachers' ratings are known to be subject to a halo effect, so that teachers tend to rate a pupil on every factor according to their general negative or positive impression of him. Teachers who rate a pupil negatively on one factor tend to rate him negatively on every other factor, and seem not to consider factors independently of one another. The primary school ratings share most biases with primary school truancy (derived from the same teachers at the same time), fewer biases with secondary school truancy (derived from other teachers at a later time) and fewest biases with self-reported truancy. This probably explains why the relationships were greatest with primary school truancy and least with self-reported truancy. Since even self-reported truancy was significantly related to all the factors, this increases our confidence that the truants really were lazy, restless, and difficult to discipline at their primary schools.

Moving on to the secondary school teachers' ratings, it was again true in almost every case that the secondary school truants were rated more negatively than the self-reported truants. However, both groups were said to be lazy, not concerned to be a credit to their parents, very untidy in class work, lacking concentration, frequently restless in class, frequently disobedient, frequently difficult to discipline, unduly resentful after criticism or punishment, quarrelsome and aggressive, showing off and seeking attention, telling lies to keep out of trouble, and persistently late. In all cases, these statements were highly significantly ($p < 0.001$) related to both self-reported and secondary school truancy. Furthermore, these statements were more likely to be applied to the primary school truants than to the remainder, although the small numbers usually did not permit the χ^2 test. It seems that all three groups of truants shared these lazy, uncaring, rebellious, and aggressive characteristics in their secondary schools.

Two other groups of factors were more characteristic of the teacher-rated truants than of the self-reported truants. First of all, the primary and secondary school truants were said to have a low position in class and to be poor readers. The self-reported truants were also likely to have a low position in class, but to a much less marked degree, and they were not significantly likely to be identified as poor readers. These results can be interpreted to indicate either that the teachers were biased against the low-achieving children and were likely to label them truants unfairly (or *vice versa*), or that the low-achieving children gave misleading results on the self-report questionnaire.

The second difference between teacher-rated and self-reported truants was that neurotic symptoms were much more likely to be ascribed to the teacher-rated truants. The secondary school truants were significantly ($p<0.01$) said to be very anxious, frequently daydreaming, always tired and washed-out and ignored by other children, but none of these factors was significantly related to self-reported truancy. The secondary school truants were highly significantly ($p < 0.001$) said to be usually gloomy and sad, diffident about competing with other children, and unable to make friends, but all these factors were only just related ($p < 0.05$) to self-reported truancy. In most respects, the primary school truants were similar to the secondary school truants on these items, but the small numbers did not permit the χ^2 significance test. These results can be interpreted either to indicate that the teachers were likely to rate anxious children as truants unfairly (or *vice versa*), or that the anxious children gave misleading results on the self-report questionnaire.

Whether or not truants are low-achieving and anxious, there seems little doubt that they are lazy, uncaring, rebellious, and aggressive. This applies to primary and secondary school truants at their primary and secondary schools. Other researchers have obtained similar results. In the National Survey, Douglas and Ross (1965) found that poor attenders at the primary school were said to be lazy by their teachers, and Douglas *et al.* (1968) found that secondary school truants were said to be both nervous and aggressive by their teachers. May (1975) found that primary school truants were said to be liars, bullies, disobedient, miserable, worrying, unpopular, and solitary by their teachers, and Hersov (1960) found that secondary school truants were said to be liars. Finally, Tyerman (1968) showed that primary school truants nominated by school attendance officers were said to be lonely and unhappy, and Croft and Grygier (1956) found that teacher-rated secondary school truants were rated unpopular both by teachers and by classmates.

FAMILY BACKGROUNDS OF TRUANTS

As mentioned earlier, most of the information about the family backgrounds of the boys in this sample was obtained in interviews between the study social workers and the boys' parents. A good deal of this information was collected while the boys were still in their primary schools, long before any of them became secondary school truants. It is therefore possible to investigate how far family background information can predict truancy. In most other researches in which truancy has been studied, with the notable exceptions of the National Survey and the National Child Development Study, family background information has only been collected after children have been identified as truants. In this kind of retrospective research, it is possible for some statements about family background to be biased by the knowledge of who is or is not a truant.

Many researchers (e.g. Belson, 1975; Kavanagh and Carroll, 1977; May, 1975; Tibbenham, 1977) have found that truants are drawn disproportionately from lower class families, although some researchers (e.g. Rutter et al., 1970) have obtained no relationship between truancy and social class. In the present study, 79 boys (19.2%) came from lower class families at age 8 or 10 or both, in that the family breadwinner's job was placed in class V on the Registrar General's scale. Table 1 shows that lower class boys were over-represented among the three groups of truants, although in fact social class was less closely related to truancy than was any other factor in this table. Truancy was not significantly related to low social class when the boy was 14.

The truants in this study tended to come from the low income families, as found by Hodges (1968). They also tended to come from large sized families, defined in this study as those containing 5 or more children by the boy's tenth birthday. Several other researchers (e.g. Hodges, 1968; May, 1975; Rutter et al., 1970; Tyerman, 1968) have noted the link between truancy and large families. The truants in this study also tended to be living in dilapidated or slum housing, and their fathers tended to have erratic job records with periods of unemployment. Having an unemployed father at age 14 was significantly related to truancy. However, truancy was not related to whether or not the mother had a full-time job, when the boy was either 8–10 or 14.

The truants were also likely to have criminal parents and delinquent siblings, and their parents were said to show poor child-rearing behaviour. This was a global rating which reflected cruel, passive, or neglecting attitudes, erratic or

Table 1. Family backgrounds and personal characteristics of truants

Factor	% of all 411 boys	% of 24 primary school truants	% of 73 secondary school truants	% of 72 self-reported truants
Low Social Class at 8–10	19.2	41.7	28.8*	29.2*
Low family income at 8	22.6	33.3	47.9***	36.1**
Large family size at 10	24.1	45.8	46.6***	37.5**
Slum housing at 8–10	36.7	54.2	58.9***	51.4**
Erratic job record of father at 8–10	12.6	33.3	30.4***	25.7***
Criminal parents at 10	25.3	62.5	46.6***	41.7***
Delinquent siblings at 10	11.2	16.7	28.8***	20.8**
Poor parental child-rearing behaviour at 8	24.2	27.3	36.6*	35.2*
Marital disharmony at 8–10	26.8	42.9	42.6**	47.1***
Low parental interest in education at 8	16.5	27.3	30.9***	35.7***
Poor parental supervision at 8	19.3	42.9	44.8***	31.9**
Separations up to 10	21.9	33.3	38.4***	31.9*
Troublesome at 8–10	22.4	75.0	45.2***	38.9***
Daring at 8–10	29.7	54.2	45.1**	45.8**
Dishonest at 10	24.9	37.5	35.6	39.3**
Low IQ at 8–10	25.1	45.8	54.8***	31.9
Low vocabulary at 10	30.9	50.0	47.9**	46.5**
Poor school leaving results at 11	23.3	38.1	39.1**	42.4***
Small at 8–10	17.8	37.5	28.8*	27.8*
Neurotic extrovert at 14	22.4	33.3	26.0	33.3*
Neurotic extrovert at 16	29.6	56.5	30.6	40.3*

$*p < 0.05$, $**p < 0.01$, $***p < 0.001$ (χ^2 test based on 2×2 table). Significance test not carried out for primary school truants, because of small numbers. Not knowns excluded in calculating all percentages.

harsh discipline, and marital conflict. Hersov (1960) found that truancy was related to inconsistent home discipline, while Tyerman (1968) found that it was related to corporal punishment by the parents. Truancy was related to marital disharmony in this study, both at 8–10 and at 14. The parents of truants showed little interest in their education, as found by other researchers (e.g. Douglas and Ross, 1965; Fogelman and Richardson, 1974; Stott, 1966). Finally, the truants tended to come from those who had been separated from their parents before their tenth birthdays for reasons other than death or hospitalization. Hersov (1960) and Hodges (1968) also found that truancy was associated with the absence of one or both parents. Broken homes for reasons other than death were related to self-reported truancy, but not to secondary school truancy.

To summarize the family backgrounds of truants, they showed a familiar but depressing picture of multiple adversities (See Chapter 2).

PERSONAL CHARACTERISTICS OF TRUANTS

The most significant predictor of secondary school and self-reported truancy was the rating of troublesomeness by teachers and peers in the primary school (see Table 1). Both groups of truants were also rated daring by parents and peers, but only the self-reported truants were rated dishonest. There was no significant tendency for either group of truants to be rated unpopular by their peers at age 8-10, in contrast to the Croft and Grygier (1956) finding mentioned above. Neither group was rated nervous by their parents at age 8. The secondary school truants were rated nervous by their parents at age 14, but the self-reported truants were not. This confirms the point made earlier, that nervous boys were likely to be identified as truants by teachers but not by self-report.

Many other researchers have noted a link between truancy and low intelligence and attainment (e.g. Cooper, 1966; Douglas *et al.*, 1968; Fogelman and Richardson, 1974; Hersov, 1960; May, 1975; Rutter *et al.*, 1970). All the groups of truants in the present research had low vocabularies on the Mill Hill test at ages 10 and 14. They also had poor junior school leaving results, based on the grades for arithmetic, English, and verbal reasoning used for secondary school selection. They also tended to leave their secondary schools at the minimum age (15 at the time, in 1968). However, only the teacher–rated truants had significantly low IQs on the Progressive Matrices test, and this was true both at 8-10 and at 14. This result is relevant to the earlier observation that low-achieving boys were more likely to be identified as truants by teachers than by self-report.

There was a significant tendency for the truants to have been relatively small at age 8-10, in agreement with Cooper's (1966) finding that truants had a less well developed physique. However, height at 14 was not related to truancy, and weight was not related to truancy at either 8-10 or 14. Those identified as neurotic extroverts on the NJMI at 14 or the EPI at 16 had a significant tendency to be self-reported truants. The same was nearly true for those identified as neurotic extroverts on the NJMI at 10, for the χ^2 value was not far off statistical significance. The individual extroversion and neuroticism scores were not related to self-reported truancy at any of the three ages. Using a similar inventory (the JEPI), Kavanagh and Carroll (1977) found that poor attenders were high on neuroticism but average on extroversion.

TRUANTS AFTER LEAVING SCHOOL

During the interview at age 18, the boys were asked about many aspects of

OUT OF SCHOOL

their lives. The self-reported and secondary school truants were different from the remainder in a number of ways. Like their fathers, they had lower status jobs and more unstable job histories (see Table 2). They were heavier gamblers and smokers, and more sexually active. They were more likely to be involved in antisocial group activity, and more likely to be tattooed. On an attitude questionnaire, they were more likely to agree with the statement 'school did me very little good'. The negative attitude of truants toward school is well known (see e.g. Belson, 1975; Kavanagh and Carroll, 1977; Mitchell and Shepherd, 1967; Stott, 1966). Indeed, Stott argued that the main reason for truanting was a dislike of school.

Table 2. Truants after leaving school

Factor (at 18)	% of all 411 boys	% of 24 primary school truants	% of 73 secondary school truants	% of 72 self-reported truants
Low job status	14.1	25.0	37.7***	30.9***
Unstable job record	23.7	37.5	52.2***	36.8**
Heavy gambling	22.4	20.8	32.9*	32.4*
Heavy smoking	26.7	50.0	47.1***	41.2**
Heavy drinking	20.1	25.0	27.1	36.8***
Driving after drinking	21.9	37.5	30.0	36.8**
Drug user	31.4	41.7	41.4	51.5***
Most sexually active	42.5	62.5	63.8***	72.7***
Motoring convictions	16.5	25.0	24.3	25.0*
Involved in antisocial groups	20.8	37.5	31.4*	35.3**
Spends time hanging about	15.7	25.0	28.6**	20.6
Tattooed	9.0	16.7	24.3***	23.5***
Hospitalized for injury	36.0	54.2	47.1*	42.6
Poor relationship with parents	22.1	33.3	35.7**	30.9
Attitude: School did me very little good	33.4	41.7	47.1*	51.5***
High score on antisocial tendency	28.3	45.8	60.0***	63.2***

*$p < 0.05$, **$p < 0.01$, ***$p < 0.001$ (χ^2 test based on 2 × 2 table). Significance test not carried out for primary school truants, because of small numbers. Not knowns excluded in calculating all percentages.

A number of results were obtained from one group of secondary truants but not the other. In comparison with the remainder, the self-reported truants were heavier drinkers, more involved in drinking and driving, more likely to have motoring convictions and more likely to have used prohibited drugs such as cannabis. The secondary school truants were more likely to have a poor relationship with their parents, to spend their time hanging about, and to have been hospitalized for an injury (See Chapter 4).

West and Farrington (1977) derived a scale of antisocial tendency at age 18 from a number of these antisocial or deviant characteristics. Although only 28.3% of the sample were identified as the most antisocial on this scale, this was true of 63.2% of the self-reported truants, and 60.0% of the secondary school truants. It seems that, after leaving school, the truants tend to develop a markedly antisocial or deviant life style.

TRUANCY AND DELINQUENCY

Many researchers have discovered a link between truancy and delinquency (e.g. Douglas *et al.*, 1968; Ferguson, 1952; Hersov, 1960; May, 1975; Stott, 1966; Tennent, 1971). This was also found in the present research. As pointed out by West and Farrington (1973), 58.3% of the 24 primary school truants were found guilty as juveniles, in comparison with 17.9% of the remainder. Secondary school truancy was significantly related to juvenile delinquency (47.9% of truants were delinquents, in comparison with 14.5% of the remainder; $\chi^2 = 39.3$, $p < 0.001$), and the same was true of self-reported truancy (44.4% as opposed to 15.3%; $\chi^2 = 29.1$, $p < 0.001$). Seven of the 11 boys with court appearances for truancy were found guilty as juveniles. Hodges (1968) had earlier noted the raised incidence of delinquency among these kinds of boys.

Both secondary school and self-reported truancy significantly predicted first convictions as a young adult (i.e. between the seventeenth and twenty-first birthdays). For example, excluding the juvenile delinquents, 26.3% of the 38 secondary school truants were first convicted as adults, in comparison with 11.5% of the remainder ($\chi^2 = 5.15$, $p < 0.025$). Blackler (1968) also demonstrated the lasting predictive power of truancy, in showing that men serving their second prison sentence were more likely to have been truants than men serving their first.

In addition to their relationships with official convictions, secondary school and self-reported truancy were also significantly related to self-reported delinquency at ages 14, 16, and 18. Belson (1975) also found a relationship between self-reported truancy and self-reported delinquency. At age 14, of course, our self-reported truancy measure was not independent of our self-reported delinquency measure, but it was only one out of 38 items. Although the figures were small, there was every indication that primary school truancy also predicted self-reported delinquency at these ages. Secondary school truancy was significantly related to self-reported delinquency at age 21 (see Farrington *et al.*, 1978), but self-reported truancy was not quite.

The two measures of truancy were also significantly related to self-reported violence at ages 14, 16, and 18, and to anti-police attitudes at ages 14 and 16 and aggressive attitudes at age 18. Only secondary school truancy was significantly related to self-reported violence and aggressive attitudes at age 21.

DIFFERENCES BETWEEN TRUANTS AND DELINQUENTS

Many of the results quoted in relation to truancy mirror results previously published in relation to delinquency, no doubt at least partly because of the overlap between truancy and delinquency. West and Farrington (1977) concluded that a constellation of adverse features of family background, including poverty, too many children, marital disharmony, inappropriate child-rearing methods, and parental criminality leads to a constellation of anti-social features at age 18, among which criminality is again likely to be one element. The results quoted in this chapter indicate that truancy often intervenes between the adverse family background at age 8 and the antisocial life style at age 18.

In agreement with the idea that truancy and juvenile delinquency are two symptoms of the same underlying problem, every significant result obtained with juvenile delinquency was also obtained with truancy. Only two significant results obtained with truancy were not obtained with juvenile delinquency. The juvenile delinquents did not tend to come from lower class families at age 8–10, and they did not tend to be neurotic extroverts at 14 or 16. However, neither of these results with truancy reached the 0.01 level of statistical significance, and so it is possible that they are due to chance rather than indicative of real differences between truants and delinquents. As supporting evidence for the contention that truancy and delinquency have the same underlying causes, and that one does not cause the other, the result of Belson (1975) showing that very little delinquency occurs while truanting can be quoted.

Given the overlap between truancy and delinquency, and the fact that in general truancy precedes convictions, another question which can be asked is whether there are any important differences between truants who become delinquents and truants who do not. Of the 116 truants identified at the secondary level by either teachers or self-report or both, 68 were convicted either as juveniles or as young adults. The delinquent truants did not seem to be more extreme in their truancy than the non-delinquent truants, since the mean school attendances were 65.3% and 67.0% respectively. However, they were more extreme in other ways.

The delinquent truants were more likely to come from low income and large sized families, to have criminal parents and delinquent siblings, to be poorly supervised by their parents, to have suffered separations from their parents during their first ten years, to have a low vocabulary at age 10, and to be rated troublesome, daring, and dishonest in their primary schools. All these factors predicted both delinquency and truancy. It seems that the delinquent truants differed in degree but not in kind from the non-delinquent truants.

THE CONTRIBUTION OF THE SCHOOL

Just as Power et al. (1967, 1972) and Reynolds et al. (1976) have argued that schools influence delinquency, Reynolds and Murgatroyd (1977) have argued that schools influence truancy. The major argument of both Power and Reynolds is that schools have dramatic differences in their delinquency (and truancy) rates which are consistent over the years and which cannot be explained by reference to differing catchment areas.

Using data from the present study, Farrington (1972) investigated the role of secondary schools in producing juvenile delinquency. On leaving their primary schools, the vast majority of the sample (335 boys) went to one of 13 schools, 8 comprehensives, 3 secondary moderns, and 2 grammar schools. Using information provided by the Inner London Education Authority, these schools were classified into high, medium, and low delinquency rate groups. The study boys attending high delinquency schools were more likely to become juvenile delinquents (35.7%) than those attending medium (22.9%) or low delinquency schools (12.8%).

On the face of it, these figures seemed to show that schools influence delinquency. However, the intakes to the three groups of schools were very different. The best predictor of juvenile delinquency was the rating of troublesomeness in the primary school by teachers and peers, and the troublesomeness ratings of boys entering the three groups of schools were very different. Of those going to high delinquency schools, 37.5% were rated most troublesome and 16.1% least troublesome, while of those going to low delinquency schools 8.3% were rated most troublesome and 55.1% least troublesome. On the basis of the troublesomeness ratings of the boys entering the schools, it was possible to calculate the expected percentage of delinquents in each group of schools. The expectations on this basis were 31.3% in the high delinquency schools, 22.9% in the medium delinquency schools and 15.2% in the low delinquency schools. A glance at the actual percentages quoted above will show that the two sets of figures were quite similar, indicating that the differences between the schools in delinquency rates were primarily due to their differing intakes.

It is possible to repeat this analysis for truancy. Truancy rates in schools are known to be significantly correlated with delinquency rates (e.g. Finlayson and Loughran, 1976; May, 1975; Reynolds et al., 1976), so the high, medium and low delinquency classification supplied by the ILEA could be regarded also as a high, medium, and low truancy classification. In agreement with this suggestion, the proportion of boys entering the high schools who became secondary truants (on either teachers' ratings or self-reports or both) was 42.9%, in comparison with 30.6% in the medium schools and 18.3% in the low schools. Coincidentally, primary school troublesomeness was the best predictor of this index of secondary school truancy, just as it had been the best predictor of juvenile delinquency.

On the basis of the known relationship between troublesomeness and truancy, and the known distribution of boys entering each group of schools over the three troublesomeness categories, it was possible to calculate the expected truancy rates in the high, medium and low schools as 37.4%, 29.6% and 22.7% respectively. The first and last of these figures are only 4–5% away from the actual truancy rates given above, indicating that the major part of the variation between the schools in truancy can be accounted for by differences in their intakes. It is possible that the remainder of the variation can be attributed to the schools. However, in view of the proportion of the variation in truancy rates which could be explained by just one of the factors present at intake, it seems unlikely that the secondary schools could be exerting a major influence on truancy.

In many ways, it is counter-intuitive to argue that secondary schools have little effect on truancy and delinquency. It may be that these 13 schools are atypical. It would be interesting to know whether Reynolds and his collaborators can still demonstrate differences between their schools after controlling for intake differences which are good predictors of truancy and delinquency. For example, Galloway (1976) showed that absenteeism rates in comprehensive schools were significantly related to absenteeism rates in their feeder primary schools. The most severe test of whether secondary schools have any effect on truancy rates would be to control for the primary school truancy rates of the children entering them.

CONCLUSIONS

Truants, like delinquents, come from family backgrounds characterized by multiple adversities and have antisocial and deviant life styles after leaving school. It seems likely that adverse backgrounds produce antisocial people, and that truancy and delinquency are two symptoms of this antisociality. There was no evidence that secondary schools had an importance influence on either truancy or delinquency.

REFERENCES

Belson, W. A. (1975) *Juvenile theft: the causal factors.* Harper and Row, London.

Blackler, C. (1968). Primary recidivism in adult men: differences between men on first and second prison sentence. *British Journal of Criminology*, **8**, 130–167.

Carroll, H. C. M. (1977). The problem of absenteeism: research studies, past and present. In (Ed.), Carroll, H. C. M., *Absenteeism in South Wales.* Faculty of Education, University College of Swansea.

Cooper, M. G. (1966). School refusal: an enquiry into the part played by school and home. *Educational Research*, **8**, 223–229.

Croft, I. J., and Grygier, T. G. (1956). Social relationships of truants and juvenile delinquents. *Human Relations*, **9**, 439–466.

Douglas, J. W. B. (1964). *The Home and the School*. MacGibbon and Kee, London.

Douglas, J. W. B., and Ross, J. M. (1965). The effects of absence on primary school performance. *British Journal of Educational Psychology*, **35**, 28–40.

Douglas, J. W. B., Ross, J. M., and Simpson, H. R. (1968). *All our future*. Peter Davies, London.

Farrington, D. P. (1972). Delinquency begins at home. *New Society*, **21**, 495–497.

Farrington, D. P., Osborn, S. G., and West, D. J. (1978). The persistence of labelling effects *British Journal of Criminology*, **18**, 277–284.

Ferguson, T. (1952). *The Young Delinquent in His Social Setting*. Oxford University Press, London.

Finlayson, D. S., and Loughran, J. L. (1976). Pupils' perceptions in high and low delinquency schools. *Educational Research*, **18**, 138–145.

Fogelman, K., and Richardson, K. (1974). School attendance: some results from the National Child Development Study. In (Ed.), Turner, B., *Truancy*. Ward Lock International, London.

Galloway, D. (1976). Size of school, socio-economic hardship, suspension rates and persistent unjustified absence from school. *British Journal of Educational Psychology*, **46**, 40–47.

Hersov, L. A. (1960). Persistent non-attendance at school. *Journal of Child Psychology and Psychiatry*, **1**, 130–136.

Hodges, V. (1968). Non-attendance at school. *Educational Research*, **11**, 58–61.

Kavanagh, A., and Carroll, H. C. M. (1977). Pupil attendance at three comprehensive schools: a study of the pupils and their families. In (Ed.), Carroll, H. C. M., *Absenteeism in South Wales*. Faculty of Education, University College of Swansea.

May, D. (1975). Truancy, school absenteeism, and delinquency. *Scottish Educational Studies*, **7**, 97–107.

Mitchell, S., and Shepherd, M. (1967). The child who dislikes going to school. *British Journal of Educational Psychology*, **37**, 32–40.

Power, M. J., Alderson, M. R., Phillipson, C. M., Shoenberg, E., and Morris, J. N. (1967). Delinquent schools? *New Society*, **10**, 542–543.

Power, M. J., Benn, R. T., and Morris, J. N. (1972). Neighbourhood, school, and juveniles before the courts. *British Journal of Criminology*, **12**, 111–132.

Reynolds, D., Jones, D., and St Leger, S. (1976). Schools do make a difference. *New Society*, **37**, 223–225.

Reynolds, D., and Murgatroyd, S. (1974). Being absent from school. *British Journal of Law and Society*, **1**, 78–81.

Reynolds, D., and Murgatroyd, S. (1977). The sociology of schooling and the absent pupil: the school as a factor in the generation of truancy. In (Ed.), Carroll, H. C. M., *Absenteeism in South Wales*, Faculty of Education, University College of Swansea.

Rutter, M., Tizard, J., and Whitmore, K. (1970). *Education, Health, and Behaviour*. Longman, London.

Stott, D. H. (1966). *Studies of Troublesome Children*. London: Tavistock.

Tennent, T. G. (1971). School non-attendance and delinquency. *Educational Research*, **13**, 185–190.

Tibbenham, A. (1977). Housing and truancy. *New Society*, **39**, 501–502.

Tyerman, M. (1968). *Truancy*. London: University of London Press.

West, D. J. (1969). *Present Conduct and Future Delinquency*. Heinemann, London.

West, D. J., and Farrington, D. P. (1973). *Who Becomes Delinquent?* Heinemann, London.

West, D. J., and Farrington, D. P. (1977). *The Delinquent Way of Life*. Heinemann, London.

Out of School
Edited by L. Hersov and I. Berg
© 1980, John Wiley & Sons, Ltd.

Chapter 4

The Long-Term Outcome of Truancy

Lee Nelken Robins and Kathryn Strother Ratcliff

While truancy has obvious importance to the child's life while in school, by interfering with his learning, another concern is its long-term implications. There is surprisingly little literature on the relationship between truancy and later outcomes. The work of Lummis (1946) showing that truancy (non-attendance on own initiative) predicted bad army conduct and prolonged civilian unemployment among 1000 consecutive men coming through a British Army Selection Centre is in fact exceptional in addressing such a concern. Certainly many efforts to predict outcomes on the basis of childhood behaviours have included truancy as one of the predictors, but truancy has constituted only one element in a rating scale. Since analyses are not presented separately for the elements of such scales, we do not know how much truancy contributed to the success of prediction. As an example, the very interesting paper by Gersten *et al.* (1976) concerning the stability of childhood behaviour over time includes 'playing hooky' as an element in a scale of delinquent behaviour. The scores on this scale are more stable from one age to another than are scores on any other of the childhood scales, but it is not possible to tell whether 'playing hooky' itself is stable, or whether the total scale score is stable only because playing hooky at one period is associated with other delinquent behaviour at another.

Since attendance is regularly recorded by schools, the number of days on which there is absence is a readily identifiable although imperfect index of the degree of truancy. If the attendance record does indeed predict outcomes reliably, it would serve as a simple screening measure for selecting children at high risk of later problems. The question that we will address in this chapter is how effective days absent might be as such a screening tool.

In our previous follow-up of child guidance clinic patients (Robins, 1966), we looked at the relationship between symptoms recorded in child guidance clinic records and diagnoses made after 436 ex-patients were approximately aged 43. Diagnosis was based on systematic interview and review of records from police, hospital, welfare and other agencies. Truancy was one of the childhood symptoms that most reliably predicted an elevated rate of antisocial personality (referred to at that time as sociopathic personality) and alcoholism. It was a significant predictor of antisocial personality and alcoholism for men, but showed no significant relationship to disorders common in women. Because truancy was associated with a wide variety of other antisocial symptoms in the clinic records, we questioned its independence in predicting later psychiatric diagnoses. We found that it did make an independent contribution. Even among highly antisocial children (defined as having six or more different kinds of antisocial behaviour), when one of those behaviours was truancy, the risk of adult antisocial personality was significantly increased. However, truancy in the absence of a large variety of childhood antisocial behaviours (when there were fewer than six such behaviours), did not significantly predict an adult diagnosis of antisocial behaviour. Although truancy was a statistically significant predictor of adult psychiatric diagnoses for these ex-child guidance clinic patients, it was not a very efficient predictor. Indeed, most truant children did not warrant a diagnosis of either antisocial personality or alcoholism as adults — only 45% did (although in the absence of truancy, only 18% were so diagnosed).

Because the follow-up study of child guidance clinic patients relied for its identification of truants on a notation in the child's psychiatric clinic record, there was no quantitative information with which to establish a threshold for the degree of truancy that should alert the family or school to concern. Further, since referral to the child guidance clinic was usually for serious antisocial behaviour, rarely truancy even when truancy was present, we could not be certain to what extent truancy in the general population would be equally ominous.

THE CURRENT STUDY

To learn more about the consequences of truancy (as well as other childhood events) in the adult lives of the general population, we selected a sample of black schoolboys from St. Louis public school records and followed them into their thirties, again with systematic interviews and an exhaustive search of records. The men in the sample were all born between 1930 and 1934, and all had IQs above the median. The upper socioeconomic group, as defined by father's occupation, was oversampled, and eight equal-sized groups representing combinations of social status, broken homes, and school problems were selected. In presenting our results, cases are weighted so that they represent the population from which these groups came: black males born in St. Louis between 1930 and 1934 who attended public schools for at least six years and had IQs of 85 or higher. (See Robins and Murphy, 1967, for a more complete description.)

Ninety-five percent (223 out of 235) were interviewed between the ages of 30 and 36, and records abstracted from hospitals, police, penal institutions, public housing, public welfare, armed forces, veterans claims records, unemployment insurance claims, etc. To evaluate truancy, school records both in elementary school and in high school were obtained and carefully scored with respect to attendance. From studying the association between these records of attendance and outcomes, as revealed in interview and our search of records, it is possible to learn in considerable detail how school absence predicts outcome. Thus we were able to develop criteria for the amount and timing of school absence that may make possible selecting for intervention those children highly likely to have difficulties in later life. The fact that our measure of truancy comes directly from the attendance records means that it is independent of the judgements of teachers. Since the evaluation of adult outcomes was done by our staff independently of the evaluation of the school record, there has been no retrospective falsification or 'halo' effects due to knowing which non-attenders turned out well or badly.

PREVIOUS FINDINGS OF THE CONSEQUENCES OF TRUANCY FOR THE PRESENT SAMPLE

The present paper will present new information about the relationship between truancy in elementary and high school and adult outcomes of those surviving into their thirties. In previous papers our concern has been restricted to the impact of elementary school truancy in this sample. We have shown that elementary school truants accounted for the excess mortality in black schoolboys, as compared with expected figures based on a national white male cohort (Robins, 1968). The excess mortality was accounted for principally by homicide, but truants also had an excess of deaths by natural causes. Among those who survived past the age of 25 and so were included in the follow-up, we have shown that elementary school truancy significantly predicted four subsequent childhood events: being held back in elementary school, dropping out of high school, leaving the parental home before age 18, and marriage before age 18 (Robins and Wish, 1977). Truancy predicted these subsequent childhood behaviours at a statistically significant level even after we took into account the number and kinds of other deviant behaviours that preceded the truancy and so might have explained the subsequent behaviour. We have also found that men who were truants in elementary school tended to marry women who truanted in elementary school and that truancy in either parent was associated with an excess rate of truancy in both sons and daughters, although transmission of truancy to the sons was more striking (Robins, Ratcliff, and West, 1979). When we compared school records of the wives and children with those of our index fathers, we found that elementary school truancy did not predict high school dropout at a statistically significant level for females in either generation, but that truancy in the sons of our subjects did predict high school dropout in just the way that it had for their fathers. This suggested that our finding in the white child guidance clinic study that truancy is a more potent predictor of outcome for males than females probably holds in black non-patient samples as well.

METHODS OF ASSESSING TRUANCY LEVELS

St. Louis school records provided number of days in attendance but seldom documented reasons for absence. Occasionally there was a notation of truancy, particularly if the student was being suspended on this account, and occasionally there was a notation of illness or the family's being out of town. When one of the latter explanations for the absence was available, we did not count the absence as a possible indicator of truancy. When there was no indication, we assumed that absence was equivalent to truancy.

Elementary school

At the time our sample was attending elementary school, the eight school years were each divided into quarters of 50 days each. We counted a quarter as truant if there were unexplained absences for more than 10 days. Thus we are considering only massed absences — missing more than 20% of school days within a ten-week period. One out of six of our sample (17%) had no truant quarters by these criteria. An additional 35% had only one or two truant quarters, and 3%, while qualifying as absent in more than two quarters, ended their truancy early, having no truant quarter after second grade. We will consider this 38% with few quarters or early termination of truancy to have had only mild truancy. The remaining 45% will be considered often truant. That is, they were absent more than 20% of days in at least three quarters, and at least one of these quarters occurred after Grade Two. Relying on attendance records incorporates absences due to non-truancy causes, but by using a criterion of 20% of the days in three quarters for our often truant group we are including only those youths with rates of absence so high that they are unlikely to be explained by illness or parents' keeping the child at home. Figures for elementary school attendance from several sources show an average attendance rate of 90% in elementary school (Tennent, 1971; Cutter et al., 1971, New York State Education Department, 1967) (See Chapter 2).

Absence in first and second graders is generally thought not to be truancy, but rather unrecorded illness or parentally instigated absence. Illnesses are supposed to decline after children have more exposure to their classmates, and parentally supported absence is supposed to decline in upper grades because parents take school attendance more seriously for older children. We were surprised, therefore, to learn that two-thirds of the children who qualified as often truant in elementary school had at least one truant quarter in first grade.

Thus, even if absence in first and second grade does occur more often because of illness or with parental consent than because of truancy, it seems to establish an attendance pattern that later is a truant one.

High school

Eight per cent of our sample did not attend high school, and for 2%, we were not able to obtain high school transcripts. Five per cent who did attend high school were expelled or sent to a reformatory while still enrolled. Although boys expelled or incarcerated had often been truant before this occurred, we chose to code this more serious problem in preference to truancy and so cannot include them in our study of high school truancy. For the remaining 85% for whom we had scored records of high school attendance, we judged truancy in high school based either on days attended or notations of truancy. Absences in high school were recorded on a semester basis. For those who attended high school the expected eight semesters or more, we judged as truant those who had absences of more than ten days per semester in at least two semesters. Those who dropped out without attending eight semesters had, of course, fewer semesters in which to show a pattern of excessive absence. For them, we accepted a single semester showing more than ten days of absence if it was a semester other than the one in which the dropout occurred. (We made the latter exception because dropping out is often a gradual tapering off of attendance in the final semester.) Among those high school attenders for whom we had information about attendance, the rate of truancy was 31%.

Association between elementary and high school truancy

We found that chances of truanting in high school (as well as chances of being expelled or sent to a reformatory) were strongly predicted by truancy in elementary school (Table 1). Only 13% of those with no truancy in elementary school became truant in high school. For those mildly truant in elementary school, the rate of high school truancy (23%) was almost twice the rate for good elementary school attenders. Those often truant in elementary school became truant in 39% of cases in high school, three times the rate for elementary non-truants.

Since elementary school truancy predicted expulsion from high school and being sent to a reformatory (10% of those often truant had either outcome, vs. 1% of the remainder), the effect of truancy in elementary school on truancy in high school is even more striking when we restrict the sample to those whose truancy was evaluated. For those often truant in elementary school, 49% were also truant in high school, 3.5 times the rate of those not truant in elementary school.

Table 1. Truancy in elementary school and high school

	Truancy in elementary school		
	None	Mild: One or two quarters or none after Grade Two	Often: Three or more quarters, at least one after Grade Two
High school experience	(37)	(82)	(98)
Did not enter high school	11%	4%	11%
Expelled or sent to reformatory	1%	1%	10%
Truant	13%	23%	39%
None of these	75%	72%	40%
Truancy among those attending and not expelled or sent to reformatory	(32)	(78)	(78)
	14%	24%	49%

JUVENILE CORRELATES OF A CONTINUATION OF TRUANCY

Although truancy in elementary school did powerfully predict truancy in high school, a number of children often truant in elementary school became good attenders in high school. In an effort to discover the difference between those who 'recovered' from truancy and those who did not, we examined their scores on a scale representing other juvenile deviant behaviours. These behaviours included being held back in elementary school, drinking before age 15, sex before age 15, use before age 18 of each of four illicit drugs (marijuana, amphetamines, barbiturates, opiates), problems with alcohol before 18, leaving the parental home before 18, arrests before 18, and marriage before 18. Information about arrests and being held back came from juvenile court, police, and school records; information about the remaining items came from interview. Overall, subjects averaged 2.3 of these eleven childhood problems.

Students who were not truant or only mildly truant in elementary school had fewer of these other deviant behaviours than did those frequently truant in elementary school. Those not truant at all or only mildly truant in elementary school had four or more of these indicators of deviance in 14% of cases, as compared with 35% of those often truant in elementary school. We found (Table 2) that juvenile deviance was associated with the continuation of truancy from grade school into high school. Children who were often truant in grade school usually truanted in high school *unless* they had very little deviant behaviour of other kinds. Juvenile deviance was also associated with *beginning* truancy in high school among those who had not truanted or were only mildly truant in grade school. Those who did little truanting in grade school rarely began truanting in high school unless they were extremely deviant in other ways, in which case almost half became truant. We can also see from Table 2

Table 2. The association between juvenile deviance and continuing truancy into high school. Percentage truant in High School, given for levels of elementary school truancy and juvenile deviance.

| | Truancy in elementary school | | | |
| | Not truant or mildly truant | | Often truant | |
Juvenile deviance score [a]	N	%	N	%
0–1	(57)	16	(26)	20
2–3	(37)	19	(23)	60
4+	(16)	44	(27)	69

[a] The juvenile deviance score is a sum of eleven items: being held back in elementary school, drinking before age 15, sex before age 15, use before age 18 of each of four illicit drugs (marijuana, amphetamines, barbiturates, opiates), problems with alcohol before 18, leaving the parental home before 18, arrests before 18, and marriage before 18.

that elementary school truancy had an impact on high school truancy even when we controlled for other childhood deviance. Those often truant in grade school were more likely to truant in high school at each level of our juvenile deviance scale, although the difference is trivial among the non-deviant.

We find, then, that elementary school truancy had a clear impact on high school attendance, but that this impact was mediated by the variety of other forms of youthful deviance. Since truancy in elementary school and its appearance in high school was associated with juvenile deviance of various kinds, we will need to be careful when we look at the impact of truancy on later outcomes that we are not simply using truancy as an indicator of the general level of juvenile deviance.

THE EFFECT OF TRUANCY ON FINAL EDUCATIONAL LEVEL

Since our sample represents the upper half of the IQ range, failure to finish high school was never attributable to a lack of adequate intelligence. In this intellectually able sample, truancy and deviance probably played an even larger role in high school completion than it does in the total population of children.

Among those who met our criteria for truancy neither in elementary nor in high school, only 3% failed to graduate from high school (Table 3). Of those often truant in elementary school whose truancy continued into high school, 75% failed to graduate. (Remember that these are all voluntary dropouts. Those expelled are not counted because we did not know whether or not they had been truant before expulsion.) While the relationship between high school truancy and dropout seems inevitable, it is of interest that dropping out of high school was also influenced by the level of elementary school truancy both among those who did and those who did not truant in high school.

Table 3. Effect of truancy on final educational level

| | Truancy in elementary and high school | | | | |
	Not truant in either	Mild in elementary, not truant in high	Often in elementary, not truant in high	None or mild in elementary, truant in high	Often in elementary, truant in high
A. Final Educational Level	(28)	(59)	(40)	(23)	(38)
High school dropout	3%	22%	29%	54%	75%
Completed technical high	8%	4%	12%	8%	8%
Completed academic high, no college	48%	29%	18%	21%	8%
Any college	41%	45%	41%	17%	9%
College graduate	13%	12%	8%	2%	2%
B. College among those completing academic high schools	(25)	(44)	(23)	(9)	(7)
	46%	61%	70%	45%	51%
C. College graduation among those entering college	(12)	(27)	(16)	(4)	(3)
	31%	26%	19%	12%	29%

Of necessity, the high rate of failure to complete high school among students truant in both elementary and high school implied that they would have a very low level of college attendance and graduation. Only 9% attended college at all, and only 2% became college graduates. Parts B and C of Table 3 show that truants' relative failure to enter and graduate from college was entirely explained by their relative failure to graduate from an academic high school. There was no regular relationship between truancy in elementary or high school and entering college among those who completed an academic high school, nor between truancy and graduating from college among those who entered college.

Having shown that truancy was associated with juvenile deviance, we may wonder whether the strong effect of truancy on high school graduation and therefore on final educational level was independent of its association with deviance. In Table 4 we note that none of the children without significant truancy was a highly deviant juvenile, and that virtually all non-truants graduated from high school. At each level of deviance, the chances of graduating from high school decreased with an increase in the amount of truancy. The difference is particularly striking for those with mild amounts of deviance, where more than 90% graduated without any significant truancy but

Table 4. The effect of truancy on high school graduation, for deviant and non-deviant children. Percentage graduating from high school, given for levels of truancy and juvenile deviance.

			Truancy in elementary and high school						
Juvenile deviance Score	Not truant in either		Mild in elementary, not truant in high		Often in elementary, not truant in high		None or mild in elementary, truant in high		Often in elementary, truant in high	
	N	%	N	%	N	%	N	%	N	%
0–1	(20)	100	(28)	89	(21)	81	(9)	75	(5)	77
2–3	(8)	90	(22)	84	(9)	74	(7)	32	(14)	40
4+	(0)	—	(9)	33	(8)	39	(7)	23	(19)	0

less than 40% graduated if they had been truant in high school. Few highly deviant children graduated, but even they showed considerable effect of truancy. Whereas a third of those who were not truant in high school did graduate despite their deviant behaviour, only 6% did so if they were truant in high school, and nongraduated if they had been both truant in high school and often truant in elementary school. Thus truancy greatly influenced high school graduation at all levels of deviance.

Since high school graduation in turn has substantial effects on job opportunities, not only in terms of prestige and salary but also in terms of job security, any effect of truancy on occupational success can be expected to be mediated to some extent through its effect on high school graduation. Opportunities for occupational success in turn will probably have important consequences for all kinds of adult problems, such as drinking, arrests, and depression. We will be interested in learning whether truancy has any additional effect on occupational success or its correlates when its effect on high school graduation is held constant. If it is found to have no further effect, this would suggest that the stigmatization of the truant as a dropout might have been more important in determining his later outcome than any effect that non-attendance at school might have had on his fund of knowledge or his competence.

THE EFFECT OF TRUANCY ON ADULT OUTCOMES

We will examine the effect of truancy on four measures of adult outcomes: earnings of less than $101/week, deviant behaviours other than drug abuse, drug abuse, and psychological status. Since higher paying jobs go to high school graduates, and since we have shown that truants often drop out before graduation, we would expect to see an effect of truancy on earnings. Since we know from previous work that juvenile deviant behaviour predicts adult deviant behaviour, and since we have shown truancy to be associated with juvenile deviant behaviour, we would also expect to find a correlation between truancy and adult deviance. There has been little in the literature to suggest that truancy ought to be associated with psychological symptoms. In fact, there has been a long-standing view that deviant behaviours (of which we can consider truancy one) and psychological symptoms are alternative ways of responding to life's problems. However, since we found no such inverse correlation between levels of deviant behaviour and psychological symptoms in our earlier work (Robins, 1966), we might expect either no relationship between truancy and psychological state in this sample or perhaps even a positive one.

Earnings

As expected, earnings were highly correlated with truancy (Table 5(A)). Almost all (85%) of those who did not truant were earning more than $100 per week at time of interview or when last employed; only about a third of those who truanted in high school were earning this much. Those who truanted only in elementary school earned less than those not truant at all. This pattern of relationships between truancy and earnings closely resembles the pattern of relationships between high school graduation and truancy, as we expected.

Adult deviant behaviour and drug use

Combining information from records and interview, we scored nine kinds of adult deviant behaviour: Alcohol abuse; marital problems; criminality; parental irresponsibility (fathering an illegitimate child, or failing to support legitimate ones); violence as indicated by getting into fights or wife and child beating; job problems as indicated by long periods of unemployment, excessive absenteeism or tardiness while working, being fired for incompetence, and never holding high status jobs; disciplinary problems in the military; 'street life', by which we refer to spending much leisure time away from home and in bars, poolrooms, or out on the streets; and drug abuse. To discover whether these behaviours all formed a single dimension of deviance, we performed a principal components factor analytic evaluation of them (Armor, 1974). We found that all except drug abuse did form a single dimension. Although drug abuse had some association with other forms of deviance, it also was associated with the psychological problems we will be discussing later, and it did not fall more clearly within the deviance dimension than within the psychological one. Among the deviance measures which did form a single dimension, the one with the smallest factor loading (i.e., least well associated with other deviance variables) was street life. Street life was also about as strongly associated with drug abuse as with the other deviance measures. We summed the eight variables which formed a single dimension by factor analysis to form an 'Adult Deviance' scale and kept drug abuse separate from both the deviance and psychological status scales.

Table 5. Truancy as a predictor of adult outcomes

	Truancy in elementary and high school				
Adult outcomes	Not truant in either (28)	Mild in elementary, not truant in high (59)	Often in elementary, not truant in high (40)	None or mild in elementary, truant in high (23)	Often in elementary, truant in high (38)
(A) Earn >$100/wk (per cent)	85%	73%	59%	32%	38%
(B) Deviance score (mean)	5.5	6.3	5.8	9.2	10.1
(C) Elements of deviance scale and drug use (per cent)					
Alcohol problems	14%	12%	12%	40%	45%
Marital problems (if married 2 + yrs)	25%	39%	27%	55%	57%
Criminality	29%	29%	25%	49%	61%
Job problems	15%	21%	23%	49%	55%
Violence	4%	18%	16%	36%	34%
Parental irresponsibility	21%	41%	50%	57%	59%
Military problems (if served)	38%	28%	30%	34%	60%
Street life	21%	29%	21%	42%	28%
Regular illicit drug use	2%	19%	20%	43%	14%
(D) Psychological status (mean)	2.2	3.1	2.6	4.1	4.0
(E) Elements of psychological status scale (per cent)					
Anxiety (2 + symptoms)	19%	33%	27%	48%	35%
Depression (2 + symptoms)	23%	42%	39%	47%	53%
Hallucinations, delusions	11%	13%	11%	17%	21%
Treatment	32%	44%	38%	53%	65%

Section (B) of Table 5 shows that truancy was indeed a good predictor of scores on the Adult Deviance scale. Those who had no significant truancy had the lowest mean score (5.5) while those who were often truant in grade school and also truant in high school had a mean score almost twice that high (10.1). Section (C) of Table 5 looks at the effect of truancy on individual deviant behaviours making up the Adult Deviance scale and on drug abuse. It will be noted that for alcohol problems, marital problems, criminality, and job problems, high school truancy had a marked effect but elementary school truancy did not (that is, in Table 5(C) there is little difference among Columns 1 to 3 or between Columns 4 and 5, but a large difference between Columns 3 and 4). Violence was also better predicted by high school than elementary school truancy, but an absence of truancy in both elementary and high school meant a virtual freedom from violence. Parental irresponsibility is the only behaviour more closely associated with elementary than high school truancy. Problems in military service were predicted by a combination of frequent truancy in both elementary and high school. Since drug abuse and participation in street life were strongly associated, it is no surprise that they have a similar pattern of relationships with truancy. Both drug abuse and street life are largely restricted to men *who became truant in high school for the first time.* Our finding of a different pattern for drug abuse than for other deviant behaviours echoes the findings of others (e.g. Johnston, 1973) that adolescent drug abuse, unlike delinquency and other forms of deviance, is not associated with early school problems or with low IQ. Rather it is associated with the onset about age 15 of precocious drinking and sexual activity. Concomitantly, truancy begins.

Psychological outcomes

To study the relationship between truancy and adult psychological status, we created an Adult Psychological Status scale composed of four subscales representing (a) the number of anxiety symptoms reported in interview, (b) the number of depressive symptoms reported in interview, (c) self-report of hallucinations (seeing or hearing something that others could not see or hear, other than the voice of a dead relative) or a report in psychiatric records of hallucinations or delusions, and (d) treatment for psychiatric problems. Table 5(D) shows a positive relationship between truancy and this adult psychological status scale. Those truant in high school had average scores almost twice as high as those who were never truant, just as we found in comparing their scores on the Adult Deviance scale. Truancy in elementary school had less effect on psychological problems than did high school truancy, again the same pattern of relationships we observed between truancy and adult deviance.

When we examine the effects of truancy on the elements of the psychological status scale (Table 5(E)), we find that high school truancy was associated with an increased level of each problem. The psychiatric care variable is somewhat contaminated with deviance, since psychiatric care includes hospitalization for the treatment of alcoholism and drug abuse. However, the fact that anxiety symptoms, depressive symptoms, and hallucinations and delusions each increased with high school truancy shows that the correlation between truancy and overall poor psychological adjustment is not an artifact of hospitalization for deviant behaviours.

DOES TRUANCY AFFECT OUTCOMES OTHER THAN THROUGH ENCOURAGING DROPOUT?

Truancy is clearly associated with each of the adult outcomes we examined. We had anticipated its relationship with earnings, based on our observation that truancy predicted high school dropout, and we considered the possibility that low earnings and other aspects of poor occupational opportunities might result in low self esteem with concurrent depressive and anxiety symptoms. Low earnings might also encourage theft to increase income and substance abuse to overcome feelings of alienation and low self esteem. It was thus possible that all these later effects of truancy might have been mediated through truancy's effect on high school graduation. To learn whether truancy had any additional long-term effects, we considered its relationship to adult outcomes separately for high school graduates and nongraduates.

While high school graduation was generally associated with an increased likelihood of earning more than $100 a week, remarkably, for children often truant in grade school who continued to be truant in high school, graduation from high school made no contribution to their earnings, so severely were earnings affected by truancy (Table 6). Truancy decreased the chances of higher earnings for graduates and nongraduates, with high school truancy

Table 6. Truancy and adult outcomes for high school graduates and dropouts

Adult outcomes	Truancy in elementary and high school			
	No truancy or mild in elementary only	Often in elementary, not truant in high	None or mild in elementary, truant in high	Often truant in elementary, truant in high
High school graduates	(74)	(28)	(11)	(10)
Earned > $100/week	79%	74%	45%	36%
Mean deviance score	5.2	5.2	7.6	6.0
Mean psychological status score	2.7	2.4	2.9	2.6
Regular illicit drug use	12%	25%	27%	0%
High school dropouts	(14)	(12)	(13)	(28)
Earned > $100/week	67%	52%	23%	40%
Mean deviance score	8.9	7.2	10.6	11.5
Mean psychological status score	3.5	3.1	5.1	4.5
Regular illicit drug use	24%	10%	56%	19%

playing the more important role. High school truancy also had a striking effect on adult deviance scores for both graduates and nongraduates, and on psychological status scores for nongraduates, although there was no such effect for graduates. Truancy initiated in high school predicted drug use only for those who failed to complete high school. Half (56%) of the nongraduates who had initiated truancy in high school used drugs regularly, in contrast to one-fourth or less of all other groups. We find, then, that truancy usually continues to show an effect even after taking into account the fact that it frequently impedes high school graduation. That is not to say that truancy's leading to dropping out of high school was not a main factor in its impact on adult outcomes. Those who graduated generally earned more and had less adult deviance and fewer psychological problems, but truancy still had an additional effect beyond its effect on graduation.

Having found that truancy continues to have an effect, even taking high school graduation into account, the final question remains: is that effect of truancy entirely due to its association with other forms of juvenile deviance?

THE EFFECT OF TRUANCY ON ADULT OUTCOME, CONTROLLING ON JUVENILE DEVIANCE AND HIGH SCHOOL GRADUATION

Needing to hold constant both deviance and high school graduation when we look at the relationship between truancy and adult outcomes strains our sample size severely. To preserve cells of a reasonable size, we divided high school dropouts and graduates at approximately their respective medians with respect to juvenile deviance. Because high school truancy was a stronger predictor of adult outcomes than elementary school truancy, we simplified our measure of truancy into those who were and who were not truant in high school. Table 7 presents results for the eight resulting subsamples with respect to their earnings, their scores on the Adult Deviance and Psychological Status scales, and their regular use of illicit drugs.

There are 16 comparisons available between high school truants and nontruants. In all but three of these 16 comparisons, truants fared worse than nontruants. Two of the three exceptions were in drug use, which we have previously noted was not regularly related to high school truancy. The third exception was in the psychological status of high school graduates free of deviance. Both truants and non-truants in this favoured group had few psychological symptoms. Indeed, aside from its effect on their earnings, truancy had little effect on the outcomes of nondeviant high school graduates. In this group, both truants and non-truants were rarely deviant adults, rarely used drugs, and were almost free of psychological problems.

Among highly deviant children, the additional effects of truancy were remarkably large in both graduates and non-graduates. For both, truancy had substantial effects on earnings and adult deviance.

To compare the relative contributions of high school truancy, graduation, and juvenile deviance to these four outcomes, we entered them into a Multiple Classification Analysis (Table 8). We found that together they explained a

Table 7. Effect of high school truancy on adult outcomes beyond that accounted for by its association with deviance and dropout

	Dropouts				Graduates			
	High Juvenile Deviance (4+)		Low or Mild Deviance (0–3)		High or Moderate Juvenile Deviance (2+)		Low Deviance (0–1)	
Adult Outcomes	High school truant (24)	Not high school truant (11)	High school truant (17)	Not high school truant (14)	High school truant (10)	Not high school truant (39)	High school truant (11)	Not high school truant (62)
Earns > $100/wk.	27%	89%	44%	54%	30%	63%	47%	79%
Uses drugs regularly	43%	18%	12%	14%	18%	32%	11%	4%
Mean deviance score	12.4	8.8	9.4	7.5	8.4	5.9	5.5	5.0
Mean psychological status score	4.9	3.9	4.4	2.7	3.4	2.8	2.2	2.5

Table 8. Multiple classification analysis of the effects of high school truancy, high
school graduation, and juvenile deviance on four adult outcomes

	Adult outcomes			
	Earnings > $100	Deviance scale	Psychological status	Drug abuse
Total explained variance	0.13	0.30	0.09	0.17
Betas for:				
high school truancy	—0.31	0.20	0.11	0.03
high school graduation	a	0.22	0.15	a
juvenile deviance	—0.12	0.26	0.11	0.47

[a]Reversed direction after adjustment for contributions of the other two predictors.

substantial amount of the variance in adult deviance (30%), 17% of the
variance in adult drug abuse, 13% of the variance in low earnings, and only
9% of the variance in psychological status.

The three predictor variables were approximately equally powerful with
respect to predicting adult deviance and psychological status. For deviance,
truancy had only a slightly lower beta value (i.e. its contribution after
adjusting for the contribution of the other two predictors) than did juvenile
deviance (0.20 vs. 0.26) and graduation (0.20 vs. 0.22). With respect to
psychological status, truancy had a beta equal to juvenile delinquency's and
slightly lower than graduation's. With respect to drug abuse, only deviance
made an independent contribution; neither high school graduation nor truancy
added to its effect. With respect to predicting low earnings, high school
truancy was the only important one of the three variables, alone accounting
for 10% of the variance after adjustment for the impact of the other two
variables, out of the 13% explained by all three.

Thus, we can conclude that high school truancy is a particularly good
childhood predictor of very low earnings, and a reasonably good predictor of
adult deviance — about as good as high school graduation or other forms of
deviance. None of our childhood predictors was very effective in predicting
psychological status, but truancy was as effective as the others. High school
truancy was not an independent predictor of adult drug abuse, as we suspected
earlier when we found that it was predictive only when there had been no
elementary school truancy and only if there was also significant deviant
behaviour of other kinds.

CONCLUSIONS AND IMPLICATIONS

We have shown that truancy had important implications for both childhood
and adult outcomes of our sample of young black men. Elementary school
truancy, often beginning in first grade, forecast continued truancy in high

school, particularly in those who had other kinds of deviant behaviour such as early drinking, early sexual activity, illicit drug use, and delinquency. Boys not truant in elementary school seldom became truant later unless they began this set of adolescent deviant behaviours at the same time. Both elementary and high school truancy were associated with dropping out of school before completing secondary education, and also with low earnings as an adult. High school truancy was strongly related to a variety of adult deviant behaviours, and somewhat associated with psychological disturbance.

These dismal outcomes for truant schoolboys were in part explained by the truants' failure to finish high school and by their concurrent adolescent deviance, but truancy itself continued to have predictive power even when these intermediary events were taken into account. In a previous paper (Robins, Ratcliff, West, 1979) we showed that in addition to the effects discussed here, those truant in elementary school tended to marry women who had been similarly truant and to produce truant sons and daughters, thus perpetuating a truant pattern in the next generation.

We do not know how generalizable these findings are to other populations, but they are sufficiently similar to our findings among our male white child guidance clinic patients of an earlier generation that we suspect them of having considerable generalizability for males.

Our findings of long-term effects of truancy could probably be duplicated with many other forms of childhood deviance. Delinquency, early drinking, fighting, etc. may each prognosticate adult problems, assortative mating with similar spouses, and the parenting of similarly affected offspring. Truancy is a special case, however, for two reasons: It is readily detectable from routinely kept school attendance records, and it typically shows itself earlier than does any other form of childhood deviant behaviour. Thus detecting children in whom to invest effort is simple, and if preventive efforts were successful, they could be expected to affect not only truancy levels, but to forestall a variety of related deviant acts that may otherwise appear later. In this sample, excessive absences were almost always detectable in the very first year of school, allowing intervention before the academic failure that frequently follows truancy occurs and makes school attendance even less attractive, thus intensifying and prolonging the truancy.

While truancy is interesting just because it presents opportunities for early intervention, there is nothing in our study to suggest that later intervention would be useless. Boys who entered secondary school with a history of prior truancy were not only at high risk of continuing their truancy there, but also of dropping out even if their truancy subsided. A review of elementary school attendance records for high school entrants would allow identifying this high risk group. Finally, we found that boys who graduated from high school despite truancy there had considerably better adult outcomes than those whose truancy led to dropping out. This suggests that it may be worth experimenting with methods for encouraging completion of high school even for this very high risk population. Of course, our findings were not based on an experiment. We do not know, therefore, whether those few who graduated despite a history of truancy had special personal assets we have not evaluated, or whether they happened to encounter a favourable home or school environment that accounted for their success. To the extent that the explanation was the latter, forms of successful intervention to allow deviant, truant children to finish high school may be discoverable.

Among high school students, there is a group who begin truanting after no school problems in elementary school. We have found such adolescents to have frequently begun engaging in early sexual experimentation, drinking, and drug abuse about the time they began truanting. This combination of behaviours forecasts dropping out of school, and after dropping out, a strong likelihood of continuing deviance and drug abuse. Such children who had no indicators of intellectual or social problems before exposure to the drug and alcohol scene in adolescence can be identified through the dramatic change in their attendance records. Given their early promise and their disastrous outcomes if their truancy culminates in dropping out, they are a group for whom intervention is particularly appropriate.

ACKNOWLEDGEMENT

This work was supported in part by USPHS grants MH 18864, MH 14677, DA 00013, DA 00259, and AA 03539.

REFERENCES

Armor, David J. (1974). Theta Reliability and Factor Scaling. In H. L. Costner, *Sociological Methodology*, 1973-1974, San Francisco: Jossey Bass, Inc. pp. 17-50.

Cutter, N. C., and E. R. Jones (1971). Evaluation of ESEA Title VIII Dropout Prevention Program 'Project KAPS' School Year, 1970-1971. Mimeo, available through Educational Resources Information Service (ERIC) Document Reproduction Service.

Gersten, J. C., Langner, T. S., Eisenberg, J. G., Simcha-Fagan, O., McCarthy, E. D. (1976). Stability and change in types of behavioral disturbance of children and adolescents, *J. Abnormal Child Psychol*, **4**, 111-127.

Johnston, Lloyd (1973). *Drugs and American Youth*. Ann Arbor: Institute for Social Research, The University of Michigan.

Lummis, Clifford (1946). The relation of school attendance to employment records, army conduct and performance in tests, *British Journal Educational Psychology*, **16**, 13-19.

New York State Education Department (1967). New York State Annual Evaluation Report for 1966-67 Fiscal Year. Albany: University of the State of New York, Mimeo, available through Educational Resources Information Service (ERIC) Document Reproduction Service.

Robins, L. N. (1966). *Deviant Children Grown Up: A Sociological and Psychiatric Study of Sociopathic Personality*. Baltimore: The Williams and Wilkins Co., 1966. Reprinted and published by Robert E. Krieger Publishing Co., Inc., Huntington, New York, 1974.

Robins, L. N. (1968). Negro homicide victims — who will they be? *Trans-action*, **5**, 15–19.

Robins, L. N., and Murphy, G. E. (1967). Drug use in a normal population of young Negro men, *American Journal of Public Health*, **57**, 1580–1596.

Robins, L. N., Ratcliff, K. S., and West, P. A. (1979). School Achievement in Two Generations: a study of 88 urban black families. In (Ed.), S. J. Shamsie, New Directions in Children's Mental Health, New York: Spectrum Publications, pp. 105–130.

Robins, L. N., and Wish, E. (1977). Childhood deviance as a developmental process: A study of 223 urban black men from birth to 18, *Social Forces*, **56**, 448–473 (1977); errata **56**: 999 (1978).

Tennent, T. G. (1971). School non-attendance and delinquency, *Educational Research*, **13**, 185–190.

Chapter 5

School Factors and Truancy

David Reynolds, Dee Jones, Selwyn St. Leger, and Steven Murgatroyd

Truancy from school is a subject about which there is much public discussion. As is to be expected, there is no shortage of opinions as to what the causes of the phenomenon are and, in addition, no shortage of opinions as to those policies that should be implemented to contain or reduce the scale of the problem. In this public discussion, suggested likely causes range from those of excessive lead in the atmosphere (Adams, 1978), general permissiveness in society and comprehensive education (Boyson, 1974), to the apparent increasing incongruity in the expectations of pupil behaviour held on the one hand by the school system and on the other hand by the parents and by the children themselves (Mays, 1973). Suggested policy options for dealing with the problem range from the development of social work teams in schools (Department of Health and Social Security, 1977) to the addition of special sanctuaries or withdrawal units for the truants, who may be thus enticed into returning to their schools (Hunkin, 1978).

Although public discussions of truancy clearly generate much heat, they rarely generate much light because they are chiefly conducted by representatives of those groups involved in the provision of educational services, who rarely have an interest in any objective, scientific assessment of the problem, its nature and its causes. In particular, discussions of truancy conducted by the teacher unions, the local education authorities, and the Department of Education and Science, tend to have a restricted focus. They locate the causes of the problem as lying in either macro-societal factors such as the nature of the class system, or in micro-societal factors such as individual family structure, family attitudes and parental standards of behaviour.

An example of this first level of analysis is given in the comments of a Director of Education, who argued recently that:

When it comes to analysing the root causes there are the widest divergencies of viewpoints and theories — the effects of a sick society, the abandonment of religious beliefs and moral values, the consequences of an unjust social

85

and economic system, or even, as I have heard it convincingly argued, as a result of damage done to the nervous system by excess lead in the urban air in which many of us are condemned to live and work.

(Adams, 1978)

The second hypothesis — that truancy is caused by factors that operate at the micro-societal level — also has wide support and is exemplified in the recent views of the President of the National Association for Social Workers in Education, who apparently believes that:

School absenteeism is following the trend in industry and commerce . . . these children manipulate their parents and the parents collude with them and keep them at home for their own purposes.

(Coombes, quoted in Hunkin, op.cit.)

Such views, which clearly locate the causes of truancy in factors other than the educational system itself, should not surprise us in view of their proponents' relationship with — and presumed commitment to — the educational system of our society.

What should surprise us, however, is that the great majority of the existing researches into truancy also neglect to study whether aspects of the educational system may cause truancy. In part, this neglect to study the school's role in the possible generation of truancy reflects the general paucity of academic research in this field that has been referred to by many writers (e.g. Evans, 1975). It has proved extremely difficult to collect valid and reliable measures of attendance itself and both national and local surveys have been regarded as invalidated by mistakes in filling up registers, by subsequent clerical errors and — some believe — by the 'rigging' of the records by form teachers, head teachers, and education authorities (Cameron, 1974). Even if valid data on attendance rates has been obtainable, it has still proved difficult to interpret. There are many possible reasons for absence that are not truancy. Pupil absence may be explicable by illness or perhaps by 'socio-medical' or 'psychosomatic' reasons (Galloway, 1976). Further absence that is not explicable by the above factors may be due to school refusal, a symptom complex that is generally argued to be separate from truancy (Hersov, 1961(a) and (b)). Furthermore, many writers (Galloway, op.cit.) believe that further refinements of simple absence data are needed to separate out those children who are absent but kept at home from the 'real' truants, who are regarded as those children who are absent without parental knowledge or permission.

The formidable difficulties involved in the collection and classification of data on attendance in general and on truancy in particular, may well be part of the explanation for the absence of a substantial body of research work into factors associated with pupil truancy.

What these difficulties do not explain, though, is the quite consistent tendency for the existing research to limit the focus of investigation to the consideration of the possible causal effects of individual factors (such as attitudes, intelligence, personality) and family factors (such as parental level of 'social deprivation', attitudes to education) with the consequent exclusion of any examination of factors connected with the educational system in general and with the character of individual schools in particular.

A review of the existing literature makes this plain (for a more comprehensive review, see Carroll, 1977). Truants have been generally found to be of somewhat lower intelligence (Cooper, 1966) and to be of substantially lower attainments (Douglas and Ross, 1965; Fogelman and Richardson, 1974), although the direction of this relationship between truancy and academic failure remains a matter of some conjecture. Truants have been described as being 'lonely, and insecure' (Tyerman, 1958) and as lacking friends (Croft and Grygier, 1956). Furthermore, it appears that — in that statement of the obvious so beloved by many writers on the subject — they don't like their schools very much (Raven, 1975; Seabrook, 1974).

Research on the family backgrounds of truants is fairly consistent in its findings. Truancy is seen to be significantly associated with lower social class (Fogelman and Richardson, op. cit.), higher than average family size (Mitchell, 1972), poverty (Galloway, op. cit.), poor housing conditions (Tibbenham, 1977), and a complex of factors that can be called social disadvantage (National Association of Chief Education Welfare Officers, 1975).

Research into the individual and family factors that are associated with truancy is thus well established (See Chapters 2 and 3), yet most of the above studies simply ignore the school, treat it as a given or openly state, as does Cooper (1966), that 'The role of the school in school refusal appeared to be a minimal one', a conclusion that is easily understandable in view of the author's total neglect to gather any data on schools. Since children — even truants — have spent much of their time in schools and since the school is the first significant area of authority relationships that the child has entered outside the home, this neglect of the school environments of truanting children is somewhat disturbing. What factors can explain it?

In part, the tendency amongst researchers to concentrate upon analysis of the family backgrounds of truants may reflect the continuing influence of past work conducted into the causes of 'school phobia'. This work, which was extensive both in America from the 1930s onwards and in Britain in the 1950s and early 1960s, attempted to relate pupil absence to factors concerned with the home, such as relationships with the mother, rather than to factors concerned with the school. Throughout this literature, the emphasis is on how the presenting problem — not going to school — may reflect other underlying problems of family relationships. Thus early American research work on truancy, which began to expand in quantity from the early 1940's onwards, adopted many of its dominant perceptions from the work on school phobia. Waldfogel *et al.* (1957) described the children's underlying problems as 'an anxiety reaction' related to 'the displacement of unconscious fears', which may have nothing to do with the school. Andriola's (1946) description of the truancy 'syndrome' sounds very like many other descriptions of school phobia, since it involves:

> . . . severe parental rejection usually by the mother and frequently involving concomitant rejection by parental substitutes such as teachers; serious marital disorder of the parents which may not be apparent to the casual observer; and strong underlying feelings of inadequacy and worthlessness on the part of the child.

Earlier work on school phobia — indicating that there may be home based explanations for behaviour in the other setting of the school — has no doubt had its influence. The psychological paradigm itself — with its emphasis on the importance of early learning experiences within the family — that has been adhered to both by Freud and Piaget, continues to emphasize the primacy of within family 'micro-level' factors. The psychological paradigm also — which permits 'qualified' practitioners to underrate individuals' own accounts of, and explanations for, their own behaviour — has had an influence in allowing the substitution of 'home-based' explanations for truancy. For example, some of Tyerman's (1958) group of truants told him that they were not at their schools because they didn't like them and instead of accepting those reasons as valid explanations, the researcher comments that:

> These reasons may be valid but it is unwise to accept truants' excuses at their face value. The limits of self deception are wide and it is easier to blame other people than oneself. Parents and children look for scapegoats and teachers are often chosen.

Quite apart from the existence of this psychological paradigm and its effects both in leading researchers to concentrate upon within-family factors and to treat truants' 'school-based' explanations as merely rationalizations of more deep-seated disturbances, other important reasons may be discerned that can explain the neglect of the school in research on truancy. Many educational researchers share a still quite prevalent societal belief that education is a social 'good' and that inability to accept this 'good' must be a consequence of some kind of 'cultural deficit' in the educational consumer. The organizations that control research workers' access to schools have also seen research into the mechanics of the system of schooling as an ideological, political, and practical threat — important work by Power (1967; 1972) into the effects of different schools in generating different levels of delinquency was stopped by the Inner London Education Authority and the National Union of Teachers before he could discover how the schools were having their differential effect.

Furthermore, nothing ensures continued neglect of an area of scientific research like past neglect by scientific researchers and there is currently no adequate body of knowledge that can guide researchers interested in 'school factors' into the most promising areas of investigation. The consequent need to measure everything about the organization of schools (since it is impossible to know from the literature which area to concentrate on) and the need for the research to still look at family and neighbourhood factors to establish whether school factors are of importance anyway, makes such research both difficult and wide ranging in scope.

The final factor that can explain the neglect of the school in research on truancy is that much educational research purports to show that individual schools have very little independent effect upon their pupils and that the crucial determinants of educational outcomes lie in the macro and micro-societal structures that determine what goes on in schools (Jencks, 1972; Bowles and Gintis, 1976). In their statistical analysis, though, these studies are usually heavily loaded with family variables rather than school variables. The school variables that are included are of the simplest — and most banal — kind, such as size of school playground or number of library books per pupil. The absence of a relationship between identifiable school factors and pupil outcome may therefore merely reflect the fact that those features of schools that do have an impact upon the pupils have not been identified or measured.

To sum up so far, we have seen that research on truancy is both relatively small in quantity, due to various entirely understandable problems, but also consistently biased in its quality towards the investigation of individual and family factors and their association with truancy. A variety of factors — an ideological belief in the value of education or the existence of the psychological paradigm — may account for this 'individualizing' of what *may* in part be institutionally caused behaviour.

However, in recent years there has begun to emerge a body of both theoretical and empirical sociological knowledge which suggests that the school system itself may be an important influence in generating truancy and other forms of pupil rebellion, and, more importantly, that there may be identifiable factors within schools that are closely associated with the development of truanting behaviour amongst their school children.

At a theoretical level, two schools of sociological theory — American 'sub-cultural' theory and both American and British 'symbolic interactionism' — have argued for the importance of considering the nature of the educational system as an active 'factor' in the causation of truancy, delinquency, and adolescent deviance of other kinds. The 'sub-cultural' theories are basically two fold — the 'blocked opportunity' hypothesis of Cloward and Ohlin (1961) and Cohen (1955), and the 'cultural conflict' hypothesis of Miller (1958) in the United States and Mays (1964) in Britain. In the blocked opportunity hypothesis, pupil deviance is seen as the result of blockages upon the attainment of highly valued success goals. The educational system and the teachers that staff it may — because of their so called middle-class assumptions as to what constitutes the 'good' pupil — deny working-class pupils status within the schools because these same pupils have not been socialized to fulfil the status requirements of middle-class society and its schools. Their chances of obtaining the success goals that they wish for through the schools are therefore much reduced and deviance may arise because of the pupils' adoption of illegitimate means to attain their success goals. Schools may contribute to this process by any processes that block off their students from the possibility of obtaining legitimate status within the school, such as by streaming (as in Hargreaves, 1967).

The 'cultural conflict' hypothesis of Miller (1958) and Mays (1964) also points to the importance of considering the role of the educational system in generating pupil deviance, which — in this case — is seen as caused by a clash between the culture of the schools and their pupils' own neighbourhood and home cultures. Mays' (1964) classic study of Liverpool sees pupil deviance and delinquency as a natural behaviour which is '. . . not so much a symptom of maladjustment as of adjustment to a sub-culture, in conflict with the culture of the city as a whole'. In this hypothesis, the educational system is seen as 'maladjusted' to the needs of its pupils and school practices like a non-relevant curriculum, a middle-class ethos, the language codes used by the teacher and some of the practices like streaming, already mentioned, may generate pupil deviance.

The interactionist school, too, has drawn attention to the ways in which the educational system can be said to generate deviance. Their concentration is on the interaction of pupils and teachers, the treatment of pupils by teachers and the labelling effect by which teacher judgments may have the effects of reinforcing and confirming problematic pupil behaviour. In this perspective the school is seen as having certain rules — rule breaking is seen as deviance. If this deviance is followed by the imposition of sanctions, the pupil may either rebel in the school or retreat from it, by truanting. The truant may then enter on a certain moral career, in which the school punishes him, he changes his self-conception, he acts differently and truants more, and in which his deviance in general and truancy in particular is further confirmed by the sanctions of the school and of outside agencies. Examples of research undertaken from this interactionist viewpoint is that of Cicourel and Kitsuse (1963) on the moral career of problem school children, that of Hargreaves, Hester, and Mellor (1975) on the labelling and definitions of certain types of children as 'trouble-makers' and studies into teacher/pupil interaction at a classroom level (see, for example, Stubbs and Delamont, 1976).

This body of theoretical formulations about the relationship between characteristics of the educational system and the generation of pupil deviance has been supplemented in recent years by a growing body of empirical research in this area, which has consistently reported the tendency for pupil problem behaviour like delinquency, truancy, or 'apathetic withdrawal' within the school (a phrase coined by Rhodes and Reiss, 1969) to be associated with educational failure within the system. Although this relationship may be explained as the common result of the influence of some other factor (like parental social class background) and although the pupil problem behaviour may cause the academic failure (as truancy does seem to affect subsequent academic attainment in the Douglas and Ross (1965) study mentioned earlier), it seems likely that the school failure is itself an independent influence on, and cause of, problematic pupil behaviour like truancy (See Chapters 3 and 4).

Hirschi (1969), for example, argues that school failure affects the commitment of the adolescent to the school and Frease (1972) believes that failure affects adolescent self-perceptions. Further supportive American evidence is produced by Stinchcombe's (1964) study of school rebellion and British evidence by Little (1977), who finds that '. . . social factors cause poor performance which in turn may generate maladjustment: further, regardless of social factors, poor educational performance is seen as a cause rather than a consequence of maladjustment.'

Both the two major theoretical positions outlined above and the empirical evidence just assessed could lead one — quite reasonably — to conclude that the educational system may well — along with other causal factors — itself cause pupil problems like truancy. Such a conclusion could only be reinforced by commonsense factors like the mounting evidence of 'bad practice' and bad results in certain schools that have been shown by recent scandals like that involving the William Tyndale school (Auld, 1976) and by consistent public concern about the functioning of the system in general. Evidence showing substantial variations between schools in their delinquency rates (Power, 1967; 1972), child guidance referral rates (Gath, 1972) and behavioural deviance rates (Rutter, 1973), is further confirming evidence that factors concerned with the organization, ethos, and functioning of the educational system may well be important causes of truancy and other pupil problems.

Over the past five years, work has been undertaken to see if — as our theories, empirical studies and 'common-sense' reasoning suggests — the individual school is an independent influence on its pupils' levels of truancy and, if so, what factors within the school can account for this influence *and* how the influence is mediated to the pupils.[1]

The area within which the research has been undertaken — a South Wales mining valley — has two principal advantages for this type of work, concerned as it is to separate out the relative effect of family, school and neighbourhood factors upon pupils' attendance and non-attendance. It is, firstly, a remarkably homogeneous community (see Reynolds, 1976; Reynolds and Murgatroyd, 1977) with very small differences in the social class composition of the catchment areas of the different schools. Within this community, historical and social accident means that we believe we have effectively controlled the effects of the intakes upon our schools. The second advantage of this particular area is the very high degree of cooperation and access that has been given to the research team, a testament in itself to the concern of the local education authority to maximize the quality of its service.

It is worth recording at the outset, though, that the choice of this area has imposed certain limitations on us. It has retained — until quite recently — grammar and secondary modern schools, whereas other areas have reorganized their systems of education upon comprehensive lines. These grammar schools have taken the top 35% of the full ability range in our community, compared to a past national average of 20%. The Welsh educational system itself has, in its ethos and functioning, certain peculiar or — more charitably — unique qualities not in evidence elsewhere. These factors make generalization of our results to other areas extremely difficult. Furthermore, the social and cultural homogeneity of our community means that our schools probably vary less than those in other areas. All these problems imposed by the area's uniqueness are the cost of its atypical homogeneity.

Our work originally concentrated upon boys only in a group of nine secondary modern schools. We found large differences in the attendance rates of the schools over the years up to 1973 (see Table 1) and in the more recent years of 1976 and 1977 (See Reynolds *et al.*, in press). These differences between good and bad attendance schools are — as Table 1 shows — remarkably consistent over the years.

These differences between the schools in their attendance rates are — as Table 2 shows — also quite closely associated with differences in the schools' rates of delinquency and academic attainment, with low attendance schools tending to have higher rates of delinquency and lower rates of academic attainment, though neither of these relationships reaches statistical significance.

It is, of course, possible that these differences in the attendance rates of the various schools could simply reflect variation between the schools in the administrative efficiency with which their records are compiled, yet our experience suggests that registers were more accurately kept (i.e. pupils who were absent being actually marked absent) in the schools with already high attendance. These official records also do not include those children who were marked present on the register but who subsequently absented themselves from lessons or the school, yet participant observation within the schools suggests that there was much more of this 'hidden' truancy in the schools with already bad attendance rates. Taking account of these two factors would, then, merely widen the differences between our schools and not narrow them.

It is also conceivable that the school differences may reflect variation in the

Table 1. Attendance rates by year and school, academic years 1966-7 to 1972-3
(Nine schools)
(All figures as percentages)

School	1966-7	1967-8	1968-9	1969-70	1970-1	1971-2	1972-3
E	88.5	89.7	90.9	90.6	90.0	87.5	87.2
	1[a]	1	2	1	2	2	2
H	88.0	87.3	91.6	88.9	90.1	88.2	85.7
	2	3	1	2	1	1	3
G	87.1	84.4	86.5	88.4	87.6	86.2	88.2
	3	5	3	3	3	3	1
I	86.3	87.9	84.2	84.6	83.0	80.0	80.0
	4	2	5	4	5	5	5
C	85.0	85.9	84.5	82.0	83.2	83.5	85.2
	5	4	4	7	4	4	4
F	83.9	82.8	83.5	82.5	80.6	77.3	79.0
	6	7	7	6	6	8	7
A	83.2	83.3	84.0	82.6	77.6	75.4	75.1
	7	6	6	5	8	9	9
B	82.7	75.4	81.3	77.5	73.0	79.0	79.3
	8	8	8	9	9	6	6
D	74.9	74.8	77.7	79.7	78.2	78.5	76.5
	9	9	9	8	7	7	8
Annual average attendance for all nine schools	83.8	82.3	84.1	83.1	81.1	80.7	80.9

Kendall coefficient of concordance, $W = 0.85$ ($P < 0.001$)
[a]Ranking of school in each year.

amount of illness at the different schools, yet self-report studies conducted with samples of fifth year pupils at eight of the nine schools show that under 10% of their total absence is explained — by them themselves — as due to illness, with only a small range in this proportion at the different schools (See Reynolds *et al.*, 1980).

Since it must be assumed that these differences between the schools reflect varying levels of truancy (defined here as absence that is not due to illness), the crucial question then becomes how much of the variation in the schools' performance is explicable by variations in the intellectual and social quality of the school input of pupils at age eleven. Table 3 shows the mean raw scores for an intake of boys that went into eight of the nine schools in Autumn 1974[3] in terms of their performance on Raven's Standard Progressive Matrices Intelligence Test (Raven, 1960), the Daniels and Diak Test of Graded Reading Experience (1974), the Watts–Vernon Reading Test (Watts and Vernon, 1947), the Vernon

Table 2. Secondary modern school performance, academic years 1966–7 to 1972–3
(Nine schools)
(All figures as percentages)

School	Attendance	Delinquency	Academic attainment[a]
E	89.1	7.4	30.4
H	88.5	4.5	52.7
G	87.0	5.2	37.9
C	84.3	8.3	21.5
I	83.6	3.8	36.5
F	81.3	7.2	18.5
A	79.9	10.5	34.8
B	78.3	8.6	26.5
D	77.2	8.1	8.4

Spearman's $r = -0.52$ (Attendance v. delinquency)
        0.55 (Attendance v. academic attainment)
[a]Academic attainment is defined as proceeding to the local Technical College at age 16.

Graded Mathematics Test (Vernon, 1971), and the Junior Eysenck Personality Inventory (Eysenck, 1965).

Simple rank order correlations of the ranked mean intake scores and the ranked mean school attendance rates (Table 4) shows a tendency for schools with higher attendance rates to have intakes of pupils with higher reading ability, higher mathematical ability and higher scores on the extroversion/introversion and neuroticism/stability sub-scales of the Junior Eysenck Personality Inventory (1965), although only the relationships between attendance and the two reading test scores reach statistical significance. Schools with higher attendance rates have intakes of slightly *lower* intelligence.[3]

The data upon the nature of the pupil intakes into our eight schools present, then, a confusing picture. Our early analysis (Reynolds *et al.*, 1976, Reynolds, 1976, Reynolds, 1977) was based only upon the Raven's Matrices test scores for each school and prompted us to claim that intake factors explained virtually none of the variance in output rates of attendance, delinquency and academic attainment, as we claimed in the article above entitled 'Schools do make a difference'. The reading and mathematical test scores suggest, however, that a substantial amount of the variation in output results is explicable by school intake differences. The personality test scores, though, show higher attendance schools to be receiving intakes of slightly more extroverted, slightly more neurotic pupils that much other research (see Carroll, *op. cit.*), suggests to be at high risk of educational failure and consequently at high risk of non-attendance. Since high attendance schools are receiving intakes that — in their intelligence and personality — are more prone to low attendance and which — in their verbal and mathematical ability — are more prone to high attendance, the picture that our full range of intake data presents is a confused one to say the least.[4]

Table 3. Secondary school attendance rates and intake characteristics
(Eight schools)

School	Attendance	Col. 1	Col. 2	Col. 3	Col. 4
E	89.1 (1)[a]	35.4 (2)	39.3 (1)	17.9 (1)	18.8 (4)
H	88.5 (2)	34.3 (5)	33.8 (4)	16.2 (2)	19.9 (3)
G	87.0 (3)	33.1 (8)	37.0 (2)	15.6 (3)	21.9 (1)
C	84.3 (4)	34.7 (3)	33.2 (5)	14.6 (4)	17.0 (6)
I	83.6 (5)	34.0 (6)	30.5 (6)	12.6 (7)	18.5 (5)
F	81.3 (6)	34.5 (4)	28.4 (7)	12.4 (8)	15.8 (7)
A	79.9 (7)	33.2 (7)	27.4 (8)	12.9 (6)	15.6 (8)
B	78.3 (8)	35.5 (1)	34.7 (3)	13.6 (5)	21.2 (2)

School	Col. 5	Col. 6	Total No. of intake[b]
E	17.6 (4)	13.6 (6)	29
H	17.1 (5)	13.8 (5)	26
G	18.0 (2)	14.0 (3)	38
C	16.8 (6)	15.0 (1)	33
I	18.1 (1)	14.0 (3)	17
F	16.3 (7)	13.3 (7)	35
A	17.8 (3)	14.0 (3)	36
B	15.7 (8)	12.2 (8)	60

[a]Ranking of school for each set of scores.
Column 1 — Ravens Standard Progressive Matrices.
Column 2 — Daniels and Dyak Test of Graded Reading Experience.
Column 3 — Watts-Vernon Test of Reading.
Column 4 — Vernon's Graded Mathematics Test.
Column 5 — Extroversion/Introversion Scale, Junior Eysenck Personality Inventory.
Column 6 — Neuroticism Scale, Junior Eysenck Personality Inventory.
[b]Response rates are above 95% for all tests overall and for all tests at each school.

Table 4. Spearman's Rank order correlations between school attendance rates and
school intake characteristics
(Eight schools)

Attendance r	Ravens' Matrices	—0.071
Attendance r	Daniels and Dyak Reading	0.595
Attendance r	Watts–Vernon Reading	0.786[a]
Attendance r	Vernon's Maths	0.309
Attendance r	JEPI — Extroversion	0.330
Attendance r	JEPI — Neuroticism	0.220

[a]$p < 0.05$

Since the variation between the schools in their attendance rates has always seemed to be unlikely to be explicable by variation in the characteristics of their intakes, a substantial programme of work has been mounted over the past six years to try and discover any possible factors that may be associated with these differences between the schools. This work has involved only eight of the original nine schools, since School D did not participate in all stages of the research.

It has been concerned with:

(1)   The validation of the existing 'output' measures of school delinquency rate, academic success rate and attendance rate.

(2)   The collection of data on further types of school output, such as school vandalism rate, pupils' occupational ambitions, etc.

(3)   The collection of data on the perceptions of the schools held by the parents of pupils at the different schools.

(4)   The collection of data on the family backgrounds and home environments of the pupils at the different schools.

(5)   The collection of data on the pupils' attitudes to their schools, their teachers, their school work etc.

(6)   The collection of data on the pupils' self-conceptions, self/other conceptions, levels of self esteem and on the norms of the pupil sub-cultures in the schools.

(7)   The collection of data on the 'process' within the schools whereby intakes of pupils are moulded into 'outputs' of varying character.

This latter set of data was collected by rating each school on a number of different dimensions, each of which is regarded as a separate school 'factor'. These factors are then grouped together into eight sub-groups, comprising sub-groups that describe the schools' staffs and headteachers (in terms of attitudes, behaviour, background, and relationships), the schools' formal organization, the schools' academic organization, the schools' pastoral care organization, the schools' system of punishments and rewards, the schools' rules and styles of rule enforcement, the schools' facilities, and the characteristics of the pupils' and teachers' classroom behaviour and interaction. The ratings were generated by participant observation within the school, both by the authors and by a specially trained 'participant observer', who was 'blind' to the differences between the schools in their output characteristics. Checks on the validity of the ratings have been provided by the local Director of Education's own ratings of the schools, which show a very high level of agreement with the research team's ratings (Reynolds *et al.*, 1980).

Analysis and discussion here will be based only on school factors grouped under three of the eight major sub-groups outlined above, which are the schools' rules and rule enforcement styles, the schools' formal organisation, and the schools' facilities. The ten school factors which fall under these sub-headings are:

RULES AND RULE ENFORCEMENT

(1) School uniform use — whether a school has compulsory uniform for its pupils in their first three years at school.

(2) School institutional control — the degree to which a school attempts to control areas of pupils' within-school behaviour and attitudes.

(3) Schools enforcement of 'no smoking' rule — the degree to which the schools, all of which had this rule, attempt to enforce it.

(4) School enforcement of 'no chewing gum' rule — the degree to which the schools, all of which had this rule, attempt to enforce it.

FORMAL ORGANIZATION

(5) Size — number of pupils (boys and girls) on roll in academic year 1974/1975.

(6) Co-option of pupils — the degree to which a school attempts to involve pupils in leadership roles (such as prefectships) or other roles within the formal school organization.

(7) Class size — number of pupils (boys and girls) in normal teaching group in academic year 1974/1975.

(8) School/parent relations — the degree to which the parents are involved with the school, as measured by proportion of parents visiting the school in a school term.

FACILITIES

(9) Age — year when main building was built.

(10) Adequacy — Director of Education's assessment of the educational suitability of the buildings, facilities, etc.

Table 5 below shows the attendance rate for each school, together with each school's scores and ratings on the ten school factors; and Table 6 below shows the rank order correlations between the school attendance rates and the school factors.

Significantly, the factors over which the schools themselves have control — numbers 1, 2, 3, 4, 6, and 8 — appear to be more closely associated with the schools' levels of attendance than those factors — size (5), class size (7), age of buildings (9), and adequacy of buildings (10) — which are to a great extent uncontrollable. The implications of this view for educational policy making are both obvious and encouraging, suggesting as they do that schools can in their attainments, be more than a pale reflection of their resource adequacy.

It will be obvious from these data that very marked differences in character exist between the schools and that many of these differences are associated with the schools' levels of attendance. In particular, schools with higher rates

Table 5. Secondary school attendance rates and ten 'school factors'
(Eight schools)

School	Attendance 1966-1974	Uniform (1 = Yes, 0 = No)	Inst. control (1 = highest)	No smoking (1 = highest)	No gum (1 = highest)	Size	Pupil co-option (1 = highest)	Av. class size	School/parent rels. (1 = closest)	Building age and adequacy (1 = most adequate)
E	89.1 (1)[a]	1	6	5	7	201	2	26.1	2	1903 4
H	88.5 (2)	1	7	7	8	136	3	22.5	4	1904 5
G	87.0 (3)	1	8	8	4	263	1	28.8	1	1906 6
C	84.3 (4)	0	5	6	5	182	4	29.1	5	1903 3
I	83.6 (5)	0	4	4	6	176	5	23.3	3	1905 2
F	81.3 (6)	0	3	3	2	355	8	30.2	6	1914 8
A	79.9 (7)	0	2	2	1	299	7	26.5	8	1912 7
B	78.3 (8)	0	1	1	3	233	6	23.9	7	1937 1

[a] Overall ranking of attencance rates.

Table 6. Spearman's rank order correlations between school attendance rates and
'school factors'
(Eight schools)

Attendance r	School uniform	0.873[a]
Attendance r	Institutional control	—0.905[a]
Attendance r	No smoking	—0.833[a]
Attendance r	No gum	—0.809[a]
Attendance r	Size	—0.500
Attendance r	Co-option of pupils	0.833[a]
Attendance r	Class size	—0.167
Attendance r	School/Parent relations	0.810[a]
Attendance r	Age of buildings	0.826[a]
Attendance r	Adequacy of facilities	—0.071

[a] $p < 0.05$

of attendance tend to be smaller, a suggestion that is in agreement with many
contemporary — and impressionistic — assessments of the causes of school
problems like truancy. The explanations for this association between the size
of educational institutions and their capacity to mobilise their pupils towards
acceptance of social and academic goals are many. It may be that small schools
make possible the development of close primary relationships between
teachers and pupils, which in turn permit the school organization's use of
interpersonal — rather than impersonal — controls. Perhaps small schools —
and the consequent small staff groups — do not 'fragment' into many discrete
and different sub-units, and therefore give a consistency of response to pupil
needs that is impossible within larger units. Maybe within small schools the
teachers know the pupils and their problems better, therefore promoting a
more 'therapeutic' or 'caring' school ethos.

Whatever the precise explanation for this association is, though, it is worth-
while noting that the relationship between size and attendance shown by this
study is based on a sample of very small schools of between 136 and 355 pupils
in size. The relationship between size and attendance can therefore hardly be
linear (since there would in that case be no pupils in schools of 750 pupils) and
is more likely to be curvilinear, with a 'threshold' above which further
increases in size are not associated with further decreases in attendance. It is
also worth noting that our findings on this subject are not supported by other
recent work into the truancy problem — Galloway's (1974) study of Sheffield
comprehensive schools concluded that: 'Large schools do not have a larger
proportion of chronic absentees than small ones, nor do they need to exclude
more pupils for unmanageable behaviour'. The work of Rutter and his team in
London comprehensives also fails to report any significant tendency for
delinquency, truancy, and behavioural deviance to be associated with larger
school size (Rutter et al., 1979).

Schools with higher rates of attendance also appear to attempt less control

of their pupils within-school lives and to make much less effort to enforce two
key rules within the school, those relating to no smoking and to no chewing of
gum. It may be, of course, that those more 'permissive' or 'tolerant' schools
need not attempt high control because their slightly more able intakes of pupils
need no such coercion. Also, it may be that these schools' low control may
reflect the fact that they have high attendance rates and therefore do not need
to *attempt* high control. It seems likely though that, in part, certain schools'
low attempted control may function as a cause of their high attendance. We
have argued elsewhere (Reynolds, 1976; 1977) that the creation of a 'truce'
with the pupils within certain schools is the result of a rational decision by the
teaching staff not to proceed against the pupils in the 'expressive' areas of
their lives, which would merely increase the risk of their pupils' alienation. The
secondary modern school — like the other service institutions of the mental
hospital or prison — has a large number of clients that have no real wish to
make use of the services provided by the institution. Its pupils have low
ambitions and are not really dependent on the school for attaining their future
desired occupations, because they do not need the instrumental rewards of
examination passes that the school offers. Pupils' decisions whether to attend
their schools — and how to behave once in them — are likely then to be based
on their experience of the school and on the relationships within it. In our
research area, schools that attempt significantly to de-limit large areas of the
pupils' behaviour as deviant are simply unlikely to be pleasurable places for
their pupils and their pupils are therefore more likely to truant.

There is — it must be said — little in the available literature on the sociology
of the school that would enable one to assess the applicability of these findings
to other educational settings. However, our concept of a 'truce' situation
within high performing schools has similarities with the notion of 'indulgency
patterns' that has been employed — notably by Gouldner (1965) — within
industrial organizations. Reciprocity and exchange apparently function to
produce the accommodation that results in smooth organizational performance.
When such accommodations are flouted, the result — as in our schools — is
conflict and absenteeism.

High attendance schools appear characterized by two further factors — high
co-option of pupils into the school organization and close school/parent
relations. High pupil co-option is attained by the appointment of school
prefects, who are allotted minor disciplinary and supervisory roles within the
school, and by the use of pupils in other roles like those of classroom
monitors, who are responsible for the giving out and receiving back of
teaching materials within lessons. Some schools further incorporate their
pupils by letting them run the sale of sweets and confectionary at break times
and others incorporate by using leadership positions within sports teams. It is
worth emphasizing that all these modes of pupil incorporation appear to be
excellent methods of ensuring social control in general and high attendance in

SCHOOL FACTORS AND TRUANCY

particular, since being given responsibility for the administration of a social structure is likely to lead pupils towards an increasing adoption of the values of that structure.

The final significant association — between high attendance and close school/parent relations — is hardly surprising. Schools with these close relations have frequent visits from parents who wish to discuss their child's progress or problems. The schools' reactions to such visits and their concern to involve parents in any important decisions about their children are both likely to increase parental commitment to their child's school and — presumably — encourage parents to insist on school attendance. Schools that encourage such 'informal' visits by parents are also further likely to secure parental commitment by the use of open days, parents' evenings and meetings of groups of parents prior to their children entering the school at age eleven and prior to leaving it at age sixteen.

In summary then, our higher attendance schools are characterized by small size, lower institutional control, less rigorous enforcement of certain key rules concerning pupil behaviour, higher co-option of pupils and closer parent/school relationships. The high-truancy schools — on the other hand — appear to be narrowly 'custodial' in orientation, with high levels of control, harsh and strict rule enforcement, and an isolation of the formal staff organization of the school from potential sources of support both amongst the pupils and parents of the school's catchment area. It is worth concluding by noting that this link between what we call 'custodialism' and the generation of adverse pupil responses to their schools has been reported before — Finlayson and Loughran (1976) have shown that teachers in high delinquency schools are perceived by their pupils as hostile and authoritarian in their dealings with their classes:

> In such a cycle of events the repressive measures which the teachers are perceived to adopt could themselves be an important factor in the contribution which high delinquency schools seem to make in inflating their delinquency problems.

American research on the pupil control orientation of teachers and the sense of alienation among students also suggests that:

> A high school imbued with a custodial pupil control orientation generally does not provide an atmosphere conducive to positive commitment on the part of students to their teachers and school; in fact it seems to make such identification more difficult.

> (Rafalides and Hoy, 1971)

CURRENT EDUCATIONAL POLICY AND TRUANCY

So far in this chapter we have suggested that certain factors in the control of the school itself — in its ethos, organisation and functioning — are associated with its rates of attendance. In this final section we move on to consider some current educational policies that have been followed in attempts to deal with the problems of truancy within comprehensive schools. The data upon which this section is based is derived from a separate study of within-school guidance practices that has been conducted — also in South Wales — from 1973 to 1977.

The thesis of this section might be briefly stated as follows: schools which admit to having a problem with pupil absenteeism (for whatever reason) tend also to be schools that have bureaucratized guidance services which emphasize the role of the middle management of the school (heads of year, heads of house, counsellors, and heads of school) in dealing with the problem, at the expense of the form teacher and the pupils' preferred pastoral teacher within the school.

In a series of papers, Murgatroyd (1974; 1976; 1977) has presented material which indicates that the claims of schools to have developed pastoral care or counselling services which attempt to achieve the humanistic goals of self-actualization, personal development and the teaching of coping strategies to pupils through the application of counselling theory tend to exaggerate the potential role of individuals within the school and they systematically de-emphasize the role of the school as an organization in generating its own problems and in determining how such problems should be interpreted and treated by members of staff.

In the first of these studies (Murgatroyd, 1974), the responses of teachers holding pastoral care posts in thirty schools in two Local Education Authorities (LEAs) to the case of truants who claimed to be truanting because they felt their schools were not good enough, were used to indicate that these staff felt that their function was to uphold the rule norms of the school as established under the 1944 Education Act. This is indicated by the fact that 60% of these staff would report the truants described above to the education welfare officer and that only 7% would accept that part of the responsibility for the child's behaviour rested with the school. Murgatroyd further indicates that the colleagues of these teachers would regard any response to such a pupil which accepted his explanation of his behaviour and based any strategy for dealing with the pupil upon it, would be 'weakening the authority of the school to decide what is and is not in the pupil's interest' and as such would be a threat to the authority structure of the school. Dealing with truants may thus be seen as an authority-indicator within the school, especially amongst staff.

In a later paper (Murgatroyd and Lewis, 1976) it was suggested that counsellors in the twenty-six schools studied were appointed on the understanding that they would operate within the law as it was understood by those who appointed them and that they would accept the procedural rules and norms of the institutions in which they were placed. Counsellors were not appointed to encourage law-breaking amongst either staff or pupils or to act contrary to the socially established and formal rules of the organization. Headmasters, pupils, and colleagues of counsellors perceive the role of the counsellor as being an agent of the school, given that he or she will behave 'properly' within the conventions of behaviour implicitly or explicitly stated to staff and that he or she will perform their duties competently. Included amongst these 'conventions' is the respect for the formal organizational structure of the school.

In the most recent study (Murgatroyd, 1977), a case study of a single school in which three counsellors are employed was used to illustrate pupil perceptions of the counsellor. When asked to indicate what the three counsellors did in the school, the 424 pupils studied provided a series of statements which they felt described the counsellors' work. When ranked by the frequency of their occurrence, the three primary functions of the counsellors in this school were seen to be (1) checking attendance registers for truants; (2) being responsible for lost property; and (3) reporting truants to the education welfare officer. Whilst the counsellors presented themselves as caring agents in the school, (which indeed they were for some pupils), they were largely perceived as 'deputies' and pupils expected them to perform the duties which they associated with middle management roles in the school. Once again, dealing with truants was seen as a function of their middle management position.

In a study of 76 schools (Murgatroyd, 1980), the level of managerial responsibility for dealing with the child observed to be truanting was studied. What was of interest was the level at which the truanting problem was dealt with in the school. If 'line-staff' are defined as those staff who occupy the posts of form tutor or who do not hold a formal position in the pastoral care structure of the school, if 'middle-management' are defined as those persons occupying specific pastoral posts in the school (i.e. head of year, head of house, counsellor), and if senior staff are defined as the Headmaster or Headmistress, Deputy Head, and the Senior Mistress, then a series of interesting tables can be constructed. Table 7, for example, presents the distribution of the 76 schools in terms of these three categories.

Table 7. Managerial responsibility for dealing with truants ($n = 76$ schools)

	Line staff	Middle management	Senior staff
Responsibility for truants	21	53	2
% of schools	28	70	2

As can be seen from this table, by far the greatest number of schools regard middle-management staff as the appropriate level for dealing with truanting behaviour, and many of these staff have the responsibility for the co-ordination of information concerning pupil absence and the referral of cases to the education welfare officer if they think that special attention is needed. The use of middle management rather than line staff appears to enhance the significance of truanting as a pupil behaviour: unlike smoking, which is generally dealt with by 'line staff', truanting is 'rewarded' (*sic*) by the attention of middle-management staff. Truanting then becomes an important form of rule-breaking behaviour on which the school feels a need to act. By responding at middle management level, the school might be regarded as reinforcing the social significance of truanting as a rule breaking act.

If other variables are added and the table is made more complex, a number of interesting facts emerge. First, those schools which indicated that they felt that they had a truanting problem tended to pursue a strategy of dealing with this at the middle management level much more than they might be expected to do, given the level at which this problem is managed in schools who felt that truanting was a minor problem. These data are given in Table 8. Indeed, if a chi-square is calculated following the combination of senior and middle management levels, the two groups of schools differ very significantly indeed ($\chi^2 = 10.63$, $p < 0.001$, on 1 df): schools who define themselves as having a truanting 'problem' tend to tackle this at a higher level of management than schools without such a problem. If the type of school is then added to Table 8 as a further variable, then it becomes clear that comprehensive schools tend to prefer to deal with truants at the middle management level far more than schools which are either grammar schools or secondary moderns.

Table 8. Managerial responsibility for dealing with truants contrasted between schools with/without a self-defined truanting problem

	Line staff	Middle management	Senior staff
Truanting a problem	2	25	2
Truanting not a problem	19	28	0

Of course, the results might be anticipated. For middle management staff have generally been appointed since the introduction of comprehensive schools. What might not be expected is that there are schools in which the role of the form tutor has actually *declined* after going comprehensive and it is in these schools that a number of problems — poor rates of attendance, high rates of cautions for delinquency, high incidence of drug taking and poor academic outputs — are admitted. The growth of middle-management in schools and the attempt of middle-management to 'deal' with these problems appears to be associated with high levels of these problems. Whether or not the growth of middle management responsibility for the truancy problem *causes* an increase in absenteeism or whether such growth in certain schools merely reflects the fact that these schools already have higher absence rates, we cannot say. All we can conclude is that this association of specific styles of school management with high levels of pupil truancy remains an interesting one, to say the least.

CONCLUSION

We began this chapter by pointing out that little of the research work that has been undertaken into the phenomenon of truancy has looked at the possible effects of the schools from which truants absent themselves. We noted, however, two sociological theories — or, more properly, one sociological and one socio-psychological theory — which held that many forms of pupil rebellion at school were actually caused by factors within the educational system, rather than by factors arising from the pupils' intelligence, personality or home background. Our own work to test this theoretical position in South Wales has, of course, all the problems that result from conducting research in an atypical area. However, within this area, large and consistent variations between schools in their levels of attendance — and, we believe, truancy — do not appear to be explicable by variation in the characteristics of their pupil intakes, whereas much more of the variation is explicable by using only a limited range of factors that describe the nature and process of the pupils' schools.

It may be, of course, that the intakes of the higher attendance schools permits them to be tolerant, incorporative, and non-custodial. It may be that the school characteristics are in part the *result* of having had high attendance rates. It also seems likely that the school characteristics may also actually *cause* some of the variation in attendance. Further analysis, using the full range of our data described above and using further current work within the same community, is in progress.[5]

Our section on current educational policy then went on to analyse and develop further material that shows the importance of analysing individual schools' responses to truancy. Such responses in the comprehensive schools have largely rested upon increasing the numbers of school personnel, like school counsellors, whose job it is to contain and reduce the truancy problem. Crucially, these policies and consequent changes, such as the relocation of responsibility for dealing with truants at the level of middle management in the schools with severe truancy problems, represent ways of attempting to 'control' truants without any fundamental changes in the nature of the schools that the truants should be attending.

It is important to remember, though, that even with our series of studies within South Wales and even with that of Rutter and his colleagues in London (Rutter *et al.*, 1979), we are still in the conjecturing stage as to which aspects of the school environment affect pupil attendance and — most importantly — how the factors concerned with the school may have their effects. Much further research is clearly required into these two linked areas.

If such work into the sociology of the school is able to generate an adequate body of theoretical and empirical knowledge, then it will have important implications for our current educational policies. These policies have largely involved a view of education in which the solution to educational problems like truancy is seen in terms of adding to the material and financial resources of the educational system. Expenditure has therefore been increased, the school life of children has been lengthened, and the number of people involved in the provision of educational services has increased rapidly. In short, the educational system has been expanded in terms of its *quantity* of resources. The implication of the new paradigm within educational research that this chapter reflects is that the same attention must now be paid to the *quality* of the educational system and of its institutions. Whilst it has been possible to defend any assessment of system or performance in the absence of clear evidence that there are independent system or school effects upon their pupils, the absence of such assessment seems increasingly indefensible as work within the new paradigm bears fruit.

At the same time as educational research is beginning — to adapt George Homans' phrase — to bring schools back in, it is to be hoped that educational policy makers will attempt the same difficult — but ultimately rewarding — task of bringing schools and their quality back into the political, social, and educational spotlight from which they have long been absent.

ACKNOWLEDGEMENT

The research reported in this chapter was undertaken at the Medical Research Council Epidemiology Unit, Cardiff.

NOTES

1. We gratefully acknowledge the co-operation of the necessarily anonymous education authority, its schools, pupils, and teachers in this programme of work.
2. It will be clear from discussion so far that the data upon pupil 'output' and on pupil 'input' is drawn from different samples of pupils. We are assuming, then, that the 1974 'input' cohort are similar in terms of mean ability, attainment, etc. to the characteristics of the 'output' cohorts when they were, in their turn, 'input' to the schools in the 1960s and early 1970s.
3. Raw scores rather than age adjusted scores are used in this analysis

since the 'input' cohorts had similar age distributions at age of testing.
4. Further work upon the intake scores is in progress.
5. As well as analysing as above the relative strength of our school factors and intake factors in the explanation of the variations in school attendance rates, we have undertaken analysis of the school and intake factors together, thereby generating a number of models which explain a significant amount of the variation in attendance.

The most successful model in terms of the proportion of variance explained is one in which school/parent relations, class size, and pupil neuroticism/ stability scores are the explanatory variables. Schools showing a high level of parental involvement, small average class sizes ($\leq$ 25) and intakes of slightly more neurotic pupils are more likely to sustain higher levels of attendance than schools with low levels of parental involvement, larger class sizes (>25), and slightly less neurotic pupils. The model is marginally improved with the addition of the second intake personality dimension (extroversion—introversion) with extroversion being positively associated with high attendance rates. The three variable model (Table 9) accounts for 62% of the variance in attendance rates and the four variable model for 64.3%. The regression fit holds good at the 5% level of probability.

Table 9. Analysis of variance table showing goodness of fit for two models

Three variable model				
Dep. var. = Attendance			Indep. var. = School parent relat./ class size/neuroticism.	
	DF	SS	MS	F
Regression	3	38.034	12.678	
			12.7900	($p<0.05$)
Residual	4	3.965	0.991	
Four variable model				
Dep.var = Attendance			Indep. var = School parent relat./class size/ neuroticism/extroversion.	
	DF	SS	MS	F
Regression	4	41.73	10.433	
			117.86	($p<0.01$)
Residual	3	0.265	0.09	

In interpreting these data, two points need to be borne in mind. First, the analysis is based on the correlation table generated by rank order correlation. Since methods do exist for converting ranks into measures, the present analysis should be regarded only as a tentative means of examining the latent structures of the data. Second, the data itself is only now being fully analysed. Since further analysis will present refinements of the models presented here (especially through an analysis of predictor variable interactions and a re-analysis of the extant data controlling for differences in the pupil characteristics of each school), these models constitute only the starting point for all further theoretical and empirical work.

REFERENCES

Adams, F. (1978). The benefits of an interdisciplinary approach to the question of disruptive pupils. *Education*, February 3rd, p. 91.

Andriola, J. (1946). The truancy syndrome. *American Journal of Orthopsychiatry*, **16**, 174–176.

Auld, M. (1976). *Report of the Committee of Inquiry into William Tyndale School*. London: Inner London Education Authority.

Bowles, S., and Gintis, H. (1976). *Schooling in Capitalist America*. Routledge and Kegan Paul, London.

Boyson, R. (1974). The need for realism. In Turner, B. (Editor), *Truancy*. Ward Lock Educational, London.

Cameron, S. (1974). Truancy survey wide open to rigging by heads, *Times Educ. Supp.*, 2nd August.

Carroll, H. C. M. (1977). *Absenteeism in South Wales*. Faculty of Education, University College of Swansea, Swansea.

Cicourel, A. V., and Kitsuse, J. I. (1963). *The Educational Decision Makers*. Bobbs Merrill, New York.

Cloward, R. A., and Ohlin, R. E. (1961). *Delinquency and Opportunity*. Routledge and Kegan Paul, London.

Cohen, A. K. (1955). *Delinquent Boys*. The Free Press, Chicago.

Cooper, M. G. (1966). School refusal: an inquiry into the part played by school and home, *Educational Research*, **8**, 223–9.

Croft, I. J., and Grygier, T. G. (1956). 'Social relationships of truants and juvenile delinquents', *Human Relations*, **9**, 439–466.

Daniels, J. C., and Diack, H. (1974). *The Standard Reading Tests*. Chatto and Windus, London.

Department of Health and Social Security (1977). *Working together for children and their families*. HMSO, London.

Douglas, J. W. B., and Ross, J. M. (1965). The effects of absence on primary school performance. *British Journal of Educational Psychology*, **35**, 28–40.

Evans, E. G. S. (1974). Truancy and school avoidance: A review of the literature, *London Educational Review*, **4**, 63–71.

Eysenck, S. B. G. (1965). *Manual of the Junior Eysenck Personality Inventory*. University Press, London.

Finlayson, D. S., and Loughran, J. I. (1976). 'Pupils' Perceptions in High and Low Delinquency Schools. *Educational Research*, **18**, 138–145.

Fogelman, K., and Richardson, K. (1974). School attendance: some results from the National Child Development Study. In Turner, B. (Ed.), *Truancy*. Ward Lock Educational, London.

Frease, D. (1972). The schools, self concept and juvenile delinquency. *British Journal of Criminology*, **12**, 133–146.

Galloway, D. (1974). Big is not to blame, *Times Educational Supplement*, 18th Jan.

Galloway, D. (1976). Size of school, socio-economic hardship, suspension rates and persistent unjustified absence from school. *British Journal of Educational Psychology*, **46**, 40–47.

Gath, D. (1972). Child guidance and delinquency in a London borough. *Psychological Medicine*, **2**, 185–191.

Gouldner, A. W. (1965). *Wildcat Strike*. Harper, New York.

Hargreaves, D. H. (1967). *Social Relations in a Secondary School*. Routledge and Kegan Paul, London.

Hargreaves, D. H., Hester, S. K., and Mellor, F. J. (1976). *Deviance in Classrooms*. Routledge and Kegan Paul, London.

Hersov, L. A. (1961a). Persistent non-attendance at school, *J. Child Psychol. Psychiat.*, **1**, 130–136.

Hersov, L. A. (1961b). Refusal to go to school, *J. Child Psychol. Psychiat.*, **1**, 137–145.

Hirschi, T. (1969). *Causes of Delinquency*. Berkeley: University of California Press.

Hunkin, J. S. (1978). Therapeutic Education in Comprehensive Schools. Unpublished paper.

Jencks, C. *et al.* (1973). *Inequality*. Allen Lane, London.

Little, A. L. (1977). Declining pupil performance and the urban environment. In Field, F. (Editor), *Education and the Urban Crisis*. Routledge and Kegan Paul, London.

Mays, J. B. (1964). *Growing Up In The City*. University Press, Liverpool.

Mays, J. B. (1973). Delinquent and maladjusted children. In Varma, Ved. P. (Ed.), *Stresses in Children*. University Press, London.

Miller, W. M. (1958). Lower class culture as a generating milieu of gang delinquency. *Journal of Social Issues*, **14**, 5–19.

Mitchell, S. (1972). The absentees. *Education North*, **9**, 22–28.

Murgatroyd, S. J. (1974). Ethical issues in secondary school counselling, *Journal of Moral Education*, **4**, 27–37.

Murgatroyd, S. J., and Lewis, G. (1976). The professionalization of counselling in education and its legal implications. *British Journal of Guidance Counselling*, **4**, 2–15.

Murgatroyd, S. J. (1977). Pupil perceptions of counsellors. *British Journal of Guidance Counselling*, **5**, No. 1.

Murgatroyd, S. J. (1980). In preparation.

National Association of Chief Education Welfare Officers (1975). *These We Serve: The Report of a Working Party Set Up to Enquire into the Causes of Absence from School*. NACEWO, Bedford.

Power, M. J., Alderson, M. R., Phillipson, C. M., Schoenberg, E., and Morris, J. N. (1967). Delinquent schools? *New Society*, **10**, 542–543.

Power, M. J., Benn, R. T., and Morris, J. N. (1972). Neighbourhood, school and juveniles before the courts, *British Journal of Criminology*, **13**, 111–132.

Rafalides, M., and Joy, W. K. (1971). Student sense of alienation and pupil control orientation of high schools, *The High School Journal*, **55**, 101–111.

Raven, J. C. (1960). *Guide to the Standard Progressive Matrices*. H. K. Lewis, London.

Raven, J. C. (1975). School rejection and its amelioration, *Research Intelligence*, **1**, 22–24.

Reynolds, D. (1976). The delinquent school. In Hammersley, M., and Woods, P. (Editors), *The Process of Schooling*. Routledge and Kegan Paul, London.

Reynolds, D., and Murgatroyd, S. J. (1977). The sociology of schooling and the absent pupil. In Carroll, H. C. M. (Ed.), *Absenteeism in South Wales*, Faculty of Education, University College of Swansea.

Reynolds, D., Jones, D., and St. Leger, S. (1976). Schools do make a difference, *New Society*, 29th July.

Reynolds, D., Jones, D., and St. Leger, S. (1980). *Schools That Fail.* Routledge and Kegan Paul. In Press.

Rhodes, A. L., and Reiss, A. J. (1969). Apathy, truancy, and delinquency as adaptations to school failure. *Social Forces,* **48**, no. 1.

Rutter, M. (1973). Why are London children so disturbed? *Proceedings of the Royal Society of Medicine,* **66**, 1221–1225.

Rutter, M., Ouston, J., Maughan, B., and Mortimore, P. (1979). *15000 Hours — Secondary Schools and their Effects on Children,* Open Books, London.

Seabrook, J. (1974). Talking to truants. In Turner, B. (Ed.), *Truancy.* Ward Lock Educational, London.

Stinchcombe, A. L. (1964). *Rebellion in a High School.* Quadrangle, Chicago.

Stubbs, M., and Delamont, S. (1976). *Explorations in Classroom Observation.* John Wiley, London.

Tibbenham, A. (1977). Housing and Truancy. *New Society,* **39**, 501–502.

Tyerman, M. J. (1958). A research into truancy. *British Journal of Educational Psychology,* **28**, 217–225.

Vernon, P. E. (1971). *Graded Arithmetic–Mathematics Test; Manual of Instructions.* University Press, London.

Waldfogel, L., Coolidge, J. C., and Hahn, P. B. (1957). The development, meaning and management of school phobia. *American Journal of Orthopsychiatry.* **27**, 754–780.

Watts, A. F., and Vernon, P. E. (1947). *Manual To The Watts–Vernon Reading Test.* Ministry of Education, London.

Out of School
Edited by L. Hersov and I. Berg
© 1980, John Wiley & Sons, Ltd.

Chapter 6

Absconding from Residential Institutions for Young Offenders

Ronald Clarke

INTRODUCTION

Delinquent children in this country who repeatedly come to the attention of the authorities tend to end up in residential care, often provided in community homes with education on the premises (CHEs). Prior to the implementation of the Children and Young Persons Act 1969, CHEs were known as approved schools, catering for broadly similar groups of children and experiencing similar problems of absconding.

The purpose of this chapter is to review the research undertaken by the present author, and David Martin, into absconding from approved schools. Account is taken of more recent studies of absconding and, in passing, some assessment is made of the practical effect of the research on the CHEs and of its relevance to more general criminology. The chapter ends by considering the relevance of findings about absconding to the apparently analogous problem of truancy.

Background to the research on absconding

Most of the research to be described was undertaken during the middle and late 1960s when the system of approved schools was still in existence. At that time, the approved school order (now abolished in favour of a care order to the local authority) was the main disposal open to the courts for those committing offences between the ages of 10–17 (and for some children subject to civil proceedings) who were thought to need an extended period of residential training. There were 121 schools — 88 for boys and 33 for girls — providing between them about 9,000 places. Four of the boys schools were regional 'classifying' centres where all boys spent a few weeks undergoing assessment on first being received into the system, and before being allocated to an appropriate 'training' school. A number of remand homes/classifying schools provided a similar assessment and allocation service for the majority of girls.

111

Children normally stayed for between one and two years in training schools and these were graded as junior, intermediate, or senior, according to the age of the children received. The schools for boys tended to be larger, usually accommodating about 100 children, while those for girls generally had places for about 30. Some of the schools were in modern purpose-built house unit accommodation, whereas others were housed in old mansions or institutional blocks. They might be located in or near large towns or cities or be in the depths of the country. Except for three small Special (Closed) Units which between them provided some 80 places for persistent absconders and very difficult boys, the schools were all 'open' establishments. Schooling and trade training was provided on the premises though different schools placed varying degrees of emphasis upon these and other aspects of the regime (cf. Dunlop, 1975; Millham *et al.*, 1975). The environment of most schools was highly structured though a few experimented with group therapy and resident self-government. Many retained the services of a consultant psychiatrist, but his role was generally to support and advise staff in day-to-day problems of handling the children rather than to provide individual psychological treatment (Evans, 1963).

Most, though not all, the boys committed to approved schools had appeared in court on a number of previous occasions and had experience of a range of different disposals (fines, probation, conditional discharge, supervision order, etc.). By and large the girls were much less delinquent (about half had no record of delinquency) and most of them had been committed because of concern over their moral development or sexual conduct (Cowie *et al.*, 1968). On the other hand, it was generally conceded that the behaviour of the girls was more difficult and disturbed than that of the boys (Cowie *et al.*, 1968; West, 1967). Only limited data on such indices as social class, employment record of parents, criminal record, and mental health of immediate relations were available, but the homes of most children left much to be desired and indeed substantial proportions (between 40–60% in various surveys) were said to come from 'broken' homes. The general level of intelligence of both boys and girls was a little below average but most were educationally retarded by as much as 2–3 years. Though relevant data are scarce, Cawson and Martell (in preparation) argue in a recent paper that there is little evidence of a marked change in the populations since CHEs replaced approved schools.

Each approved school maintained records of unauthorized absence which distinguished between absences resulting in boys or girls being returned to the school before midnight on the day of running away, which were known as 'boundbreakings' and those which did not, which were known as 'abscondings'. In fact most of those who ran away were returned to their schools within a day or two and we did not follow official practice in our research, but called all unauthorized absences 'abscondings'. Following our usage there were 2,682 abscondings from boys schools in 1956 (when records were first kept) and

11,557 in 1971 (the last year for which official figures were available). About 40% of boys and 60% of girls absconded at least once from their schools and we estimated that about 5% of boys and 10% of girls could be regarded as persistent absconders. These figures reveal a considerable problem for the schools. Absconding is disruptive of school discipline, is upsetting to staff who may see it as a rejection of the care they provide, and is a source of friction with the local community because absconders may steal food and money or take cars to make good their escape. More worrying is that boys and girls who are 'on the run' are exposed to the dangers of sexual and other kinds of exploitation. Absconding was also the main factor in the transfer or recommittal of boys and girls to other approved schools or to borstal. Figures for absconding from CHEs are not available, but it seems on the basis of various items of informal evidence that the problem is certainly no better than it was in 1971.

An important objective of the research we undertook was to find ways of reducing absconding from the schools without undermining their fundamentally 'open' traditions. The work consisted of a series of separate studies involving different samples of boys and, in one case, of girls. Many of the studies were undertaken in one boys' classifying school though others were mounted in individual training schools. Most of the research has been reported in detail in Clarke and Martin (1971a) but some of the later studies have been reported in journal articles and these are referred to at appropriate points below.

A SUMMARY OF THE FINDINGS

Individual differences and absconding

When we began the research we were recently-qualified clinical psychologists, employed by a classifying school whose express function was to undertake detailed assessments of individual boys and to make recommendations about their training and prognoses about their response. It may not be surprising, therefore, that the initial aim of the research was to find the distinguishing characteristics of boys who abscond. It seemed likely that those who absconded would be impelled to do so by some feature of their personalities which, in turn, might have resulted from their early experience or upbringing. This too was the general assumption on which most previous studies of absconding had proceeded though, it must be admitted, without much success. In particular, there was little consistency in the personality traits that were said to be related to absconding, and in all cases the 'findings' might have resulted from the bias of raters who knew which boys had absconded and which had not.

We began by undertaking comparisons between groups of boys who subsequently absconded from training school and boys who did not on the basis of 'hard' information recorded in the boys' files. Included in the studies we undertook or in studies undertaken by others — notably Wilkins' (unpublished) attempt to repeat the famous borstal prediction study (Mannheim and Wilkins, 1955) for the approved school population — were a very large number of variables related to: the boy's age, height, weight, IQ, and reading age; his home background (broken home, area of residence, type of accommodation, number of siblings and birth order, age of parents, criminality or mental illness in family, etc.); delinquency history (number of previous court appearances, age at first court appearance, current offence, previous court disposals, etc.); psychiatric history (e.g. enuresis, referral to child guidance clinic, psychiatric diagnosis); school and, where appropriate, work record (truancy, number of jobs held, type and number of schools attended, etc.).

There were very few differences between absconders and others. Both groups were of similar intelligence, educational attainments, and build, and there were no differences in home background, psychiatric histories, and work or school records. (It is worth noting in the present context that the large majority of boys committed to approved school were said to have extensive records of truancy.) Indeed there were only three positive findings: first, absconders were very slightly more 'delinquent' than other boys in that they tended to have appeared in court for the first time at an earlier age and had also appeared slightly more often and at shorter intervals of time; second, older boys tended to abscond at a faster rate though no greater a proportion of them absconded than of younger boys; third, and perhaps not unexpectedly, more absconders than other boys had a history of running away from some other form of residential provision (such as a children's home or remand home).

In view of the almost unshakeable belief of most of those working in the schools that absconders were of a distinct personality type, it came as a surprise that so few differences were found. Indeed, there was other evidence, apart from the beliefs of staff, that absconders constituted a 'special' group of boys in that abscondings were not distributed randomly among the population (i.e. they did not fit a *Poisson* curve). It seemed likely, therefore, that more direct measures of personality obtained through standardized tests might more successfully differentiate absconders from others. Accordingly we set about comparing the performance of absconders and others on a number of paper-and-pencil tests which between them covered a wide range of personality variables. These were the Junior Maudsley Personality Inventory (Furneaux and Gibson, 1961), the Gibson Spiral Maze (Gibson, 1965), the Jessness Inventory (Jessness, 1963), Cattell's HSPQ (Cattell and Beloff, 1962), and a version of Osgood's Semantic Differential (Osgood, Suci, and Tannenbaum, 1957). No differences were found on any of the tests between absconders and non-absconders. Two further studies were undertaken: one (using the Junior

Eysenck Personality Inventory (Eysenck, 1965)) to see if there was any evidence of an interaction between type of personality and type of training school attended in producing absconding, and the other (using the Spiral Maze) to see if it made any difference whether boys were tested in the training rather than in the classifying school. The results were again negative and the general conclusion to all this work was that absconders and non-absconders from approved schools were remarkably similar groups; perhaps the best (though still weak) predictor of future absconding was a record of previous absconding.

The contribution of the school and the wider environment

By this time we might have become rather discouraged had we not already begun work on a more productive front. We made use of daily records of absconding in order to study the relationship between absconding and variables of the school and the wider environment. Investigation was limited, however, to variables about which information could be abstracted easily from records that were routinely kept by schools, such as records of admission and release, numbers on roll, staff duty rotas, punishment records, and the daily log. Nevertheless we soon found a number of relationships with absconding.

First, and this had been noticed by others, absconding was considerably more likely to occur in the first few weeks after admission and during the few days immediately after return from home leave. This effect has usually been attributed to the 'admission crisis', a period of unhappiness and anxiety experienced by boys recently removed, or removed once again, from their familiar surroundings.

Secondly, it was found that boys admitted in busy periods (see Table 1) or who were accommodated in house units which were unusually full, and boys who were admitted close in time to, or in the company of, others with a record of absconding from some previous residential placement (Table 2), were more likely to abscond themselves. These findings suggested, first, that if a boy is not helped to settle into the school by the staff he will be more likely to abscond and, second, that there is an 'infectious' element in the behaviour; boys with a previous record of absconding are likely to influence others to adopt the behaviour.

Thirdly, by making use of local meteorological data we found some relationship between absconding and weather conditions. For obvious reasons perhaps, absconding was lower than might otherwise have been expected in the coldest months of December–February (see Figure 1) and was significantly higher in particular months which had either been unusually sunny or unusually dull for the time of year. For example, if an especially sunny March or very dull August had occurred, absconding rates were significantly higher. This might have been because dull weather could make confinement

Table 1. Time span of admission in relation to absconding by each admission group of 10 boys (300 consecutive admissions to one training school). (Crown copyright, reproduced with the permission of the Controller of Her Majesty's Stationery Office)

No. of weeks during which group admitted	No. of admission groups	Mean of groups' abscondings
3	1	21.00
4	6	13.17
5	5	12.20
6	5	7.20
7	5	7.00
8	2	3.00
9	3	8.33
10	3	7.67
All	30	9.53

$\chi^2 = 42.30$, $p < 0.01$

Table 2. Previous absconders in each admission group of 10 boys in relation to absconding by other members of the group (300 consecutive admissions to one training school). (Crown copyright, reproduced with the permission of the Controller of Her Majesty's Office)

No. of previous absconders in group	No. of admission groups	Mean abscondings by boys with no previous record
0	10	0.58
1	7	0.77
2	9	1.10
3	4	1.00
	30	0.82

$\chi^2 = 15.02$, $p < 0.01$

depressing, whereas the sun could make the outside world and freedom especially tempting. (Temperature and rainfall bore no relationship to absconding.)

Fourthly, there was some evidence that if a boy (especially an older one) were caned for absconding this had a deterrent effect on absconding by other boys (see Table 3). The interest of this finding had not so much to do with the rights and wrongs of corporal punishment (despite this result, the use of the cane in the school concerned greatly decreased in the period following the research as it did in other approved schools), but because it added weight to the conclusion that the climate of the school and the way it was run were of fundamental importance in absconding.

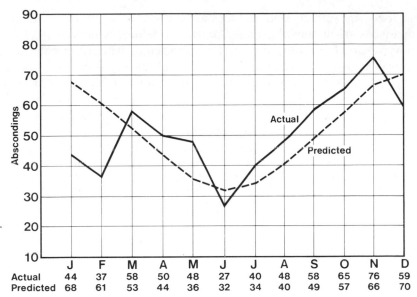

	J	F	M	A	M	J	J	A	S	O	N	D
Actual	44	37	58	50	48	27	40	48	58	65	76	59
Predicted	68	61	53	44	36	32	34	40	49	57	66	70

Figure 1. Number of actual abscondings from Kingswood and number predicted from hours of darkness for each month taking 5 years 1960–64. (Crown copyright, reproduced with the permission of the Controller of Her Majesty's Stationery Office)

Table 3. Interval between absconder's return and next absconding by any boy (for all 'senior' boys absconding from one classifying school during 1960–64). (Crown copyright, reproduced with the permission of the Controller of Her Majesty's Stationery Office)

		Mean days between absconder's return and next absconding by any boy	Standard deviation
Caned	237	10.42	10.22
Not caned	131	7.86	7.84

Standard error of difference between means = 0.95, $p < 0.01$

The most striking evidence of the power of the school environment was provided, however, by a study of the variations in absconding rates between different schools. This study, which was undertaken rather late in the course of the research, was made possible when tables showing the yearly absconding rates (numbers of abscondings expressed as a percentage of the average number of boys on roll) for each approved school were made available to us by the Home Office. As most schools simply accepted children from a local catchment area, their intakes were rather similar and the few schools which 'specialized' in certain kinds of boys were excluded from the analysis. Comparisons of absconding rates for the remaining schools (which were separately made for junior, intermediate, and senior schools) revealed a very considerable range in absconding — some schools having rates *five or six times* greater than others catering for apparently comparable children. These variations between schools were relatively stable in that schools with high rates at one time were more likely to have high rates at another. The rates for senior schools during 1964–1966 are shown in Table 4.

Table 4. Absconding rates for senior boys' training schools in 1964 and 1966. (Crown copyright, reproduced with the permission of the Controller of Her Majesty's Stationery Office)

School	Absconding rate	
	1964	1966
1	10	10
2	13	38
3	14	14
4	21	18
5	21	23
6	22	14
7	22	21
8	24	29
9	25	33
10	26	37
11	27	25
12	28	47
13	29	45
14	32	43
15	34	26
16	46	27
17	75	59
Average	27.6	29.9

Correlation (Spearman's coefficient) $= 0.65, p < 0.01$

Unfortunately we did not have the resources to compare approved schools with differing styles of management, differing treatment philosophies, and corresponding variations in routine and staff–child relationships, to see what light could be thrown upon the reasons for variations in absconding. The need for such research was underlined by publication of Sinclair's (1971) study of probation hostels in which he showed that their widely differing 'failure' rates (each boy leaving as a result of absconding or an offence was defined a 'failure') had little to do with the differences between the groups of boys admitted to each hostel, but had much to do with differences in the way in which the hostels were run. Wardens who were kind but strict in their dealings with the boys and who were in agreement with their wives about policy had the lowest absconding rates. The situation in approved schools which were much larger and employed many more staff, might have been rather more complicated though, as we shall see later, there may be some close parallels with Sinclair's findings.

Opportunity and absconding

The opportunity variable is sufficiently important in prevention and in its possible relevance to other deviant behaviour (including truancy), to deserve separate discussion. Some previous authors, notably Hildebrand (1969), had thought opportunity to be an important factor in absconding. He reported that most absconding from the Californian training school he studied took place after dark when it was easier to run away and that, despite careful selection of suitable boys, more absconding occurred from dormitories that were less secure. The greater risk of absconding identified in the present research among boys admitted in busy periods and accommodated in very full house units, might, in part, have resulted from greater opportunities to abscond when over-stretched staff were unable to keep adequate watch. Similarly, the fact that boys exposed to the example or the influence of confirmed absconders early in their careers were themselves more likely to abscond, might be construed as the operation of a different kind of opportunity factor. In addition, the marked variations we found in absconding between different days of the week (with the peaks being on different days at different schools) may well have had something to do with daily variations in routine and corresponding variations in opportunity.

The importance of opportunity was really brought home to us, however, by a study we undertook of the seasonal variation in absconding at one classifying school during 1960–1964. This variation was consistent and very marked, rising to a peak in the Autumn and dropping to a low in the Summer (see Figure 1). It could not be explained by different kinds or different numbers of boys being in the school at different times. (The school had no holidays and, because of demand for places, was more or less full throughout the period studied.) As can be seen from Figure 1, the variation closely paralleled hours of darkness except for the coldest months of December–February. Most of the variation seemed to be accounted for by the additional absconding taking place between the hours of 6.00–9.00 p.m. during the months of October–March (see Table 5). This suggests that it was the opportunity afforded by cover of darkness in the 'winter' evenings that provided the explanation. If so, opportunity is indeed a powerful determinant of absconding behaviour: there was about *two and a half times* as much absconding on winter evenings as on summer evenings.

Table 5. Number of abscondings from one classifying school taking place 6.00–9.00 p.m. during the summer and winter months 1960–64. (Crown copyright, reproduced with the permission of the Controller of Her Majesty's Stationery Office)

Time of abscondings	April to September	October to March
6.00 to 9.00 p.m.	64	150
All other times	207	189
Total	271	339

χ^2 (with Yates' correction) $= 27.25, p < 0.01$

Learning and absconding

It seemed to us from these results that environmental variables were related to absconding in two main ways: they either provided opportunities for absconding or they were the source of feelings of anxiety and distress which in turn fuelled absconding. In behaviourist terms, the environment provided both the cues and motivating stimuli for the behaviour. This perspective led us to consider whether a deeper understanding of absconding could be achieved by seeing it in terms of social learning theory — indeed whether absconding might be regarded as learned behaviour. The fact that absconders were more likely to have had a previous record of absconding, was consistent with the hypothesis that those who absconded repeatedly were not necessarily impelled to do so by some deep-seated trait of personality, but because they had learned to do so under particular conditions of (i) stress and opportunity and (ii) reinforcements for the behaviour.

We undertook two studies to test this hypothesis. In the first of these, the actual frequency distribution of abscondings among a population of training school boys was compared with a theoretical distribution predicted on the basis that learning, rather than individual differences, was the source of the variation among boys in numbers of abscondings. Unfortunately, difficult technical problems made the results of this work equivocal (Green and Martin, 1973). In the second study, two groups of persistent absconders, one of 84 girls in six training schools and the other of 85 boys in five schools, were considered. All subjects had absconded at least six times and the principal data were the time intervals between these abscondings.

On the grounds that learning would increase the *probability* of absconding in a given situation and that it would, through *stimulus generalization*, increase the range of situations in which absconding might occur, we predicted that the more often a boy or girl had absconded, the shorter would be the interval between recovery and the next absconding. In that absconding was generally at a peak after admission, this prediction might have seemed to go against existing knowledge but, by and large, it was confirmed. The decline in intervals for both boys and girls was statistically significant and, moreover, analysis of variance showed that it fitted a typical exponential learning curve, with most 'learning' taking place as a result of earlier rather than later abscondings (see Figure 2). No decline in intervals was found, however, for certain groups: boys and girls aged over 14½ and those with previous absconding experience tended to abscond at a steady but high rate. We argued that learning for these groups may have taken place elsewhere and consequently their learning curves were being sampled closer to the asymptote than those of other groups. In addition, the intervals between abscondings at certain schools did not show a decrease, but this was anticipated on the grounds that learning (and absconding) are largely under the influence of environmental conditions, and that schools provide widely differing environments. In other words, the environment in some schools brought absconding and the reinforcements for absconding under control, whereas in other schools, it allowed a habit of absconding to develop quite rapidly.

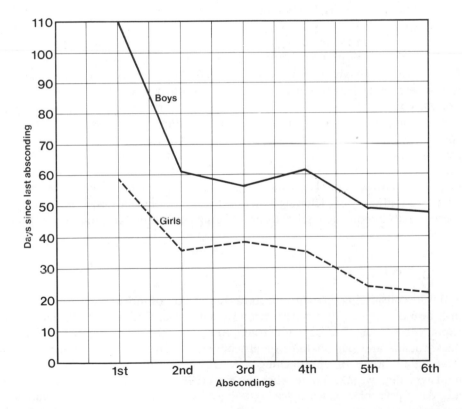

Figure 2. Mean interval between abscondings for 85 boy and 84 girl persistent absconders. (Crown copyright, reproduced with the permission of the Controller of Her Majesty's Stationery Office)

Absconding and further delinquency

A final topic covered in the research concerned the relationship between absconding and further offending. There was some suggestive evidence in Wilkins' (unpublished) study of an association between absconding during the training period and re-offending *after* release from the school. In brief, this consisted of the fact that he could not devise an efficient prediction equation for reconviction after release if he relied solely on information about boys before they started training. Such a predictor was made possible, however, if he included information about the boy's absconding during training. It seemed to us that if, as we had come to believe, absconding was mainly determined by school environment yet was associated with re-offending, this was probably because absconding had in some way increased the boy's chances of subsequent crime. It could be that by *absconding* a boy was strengthening his delinquent orientation; more likely, we thought, the offences he committed during absconding were confirming him further in his delinquency.

After the main body of the work had been completed the present author, in collaboration with Ian Sinclair, had the opportunity to collect some additional evidence about absconding and further offending. In the study (Sinclair and Clarke, 1973) the absconding records of 66 boys' schools were correlated (separately for each age-category of school) with their reconviction rates, while holding constant certain intake factors associated with reconviction (means of the IQs and previous court appearances of boys admitted). As expected, it was found that, with intake variables controlled, schools with high absconding rates also had high reconviction rates. The relationship was not a strong one, however, as it accounted for only about 10% of the variance in reconviction rates between the schools of each age category and it could not have been demonstrated without including so many schools in the analysis. It is unlikely, therefore, that reducing a school's absconding rate would have much effect on its reconviction rate.

A model of absconding

Before considering their current status in the light of more recent research, it may be useful to say what construction we put on our findings. Our attempt to explain absconding had begun by trying to identify those characteristics in the backgrounds and personalities of absconders which might distinguish them from other boys. In approaching the subject in this way, it seems with hindsight that we had made what Tizard (1976) has described as the usual mistake of psychologists when dealing with problems in the social, educational, or industrial fields: we had set out to explain a complex piece of social behaviour solely in terms of 'fixed' psychological characteristics. Because this approach ignored the situational and environmental context of the behaviour and the more dynamic psychological processes it was largely unproductive, as it has so often been before (Mischel, 1968). Absconders differed hardly at all from other boys except in their records of previous abscondings from other residential establishments.

Studying the environmental context of the behaviour was, however, considerably more fruitful: schools were found to vary greatly in the proportion of boys absconding and we found many environmental variables to be related to absconding — either, it seemed, because they mediated opportunities to abscond or because they were the source of feelings of unhappiness or anxiety which fuelled the behaviour. There was evidence also that children could learn to abscond and that this, again, was mediated by the school environment. In short we had progressed from a simplistic 'trait' model of the behaviour to an altogether more complex position that we have described elsewhere (Clarke and Martin, 1975) as an 'environmental/learning' model of absconding. This we summarized as follows:

We believe that the main reason why boys (and girls) feel impelled to run away from the school is that they have met or been placed in a situation that makes them unhappy or anxious, and absconding is a way of dealing with these feelings. There are a great many situations in which a boy could be made anxious; it may be because he has been bullied, because he is in trouble with the staff, because a friend has left the school . . . . In a school that is administered with sensitivity and skill many of these situations can be prevented, and the harmful effects of those outside the control of the school can be cushioned by action on the part of the staff.

Even in the best-run schools, however, all boys will from time to time encounter situations that make them unhappy. But not all boys run away and this is because absconding is only one of a number of competing responses to feelings of misery and anxiety. For example, a boy who is miserable may deal with his feelings by picking a fight with another boy . . . he may share his feelings with another boy or a member of staff . . . . Which of these competing responses he makes will depend on the variety of internal and environmental cues he experiences at the time . . . . If he has not experienced directly comparable situations, the most influential cues may be . . . the opportunities open to him to abscond (or perform a competing response) . . . .

The experiences consequent upon absconding, if it occurs, will help to determine whether or not the boy will abscond again when placed in a similar position. Because previous absconding predicts more rather than less absconding, it seems likely that absconding is more often rewarded than punished. The simple relief of getting away from an anxiety-provoking situation in the school might be a sufficiently powerful reinforcement in some cases, but there are other ways in which a boy could find absconding rewarding. He may initially be welcomed at home, he may enjoy himself while away from the school, and on his return he might have some brief prestige among the other boys. The probability of repeating the behaviour could be lowered through being caught quickly, having a miserable time on the run, or even, perhaps, through being caned on return to the school. It is clear that . . . some boys could through an accidental combination of circumstances develop a strong absconding habit while others never get to practise the behaviour at all.

(Crown copyright, reproduced with the permission of the Controller of Her Majesty's Stationery Office)

This model of absconding is depicted in Figure 3.

CURRENT STATUS OF THE 'ENVIRONMENTAL/LEARNING' MODEL

In the few years since the completion of our research, a number of other studies have been reported which may call for some re-appraisal of our position.

Individual differences

A number of these studies have commented directly upon the part played by individual differences in absconding though they do not seem to have added much to existing knowledge. Millham *et al.* (1977) in reviewing not only our research and earlier work but also their own more recent study and those of Laverack (1974) and Porteous and McLoughlin (1974) concluded: 'In short, all of these studies have been unable to establish any predisposition to abscond stemming from personality factors and all find that it is the most delinquent and those who have absconded from previous placement that present the greatest risk.'

Brown *et al.* (1978), however, believe that the failure to find differences in scores on standardized personality tests has resulted from the fact that different 'types' of absconders, for example those absconding alone and those absconding in a group, have not been separately studied. In their study of absconders from one assessment centre using Cattell's HSPQ (Cattell and Beloff, 1962), they found (i) that 'shy' boys had a higher probability of absconding alone, (ii) that 'group dependent' boys had a higher overall probability of absconding, but especially in a group, and (iii) that 'relaxed' boys were more likely to abscond and not to return from leave. However, the sample size was small (a total of 148 boys, 73 of whom absconded), the statistical tests were many, the differences found were few, and, of course, no

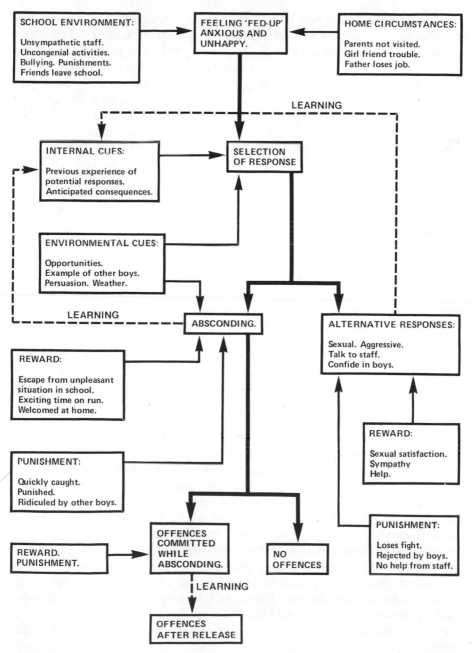

Figure 3. The development of absconding and its relationship with offending after release. (Crown copyright, reproduced with the permission of the Controller of Her Majesty's Stationery Office)

replication of the study was undertaken. Moreover, apart from a distinction between persistent and other absconders, we have found it extremely difficult in our own work to establish 'types' of absconder: for example boys who abscond alone on one occasion may well abscond in a group on another.

Finally, Laycock (1977) using a large sample of 1103 boys was unable to find any differences between those absconding from open or closed borstals and their non-absconding peers on three tests of personality — the Foulds HDHQ (Foulds, Cain, and Hope, 1967), the Maudsley Personality Inventory (Eysenck, 1959), and the Smalley Inventory (Smalley, 1964).

Opportunity

Laycock did find, however, that boys committed to open borstals for 'motor vehicle' offences (including taking and driving away, theft of a motor vehicle, driving while disqualified, being carried in a stolen vehicle, and driving without insurance) were more than *twice* as likely to abscond as boys committed for other offences. One possible explanation she suggests for this finding, was that motor vehicle offenders can drive and this might make it easier for them to get away from the vicinity of the borstal. If so, this could be seen as an interesting way in which an 'opportunity' variable plays a part in absconding, though it is a little surprising that her finding in open borstals has not so far been confirmed in any studies of approved school and CHE samples. Nor did she find it to hold in closed borstals though the main problem for those escaping from closed borstal may be getting out of the institution rather than escaping from its vicinity — in which case driving skills may not be so important. (Other sorts of opportunities may still be important, however, in explaining absconding from closed borstals.)

Further observations that are relevant to the role of opportunity appear in three other studies. First, Millham *et al.* (1977) found that schools which imposed restrictions 'on an individual's choice, movement, privacy, and relationships' and thereby presumably also restricted opportunities to abscond, had generally lower rates of absconding. Next, using data from the same classifying school in which we studied seasonal variation but for later years, Marie Johnston (personal communication) showed that this variation in absconding had markedly decreased and she concluded that we had overplayed the role of opportunity. However, there had been a threefold increase in the overall rate of absconding from the school by the time of her study and under such conditions, with perhaps a much lower threshold for the absconding response, behaviour might be less affected by the particular opportunities provided by cover of darkness. This does not mean, of course, that opportunities mediated in other ways were not continuing to play as great a part as before.

Finally, Laverack (1974) also investigated the time of day at which abscondings occur in order to test for the effect of opportunity. The interpretation of his study is complicated by the fact that it was undertaken in a training school which, presumably, had holiday periods. Nevertheless he found that: 'A large number of abscondings (23% of the total recorded) took place between 6.00–8.30 p.m. This is the period after tea and before supper when the boys have a good deal of freedom and therefore both 'opportunity factor' and boredom could be operating.' He also found that some 45% more abscondings occurred in this period during the 'dark' months of October–March than for the months of April–September. He failed, however, to replicate our findings of an 'infectious' element in absconding and of high absconding among boys admitted in busy periods, both of which we had argued might in different ways be seen as consequences of opportunity. Despite this he still believes that an important reason for the high rate of absconding from the school was 'the amount of physical freedom allowed the boys'.

The school and the wider environment

By and large there has been little quarrel, even by such determined psychometricians as Brown and his colleagues, with the view that, in addition to opportunity, other variables of the school and wider environment play an important part in absconding. After studying one maximum security institution for boys in Ohio, Bartollas (1975) while agreeing with Lubeck and Empey (1968) that absconding results from an interplay between personal and environmental factors concludes that: 'It is our central thesis that a boy becomes a runaway at this institution when he is faced with an unmanageable problem which he feels is unshareable'. He quotes the case of a new entrant impelled to abscond as a result of aggressive sexual approaches from established inmates.

Other recent studies have begun to tease out some of the particular school variables that are implicated. Dunlop (1975) found that of the 8 intermediate approved schools she studied, those which laid emphasis on trade-training and on responsible behaviour tended to have lower absconding rates. In their controlled comparison of a house unit run as a therapeutic community with one run on traditional approved school lines, Cornish and Clarke (1975) found that boys in the permissive 'therapeutic' regime were more likely to abscond or damage the furniture and fittings. Chase (1975) reported that a group of 45 boys who *permanently* absconded from New York State residential programmes in 1971 rated their institutions on the Moos Correctional Institutions Environment Scale (Moos, 1974) as being somewhat stressful. Specifically, the staff were seen to exercise close control over behaviour and to stress personal problems and inadequacies without allowing the boys to express their anxieties or concerns. A difficulty of interpreting these results is that institutions which were generally seen in this light by residents did not have higher absconding rates overall. Chase believes, however, that personality variables are also implicated in that the absconders obtained higher Manifest Aggression scores on the Jessness Inventory (Jessness, 1963). Millham *et al.* (1977) found that of the 17 approved schools they studied, those with lower absconding rates tended, according to interviews with the boys, to have good pastoral care systems and to foster a climate in which boys felt able to discuss their personal problems with staff. There also tended to be lower absconding rates among the schools which attempted (again according to interviews with boys) to exercise closer control and to influence boys' behaviour in areas such as moral behaviour, sensitivity to others' feelings and application to work. (Their results must be treated with a little caution, however, as it is not clear from their report that variations in intake had been adequately controlled). Finally, Martin (1977) in an ingenious study undertaken at St. Charles Youth Treatment Centre has shown that staff who believe that problem behaviour is 'internally-caused' and who therefore presumably expect 'acting-out' to occur, experience more incidents of difficult and disruptive behaviour (including absconding) than staff who expect reasonable behaviour and respect.

It is clear that we are still a long way from a full understanding of the kinds of regimes and policies which promote absconding or bring it under a degree of control. The variables implicated, especially perhaps those which mediate opportunities, will undoubtedly differ from school to school, but there is sufficient agreement between the findings reported in this section and Sinclair's (1971) findings in probation hostels to accord the following proposition more than the status of a hypothesis: *institutional regimes which succeed in combining a degree of structure and discipline with a climate in which boys can seek the help of staff with their personal problems are likely to experience fewer problems of absconding.*

Learning and future delinquency

Millham *et al.* (1977 and 1978) are not persuaded that it is useful to see absconding as learned behaviour, or that absconding contributes to subsequent delinquency. The fact that a significant minority of boys do *not* continue to abscond when placed in a different institution, is seen by them as weakening the explanatory value of a learning perspective: 'If unlearning can be so frequent and haphazard, then learning theory is robbed of much of its reliability and validity'. The habits acquired through learning are not, however, as fixed and immutable as Millham and his colleagues seem to expect. On the contrary, the continued expression of the behaviour depends on the repeated presentation of appropriate motivating and cueing stimuli and also, by and large, on continued reinforcement. These might not be so forthcoming in a new institutional environment.

Millham *et al.* suggest that interactionist or 'labelling' theory might provide a more useful vehicle for explaining the emergence of persistent absconding.

Under this, an absconder becomes a persistent absconder through being stigmatized as deviant by staff (and sometimes also by other boys) and by being punished or deprived of privileges and status. Leaving aside the point that a process of 'labelling' and its effects could easily be assimilated into a learning theory account, there are some particular difficulties with the inter-actionist perspective. For example, since a great many boys abscond only once or twice it might be inferred that real stigmatization occurs only after later abscondings. Consequently, it would be expected that the intervals between abscondings for persistent absconders would decrease more noticeably after *later* abscondings rather than, as we found, after *earlier* ones (see Figure 2).

Millham *et al.*'s criticism of the link we suggest between absconding and re-offending has perhaps more weight. Essentially it rests on the observation that of the 17 schools that they studied, 3 had *low* reconviction rates but *high* absconding rates. They argue that absconding rates and reconviction rates are separate effects of school regimes. A generally ineffective regime will tend to have both high absconding and high reconviction rates while a generally effective regime will tend to have low rates of both — hence the statistical association. That the reconviction rate is not the *result* of the absconding rate, however (they say), is demonstrated by the not so rare instances of schools where absconding is high and reconviction low. For example, a regime may be generally effective in reducing reconviction and at the same time be unusually tolerant of its few persistent absconders, allowing them to remain at the school rather than transferring them, and putting up with their many abscondings. Unfortunately for their position, Millham *et al.* did not show that the *absconders* from these schools had a no greater likelihood of being reconvicted than the other boys. Nevertheless their argument has a certain force, at least as an alternative explanation, especially given the rather slender evidence of an association between absconding and further offending that we found in our work. Perhaps the question will only be settled if a further study is undertaken of the reconviction records of the two groups of boys from a number of schools who abscond equally often, but one group of which commits more offences during absconding.

Summary of the present position

In brief it would seem that the view of absconding summarized in Figure 3 has stood up quite well to evidence from later research. Some researchers would prefer to see greater weight attached to pre-disposing personality factors, but there has been little quarrel with the great importance attached to environment. There is now greater recognition that the particular variables of school regime that are implicated (especially those mediating opportunity) may differ from school to school and from time to time in the same school, though there is a developing consensus that schools which combine warmth with strictness enjoy lower absconding. The value of seeing the behaviour as a learned and finally habitual response to environmentally-induced stress does not appear to have been seriously put in doubt, though the link between absconding and further offending has perhaps been more effectively questioned.

PREVENTION OF ABSCONDING

Our hope that practical suggestions for prevention would result from the research seemed to us to have been realized and in the main report of our work, as well as in a brief abstract published in the appropriate professional journal, (Clarke and Martin, 1971b) we discussed measures for reducing casual absconding and for the management of persistent absconders.

In dealing with the former problem, we urged schools to consider ways of reducing the often fortuitous stresses and anxieties that motivate the behaviour. We made some specific suggestions for alleviating the 'admission crisis', for spacing out admissions to training schools, and for making holidays fit the needs of the boys rather than those of the institution. Apart from reducing the motivation to abscond, we thought it important also for the schools to consider the means (including an increase in staff ratios at critical periods such as winter evenings, the locking of external doors at night, and the reduction of exit points from the grounds) by which opportunities for absconding might be reduced, since much casual but harmful absconding might be eliminated in this way.

Our main suggestion for dealing with persistent absconding was that boys who showed early signs of this (or who had a record of absconding from some other institution) should be placed sooner, rather than later, in one of the three Special (Closed) Units or similar provision. Placement in these units was generally delayed until a boy had shown himself unable to settle in two or three open training schools, but on our evidence this was probably too late since he would by that time have acquired an absconding 'habit' and, moreover, might have increased his chances of future offending. We also suggested that training schools themselves might experiment with gradations of security so that boys and girls who were likely to abscond could be started-off in secure conditions but, subject to their response, might then be tried in semi-secure and, later, in open provision.

So far as we are aware, however, few of these suggestions have been taken up. It is true that the St. Charles Youth Treatment Centre (designed to accommodate the most disturbed group of children requiring residential care) was intended to have house units of differing security, and that there had been a marked increase in the number of secure places in CHEs (these should number some 260 by 1980). But these developments seem to have been independent of our findings, carried out under pressure to accommodate the increasing number of persistent absconders we predicted rather than to provide resources for the earlier, preventive handling of potentially habitual absconders. Except for some isolated instances of modifications being undertaken to individual school regimes (e.g. Tutt, 1971) the research appears to have had little practical effect. This is particularly disappointing in relation to the prevention of casual absconding where the measures we proposed would be relatively simple and cheap to implement.

One reason for the limited response may have been that the results arrived at the wrong time, into an unfavourable climate. They became available just at the point when approved schools were about to be absorbed into the wider system of community homes and when there was an understandable (though unfounded) optimism in certain official quarters that the problems of the schools were about to be solved. In addition, the apparently authoritarian emphasis of a piece of research which set out to find ways of 'stopping' absconding and which, moreover, was sometimes caricatured as advocating that boys should be beaten and locked-up to achieve this, was not in tune with the heady liberalism and superficially more 'caring' ethos that pervaded much child care thinking at those times. 'After all', the argument ran, 'any child would want to escape from such outmoded institutions'.

It was disappointing to us, though hardly surprising, that the Community Homes Regulations 1972 contained no requirement for abscondings to be recorded as a matter of routine as they had been in the former approved schools. Apart from the fact that these statistics are an aid to good management and may provide a sensitive index of school climate, their lack means that the comparative studies of CHEs which are necessary and which have not so far been undertaken will be much more difficult to do.

Another reason for the lack of practical effect may have to do with the uneasy relationship between research and practice. Practitioners are often confused by research. They have difficulties in coping with technical language, and it often seems to them that there is disagreement in the research literature about explanations (for example about the link between absconding and future delinquency) and about remedies. Moreover, the information from research is always imperfect and has to be supplemented by thinking, but practitioners are reluctant to generalize on the basis of research findings. Thus, our general conclusions that much could be done to reduce absconding by reducing opportunities and sources of anxiety could have been of much more use to imaginative staff than the particular findings about such things as rate of admission or seasonal variation, about which there may be disagreement among researchers over detail, but little over principle.

Even if those responsible for running the schools had wished to make more use of the research, however, introducing change into institutions is notoriously difficult. Alterations in routine or practice can have so many repercussions that the progenitors of change have to be very determined and they have to persuade key members of staff that solving the problem justifies the effort involved. In the case of absconding, this would not always be easy to do. Staff with child care training in particular tended to be opposed to any changes, such as an increase in security, which they thought might increase the penal overtones of the regime. They also tended, in line with psychoanalytic theory, to argue that it was preferable for a boy to 'act-out' his anxieties by absconding than in some potentially more harmful or violent manner. In addition, they sometimes also made the point that, while some 11,500 abscondings in 1971 seems to represent a considerable problem, most absconders are returned to the school within a day or two of running away and they therefore spend the overwhelming bulk of their training actually under the care of the school.

RELEVANCE OF THE ABSCONDING RESEARCH TO GENERAL CRIMINOLOGY

Before examining the relevance of this work to truancy, it may be worth briefly considering its relevance to more general criminological theory. First, it constitutes a reminder that developmental theories of crime, in particular those implicating personality variables, are likely to be of only limited explanatory value (This argument is developed more fully in Clarke, 1977).

Second, it has reinforced other work, notably that of Sinclair (1971), in drawing attention to the importance of current environment in determining delinquent conduct. This, as Sinclair compellingly argued, has implications for penal treatment. If institutional environments are so powerful in determining the deviant behaviour (such as absconding) of those they accommodate, irrespective of their past experience, we might expect the post-treatment environment to exert a correspondingly powerful influence on criminal behaviour. This provides a cogent explanation for the almost uniformly disappointing results of penal treatments (cf. Cornish and Clarke, 1975; Brody, 1976; Clarke and Cornish, 1978): whether institutional or non-institutional, these proceed on the premise that offending is largely the expression of long-standing anti-social attitudes or maladjusted personality.

Finally, the research into absconding suggests that opportunity is a particular environmental variable that would repay closer study by criminologists. As the present author together with some Home Office Research Unit colleagues (Mayhew et al., 1976) has recently argued, opportunity-reducing measures may at present afford the most manageable way of preventing crime.

ABSCONDING AND TRUANCY

The body of research into absconding described above, especially insofar as it has dealt with the effect of differing institutional environments, has had considerable explanatory power and it may hold some lessons for the study of truancy. In view of the present author's limited acquaintance with the research literature on truancy, it may be safer for others to draw the relevant inferences. However, there are some important differences that may limit the transferability of the absconding research between absconding and truancy and between the settings in which they occur, and most of the discussion below will be concerned wtih these differences. But if there is a single point arising from the present research which may have equal importance for an understanding of truancy and its prevention, it concerns the role of opportunity. This seems largely to have been neglected (though Boyson, 1974, has listed various techniques for tightening-up registration procedures and for checking on the movements of pupils during the day) and is a topic which should be more closely analysed by those concerned with truancy.

One other important finding regarding absconding was that it seemed to be more powerfully related to environmental factors than to individual differences. It is tempting to suggest that the same may be true of truancy, especially as this would be generally consistent with the views of an influential and developing school of social learning theorists (Mischel, 1968, 1973; Bandura, 1973). But one must be a little cautious. While truants from ordinary day schools are somewhat more delinquent than their peers (see Chapter 3) the majority of children in CHEs are drawn from the most delinquent and deprived segments of the population. Consequently the spectrum of children in CHEs is likely to be in many respects rather narrower than that of children of the same ages in ordinary schools. A greater variety of children in ordinary schools may thus mean that individual differences may assume greater weight in the causal explanation of deviant conduct. In turn, learning theory may be of less weight in explaining its persistence. Whether or not this is so, it is worth recalling that 'habits' of absconding can be broken by a change of environment. Moreover, the acquisition of a 'deviant habit' of truancy may not imply that a boy or girl will be more likely to develop a generally deviant orientation in later life (though while truanting he or she may be more likely to commit offences): the causal link between absconding and future crime was found to be at best a weak one.

Residential institutions exercise round-the-clock care over their charges, whereas pupils spend only a small part of their day in schools. This means that the institutional environment will inevitably play a larger part in absconding and, on the other hand, that pressures and forces current in the home environment may be correspondingly more influential in truancy. Comparative studies of day school environments (assuming that adequate records of truancy were available), similar to those that have been conducted in residential institutions would, however, be no less worth undertaking (cf. Mortimore, 1977). In particular, it would be interesting to see how far schools in which the staff were perceived by the pupils as kind but strict had lower rates of truancy. Davies and Sinclair (1971) have provided suggestive evidence that a combination of warmth and strictness produces not only good behaviour in residential institutions for young offenders but also in the family.

Finally, it should be recognized that absconding is generally regarded as a greater problem for residential institutions such as CHEs than truancy is for the great majority of schools. This is not simply because absconders have to find food and shelter and are therefore at risk of offending and coming to harm, but because absconding is evidence that the institution is failing in its primary tasks of care, control, and rehabilitation. The major goals of day schools are educational rather than correctional or even pastoral. This difference in the salience of the problem may account for the relatively much greater attention (in view of the numbers of children involved) that appears to have been given by researchers to absconding than to truancy. More important, the differences in the scale of the problem for each type of institution has policy implications. For what chance is there of persuading ordinary day schools to make changes in routine or practice to deal with what will for most of them be the comparatively trivial problem of truancy when so little account of the absconding research appears to have been taken by residential institutions? Would it be better, after all, to concentrate research effort on those factors in the child and in his home which may be more amenable to modification or treatment? These questions cannot be answered here, but they may be worth pondering further by those engaged in truancy research — especially those seeking practical results.

ACKNOWLEDGEMENT

I am grateful to Dr David Martin for his helpful comments on the draft of this chapter.

REFERENCES

Bandura, A. (1973). *Aggression: A Social Learning Analysis.* Prentice Hall, New York.
Bartollas, C. (1975). Runaways at the Training Institution Central Ohio. *Canadian Journal of Criminology and Corrections*, **17**, 221–235.
Boyson, R. (1974). The need for realism. In: Turner, B. (Ed.) *Truancy.* Ward Lock, London.
Brody, S. R. (1976). *The Effectiveness of Sentencing — A Review of the Literature.* Home Office Research Study No. 35. HMSO, London.
Brown, B. J., Druce, N. R., and Sawyer, C. E. (1978). Individual differences and absconding behaviour. *British Journal of Criminology*, **18**, 62–70.
Cattell, R. B., and Beloff, H. (1962). *Handbook for the JR-SR High School Personality Questionnaire.* Institute for Personality and Ability Testing, Champaign, Illinois.
Cawson, P., and Martell, M. (in preparation). Children referred to closed units. Social Research Branch, Department of Health and Social Security.
Chase, M. M. (1975). The impact of correctional programs: absconding. In: Moos, R. H. M. (Ed.), *Evaluating Correctional and Community Settings.* Wiley–Interscience, New York.

Clarke, R. V. G. (1977). Psychology and crime. *Bulletin of the British Psychological Society*, **30**, 280-3.

Clarke, R. V. G., and Cornish, D. B. (1978). The effectiveness of residential treatment for delinquents. In: Hersov, L. A., Berger, M., and Schaffer, D. (Eds.) *Aggression and Anti-social Behaviour in Childhood and Adolescence*. Pergamon, London.

Clarke, R. V. G., and Martin, D. N. (1971a). *Absconding from Approved Schools*. Home Office Research Study No. 12. HMSO, London.

Clarke, R. V. G., and Martin, D. N. (1971b). Absconding. *Community Schools Gazette*, **LXIV**, 702-6.

Clarke, R. V. G., and Martin, D. N. (1975). A study of absconding and its implications for the residential treatment of delinquents. In: Tizard, J., Sinclair, I. A. C., and Clarke, R. V. G. (Eds.), *Varieties of Residential Experience*. Routledge and Kegan Paul, London.

Cornish, D. B., and Clarke, R. V. G. (1975). *Residential Treatment and its Effects on Delinquency*. Home Office Research Study No. 32. HMSO, London.

Cowie, J., Cowie, V., and Slater, E. (1968). *Delinquency in Girls*. Heinemann, London.

Davies, M., and Sinclair, I. A. C. (1971). Families, hostels, and delinquents, an attempt to assess cause and effect. *British Journal of Criminology*, **11**, 213-29.

Dunlop, A. (1975). *The Approved School Experience*. Home Office Research Study No. 25. HMSO, London.

Evans, J. (1963). Has the psychiatrist a useful function in an approved school? *British Journal of Criminology*, **4**, 127-144.

Eysenck, H. J. (1959). *Manual of the Maudsley Personality Inventory*, University of London Press, London.

Eysenck, S. (1965). *The Junior Eysenck Personality Inventory*, University of London Press, London.

Foulds, G. A., Cain, T. M., and Hope, K. (1967). *Manual of the Hostility and Direction of Hostility Questionnaire*, University of London Press, London.

Furneaux, W. D., and Gibson, H. B. (1961). A children's personality inventory designed to measure neuroticism and introversion. *British Journal of Educational Psychology*, **31**, 204-207.

Gibson, H. B. (1965). *Manual of the Gibson Spiral Maze*, University of London Press, London.

Green, J. R., and Martin, D. N. (1973). Absconding from approved schools as learned behaviour: a statistical study. *Journal of Research in Crime and Delinquency*, **10**, 73-86.

Hildebrand, R. J. (1969). The anatomy of escape. *Federal Probation*, **XXXIII**, 58-66.

Jessness, C. F. (1963). *Redevelopment and Revalidation of the Jessness Inventory*. Sacramento, California Youth Authority Research Report No. 35.

Laverack, K. (1974). Absconding from Kneesworth House. *Community Schools Gazette*, **LXVIII**, 5-24.

Laycock, G. K. (1977). *Absconding from Borstals*. Home Office Research Study No. 41. HMSO, London.

Lubeck, S. G., and Empey, L. T. (1968). Mediatory *versus* total institution: the case of the runaway. *Social Problems*, **16**, 242-260.

Mannheim, H., and Wilkins, L. T. (1955). *Prediction Methods in Relation to Borstal Training*. HMSO, London.

Martin, D. N. (1977). Disruptive behaviour and staff attitudes at the St. Charles Youth Treatment Centre. *Journal of Child Psychology and Psychiatry*, **18**, 221-228.

Mayhew, P., Clarke, R. V. G., Sturman, A., and Hough, J. M. (1976). *Crime as Opportunity*. Home Office Research Study No. 34. HMSO, London.

Millham, S., Bullock, R., and Cherrett, P. (1975). *After Grace — Teeth: A Comparative Study of the Residential Experience of Boys in Approved Schools.* Chaucer Publishing Co. Ltd., London.

Millham, S., Bullock, R., and Hosie, K. (1978). *Locking up Children: Secure Provision within the Child-Care System.* Saxon House, Farnborough, Hants.

Millham, S., Bullock, R., Hosie, K., and Frankenburg, R. (1977). Absconding. *Community Schools Gazette,* **LXXI,** 281–291, 325–337.

Mischel, W. (1968). *Personality and Assessment.* Wiley, New York.

Mischel, W. (1973). Towards a cognitive social learning reconceptualization of personality. *Psychological Review,* **80,** 252–283.

Moos, R. (1974). *Correctional Institutions Environment Scale Manual,* Palo Alto, Consulting Psychologists Press, California.

Mortimore, P. (1977). Schools as institutions. *Educational Research,* **20,** 61–8.

Osgood, C. E., Suci, G. J., and Tannenbaum, F. H. (1957). *The Measurement of Meaning,* University of Illinois Press, Urbana, Illinois.

Porteous, M. A., and McLoughlin, C. S. (1974). A comparison of absconders and non-absconders from an assessment centre. *Community Schools Gazette,* **LXVII,** 681–699.

Sinclair, I. A. C. (1971). *Hostels for Probationers.* Home Office Research Study No. 6. HMSO, London.

Sinclair, I. A. C., and Clarke, R. V. G. (1973). Acting-out behaviour and its significance for the residential treatment of delinquents. *Journal of Child Psychology and Psychiatry,* **14,** 283–291.

Smalley, R. (1964). *Some Psychological Factors in Selection for Borstal training.* Unpublished MA thesis, University of London.

Tizard, J. (1976). Psychology and social policy. *Bulletin of the British Psychological Society,* **29,** 225–233.

Tutt, N. (1971). Towards reducing absconding. *Community Schools Gazette,* **LXV,** 65–68.

West, D. J. (1967). *The Young Offender.* Penguin Books, Harmondsworth, Middx.

Wilkins, L. T. (unpublished). Prediction methods in relation to approved school training. Unpublished Home Office Research Unit report.

Chapter 7

Absence from School and the Law

Ian Berg

Education has been compulsory in Britain for a century (Tennent, 1970). In the latter part of the 19th century Parliament made it necessary for local authorities to see that children went to school. Four major Acts of Parliament and several amendments to them have specifically referred to attendance at school (Fogelman and Richardson, 1974). Thus the Education Act of 1944 put the onus on parents of ensuring their child receives a full time education. The local authority could proceed against them if they failed to do so (Section 40). A child who fails to attend school regularly may be taken to a juvenile court at the request of the magistrates concerned with the prosecution of their parents or they can be brought there directly by the local Education Department under Section 11 of the Education Act 1953.

As the law stands at present, parents can be convicted of failure to ensure that their child attends school regularly, even if they have made reasonable efforts to ensure the child goes and are not even aware the child is absent. The court need only to have evidence of failure to attend (Dutchman-Smith, 1971). The Children and Young Persons' Act 1969 states that before proceeding against parents, local authorities should consider whether the child should be taken to a juvenile court instead or as well as the parents (Section 1 of the Act).

ENFORCEMENT OF THE LAW

School

Truants, using the term somewhat loosely to refer to children who fail to attend school regularly without adequate reason, are normally first identified by the school. The process of deciding what are acceptable excuses and the methods employed to check whether children are, in fact, at school, must vary a great deal depending on circumstances. At one extreme are the schools that are determined to cut down truancy rates to as low a level as possible. Dr. Rhodes Boyson (1974) who was headmaster of a large London Comprehensive

School, Highbury Grove, described how the problem was tackled there. Regular contact was maintained with parents. The school was in touch with the family the moment there was an unexpected absence. Random checks were carried out so that youngsters could not slip away after registration. Rewards were given to individuals and groups of children whose attendance records were exceptionally good. At the other extreme are schools who, for various reasons do not appear to take the same amount of trouble (Williams, 1974). The school may be somewhat spread out geographically, giving young people more chance of leaving unobtrusively whilst transferring from a class in one building to one in another. Inadequate facilities and insufficient staff to cope with exceptionally disruptive youngsters may tempt head teachers to turn a blind eye when they are absent. Another factor is that high truancy rates reflect badly on a school. As levels of absence rise there comes a point when teachers may be disinclined to check with any greater thoroughness.

Police

Although from time to time they make special efforts to round up children who are roaming the streets during school hours, the police are not often directly involved with this problem. However, in view of the fact that truants and youngsters who commit indictable offences tend to form closely over-lapping groups, with similar problems otherwise and with similar background features (Tennent 1970, 1971), the police do help with the problem of truancy insofar as they deal with juvenile delinquency in general.

The Educational Welfare Service

The Educational Welfare Officer (EWO) is the social worker employed by Education Authorities who is most concerned with unjustifiable absence from school. They investigate children who are away without good reason. Legally, they are empowered to approach the child's family and make enquiries, and therefore provide a useful link between home and school. When it appears that the amount of unexplained absence justifies legal action it is the EWO who initiates proceedings in this direction. Different approaches are adopted in different parts of the country. Warning letters may be sent to parents, they are sometimes asked to appear before a school attendance panel to explain why their child is away so much. Finally, the Educational Welfare Service initiates prosecution of parents and/or child by the courts, if all else fails.

This service has additional functions. It is concerned with helping socially deprived families in many areas, in providing transport to school where necessary and in arranging for the provision of free meals at the school if the child is entitled to them. The EWO is a case worker who supports families.

Nevertheless, it is the particular role of enforcing school attendance which characterizes the service (Clark, 1976).

PROTECTION FROM LEGAL PROCEEDINGS

Truants may be protected from prosecution for failure to attend school in various ways. The educational system may itself provide the means. Insofar as it can arrange for less demanding forms of schooling such as special classes or home tuition which the truant finds acceptable as a substitute for normal school and the authority is prepared to count as such, legal action is prevented.

Social workers may be able to forestall prosecution of youngsters who truant and who are under supervision by or in care with local authorities. It is unlikely that children in this situation could be taken to court without the agreement of the social worker looking after them. Social service departments are concerned with the child, often as a member of a family with severe social problems. School attendance may take a low priority in the opinion of the social worker who is trying to help when weighed against the other difficulties besetting the child. Prosecution can be seen as interfering with the relationship the worker is trying to maintain with the family. Added to this is the view of some social workers that schools often fail to meet the needs of young people and that it is wrong to force them to attend schools where they cannot cope.

Referral to medical agencies also affords some protection against prosecution since there is then an assumption that the child could be suffering from an illness requiring a treatment approach and should not be subjected to the normal legal consequences of failure to attend school. Yet, as far as juvenile delinquency in general is concerned, it looks as though clinic referral may be somewhat fortuitous. In one survey, it was found that children taken to court and those attending a child guidance clinic had very similar features (Gath, Cooper, and Gattoni, 1972). However, increasingly, medical services are finding that it is better to work alongside other agencies rather than providing a shelter from the usual consequences of antisocial behaviour. Social workers and probation officers may be actively brought into the process of therapy. Children may be treated in clinics even after they have been taken into care by the local authority. Although what has been said applies mostly to the large group of truants whose antisocial behaviour is often associated with educational and social problems, it also applies to a limited extent to school phobic youngsters. This is especially the case when anxiety and its associated physical symptoms are less evident than adamant refusal. Effective treatment of phobic avoidance often requires some exposure to the feared situation to help overcome the fears. It can be helpful to have the support of the educational welfare service, and even the courts, when parents will not allow even a reasonable amount of pressure to be brought on the child to secure school attendance (Eisenberg, 1958).

TRUANCY AND THE COURTS

Prosecution of Parents

It has been reported (Tennent, 1970) that studies have not shown any clear relationship between the prosecution of parents and the taking of children to court for truancy; one study indicated that there might be an inverse relationship, but another one did not.

Children coming to juvenile court

(a) Frequency

Children are not prosecuted for truancy under criminal proceedings, as they are for offences against the law. Instead they are brought before juvenile court magistrates under care proceedings. In a survey carried out in London (Tennent 1970), it was found that two per thousand children from the normal school population were taken to court for truancy over the period of one year. The proportion of 14 year olds brought to court was seven per thousand and that was the age group most frequently dealt with in this way. Approximately equal numbers of boys and girls aged 13 to 15 appeared in court for truancy, although youngsters prosecuted for offences tend to show a predominance of boys over girls of about ten to one.

(b) Court procedures

(i) adjournment. In the study mentioned (Tennent 1970) it was found that magistrates tended to adjourn the case several times in the hope of school attendance improving before coming to a decision about disposal. It was also reported that a previous investigation undertaken by Bedford College in London had shown that adjourning the case to allow a trial of attendance was of little value. However, a retrospective survey carried out in Leeds, a large city in the north of England (Berg, Hullin, McGuire, and Tyrer, 1977) indicated that the procedure of repeated adjournments was the main method of dealing with truants in juvenile courts there and that it appeared to be more effective in getting them back to school than a supervision order.

(ii) supervision. In the London survey Tennent (1970) found that about half the truants coming to juvenile court were eventually made subject to a supervision order. The north of England study, in contrast, found that only a fifth of truants were dealt with in this way. This was because magistrates in the city investigated were convinced that adjournment was generally the more effective procedure. The Leeds investigation showed that the youngsters

placed on supervision tended to be those who came from broken homes. Yet it was just these children who had particular difficulty in getting back to school. Insofar as it provides a social worker from the local authority social services department, or a probation officer, to give the child personal attention throughout the duration of the order, magistrates must have thought that a supervision order might have gone some way towards making up for the deficiencies in the home circumstances. But this assumption appears to have been incorrect.

(iii) residential placements. About a tenth of truants in Tennent's (1970) survey who appeared in court eventually went into 'care'. In another investigation (Tennent, 1971) it was found that a third of boys aged 12 to 15 brought to court for failure to attend school were sent to a remand centre (as the law stands at present, children are sent to assessment centres on interim care orders but the end result is the same). The decision to send them there was taken after an average of 3.5 court appearances. Few differences were found between those remanded and those not. Committing offences or having brothers or sisters who had committed offences made a remand in custody more likely. The children who were placed in a remand centre were more likely to be placed in a long-stay institution such as an approved school, subsequently.

In the Leeds survey (Berg, Hullin, McGuire and Tyrer 1977) about 15% of the truants coming to court were placed in 'care' almost immediately and a further 20% after several weeks of repeated adjournments. At least two thirds of those taken into 'care' went to a residential institution of some kind. It was found that about 40% of youngsters not put on care orders immediately, or placed on supervision orders, were sent to assessment centres for a period of three weeks on an interim care order. More of those put on interim care orders eventually went into care than those who were not subject to them.

THE EVALUATION OF
TWO COURT PROCEDURES IN TRUANCY

Another investigation was carried out in the city of Leeds to evaluate the use of two judicial procedures on truants brought to court (Berg, Consterdine, Hullin, McGuire, and Tyrer, 1978). The procedures were adjournment and supervision. When the first of these was employed, the case was repeatedly adjourned and the child had to come back to court at varying intervals, after a week, a fortnight, or several weeks, depending on progress in returning to school. When attendance was good the intervals between court appearances were made longer and when it was poor the child was brought back more often. If improvement nevertheless failed to occur, placement in a residential assessment centre for a three week period could be arranged. If all else failed, it was possible to put the child on a full care order. It was then up to the social services department to send the child to a community home, with or without residential schooling, if it was considered appropriate. When supervision was used the magistrate made a supervision order. A social worker from the social services department or a probation officer then became responsible for the supervision of the child. No further court appearances were arranged unless the supervising social worker felt that supervision had failed and wanted further action on the part of the juvenile court such as the making of a care order so that a residential placement could be arranged.

Children taken to juvenile court for failure to attend school were considered for inclusion in the trial over the period of about a year. Three courts dealt with truants and were concerned with the evaluation. Several magistrates sat in each court for a few months at a time with about a dozen others sitting from time to time. Only one child from any particular family was included. Youngsters with less than six months to go before reaching school leaving age were excluded. When circumstances, such as social factors of overriding importance, the existence of offences which needed to be taken into consideration or the child's adamant refusal to even consider returning to school, appeared to require a particular course of action, the child was not taken into the trial of the two procedures. In all, 96 children were included and 69 excluded, for the foregoing reasons. Once the case was proved and there was no reason not to include the child in the study, a random allocation to either adjournment or supervision was carried out. In this way 45 children were put on adjournment and 51 were made subject to a supervision order entirely at random.

Before coming to court both groups of children had been away from school about 75% of the time, on average, over a three month period. In the first six months after their first court appearance the adjourned group were away 35% of the time and the supervised group were off school 50% of the time. The proportions were 25% and 50% respectively in the subsequent six month period. These differences were statistically significant ($P < 0.01$). Whether the truants were boys or girls did not affect these findings. Nor did their age although in both groups older youngsters of 14 or more tended to be off school to a greater extent than younger children.

As well as absence from school, convictions for offences, such as stealing, were looked at as a measure of outcome. The average number of offences per child before the first appearance in court was 1.2 for adjourned children and 1.0 for supervised youngsters. In the six months period afterwards it was 0.2 in the adjourned group and 0.9 in the supervised group. Not surprisingly, boys had more offences, 1.6 per child, than girls, 0.4 per child, on average, but this was the same in both groups. Again the marked improvement in the adjourned group was statistically significant ($P < 0.05$).

This appeared to be the first time a randomly controlled trial of judicial procedures had been attempted in Britain (Walker, 1972; Farrington, 1978) and the results seemed to be clear cut. The two groups of truants were compared on a variety of background variables to be sure that by chance particularly disadvantaged individuals had not been allocated to the supervision group. There was no evidence that this had happened. There was a similar proportion of boys and girls in the two groups and the age distribution was similar. Type of schools, as indicated by size of classes and proportion of children on free school meals, did not differ between the two groups. If anything, the adjourned cases were somewhat disadvantaged by having more individuals from broken homes and more youngsters from parts of the city with a high immigrant population.

Another comparison between adjourned and supervised cases was in psychiatric disturbance. This was measured in 36 of the adjourned and 47 of the supervised children by questionnaires completed by teachers. They were the Rutter Scale B (Rutter 1967) and the Conners Teacher Rating Scale (Conners 1969). Controls were taken from the same schools. The assessments were made 3 months after the truants' first court appearance. The 83 truants were more disturbed than the controls, to a significant extent, on the three Rutter Scale B scores and 4 of the 5 Conners Teacher Rating Scale factor scores. The two groups of truants did not differ significantly from each other. The total group of truants had a total (T) score on the Rutter Scale B of 16.4 compared to 6.8 in the case of the controls ($P < 0.001$). 82% of truants had a T score of 9 or more on the B scale compared to only 27% of controls. ($P < 0.001$).

The adjourned cases came to court seven times on average during the first six months after their first appearance. Interim care orders were made on 13 of them. Seven of the supervised children were brought back to court by their social workers because of failure to make progress. Four children in each group eventually went to community homes after being put on full care orders. Institution placements were thus also similar in the two groups.

It might be argued that the truants came from schools that were in some way atypical with regard to attendance rates. The school attendance of the control group used for the assessment of psychiatric disturbance was looked at. The mean absence rate was 14%. This was very similar to the average absence rate for secondary schools in the city found whilst the study was being carried out. The schools the truants went to thus appeared to be representative of those in the city as a whole with regard to rates of absence.

There are a number of factors which could explain the superiority of adjournment over supervision in the management of truancy by juvenile courts. One is the effect on the family. A parent has to accompany a child appearing in court. This may necessitate the father or mother taking time off work. The fact that adjournment requires frequent court appearances means that there are more demands made on the family. Another factor is the effect on the educational welfare officer. With adjournment the EWO remains very much involved with the case. Once a supervision order has been made, however, the EWO needs the cooperation of the child's social worker in arranging for further appearances in court if progress fails to occur. It is probably true to say that EWOs are much more concerned with the limited problem of getting a child back to school than social services social workers or probation officers who see themselves as having a much wider role. A third factor is the effect on the child. The experience of repeated court attendances may well have more impact on the child than occasional chats with a sympathetic social worker. Improvement in the commission of indictable offences may reflect similar influences to those responsible for more satisfactory school attendances and also the effect of being in school keeping the child occupied and out of mischief.

TRUANCY AND COURT APPEARANCE

An investigation of boys remanded in custody after coming to court for failure to attend school (Tennent,1969), looking at their clinical features, suggested that neurotic features and even frank school refusal occurred as well as the antisocial behaviour which is often found to be associated with truancy (Hersov, 1960).

A similar study was carried out on 84 of the 96 children on whom the two court procedures mentioned above were evaluated (Berg, Butler, Hullin, Smith, and Tyrer, 1978). Social reports produced before they first appeared in court for failure to attend school were available on this group. However, they appeared to be a representative sample of the original cases since no significant differences were found on a variety of background features. The reports were rated by two sets of raters quite independently on 42 items covering the domestic situation, problems shown by the child and social work involvement. Reliability appeared to be quite satisfactory.

The method of principal component factor analysis was used to see if the sort of truancy resulting in a court appearance is a homogeneous condition. This was not found to be so. At least three independent sets of features appear to be involved in most cases. One involves antisocial and education problems and can be called 'clinical truancy' for that reason. A second set is concerned with adverse social factors and parental complicity and can be equated with 'school withdrawal'. A third includes a tendency to social isolation and may very tentatively be called 'school refusal'.

Individuals were plotted on scatter diagrams using two factors at any one time as coordinates. There was no evidence that they tended to cluster close to one of the coordinates. It thus appeared that most cases had features made up of all three underlying tendencies present to varying extents.

Scores on teachers' questionnaires measuring psychiatric disturbance obtained during the trial of the two court procedures helped to confirm the validity of the 3 factors. The 'clinical truancy' component correlated significantly with the Rutter Scale B antisocial subscale ($r = 0.3$, $P < 0.05$) and the 'school refusal' component correlated inversely to a significant extent with both the Rutter anti-social subscale ($r = -0.3$, $P < 0.05$) and the Conners Teachers Rating Scale *conduct problem* subscale ($r = -0.4$, $P < 0.05$).

COMMENTS

The legal obligations involved in school attendance have undoubtedly affected the way in which problems of going to school are dealt with by educational, medical, and social agencies.

The school system has the responsibility of providing suitable education for all children, including those with special needs, and this duty even extends to those who find it difficult to attend school. It is obviously highly desirable for children to acquire habits of regular attendance and to learn to conform with the routines of school life, so as to prepare them for work when they grow up, and the more schools can bring this about by providing their pupils with rewarding experiences, so that they want to come, the better it will be for all concerned. To have any hope of bringing about this desirable state of affairs the education provided would probably have to be much more varied and much more tailored to individual needs than it is at present. To some extent efforts to motivate children to attend school by promoting pleasurable individualized tuition are interfered with by the legal responsibilities of education authorities to monitor attendance, scrutinize excuses for absence, and pursue truants.

This conflict between helping children who have problems in attending school and threatening them with legal sanctions if they do not go is even more pronounced when it comes to the educational welfare service, since this agency is still more identified in people's minds with a coercive than with a helping role. The educational welfare officer has a primary task of supplying free school meals, clothing grants and arranging transport, when these are required, to get a child to school adequately clad and fed. The EWO also functions as a counsellor assisting the families of truants on a personal basis. Nevertheless, the main work of this service is the identification of truancy and the implementation of legal sanctions to counter it. There are historical and organizational reasons why this is so. Traditionally, educational welfare officers have been older men, recruited from authoritarian organizations such as the armed services, without specific training for the job and employed by education rather than social service departments. Because of poor levels of staffing and lack of clerical assistance they have had to concentrate on the most urgent and demanding aspects of their work and this has only served to emphasize the stereotype of the 'truant-catcher'. The amount of time required to collect evidence, attend court and deal with prosecutions limits the number of severe truants any EWO can deal with simultaneously in this way. It is not clear just how it is decided which children are in fact taken to court. Undoubtedly, one reason for doing so is to impress other absentees in the neighbourhood that court action may result from truancy, that is to use prosecution to try and prevent the problem occurring in others. Presumably, the severity and persistence of absenteeism are the reasons for most truants being taken to court (Clark, 1976).

Medical and social services are in much less conflict in regard to the use of legal procedures in getting children with attendance problems back to school since they do not have the statutory obligations of the Education Department. In fact, as has already been mentioned, they can protect children from the law. This happens by labelling them as ill requiring treatment, rather than deviant needing pressure to return to school. Doctors are able to involve the educational welfare service when they consider that this would be a helpful adjunct to their therapy.

It is not clear how much the prosecution of parents has contributed in the past to alleviating the problem of truancy. The recent increase in penalties in Britain including large fines and even imprisonment of a parent may change the situation in the future.

Once children are brought to court it would seem that repeated adjournments are more effective in helping them than supervision orders. It was a significant achievement to be able to establish this by a randomized controlled trial, (Farrington, 1978). The justification for such controlled investigations of court procedures has been discussed elsewhere (Berg, Hullin, and McGuire, 1978). Suffice it to say that it is obviously in the interest of the children affected to find the most effective ways of helping them overcome their difficulties. This has been an established principle in the medical field for many years. It seems only right that the scientific evaluation of procedures should become acceptable in the legal sphere as well.

There is no evidence that the children actually brought to court for failure to attend school fall into clearly delineated types of cases familiar to the clinician (Hersov, 1960). The stereotyped clinical pictures of the truant, the school phobic child and the youngster kept home by socially deviant parents are represented more as tendencies affecting any child to some extent, the amount of each determining the characteristics shown in any particular instance.

REFERENCES

Berg, I., Hullin, R., McGuire, R., and Tyrer, S. (1977). Truancy and the courts: research note. *Journal of Child Psychology and Psychiatry*, **18**, 359–365.

Berg, I., Consterdine, M., Hullin, R., McGuire, R., and Tyrer, S. (1978). A randomly controlled trial of two court procedures in truancy. *British Journal of Criminology*, **18**, 232–244.

Berg, I., Butler, A., Hullin, R., Smith, R., and Tyrer, S. (1978). Features of children taken to juvenile court for failure to attend school. *Psychological Medicine*, **8**, 447–453.

Berg, I., Hullin, R., and McGuire, R. (1978). A randomly controlled trial of two court procedures in truancy. In *Psychology, Law and Legal Processes*. (Ed.), K. Hawkins and S. Lloyd-Bostock. Macmillans, London.

Boyson, R. (1974). The need for realism. In (Ed.), B. Turner, *Truancy*. Ward Lock Educational, London, pp. 52–61.

Clark, J. (1976). *Educational Welfare Officers*. Dissertation for M.A. in Education, University of London.

Conners, C. K. (1969). A teacher rating scale for use in drug studies with children. *American Journal of Psychiatry*, 126, 884–888.

Dutchman-Smith, M. (1971). Section 40 of the Education Act 1944. *British Journal of Criminology*, 1, 85–87.

Eisenberg, L. (1958). School phobia: a study in the communication of anxiety. *American Journal of Psychiatry*, 14, 712–718.

Farrington, D. P. (1978). The effectiveness of sentences *Justice of the Peace*, 142, 68–71.

Fogelman, K. and Richardson, K. (1974). School attendance: some results from the National Child Development Study. In (Ed.), B. Turner, *Truancy*. Ward Lock Educational, London, pp. 29–51.

Gath, D., Cooper, B., and Gattoni, F. E. G. (1972). Child Guidance and Delinquency London Borough. *Psychological Medicine*, 2, 185–191.

Hersov, L. A. (1960). Persistent non-attendance at school. *Journal of Child Psychology and Psychiatry*, 1, 130–136.

Rutter, M. (1967). A children's behaviour questionnaire for completion by teachers: preliminary findings. *Journal of Child Psychology and Psychiatry*, 8, 1–11.

Tennent, T. G. (1969). *School Non-attendance and Delinquency*. MD Thesis. University of Oxford.

Tennent, T. G. (1970). The use of Section 40 of the Education Act by the London Juvenile Court. *British Journal of Criminology*, 9, 175–180.

Tennent, T. G. (1971). School non-attendance and delinquency. *Journal of Educational Research*, 13, 185–190.

Walker, N. (1972). *Sentencing in a Rational Society*. Penguin Books, London.

Williams, P. (1974). Collecting the figures in *Truancy*. B. Turner, (Ed.) Ward Lock Educational, London. pp. 20–28.

Out of School
Edited by L. Hersov and I. Berg
© 1980, John Wiley & Sons, Ltd.

Chapter 8

Problems in the Assessment and Management of Persistent Absenteeism from School

David Galloway

INTRODUCTION

There is no lack of strongly held beliefs about the prevalence and causes of poor school attendance. Kline's (1897) comparison of truancy with the migratory instinct in animals was probably never taken very seriously; in contrast, the 'Tom Sawyer' theory of truancy as a healthy, boyish rebellion against the monotony of school persists. This picture of the truant as a cheerful, well-adjusted young rebel from a stable home and caring, if traditional, school, might possibly apply to occasional absentees, but all the available evidence is against it applying to those who are persistently absent.

PROBLEMS OF DEFINITION

Different formulations

The term 'truancy' is used in different ways (See Chapter 2 and 3). Thus, Reynolds and Murgatroyd (1977) use it to describe overall absentee rates; in contrast, Galloway (1976a) reserves the term 'truancy' for those pupils who are absent from school without their parents' knowledge or consent.

There are conflicting views over the psychological implications of absence for the individual. It may be seen as a symptom of psychiatric disturbance in the child, perhaps resulting from temperamental vulnerability or from disturbed family relationships; within this model the child or his family should be offered treatment for the presenting symptom or its underlying causes. This view has often been favoured by psychologists and psychiatrists. On the other hand, absenteeism may be viewed from a sociological perspective. Here the emphasis is not on the individual, but rather on the individual's reaction to the conflicting or inconsistent expectations he experiences from society or at

149

school (Gutfreund, 1975; Reynolds and Murgatroyd, 1977). It may consequently imply a need for changes in the family, school or social situation in which the child lives, to bring about better attendance. A view, widely held by teachers, psychologists and psychiatrists, is that whilst a minority of absentees may require psychiatric treatment, the majority of cases reflect an irresponsible or indifferent attitude towards education, in which case legal intervention may be appropriate to enforce attendance.

Differential diagnosis

Psychiatric diagnosis has tended to define truancy as absence without parental knowledge or consent, it distinguishes between children whose absences are due to truancy, school refusal, and voluntary withholding by a parent. Hersov (1977) has noted that children in the latter group, also known as the 'parent-condoned' category, are relatively seldom referred for specialist advice. Within this diagnostic framework, truancy is seen as part of a wider conduct disorder; truants constitute a high risk group for other forms of delinquency (Tennent, 1971; May, 1975). They tend to have bad school reports, to be socially isolated and to be below average both in their intelligence and their educational attainments (Hersov, 1960). In contrast, school refusal (or school phobia) is seen as a neurotic disorder indicative of disturbed family relationships. The child is less likely to suffer intellectual or educational retardation. He may experience difficulty in relating with his peers and symptoms of separation anxiety are likely.

The validity of distinguishing truancy from school refusal has been questioned. Tyerman (1968), for example, argues that a clear distinction is not possible and the two groups lie on a continuum of reasons for absence. As prosecutions against parents for withholding their children from school are five times as common as for truancy (Tyerman, 1968) it is perhaps surprising that the literature does not appear to contain detailed studies of the personal and family characteristics of the most numerous group of absentees.

Other reasons for absence

The differential diagnoses described above do not cover other possible reasons for absence other than recognized illness. Some children are excluded from school on account of infestation, and an unknown number are absent due to lack of appropriate clothing, usually shoes or school uniform. At least in the U.K. the latter are regarded as illegal absences, and the child's parents are liable to prosecution. Similarly, a few pupils are excluded for behavioural reasons; in 1976–1977, 70 pupils missed over three weeks for this reason in Sheffield, a city with a total school population of 107,000. More importantly, the 'withheld' group probably includes not only children whose parents wish them to stay at home but also many instances where the parent knows about the absence, yet lacks the will or the strength to insist on return. The point at which this merges into the psychiatric category of school refusal remains an open question.

PREVALENCE OF PERSISTENT ABSENCE

Occasional absences

The figures from epidemiological research (see Chapters 2 and 3) do not generally include 'hidden truancy' — pupils who depart after registration. Figures on hidden truancy are understandably hard to obtain. Also it is clear that many of the statistics disguise the number of pupils who are occasionally absent for a variety of unjustified reasons. In America, Karweit (1973) found attendance rates declined on rainy days, while Jackson (1978) has noted a highly significant rise in absence rates on Fridays. In the same study, carried out in a comprehensive school known to have an exceptionally high overall attendance rate, 78 out of 312 14–15 year olds were shown to have missed at least one half day in 10 or more out of 37 weeks in the school year, excluding full week absences; of these a significantly higher proportion were boys.

Persistent absence

Carroll (1977b) has pointed out that identical attendance records can obscure quite different attendance patterns. Taking two improbable extremes, a 90 per cent attendance figure for a school could mean that 90 per cent attended all the time and 10 per cent none of the time, or that all pupils attended only 90 per cent of the time. The distinction is important for theoretical and practical reasons. Whereas chronic but sporadic absence may suggest the possibility of precipitating factors within the school, such as anxiety or resentment associated with certain teachers or certain subjects, persistent absence may pose additional problems such as educational retardation or psycho-social factors in the child or his family.

PERSISTENT ABSENTEEISM IN SHEFFIELD (1)

Introduction and method

To throw further light on the incidence and nature of persistent absenteeism, Sheffield Education Department carried out annual surveys in 1973 and 1974 (Galloway, 1976a; 1976b). Head teachers provided details about all pupils missing more than 50 per cent of attendances in the course of a six week period (1973) and a 14 week period (1974). An officer from the

Education Department's support service responsible for school attendance (known as the education welfare service) then stated whether more than half of each child's absence was due to illness. If not, he stated which of seven categories accounted for the greatest proportion of absences. Cases where more than half the absence was due to illness were not included in the subsequent analysis of results.

Results

Table 1 shows the prevalence of persistent unjustified absence in each age group. It will be seen that prevalence rates are remarkably constant from the start of compulsory education until the age of 12, after which there is a rapid increase with a peak in the final year.

Table 1. Prevalence of persistent unjustified absence. (Reproduced by permission of the Controller of Her Majesty's Stationery Office)

1973: 6 weeks in the Autumn term; 30 secondary school catchment areas
1974: 14 weeks in the Autumn term; 36 secondary school catchment areas

School	Age Group	1973		1974	
		No. of Absentees	% of total on roll in each age group	No. of Absentees	% of total on roll in each age group
Infant or First	5	24	0.6	11	0.4
	6	40	0.5	17	0.2
	7	18	0.2	24	0.3
	8	25	0.3	21	0.2
	9	26	0.3	22	0.2
Junior or Middle	10	33	0.4	11	0.1
	11	30	0.4	30	0.3
	12	37	1.0	15	0.4
Primary Schools	Total	233	0.4	151 (139[a])	0.3
Comprehensive	12	15	0.5	21	0.4
	13	89	1.3	74	0.8
	14	91	1.4	137	1.7
	15	154	2.3	138	1.8
	16	290	4.4	302	3.9
Secondary Schools	Total	639	2.1	672 (598[a])	1.8

[a]Total from the 30 schools in 1973 survey

Table 2 shows the categories into which their educational social workers placed the pupils. The categories were reached in discussion with senior members of the service, and were intended to be meaningful to the officers concerned rather than to follow traditional diagnostic categories. Hence, category 6, 'psychosomatic illness' almost certainly includes children presenting with 'somatic disguise' of school refusal. Officers were expected to tick psychosomatic illness only when the diagnostic assessment had been made by a doctor. The wording of the school phobia category deliberately focussed attention on severe home problems as described in much of the psychiatric literature, in order to exclude children whose absence was due simply to dislike of some aspect of school in which case the children should generally have been included in categories 1, 4, or 5. As each family was usually known to only one officer, there was no evidence either on the reliability or the validity of the ratings. Nevertheless, it is of considerable interest that over 16 per cent of primary school absentees and 26 per cent from secondary schools were thought to be absent with their parents' knowledge, but without their active consent.

Table 2. Reasons for persistent absenteeism (excluding prolonged organic illness). (Reproduced by permission of the Controller of Her Majesty's Stationery Office)

	Primary schools percentage		Secondary schools percentage	
	1973	1974	1973	1974
1 With parents' knowledge, consent, and approval	24.2	19.2	24.3	15.4
2 Socio-medical reasons — child is excluded from school for reasons such as infestation, scabies, etc.	10.5	6.6	2.7	3.0
3 'School phobia'. Non-attendance is associated with severe relationship difficulties in the home	1.2	4.0	4.2	3.5
4 Parents unable or unwilling to insist on return — child is at home with parents' knowledge but not with their active consent	16.1	18.6	26.0	31.3
5 Truancy — child is absent without parents' knowledge or consent	2.4	2.0	11.2	15.4
6 Psychosomatic illness	4.4	1.3	3.8	4.7
7 Mixed — part of the child's absence is due to illness but one or more of the other factors is also relevant	41.2	48.3	27.8	26.7
		100		100

Analysis of absentee rates in each secondary school against a number of school and community variables showed a significant positive correlation with poverty in the school's catchment area as reflected in the number of pupils receiving free school meals. In contrast, no association was found with the school's size, nor with the number of pupils excluded on disciplinary grounds. Yet although free school meal rates of schools predicted *how many* children might be persistent absentees, further analysis has shown that the pupils known to be eligible for free meals were not more likely to be persistent absentees than their peers who were not. This suggests the possibility of contributory factors within the schools concerned. Transfer to a new and larger secondary school did not *per se* seem to be a cause of higher absence rates. Children who transferred to a secondary school at age 11 were not more likely to become persistent absentees than their exact contemporaries who remained at middle schools for a further year of primary education. Analysis of the boy–girl ratio in the 1974 survey showed a non-significant excess of girls, a trend noted by Shepherd *et al.* (1971) (see Chapter 1). On the other hand, when the categories of absence were broken down by sex, truancy was seen to be almost twice as common in secondary school boys as in girls, while the reverse applied to pupils remaining at home with their parents' knowledge, consent, and approval.

The prevalence surveys summarized here show that truancy and school phobia were together thought to account for less than 20 per cent of absences, while absence with parental knowledge, with or without active consent, accounted for more than six times as many primary school absentees and well over twice as many in secondary schools.

PERSISTENT ABSENTEEISM IN SHEFFIELD (2)

Rationale and method

Following these results, a more detailed study aimed to answer three questions: (1) How many of this 'silent majority' of absentees who are not referred for specialist advice share the characteristics of truants or school refusers? (2) Do absentees in this area who are referred to psychological and psychiatric support services differ from absentees who are not? (3) As persistent absence is so much more widespread in secondary schools, is there evidence that, compared with absences from primary school, secondary school absenteeism is less influenced by family and psychological factors, and more influenced by school and community factors?

Four samples were selected: (1) all pupils at one secondary school who missed 50 per cent of attendances in the previous autumn term without adequate reason; (2) all pupils who missed a similar amount of time from the secondary school's feeding primary schools; (3) all pupils known to have been referred to the Education Department's Psychological Service in a larger, but overlapping area within a two year period, for advice or treatment on school attendance problems; (4) good attenders selected from the same class as some of the secondary school absentees and one of the primary schools.

Pupils in the secondary and primary school absentee samples who had been referred to a psychologist on account of school attendance problems were included only in the 'referred' sample. The secondary school catchment area had a high incidence of social problems, with few owner occupied houses. Over 90 per cent of parents from each of the original absentee samples agreed to be interviewed, but only 74 per cent of the good attenders' parents.

Results

Table 3 shows relatively few items from the histories reported at parent interview distinguishing the three groups of absentees. In statistical analysis the log-likelihood ratio statistic was preferred to the more familiar chi square, to which it approximates, for reasons explained by Gabriel (1966). Parents of secondary absentees were more likely to report fear of a teacher or dislike of a subject as a contributory cause of their child's absence than those of the younger children. The only item on which all secondary absentees differed significantly from the referred group was difficulty in social relationships at school. The only item on which the primary children differed from both the other absentee groups was a history of 'socio-medical' problems (usually infestation). More differences were found between the three absentee groups and the good attenders. The only discriminatory item which might generally be described as a 'neurotic' symptom was fear of harm befalling the parent, with associated reluctance to leave home.

Parents in each sample were asked to complete the Malaise Inventory (Rutter et al., 1970). This questionnaire has been shown to have reasonably high validity in predicting psychiatric disorder (Chadwick, 1976). Although the differences between the Sheffield samples did not reach statistical significance (Table 4), there was a noticeable trend for the mothers of secondary absentees to show higher rates of reported disorder, as assessed by a score of more than 6. The three absentee groups, though not the good attenders, had significantly higher scores than the full control sample in Chadwick's study. In fact, the rate of disorder in the absentee groups is similar to that of the group with psychiatric disorder in the Isle of Wight investigation (Rutter et al., 1970). That this should be reflected in the children's school attendance is not altogether surprising in view of the association between parental ill-health and childhood disorder (Rutter, 1966).

The surveys summarized here are consistent with the epidemiological literature on the prevalence of maladjustment (Davie et al., 1972) and psychiatric disorder (Rutter et al., 1970, 1975a). The total prevalence of illegal absence from school is considerably higher than studies of clinic referrals would suggest. How far the largest groups of pupils remaining at home with their parents' knowledge, sometimes with their active consent and sometimes without it, differ from the traditional diagnostic categories of truancy and

Table 3. Information reported at Parent Interview

	Secondary school absentees N = 39 (%)	Primary school absentees N = 20 (%)	Absentees Referred for psychological advice N = 20 (%)	Good attenders N = 23 (%)	Overall log-likelihood-ratio (d.f. = 3)	Comparison of sub-groups (d.f. = 3) +
Physical symptoms associated with school attendance	8 (20.5)	3 (15.0)	8 (40.0)	4 (17.4)	4.2 NS	
Eating difficulties	6 (15.4)	5 (25.0)	5 (25.0)	4 (17.4)	1.2 NS	
Abdominal pains	18 (46.2)	7 (35.0)	5 (25.0)	3 (13.0)	8.4 ($p < 0.05$)	
Sleep disturbance	9 (23.1)	0 (0)	6 (30.0)	3 (13.0)	7.9 ($p < 0.05$)	
Fear of harm befalling parent	14 (35.9)	9 (45.0)	9 (45.0)	2 (8.7)	10.3 ($p < 0.01$)	Groups P and G ($p < 0.05$) Groups R and G ($p < 0.05$)
Enuresis	8 (20.5)	3 (15.0)	4 (20.0)	1 (4.4)	3.9 NS	
Stealing	11 (28.2)	6 (30.0)	10 (50.0)	2 (8.7)	9.6 ($p < 0.05$)	Groups R and G ($p < 0.05$)
Lying	5 (12.8)	4 (20.0)	9 (45.0)	2 (8.7)	10.0 ($p < 0.05$)	Groups R and C ($p < 0.05$)
Wandering, coming home late, etc.	10 (25.6)	5 (25.0)	7 (35.0)	3 (13.0)	3.0 NS	
Complaints of	10 (25.6)	9 (45.0)	8 (40.0)	7 (30.4)	2.7 NS	

						Group comparisons			
				3 (21.7)	(p<0.001)		(p<0.001)		(p<0.01)
Dislike of a particular subject	18 (46.2)	1 (5.0)	7 (35.0)	9 (39.1)	12.7 (p<0.001)	Groups S and P (p<0.01)			
Sense of educational failure	6 (15.4)	2 (10.0)	5 (25.0)	4 (17.4)	1.7 NS				
Difficulty in social relationships at school	5 (12.8)	3 (15.0)	11 (55.0)	1 (4.4)	18.4 (p<0.001)	Groups S and R (p<0.01)	Groups R and G (p<0.01)		
Anxiety about sex (e.g. showers, boy–girl relationships)	7 (18.0)	1 (5.0)	5 (25.0)	4 (17.4)	3.5 NS				
Influence of peers	11 (28.2)	3 (15.0)	7 (35.0)	7 (30.4)	2.4 NS				
Socio-medical problems (e.g. infestation)	11 (28.2)	14 (70.0)	3 (15.0)	0 (0)	28.9 (p<0.001)	Groups S and P (p<0.05)	Groups R and P (p<0.01)	Groups P and G (p<0.001)	Groups S and G (p<0.05)
Kept at home to help look after parents or siblings	17 (43.6)	3 (15.0)	2 (10.0)	1 (4.4)	17.3 (p<0.001)	Groups S and G (p<0.01)			
Known to other specialist agencies (e.g. social work)	18 (46.2)	7 (35.0)	14 (70.0)	2 (8.7)	19.7 (p<0.001)	Groups S and G (p<0.02)	Groups R and G (p<0.001)		
Have been in Care	11 (28.2)	2 (10.0)	9 (45.0)	3 (13.0)	8.9 (p<0.05)				
Parent has met child's teachers	13 (33.3)	14 (70.0)	13 (65.0)	13 (56.5)	9.8 (p<0.05)				

Table 4. Mothers' scores on malaise inventory

	S secondary school absentees ($N=36$)%	P primary school absentees ($N=16$)%	R absentees referred for psychological advice ($N=18$)%	G Good attenders ($N=19$)%	IOW (1) Isle of Wight mothers: pure control ($N=150$)%	IOW (2) Isle of Wight mothers: psychiatric group ($N=79$)%	Log-likelihood ratio statistic d.f. = 5	Comparison of sub-groups d.f. = 5
Score ≥ 7	20 (56)	11 (69)	8 (45)	6 (32)	8 (5)	47 (60)	110 ($p < 0.001$)	Groups S and IOW (1) ($p < 0.001$) Groups P and IOW (1) ($p < 0.001$) Groups R and IOW (1) ($p < 0.01$) Groups IOW (1) and IOW (2) ($p < 0.001$)

school refusal remains an open question, though our work does suggest that the area of overlap is considerable. Less disputable, however, is the high level of possible psychiatric disorder in the mothers of all our absentee samples. How far this is causally related to their children's symptoms and attendance problems is not yet clear. Mothers of good attenders also had a fairly high rate of possible disorder, though their scores tended to be lower than in the absentee groups.

Interviews both with the parents and children in the absentee samples showed a considerable overlap between different reasons for absence, suggesting that the categories in Table 1 over-simplify the true position. Some of the pupils who remained at home, with or without their parents' active consent, admitted to some truancy. Further, some of the children whose absences were actively condoned by their parents showed the behaviours characteristic of school phobia/refusal in the psychiatric literature.

MANAGEMENT

Roles for the psychological/psychiatric team

The psychological support services have two potential roles: (1) as therapists for individuals, and (2) as consultants to advise on management. In practice, these roles are not mutually exclusive, yet the distinction should be recognized in planning a network of services.

The generally favourable outcomes of treatment for school refusal (Hersov, 1977) point to the value of a clinic-based service for families which are able to attend regularly. The study reported above suggests that symptoms associated with school refusal may be more prevalent than has previously been assumed, particularly in inner-city areas which are known from other research to have high rates of psychiatric disorder (Rutter *et al.*, 1975a) and social malaise (Wedge and Prosser, 1973). Unfortunately, these are the areas where families may be most likely to have difficulty in keeping clinic or hospital appointments. One obvious reason for this is that many parents face so many social and medical problems that insistence on their anxious or resistant children attending school is a long way down their list of priorities; another is that their own childhood may not have led them to see education as a partnership between school and home.

In such areas, when teachers and social workers may understandably feel overwhelmed by the number of children and families with special needs, clinicians may wish to allocate time for what is essentially an advisory service for teachers and other professional personnel rather than a treatment service. Such a service has an important implication for referral. In a treatment service, it makes sense to encourage the referral of cases with the best prognosis for the available treatments. This generally implies children with neurotic disorders such as school phobics or refusers, rather than conduct disorders such as truants (Robins, 1966; Levitt, 1963). An advisory service, in contrast, would encourage referral of pupils who were most disruptive and disturbing to the teachers, and explore ways of helping them within the school or community.

Multi-dimensional assessment

A child may be absent because he is embarrassed by his educational backwardness, frightened of a particular teacher, unskilled in social relationships with other children, worried about his parents' or siblings' health, worried about the disintegration of his home, anxious about his own physical development (for example, when puberty is delayed), easily led by more dominant or delinquent peers, and so on. Hersov's (1977) review of school refusal shows that this is probably 'not a true clinical entity with a uniform aetiology, psychopathology, course, prognosis, and treatment, but rather a collection of symptoms or a syndrome occurring against a background of a variety of psychiatric disorders'. In other words, assessment should examine the possibility of social, educational, and psychological factors both within the child and the family.

How this is achieved in practice will depend on the organization of local resources. Traditionally, child guidance or child psychiatric teams consist of psychiatrist, educational psychologist, and psychiatric social worker and sometimes a child psychotherapist. In principle this team is well placed to assess psychiatric, educational, and social factors. The centralized clinic team has, however, come under considerable attack (Tizard, 1973; Loxley, 1974) and is being replaced in many areas by a more loosely knit network of services as proposed by the Court Committee on Child Health Services (DHSS, 1976).

In practice, it is as difficult to distinguish the relative contributions of different potential causes in cases of poor school attendance as with any other presenting symptom. For two reasons this problem is particularly acute in assessing the significance of school variables: first, these are frequently emphasised by clients and second, schools which appear very similar to an outside visitor may provide quite different experiences for vulnerable children who attend them. Similarly, schools vary — quite understandably — in their ability to cater for the individual needs of a pupil who, from their point of view, may persistently have rejected everything they have offered in the past (See Chapter 5).

Community-based assessment

A model which is gaining favour in a number of local education authorities in England, is for the support services of school health, educational psychology and educational welfare to base themselves on secondary school catchment areas. As the support service responsible for cases of poor attendance, educational social workers (educational welfare officers) co-operate with teachers in preliminary investigations. Ideally, these include a home visit, generally from the educational social worker, to identify contributory problems at home, and an interview with the child about possible difficulties at school. Sometimes study of the attendance register shows a consistent pattern of absences, for example from certain subjects, or at the start of the week. When a pupil has frequent absences due to minor illness, advice is sought from the schools' visiting medical officer who may involve the educational psychologist or child psychiatrist if he thinks the illnesses may be symptomatic of other problems. Other children may be referred directly to the visiting educational psychologist or discussed informally with him at a weekly staff meeting on pupils' welfare.

A development in Liverpool has extended this approach. Each area has a social education team, headed by an 'education guidance officer' whose job is to co-ordinate the efforts of all the available educational, social work and medical agencies to help both child and school (Brandon, 1974). Although the teams are based in the Education Department, it is hoped that they will be able to draw on the skills of other personnel, and thus prevent overlap in service provision. It is not clear how far this has in fact been possible, and the emphasis seems to be somewhat heavily on the child's and family's problems rather than on contributory factors in school. Nevertheless, the social education team constitutes an interesting attempt to extend and co-ordinate the available resources for dealing with truancy and related problems.

The scope and limitations of 'clinical' treatment

Ever since Broadwin's classic paper (1932), school phobia (or school refusal) has attracted consistent attention from psychiatrists and psychologists (See Chapter 12). Numerous papers have described the syndrome and many different forms of treatment. Although truancy is widely agreed to be more widespread than school refusal, even when the former term is restricted to children absent from school without their parents' knowledge or consent, its treatment appears to have received remarkably little attention from psychologists and psychiatrists; clinical studies are notable only for their absence. There are a number of possible reasons for this: (1) truancy is usually regarded as just one aspect of a more wide-ranging conduct disorder, while school refusal is often seen as the main expression of a neurotic disorder; (2) conduct disorders are less amenable to clinic-based treatments than neurotic disorders, and have a worse prognosis (Levitt, 1963; Robins, 1966); (3) truants and their families may be less likely to co-operate in clinic-based intervention than school refusers who are referred for treatment, perhaps due to differences in social class attitudes to treatment (Hersov, 1960).

The first of these possibilities merits further discussion. While there is a detailed theoretical literature on school refusal, the same is not true of truancy or other forms of absenteeism. While clinicians are in general agreement about the neurotic nature of school refusal, they have differed on points of detail, for instance the relative significance of depression, separation anxiety, and avoidance conditioning (Davidson, 1961; Chazan, 1962; Ross, 1972). The point is that the theoretical and diagnostic literature provides a number of conceptual frameworks on which to base treatment programmes.

Studies reviewed by Yule (1977) (See Chapter 14) suggest that approaches derived from behaviour therapy and modification have been successful in treating a variety of problems, both in home and school settings. The common conceptual background to these studies is that treatment is based on a behavioural analysis which seeks to describe how the child and people in his environment interact with each other in creating or maintaining the presenting problem. This approach lends itself to the study and treatment of a problem in which there is often a complex interaction between family, environmental, temperamental, and school variables. Viewed in this way, clinic treatments could have an important role in the treatment of some truants, but are not likely to be effective unless combined with other approaches which tackle the problem in its social context. A case history will illustrate this approach.

Case history — Albert

Albert was referred at the age of 15 with a long history of truancy and delinquency. His offences were sometimes committed on his own, sometimes in company. He was of low average intelligence, severely retarded educationally, and had few friends. His parents were concerned about him, but his mother suffered from depression and his father worked long hours. His mother reported that her depression had started after the death, from acute leukaemia, of Albert's older sister, to whom he had been very close. This happened two months after he started his secondary education. Perhaps understandably, his parents were relieved, rather than concerned, that he showed no grief. In a family interview Albert astonished his parents by bursting into tears when asked if he had been close to his sister.

A provisional formulation saw Albert's *initial* truancy as a response to unresolved grief and associated anxiety about his mother's health. They were offered separate interviews using a modified version of the approach described by Ramsay (1977) for treating grief reaction. However, it was felt that Albert's *current* truancy was maintained by secondary factors, mainly his social isolation and educational retardation. This highlighted two problems in his school's provision for pupil welfare: (1) that class teachers were encouraged to pass all 'welfare' problems to the Head of Year (the teacher responsible for each age group) whose time was mainly spent investigating cases of disruptive behaviour (See Chapter 8); (2) the school currently had no remedial teaching facilities for 15 and 16 year olds. Arrangements were made to tackle the immediate problem by drawing up an individual time-table in co-operation with Albert; this enabled him to receive — at considerable administrative inconvenience — some remedial teaching, and an unusual number of woodwork and PE lessons — subjects which he enjoyed and were taught by teachers he liked. The broader issues were discussed in a series of meetings of senior staff, when future policy was under consideration.

School and community based treatment

Treatment at school within ordinary classes

Brooks (1974) has described the use of 'contingency contracts' with truants. The use of contingency contracts lends itself to the assessment procedures suggested above, since the contract can be tailor-made to deal with problems arising in — or caused by — factors at home, at school or in the community. Brooks' contracts were drawn up by a school counsellor and involved a written contract between pupil, parent, and school in which school attendance was reinforced by previously agreed rewards.

Brooks reported improvement, but his cases seem to have been relatively straightforward. It was not necessary for the contract to specify active intervention from the school, for example in teaching the pupil to read more fluently by providing an individualized remedial programme. Another approach is described by Boyson (1974). He appears to be in some doubt as to whether responsibility for truancy lies primarily with slack teachers, neglectful parents or subversive administrators, but describes his own approach as 'regular if not eternal vigilance'; staff at his school made frequent spot checks for hidden truancy, with immediate 'phone calls to parents — at work if necessary — whenever any unexplained absence was discovered.

Whether this approach is seen as coercive or caring may depend on one's point of view. The same may be said of the role of school counsellors and teachers with positions of special responsibility for pastoral care. Reynolds and Murgatroyd (1977) have argued that these appointments exaggerate the influence of individual staff and underestimate the capacity of the school's internal organization in generating its own problems. Counselling procedures have nevertheless been used both by teachers and by outside personnel in attempts to improve attendance. Some small-scale studies wtih truants have obtained results which justify cautious optimism, though the follow-up periods were rather short. (Law, 1973; Sassi, 1973; Cain, 1974; Beaumont, 1976; Tumelty, 1976). A more wide-ranging action research project (Rose and

Marshall, 1974) has suggested that attendance may be improved and delinquency reduced when counsellors or social workers are introduced into schools.

While the clinical literature on treatment has concentrated on school refusal, the few published descriptions of school-based treatment have concentrated on truancy. One of the few studies which focusses on poor attenders without discriminating truants from other absentees compared the efficacy of three behaviour modification procedures with elementary (primary) school children (Morgan, 1975). A combination of material rewards and social reinforcement from peers was found to be the most effective procedure, though the follow-up period was very short. In view of the complexity of reasons for illegal absence, it is doubtful whether the arbitrary application of behaviour modification techniques is justified, though they can certainly form part of a programme based on a careful assessment of the presenting problem (Galloway, 1977).

Special units in ordinary schools

Special units for problem pupils could legitimately be described as the only current growth area in British education. Many of them cater *inter alia* for truants and school refusers. Teachers' opinions about basing these units in ordinary schools are divided. Some believe their primary focus should be on therapy, others on deterrence; while some emphasize the need to protect the conforming majority from undesirable influences (Lodge, 1977) others stress the therapeutic and rehabilitative function, and encourage social workers, psychologists, and psychiatrists to participate in the overall planning and more immediate recommendations for individual children (Jones, 1973; 1974). Some head teachers, however, oppose the introduction of any form of unit for absentees or disruptive pupils. Three reasons are commonly put forward: (1) the existence of such a unit 'normalizes' deviant behaviour in the eyes of pupils, and thus reduces the potential influences of group pressure from the conforming majority; (2) it is as unsound educationally to separate problem pupils from their peers as it is to cream off the academic elite into grammar schools; (3) the units reduce the commitment of class teachers and subject teachers to handle problems themselves, with consequent reluctance to co-operate in a pupil's return from the unit (See Chapter 9).

A growing number of head teachers appear to think these obstacles can be overcome. Following the early reports (Boxall, 1973; Jones, 1973, 1974; Labon, 1973) over 200 schools have established special groups (Berger and Mitchell, 1978). How many of these cater for truants as well as disruptive pupils is not known, nor is there yet any reliable body of information about their methods or their results.

Special units outside ordinary schools

Parallelling the development of special units in ordinary schools has been a similar development in which units have been established to take 'hard-core' cases from a number of different schools. Some of these cater primarily for delinquent or disruptive adolescents, but generally find that many of their clients have had school attendance problems. Others cater primarily for truants. No consensus has yet emerged regarding responsibility for these centres. Some are set up by the local education department and are run exclusively by teachers; others are set up by social work departments, with teachers seconded from the education department. In Scotland, provision of day units for truants has been encouraged by the Pack Report, in preference to residential provision (Scottish Education Department, 1977).

Rowan (1976) has noted that children are always accepted for outside units on the understanding that they remain on the register of their ordinary school, to which it is hoped they will eventually return. Although they share the common aim of providing an effective alternative to orthodox schooling, they vary widely in their methods. The Islington Centre in London caters for truants referred by local secondary schools (Grunsell, 1978). Their relatively unstructured approach tolerates a wide range of disturbed behaviour within an accepting framework reminiscent of some of the pioneer workers for maladjusted children. The Hammersmith Teenage Project (NACRO, 1978) also caters for truants, though truancy is secondary to a history of delinquency as a criterion for admission. This project breaks new ground in the treatment of truants (and offenders) in England by employing as staff people who had themselves been in trouble as adolescents. Having similar backgrounds and problems to the project's youngsters, it was hoped that these workers would provide more acceptable identification figures and thus offer a model of successful emergence from an incipient criminal career.

The majority of special units and centres catering for truants appear to operate on relatively unstructured lines. Descriptive accounts are not hard to find, and evaluative studies are almost non-existent. One consistent trend from the small available literature is that successful return to school is seldom achieved. The Islington Centre and the Hammersmith Project had to dismiss this as impractical for most children. This may have been due to the disturbance in the pupils; alternatively, it may be attributable to the units providing so radical an alternative to conventional education that realistic pressure to return would have run counter to their practice and philosophy. A third possibility is that the schools themselves may have been less than enthusiastic about the return of their poor attenders. Follow-up studies on the subsequent careers of truants who have attended such centres, compared with truants who remained in conventional education, are urgently needed.

An exception to the general lack of success in returning pupils to school is the Hungerford Centre in London (Lane, 1977a, 1977b). The centre offers short-term treatment based on a contract between each child, the centre's staff and the referring school. Significantly, the referring school is involved in drawing up the contract which can, when necessary, specify what the school should do to facilitate the pupil's return. The child is expected to keep to his contract and can see whether the centre and his school keep to theirs. Training and advice is offered to the ordinary school's teachers and the child is consciously taught how to cope with the situations that had previously led to confrontation or escape. The centre caters primarily for disruptive pupils, some of whom, nevertheless, have attendance problems. This would seem a logical and promising avenue for further research, particularly if pupils' families can also be involved in the contract.

CONCLUSIONS

The efficacy of clinic-based treatment is not in doubt for many cases of acute school refusal associated with a neurotic disorder. It is not clear whether the same procedures will be effective when similar symptoms are associated with the severe social problems prevailing in the area of our study. The school-based team of educational psychologist, education social worker (or welfare officer) and specialist teachers should be able to carry out initial assessment, giving greater attention to the potential influence of school — positive or negative — than is possible for a clinic-based team. When appropriate the more specialized skills of psychiatrists and other casework or medical services are naturally available through normal referral channels.

Similar choices face educational administrators in allocating resources to the treatment of absenteeism: should they be channelled into special units which may provide an intensive treatment service for a small minority of absentees, usually hard-core truants, or should the available funds be allocated to encourage schools themselves to cater more successfully for their absentees? In this connection there is an urgent need for research into the progress of pupils admitted to special units, particularly those which are separate from ordinary schools. One of the few relatively consistent trends to emerge from the literature is that return to school is more often an ideal than a reality.

Study of persistent absence from school reveals a complex inter-relationship between factors in the school, the local community, the family and the child himself. Hence treatment of the individual, alone or with his family, has a good prognosis only when school and community factors appear insignificant as in some cases of school refusal, or their influence can be overcome in the course of treatment. No single approach — counselling, social workers in schools, special units within schools, special centres independent of schools — is likely to succeed unless based on the recognition that a solution to a many facetted problem will require close co-ordination and co-operation between schools and the various advisory, casework and treatment agencies.

ACKNOWLEDGEMENTS

I am grateful to colleagues in Sheffield Education Department and Sheffield School Health Psychiatry Service for criticisms of an earlier draft of this chapter; also to Dr. Oliver Chadwick for permission to quote from his data on the Malaise Inventory, to Professor Loynes for his advice on statistical analysis and to Mr. Graham Dawson for carrying out computer programming. Part of the second study reported here was carried out with the help of a grant from the Department of Education and Science.

REFERENCES

Beaumont, G. R. (1976). A comparison of the effects of behavioural counselling and teacher support on the attendance of truants. *Unpublished Diploma School Counsellors Dissertation*, University College, Swansea.

Berger, M., and Mitchell, C. (1978). Multitude of sin-bins. *Times Educational Supplement*, 7th July.

Boxall, M. (1973). Nurture Groups. *Concern*, 13, 9–11.

Boyson, R. (1974). The need for realism. In (Ed.) Turner, B., *Truancy*. Ward Lock Educational, London.

Brandon, R. (1974). Local authority experiment. Liverpool. In (Ed.) Turner, B., *Truancy*. Ward Lock Educational, London. pp. 113–121.

Bransby, E. R. (1951). A study of absence from school. *Medical Officer*, 86, 223–230.

Broadwin, I. T. (1932). A contribution to the study of truancy. *American Journal of Orthopsychiatry*, 2, 253–259.

Brooks, D. B. (1974). Contingency contracts with truants. *Personnel Guidance Journal*, 52, 315–320.

Cain, J. (1974). A study of the effect of counselling on pupils displaying an irregular pattern of school attendance. *Unpublished Diploma School Counselling Dissertation*, University College of Swansea.

Carroll, H. C. M. (1977a). A cross-sectional and longitudinal study of poor and good attenders in a comprehensive school. In (Ed.) Carroll, H. C. M., *Absenteeism in South Wales*. University College of Swansea.

Carroll, H. C. M. (1977b). The problem of absenteeism. In (Ed.) Carroll, H. C. M., *Absenteeism in South Wales*. University College of Swansea.

Chadwick, O. (1976). *Personal Communication*.

Chazan, M. (1962). School phobia. *British Journal of Educational Psychology*, 32, 209–217.

Davidson, S. (1960). School phobia as a manifestation of family disturbance. Its structure and treatment. *Journal of Child Psychology and Psychiatry*, 1, 270–287.

Davie, R., Butler, M. and Goldstein, H. (1972). *From Birth to Seven*. Longman, London.

Department of Education and Science (1967). Children and their Primary Schools. *Report of the Central Advisory Council for Education (England)*. HMSO, London.

Department of Education and Science (1974). *Results of School Absence Survey*. Press Notice, 25th July.

Department of Health and Social Security (1976). *Fit for the Future: Report of the Committee on the Child Health Services.* (The Court Report) Vols. I and II. HMSO, London.

Fogelman, K. (Ed.) (1976). *Britain's Sixteen-Year-Olds.* National Children's Bureau, London.

Fogelman, K. (1978). School attendance, attainment and behaviour. *British Journal of Educational Psychology*, **48**, 148–158.

Gabriel, K. R. (1966). Simultaneous test procedures for multiple comparisons on categorical date. *Journal of the American Statistical Association*, **61**, 1081–1096.

Galloway, D. M. (1976a). Size of school, socio-economic hardship, suspension rates and persistent unjustified absence from school. *British Journal of Educational Psychology*, **46**, 40–47.

Galloway, D. M. (1976b). Persistent unjustified absence from school. *Trends in Education*, 1976/4, 22–27.

Galloway, D. M. (1977) Application of behavioural analysis and behaviour modification in school psychological service practice. *British Association Behavioural Psychotherapy Bulletin*, **5**, 63–66.

Grunsell, R. (1978). Born to be Invisible: *The Story of a School for Truants*, Macmillan Education, London.

Gutfreund, R. (1975). Resolving the problem. *Youth in Society*, May/June, 12–15.

Hersov, L. (1960). Persistent non-attendance at school. *Journal of Child Psychology and Psychiatry*, **1**, 130–136.

Hersov, L. (1977). School refusal. In (Eds.) Rutter, M., and Hersov, L. *Child Psychiatry: Modern Approaches.* Blackwell, Oxford. pp. 455–486.

Jackson, D. (1978). A comparative study of the perceptions of their school of frequent absentees and regular attenders. *Unpublished M.Ed. Thesis*, University of Sheffield.

Jones, N. (1973). Special adjustment units in comprehensive schools: I Needs and resources. II Structure and function. *Therapeutic Education*, **1**, No. 2, 23–31.

Jones, N. (1974). Special adjustment units in comprehensive schools: III Selection of Children. *Therapeutic Education*, **2**, No. 2, 21–62.

Karweit, N. L. (1973). Rainy days and Mondays: An analysis of factors related to absence from school. Report No. 162: Baltimore: Johns Hopkins University, Centre for the Study of Social Organization of Schools.

Kline, L. W. (1897). Truancy as related to the migratory instinct. *Pedagogical Seminary*, **5**, 381–385.

Labon, D. (1973). Helping maladjusted children in primary schools. *Therapeutic Education*, **1**, No. 2, 14–22.

Lane, D. A. (1977a). Aspects of the use of behaviour modification in secondary schools. *British Association for Behavioural Psychotherapy Bulletin*, **5**, 76–79.

Lane, D. A., and Millar, R. (1977b). Dealing with behaviour problems in school: a new development. *Community Health*, **8**, 155–158.

Law, B. (1973). An alternative to truancy. *British Journal of Guidance Counselling*, **1**, 91–96.

Levitt, E. E. (1963). Psychotherapy with children: A further evaluation *Behaviour Research and Therapy*, **1**, 45–51.

Lodge, B. (1977). Call to isolate the classroom thugs. *Times Educational Supplement*, 15th April.

Loxley, F. D. (1974). Beyond child guidance. *British Psychological Society Division of Educational and Child Psychology Occasional Papers*, 283–288.

May, D. (1975). Truancy, school absenteeism and delinquency. *Scottish Educational Studies*, **7**, 97–107.

Morgan, R. R. (1975). An exploratory study of three procedures to encourage school attendance. *Psychology in Schools*, **12**, 209–215.

National Association for the Care and Rehabilitation of Offenders (1978). *The Hammersmith Teenage Project*. Barry Rose, Chichester.

Norris, V. (1951). Health of the schoolchild. *British Journal of Social Medicine*, **5**, 145.

Ramsay, R. W. (1977). Behavioural approaches to bereavement. *Behaviour Research and Therapy*, **15**, 131–135.

Reynolds, D. and Murgatroyd, S. (1977). The sociology of schooling and the absent pupil: the school as a factor in the generation of truancy. In (Ed.) Carroll, H. C. M., *Absenteeism in South Wales*. University College of Swansea.

Robins, L. N. (1966). *Deviant Children Grown Up*. Williams and Wilkins, Baltimore.

Rose, G., and Marshall, T. F. (1974). *Counselling and School Social Work*, Wiley, Chichester.

Ross, A. O. (1972). Behaviour therapy. In Wolman, B. B. (Ed.), *Manual of Child Psychopathology*. McGraw-Hill, New York.

Rowan, P. (1976). Short-term sanctuary. *Times Educational Supplement*, 2nd April, 21–24.

Rutter, M. (1966). Children of Sick Parents: an Environmental and Psychiatric Study. *Maudsley Monograph*, No. 16. Oxford University Press, Oxford.

Rutter, M. (1967). A children's behaviour questionnaire for completion by teachers: preliminary findings. *Journal of Child Psychology and Psychiatry*, **8**, 1–11.

Rutter, M., Tizard, J. and Whitmore, K. (Eds.) (1970). *Education, Health, and Behaviour*. Longman, London.

Rutter, M., Cox, A., Tupling, C., Berger, M., and Yule, W. (1975a). Attainment and adjustment in two geographical areas: I The prevalence of psychiatric disorder. *British Journal of Psychiatry*. **126**, 493–509.

Rutter, M., Yule, B., Quinton, D., Towlands, O., Yule, W., and Berger, M. (1975b). Attainment and adjustment in two geographical areas: III Some factors accounting for area differences. *British Journal of Psychiatry*, **126**, 520–533.

Rutter, M., Graham, P., Chadwick, O. F. D., and Yule, W. (1976). Adolescent turmoil: fact or fiction. *Journal of Child Psychology and Psychiatry*, **17**, 35–36.

Sassi, L. C. F. (1973). The effect of counselling on school truants. *Unpublished Diploma School Counselling Dissertation*, University College, Swansea.

Scottish Education Department (1977). Truancy and Indiscipline in Schools in Scotland. *The Pack Report*. HMSO, London.

Shepherd, M., Oppenheim, B., and Mitchell, S. (1971). *Childhood Behaviour and Mental Health*. University of London Press, London.

Tennent, T. G. (1971). School non-attendance and delinquency. *Educational Research*, **13**, 185–190.

Tizard, J. (1973). Maladjusted children and the child guidance service. *London Educational Review*, **2**, 22–37.

Tumelty, A. (1976). A study of the effectiveness of peer counselling of school truants. *Unpublished Diploma School Counselling Dissertation*, University College, Swansea.

Tyerman, M. J. (1968). *Truancy*. University of London Press, London.

Wedge, P. and Prosser, H. (1973). *Born to Fail*. Arrow Books, London.

Yule, W. (1977). Behavioural treatment of children and adolescents with conduct disorders. In: Hersov, L., Berger, M., and Shaffer, D. (Eds.) *Aggression and Anti-social Behaviour in Childhood and Adolescence*. Pergamon, Oxford. pp. 115–141.

Chapter 9

The School's view of persistent non-attendance

Anne Jones

INTRODUCTION

From the school's point of view, non-attendance feels like rejection by the pupil and therefore produces considerable anxiety and guilt among teachers. Schools rarely publish attendance figures — even the few brave enough to publish exam results, usually maintain a discreet silence about attendance. However, some official 'unnamed' surveys exist. Apart from the Department of Education and Science (1974) Survey, there are also regular reports from Local Authorities such as the Inner London Education Authority (ILEA, 1975). This states that the *average* attendance figure for an ILEA secondary school in 1974 was 84.6%. In 1976 the overall average attendance was 86.9%, a substantial improvement, which has been maintained. These figures gave London Head Teachers some idea of how their attendance figures were comparatively, a comfort for some and a goal for others.

Taking the figures as a rough guide to the size of the problem in 1974 (and not only for London schools), we can draw some conclusions. An *average* figure of 84.6% in 1974 must mean that many schools were then running at a non-attendance rate of over 20%.[1] Illness to cause absenteeism on this scale is virtually impossible in the age of antibiotics and the National Health Service, except in a sudden epidemic such as the 'red flu' of 1978. Pupils (and sometimes even staff) miss school for apparently trivial reasons. Schools can easily attribute absenteeism to their catchment area, the low socio-economic status of their pupils, ill health, poor housing, financial hardship, and parental attitudes. This argument is used in favour of *not* printing statistics, since some schools are unfairly handicapped from the start. However, it is now becoming recognized that attendance patterns and deviancy rates vary greatly within similarly matched areas and schools (Carroll, 1977).

This justifies teachers' anxiety and guilt to some extent. The nature of the experience offered by the school is a key factor in determining whether or not a pupil attends (See Chapter 5). In order to cope realistically with non-attenders, teachers need more objective analysis of the reasons for non-attendance, viewed from both within the schools and from outside. Teachers need to discard unnecessary guilt, for they have enough other problems but, equally, they need to face what they themselves can do.

WHAT ARE SCHOOLS FOR?

One of the first things schools can do is to recognize that non-attendance at school is a problem of our society in which absenteeism from work also figures. To argue that the workers of today are the pupils of yesterday and to say that they must have learnt their bad habits at school would be to tackle the wrong issue. The real malaise lies deeper: in attitudes towards oneself, work, responsibility, authority, and others; but in the last decade schools have been mopping up and trying to deal with problems which rightfully belong elsewhere. They have taken up for parents, and for society, the role of defenders of moral values and protectors of the *status quo*. Further, teachers have tried to be all things to all pupils: parents, friends, social workers. They have been confused about the aims of schools, which have in some instances too often ended as a combination of soup kitchen, social club, and welfare agency. The result has immobilized many schools, with the burden of the non-attender adding to the sense of failure. If there is a failure, it comes from not having defined the task of the school and from not setting realistic limits to that task. I contend that one of the major reasons for non-attendance is that pupils cannot cope with this confusion about the purpose of schooling. I am certain that if schools were clearer about their purpose and if pupils shared this clear understanding, then many incipient non-attenders would be encouraged to stay in school.

However, uncertainty about the purpose of schooling is not confined to teachers: it comes from society itself and is simply reflected in schools. Society is ambivalent about schools, on the one hand querying whether they serve any useful purpose except ineffectual child-minding, on the other hand expecting far too much of them in both teaching and instilling standards of behaviour. Schools are the victims of this ambivalent attitude.

Studies of families of children who do not attend school (Carroll, 1978) suggest that chronic non-attenders are likely to have one or more key factors in their background: (1) one-parent families; (2) above average number of children (e.g. 5 +); (3) one or both parents chronically ill; (4) poor housing; (5) parent(s) unemployed, certainly of low socio-economic status; (6) low intellectual attainment levels; (7) negative attitudes to school; (8) clash of values with the school. With such situations at home, children are caught in a vicious circle. The more they are absent from school, the harder it is for them to come back, to join in, to catch up and to keep up with their peer group, to feel part of the school.

FAMILY FACTORS IN ABSENTEEISM/NON-ATTENDANCE

Absenteeism often begins for simple reasons of economic necessity and survival of the family unit. This is particularly true in one-parent families when the main breadwinner is the mother, who often holds an unskilled poorly-paid job. 'Justifiable' pupil absence may occur when a child stays at home to look after a sick parent or siblings, or to open the door for the gasman and other servicing agencies.

It is a sad reflection on our society that we have not found a way of *valuing* the contribution that children can make to the stability of family life. Absenteeism for these reasons may become an issue leading to Court appearance. Yet often, curiously enough, many pupils may be already carrying far greater domestic responsibilities on a regular basis than the adults (be they parents or teachers) who are supposedly looking after them and helping them to 'grow up'. The implications for social policy, particularly with reference to one-parent families, are considerable, but not within the scope of this book. The implications for schools are serious: we constantly underestimate the 'adult' qualities in our pupils and the extent to which they can take responsibility for themselves and for others, imagine (particularly if they come from 'deprived' backgrounds) that they are not capable of doing things for themselves, and that they need to be organized and controlled by teachers. Some of the pupils who fail to attend school do so because they find this attitude (when it exists) to be insulting and irritating. In these circumstances they see their teachers as immature, uninteresting, and unnecessarily repressive.

Ironically, the pupils who come from the most 'difficult' homes may be among the most resilient and mature of the school population: they may be far more capable of coping with life than the pupils who attend out of passive obedience but no real commitment. My hunch is that some of these capable non-attenders would come if schools recognized and used their pupil's coping qualities. Of course, some pupils with difficult home backgrounds *are* crippled emotionally by the pull of the family problems. Schools lack a sensitive, realistic and accurate way of analysing the needs of a *particular* child in a *particular* family situation. At the moment, teacher expectations, education welfare back-up and child guidance interventions are too often blunt instruments used somewhat indiscriminately.

As far as parental attitudes towards education in disadvantaged families are concerned, I accept that there is frequently a clash of values between school and home. However, it seems to me that the clash is not about *educational* values so much as the treatment of pupils. I have never met parents who did not want their child to leave school equipped with basic skills and preferably some qualifications. What they dislike is the school's being totally judgmental and denying in them (as well as in their children) those positive qualities which are in fact supportive to learning. Thus, schools have to find a way to give parents the facts without rejecting, denying, or distorting the parents' positive role. The parent may want understanding of the difficulties faced at home, but he or she does not really want these made an excuse. It is easy for teachers to collude with parents and thereby exacerbate rather than alleviate their problems. This is another problem which schools need help in facing.

In cases where the child is used to meet the parents' dependency needs, it is very difficult for the school to intervene effectively. These children and families most certainly need help. The main problem will be to gain access to this family and, even more serious, to persuade the family to want or to use the help offered — maybe they are satisfied to remain as they are. Insistence on going to school — or worse still, going for treatment — may be seen not as a helpful move, but as punishment or rejection of the child or of the parent. Clearly, schools cannot be blamed for failure, in such extreme cases, since they are hardly ever allowed to begin. Whatever they do when the child is 'wheeled in' by a conscientious social worker or education welfare officer too often is still rejected by the unwilling pupil. A personal reception into school, an individual time table, some individual tuition in a special unit, counselling, these measures may make no impact on some pupils. They will still not wish to come, saying adamantly that the school is 'no good'. Such psychologically disturbed children and their families probably need intensive clinic or hospital treatment before schools can help. For their part, more schools need to develop flexible strategies for non-attenders returning: it is too much ever to expect them to fit straight away into a 'normal' time-table. More of this later.

More commonly, pupils who are frequently absent are not 'emotionally disturbed' in the clinical sense: socio-economic and psychological factors will be intertwined. It is worth mentioning that when parents' motivation towards sending their children to school is strong enough, many existing socio-economic and psychological problems are overcome. For example, working mothers who are the sole source of income in the family commonly send their children to school even if they are suffering from coughs, colds, etc. They cannot afford to lose pay. They also often want their children to do well at school so that they will not have to take an unskilled, low-paid job like their mothers. These mothers steamroll over most minor illnesses and other possible reasons for missing school. Only occasionally do their children develop more serious illness, although they may sometimes suffer from other behavioural difficulties. Clearly, the question of parental attitude to attendance is of paramount importance. It can easily be the pampered darling who is encouraged to stay away.

THE SCHOOL'S ROLE IN INFLUENCING ATTENDANCE

Although correlations between socio-economic background and non-attendance do correlate statistically, judgements about these factors must not be allowed to prejudice teachers. Teachers' attitudes and expectations also influence pupils' behaviour immeasurably. In schools we have to start from the assumption that all pupils want to come to school because it is worth coming! If we expect them to fail because they have problems, that will surely happen. Remember the law of diminishing expectations: 'blessed is he who expecteth nothing for he shall not be disappointed'.

I propose now to look in more detail at what was happening in schools in the early '70s and, on the basis of that experience, to make some suggestions about how schools can reduce non-attendance.

(a) Teacher influences

Teacher attitude and teacher reliability are obviously key factors. Teacher stability (rather, instability) was certainly a major problem in the early '70s in Britain. Since the Houghton pay award in 1975 and the changed economic climate, this particular problem has reversed. In the early '70s the daily task facing any school was survival in the classroom: finding enough adult bodies to cover every class. Now the major task is survival at all: the teachers are there (in truth, not all of them would be re-appointed were they to apply for their present jobs now) but the *pupil* population is falling rapidly. Schools have suddenly to demonstrate that they have a philosophy and a purpose, and that they achieve this purpose. The effects of this will be to streamline what schools offer and, ultimately, to reaffirm the *value* of schools to the growing pupil. This in itself will improve attendance rates.

(b) Extra provisions

Part of the streamlining will include simplifying the basic structure of the schools. In the mounting panic and the affluence of the late '60s and early '70s, there was a tendency to 'add on' extra provision whenever a school discerned a problem. School counsellors, sanctuaries, sinbins, special units, social workers, nurture groups, withdrawal groups, offsite centres, onsite units: all of this special provision *can* work splendidly, and in many cases is still needed, but these extras can confuse and undermine the *main* body of the school if it is not functioning properly. In other words, the hard centre core of the institution must be in good order if it is to benefit from its splendid accessories.

This trend toward adding extras was part of an attitude to schooling, exacerbated by the research of sociologists and the effects of a consumer society — an attitude that schools had to make themselves exciting, relevant, enjoyable, attractive, comfortable, and undemanding in order to 'compete' with life outside school. Even then, some children preferred the streets. There was also a touch of the 'over-indulgent' parent about this phase, as if schools felt guilty about their failure to attract or interest their pupils and so gave more and more 'goodies'. The child knows that all is not well but takes advantage of the parental weakness and becomes more spoilt and soft, not more resilient and strong. Although I am over-stating the situation, I do believe that this fundamental attitude in schools did not help their cause. I further believe that the basic *attitudes* and assumptions within an institution like a school have greater influence upon pupils than does the organization or structure.

(c) Pastoral care systems

Within the main structure of schools there also developed another phenomenon which, despite good intentions, has not entirely helped its clients, the pupils. This phenomenon was the growth of the 'Pastoral Care' systems. Elaborate networks of 'helping' senior staff were established, usually based on a 'house' system or a 'year' system, and occasionally supplemented by a school counsellor. A Head of House is responsible for the 'pastoral care' of a cross-section of the school population, i.e. a kind of family group, including all siblings and pupils of all ages. A Head of Year is responsible for the pastoral care of a 'year', one cohort of pupils of the same age. In large schools there are also Deputy Heads of House or Year. The success of the House or Year System depends, in my view, upon how its function is perceived and carried out. If the House/Year system is seen as totally separate from the academic system, there can develop an unhealthy splitting: the pastoral system becomes the loving, caring, all-forgiving parent; the academic system the demanding, rejecting, punishing parent. The pupils not only feel this split but also may play off one against the other. Even teachers may behave quite differently in their roles as form tutor and as subject class teacher. Thus, in schools where caring and demanding, loving, and learning have become split, there is a serious problem which I am sure causes confusion and conflict for pupils, a few of whom will stay away as a result.

As in the family, where children sometimes act out certain situations on behalf of their parents, so in schools pupils sometimes unwittingly act out the dramas, tensions, and conflicts of the staff. The staff of a school must recognize, integrate and use their whole selves and not take up polarized partial roles. In other words, the development of a mature, integrated, and balanced staff group is as essential to the growth and effectiveness of a school as is its basic sense of cohesiveness and purpose. Schools often avoid dealing with their inter-staff conflicts, instead allowing a few 'deviant' staff members or pupils to carry these for them. Until schools learn to recognize, handle and use their differences in a mature way, pupils will be victims or pawns in a system which is not serving their best interests. Some pupils may refuse to play this game and stay away.

(d) The pursuit of relevance

Another feature of the late '60s and early '70s which has in some ways been a blind alley is the pursuit of 'relevance'. This was part of the attempt of schools to 'attract' pupils into learning. But this philosophy may still miss the point: as one pupil put it 'school is still a bloody school'. Venables (1971) makes the point that some pupils reject school not because of relevance but because they cannot accept the terms on which it is offered. This brings us back to the basic attitude of the school and its staff, which may often be classified as 'conditional positive regard' — we approve of you only if you do what we say when we say it. Thus the 'relevance' is cancelled by rejection of the basic terms of the offer.

Furthermore, the vogue for basing much of the school curriculum on the 'here and now' social situation in which the pupils live, often serves only to encapsulate those pupils in a circle of deprivation. Many of them find this denigrating and depressing rather than stimulating. And if the methods used do not mobilize a pupil's energy and enthusiasm for learning, then to study 'myself in my community' is just as 'boring' to study as the Roman Invasion of Britain — possibly more so. Given ineffectual methods, the pursuit of relevance in the curriculum has attracted no more pupil votes than the traditional curriculum. In fact, it may have lost some, for at least parents and pupils, rightly or wrongly, could more easily see the value of the old curriculum and methods.

(e) The challenge of learning

The real point is that current teaching methods do not sufficiently engage pupils in the *challenge* of learning. The prevailing culture has become 'do it for you' rather than 'do it yourself', even in classes purporting to use 'modern methods'. At worst, individualized learning means filling in someone else's watered-down worksheet, and group learning becomes gossiping while one member of the group does the work for the others. Schools may have developed into an even more passive dependent culture than they were in the 'bad old days'. I suspect that in too many schools we do not demand enough of our pupils, we do not challenge them to do *more* (rather than less), we do not allow them to make mistakes and learn from them, we overorganize and overrule them, and we discourage them by not sufficiently recognizing their individual differences, their maturity, their ability to take responsibility. This ethos does not encourage pupils with drive and initiative but actively discourages them. Hence, some of the most challenging pupils are those who react with fight (i.e. deviant, disruptive, aggressive behaviour) or flight (i.e. absenteeism). The Grubb Institute's work (1977) on this topic bears out these points.

Schools need enough structure for pupils to feel secure, but also need to channel pupils' fighting energy into their work and their contribution to the running of the school, to the school community. I was fascinated recently to hear a colleague report that among his school leavers, the ones who had truanted or otherwise deviated were the ones who had had the greatest success and shown the greatest initiative in getting jobs. The 'healthy' deviants in some ways have learnt to cope with life better than those pupils who have, with incredible patience, glided through school on a conveyer belt. I am sure my colleague's is not an isolated example. The implications for the future of schools are considerable, though the best way to change the prevailing ethos is not obvious, nor will it be easy.

(f) The role of the form teacher

In recent years schools have prided themselves on their 'pastoral care' systems. It therefore comes as a shock when talking to pupils who have recently left school to discover how many of them feel that no one adult in the school really knew them. For example, here are some quotations from young school leavers broadcast in a BBC programme called *The School Years* in December 1977.

'Well, adults at work sort of seem to understand you more than what teachers do. Although the teachers' job is to understand you, I don't think they understand you as much as when you go to work.'

'When you go to work there's more responsibility on you, like before you were someone else's responsibility, the teachers were responsible for you, but now you have your own responsibilities about going to work and earning your own money.'

'When I started work I thought — I don't know anyone here — I wonder if they're going to like me or not. But they look at you in a much more adult fashion, so they treat you as adults, so you got on alright with them.'

The paradox here, which we teachers need to grasp, is that where they were responsible for themselves and treated as adults, these young people felt known, understood, and accepted, whereas with the teachers who kept them in a dependent relationship they felt neither autonomous nor understood.

I suspect that this situation may arise from teachers feeling harassed, being concerned with 'doing' rather than 'being', mistaking organization and control for relating and growth. It is frightening to a teacher to have a class of thirty (even twenty) 'out of control': in rightly wanting some degree of law and order, many teachers, having established it, fail to give themselves the opportunity to make a deep relationship with the pupils in their form. I say 'in their form' because it would be unrealistic and misplaced for this to be the aim of every teacher of every pupil. But it is surprising how many *form tutors* have never *listened* to the pupils in their form or got pupils to talk about their views of themselves. My own experience is that pupils are willing to talk to an adult who is genuinely interested in their growth and development. They do not want their teacher to be their friend, but to be an adult relating in an emphatic, unobtrusive non-judgmental way. In fact, pupils respond enthusiastically to form teachers who have the counselling qualities of empathy, genuineness, and non-possessive warmth. Those pupils who have problems in relationships at home are much more likely to come to school if they feel that their form teacher is a dependable adult who knows them, respects and gives them room to grow in their own way. I would therefore submit that if form tutors were given more training in the possibilities and the limitations of their role, this might encourage pupils who feel alienated, unrecognized and unloved to attend rather than to absent themselves.

(g) The main task of schools

What can schools do about these issues? First, they need to reaffirm their belief in their value and purpose, to come to terms with their own identity problem. Schools have something to offer which is specific, useful, enriching, and needed. Schools need to be clear about their main task and concentrate on doing that well. Pupils want to come if they lose out by not coming. Schools have to learn to say 'No' when they are asked to take responsibility for matters for which they have neither the training nor the time; only then will they clearly demonstrate their skill in doing their real job. Many pupils will be helped to overcome their socio-economic problems if they are really well taught.

When schools feel a sense of purpose, of identity, of value, then they are not afraid to make demands upon their pupils. These demands not only increase the esteem the pupils feel for the school and their desire to be identified with the school, but they also help the pupils to engage actively in the learning process, to use their energy in constructive ways and ultimately to grow in confidence. The demands made by school are not meant to be negative or punitive, but *caring* about pupils includes offering and demanding the best possible. The compulsory nature of schooling, till 16, has put schools in a supplicant's role: the more we plead with our pupils to come, the less they want to. When school is recognized as a valuable experience, few pupils want to stay away. Society must devise other ways of helping those who still do not want to come.

Within the schools themselves, there has to be a constant monitoring. Is the school doing what it says it is doing or is a hidden curriculum giving double messages to the pupils? Does the school activate and use the pupils' energies and resources? Are the pupils' needs put first or have the needs of the staff or the system taken over? What is the overall ethos of the school? Is the activity purposeful or is it chaotic? Is there sufficient structure and stability, or is there too much? What kind of relationship is there between staff and pupils? Is there any sense of corporate identity, of belonging, of pride in belonging? Do all the members of the school community have a clear idea of their role and function? Is the school open to help from outside, or is it defensive and insular? Is the school genuine even if it sometimes makes mistakes? These are the sorts of questions which have to be worked on continually if a school is to remain alive and well and its pupils are to attend and develop.

AN APPROACH TO THE PROBLEMS OF NON-ATTENDANCE

In the last part of this chapter I should like to be more specific and discuss some of the work at the school of which I am Head — Vauxhall Manor School in South London. In 1973 the attendance figures had become a cause of concern, and a project was set up between the school, the education welfare and the social services. Extra workers from the two outside agencies were allocated to survey all second-year pupils. They analysed and identified the background factors influencing attendance and also attempted various kinds of intervention to see which was most effective: extra casework intervention, more education welfare officer visits, and intensive group work in school. The project was imaginative but not easy to carry out. It was difficult to get accurate information about pupils' backgrounds without breaking the confidentiality of records. It was also difficult to find measures for evaluating the effectiveness of group work or casework interventions. The attendance of the girls who were given special extra help varied enormously: some improved and some got worse. As the social worker stated, this mainly proved that no two cases of non-attendance are alike! The research project did illustrate that attempting to improve attendance by individual efforts was to throw workers into a bottomless pit. The demand on the extra resources was infinite and however much extra was done, it was still not enough. Clearly, we had at the school (and still have) an above average number of girls who score highly on any statistician's index of social deprivation. We could have used a dozen social workers and education welfare officers and still not got very far. It became clear to us that, valuable as this extra help was, we had to tackle the problem from the school end as well. It was not, in my view, until this was done, that the attendance figures began to improve. By then the formal part of the project had ended, but we were fortunate in being able to keep the social worker for another whole year. During this time tremendous advances were made in her work, because by then we better understood how to use her help.

In tackling the problem of attendance from the school end, we were much helped by consultations with governors, staff, and pupils. In fact, the governors had set up the original working party which led to establishment of the project. The governors' recommendations in 1973 were, among others, that efforts should be made to reduce the number of teachers that pupils have; that closer links between home and school should be encouraged; that early diagnosis and follow-up of incipient non-attenders should be introduced, if necessary by employing a teacher social worker; that a 're-entry zone' should be established, a special unit for girls returning after a period of absence; that alternative educational provision should be made for older pupils who had opted out completely; and that a short stay in a residential hostel should be set up for girls experiencing temporary but acute home problems. This clear brief was accepted. It took another three years to implement: all the recommendations have been carried out except for the short stay hostel. However, a local hostel has recently been set up for the whole area which meets this need.

(a) Introducing pupils to school

This is what we now do. Firstly we make a particular effort to help first-year pupils arriving at the school to feel happy and secure and to identify with the school. The eleven-year-olds spend nearly half the week in their own form room, and are taught by far fewer teachers than before. We have achieved this by integrating certain subjects. For example: history, geography, religious education, and social studies are now called Liberal Studies and taught for eight periods, not as separate subjects of two periods each. We also teach several subjects in sessions; instead of single or double lessons, we give the subject a whole morning or afternoon. This cuts down unnecessary movement, which can be unsettling. It also allows pupils to get into the subject in greater depth and gives the teacher a chance to get to know her pupils better. In addition, the form can take a greater pride in its form room, which is usually decorated with displays of work and hobbies. The first years have priority as far as stability of room and teacher is concerned, but throughout the lower school the basic teaching unit is the form. Continuity of subject teacher is given priority too from one year to the next, so that at the beginning of the academic year the class does not waste time and energy adjusting to a new teacher. The Heads of Years move up with their years so that they can build up their knowledge of girls and their families. All this helps not only to increase learning opportunities but also to give the pupils continuity of care and of relationships with adults. This is always important but particularly so if pupils lack this at home. It is one of the factors which can encourage an insecure child to attend. Many secondary schools now take these measures as well as those set out in the following sections.

(b) Fostering identification with the school

Another important aspect of the school is how well cared for, attractive and smart the buildings are — not glossy necessarily, but certainly tidy, free from vandalism and full of pupils' work and treasured posters. The standard of display throughout the school has improved in recent years, another indication that the pupils feel more trusting and trusted. After school three evenings a week the End On Club meets between 3.30 and 5.30, providing wide ranges of educational and recreational activities. This voluntary activity is well supported by the girls who, again, are helped to feel they belong to the school and are given something constructive to do in that arid time of day after school and before their parent comes in from work.

A further measure which helps the girls enormously in feeling they are full members of the school community is the provision of many outings and the school journey. Many of our pupils have never been away from their parents for a holiday; some have not travelled much, not even in London. So we build into our normal lessons a programme of visits and outings. Visiting a museum or gallery not only expands intellectual horizons but it also gives the girls confidence to go again or to try others. The school journey itself, a week away at a holiday camp with a planned programme of outings and activities, is one of the best confidence boosters we know. For those first-year pupils who do not go on the school journey, possibly because they are afraid of leaving home (not usually for financial reasons, since the grant system is generous), we offer a special programme of outings in London. For older girls there are also 'year journeys', field studies trips and journeys to the Continent.

(c) Contact with families

We make a great effort to get to know whoever is responsible for our pupils at home. In Junior Schools parents have easy access to the class teacher but in Secondary Schools it can be more difficult for parents to gain informal access. We get around this by offering an interview before the pupils come, by making it clear that parents really are welcome at any time, and particularly by our system of giving out reports: we do not send out reports but instead invite parents up to read and discuss what the teachers have said — and in Lower School the majority of parents respond. The benefits are enormous. It is less work to send for parents only when their children are in trouble but this method provides an opportunity for positive interchange. When parents come, particularly parents on their own, they often confide their own difficulties. We listen and we put them in touch with the agency that can best help them. When a girl is unsettled and disturbed in school, we ask her parents to come up as early as possible. The response to this is heartening: parents are relieved to know that we care and pleased when we do not tolerate antisocial behaviour. Together we discuss what best might be done to help the pupil benefit from her education. In other words, we do our best to keep communications between home and school genuine, preventive rather than remedial, and two-way.

Given the importance of parental attitudes to education, this must be a factor in encouraging good attendance.

(d) Special provision

In addition to these measures affecting main school structure, provision and attitude, we have also set up some special provision to help girls with difficulties. We now have a school counsellor, a school social worker, and two special units, one in Lower School and one in Upper School, in separate buildings, each with different functions. All this is in addition to the normal Head of Year/Form Teacher provision and Education Welfare Service support.

(i) The school counsellor

Our school counsellor provides individual and group counselling for those girls who want to talk through their feelings and problems. Some of the girls seek out the counsellor themselves, others are referred by staff. The counsellor, in turn, works closely with the form tutors and of course makes referrals to other agencies as appropriate. This is not the place for a detailed explanation or analysis of the counsellor's work; my views have already appeared elsewhere (Jones, 1977). However, our counsellor's work is much appreciated by pupils and staff and, although not solely or even directly linked with attendance problems, clearly is a factor in encouraging certain girls to come to school.

(ii) The school social worker

The school social worker has a different brief. Whilst the counsellor rarely makes home visits and only occasionally sees parents in school, the social worker is our direct line of communication between school and home. She makes home visits whenever we feel such intervention to be necessary. The only restriction here (apart from limited time) is that we do clear the lines of communication with the education welfare service so that there is no unnecessary overlap or confusion between the two services. In fact, the education welfare services and the social services, although wary at first, now welcome this extra help. We have taken care to define the roles of these workers and to ensure that they have regular contact with each other. These factors are important in using resources economically and effectively. Again, the school social worker's role is not confined to attendance problems, but clearly has bearing on them. Having these two specialist workers 'on site' also removes some of the anxiety of the teaching staff, who know that their pupils need extra help and support but who cannot undertake this in the depth required on top of their normal teaching commitments. The school social worker obviously can play a key role in helping to support non-attenders returning after a long absence, but this job also has to be undertaken by the form teacher. In other words, no one provision solves all problems: there has to be team work, co-operation and partnership if our extra measures are to have any effect.

(iii) Special units

The two special units differ from each other in nature. The Lower School unit was set up in 1973 in a house near the school to help pupils suffering from 'cultural shock'. At the time the school was receiving a constant stream of new pupils from abroad, many of whom did not speak English. Not only did they have the problem of learning English as a foreign language, but they also needed help in adjusting to a totally new way of life. This unit has succeeded in helping such girls to integrate with the school and with our society. It has also taken on some girls with learning and behavioural difficulties, who need more individual attention and help than can be provided in the 'normal' classroom. This provision is over and above 'normal' remedial work for girls with specific learning difficulties, which in our system is to withdraw girls from ordinary lessons in very small groups for help in learning to read. But in the Bonnington Square unit there are girls who need more help than this, possibly because they are going through an unsettled stage, are rather too attention-seeking and demanding for the normal classroom. None of these girls go to the unit full time but, rather, on a part-time sessional basis, as for a 'tutorial' class. In addition to our own resources, naturally we use the resources of the Authority as fully as possible: namely their classes for English as a foreign language, their tutorial classes and their education guidance unit. In all cases the aim is to give the girls sufficient skills, confidence, and motivation to return fully to the main part of the school and to be able to cope with it. Obviously we do not succeed in all cases, but we have had some encouraging successes.

The special unit in Upper School has a different purpose, although it includes many of the same features. It is a frequent pattern in our school (and no doubt in many others) for some girls to attend reasonably well in the first two years but for their attendance to drop off dramatically in the third year. We have in some cases, through the efforts of the welfare service and our own social worker, managed to recapture some of these girls in the fourth year. Our school is on two main sites, with girls transferring to Upper School at the beginning of their fourth year. The unit is set up to help rehabilitate these pupils who have been lost and found again. When a girl has been away for a long time, she is nervous and insecure; she has also fallen behind in her work. In the unit she can be given help with basic skills, and her confidence can be built up. We design a programme for each girl. Ideally she will register with her form and go to some normal lessons, but she will also go to the unit for as many sessions as seems appropriate. She will spend gradually less time in the unit and more in class until she is able to return full time to normal classes. There is some advantage in having this particular unit *inside* the main building so that the geographical and social distance between the unit and the main school is kept to a minimum.

It must be stated that though we have had some notable successes, we inevitably do not succeed in rehabilitating all our pupils. Some continue to need a little help from the unit, and others again break the attendance pattern. But the unit is an important and necessary provision for the successful re-entry of girls who have been absent, providing an on-site intermediate zone. The unit also takes on a number of pupils who have become unsettled and disorientated, especially with the increased emphasis in Upper School on academic work and the start of examination courses. For them too, the unit performs a valuable service in boosting skills and confidence. There are usually no more than 6 to 8 pupils in this unit at one time.

I learnt in my last school (Jones, 1976) that running separate groups for phobics and deviants was hazardous: too often the deviants deviated and the phobics didn't come! A mixture of pupils (i.e not all chronic non-attenders in one group) ensures that there will be *some* pupils to teach. Furthermore, it helps the pupils returning if they can mix with a small number of pupils with different predominating characteristics — this is one of the factors in school and in life that they have to readjust to. As in Lower School, there is also provision in Upper School for pupils who need help with basic skills, but who are otherwise calm and settled. The Upper School unit worker joins the team of the form tutors, the Heads of Year, the Counsellor, the school social worker and the education welfare officer — all closely co-ordinating their efforts.

(iv) The education welfare officer

The education welfare officer herself, although hard pressed, comes in to see each Head of Year each week. This maintains a constant dialogue between the school and the agency responsible for getting pupils back into school. We value this two-way contact as supportive and informative. Ideally, more than one EWO would be attached to the school to work intensively on follow-up: when we had the social worker seconded to work intensively with borderline attenders in the last year, their attendance improved dramatically. We could not have maintained this level of attendance in that year without the additional help. We are therefore convinced that, even though we have done a lot within the school to improve attendance, we could still use, and would welcome, further intensive help from other agencies. Unfortunately, resources are scarce and overstretched in all professional services — and particularly in an inner

city area like ours, which is outstanding in its degree of deprivation and therefore strains all the services.

(e) Results

The attendance rate in our school has certainly improved dramatically. The
September figures for the last few years are as follows:

September 1974 — 77.05%
September 1976 — 85.00%
September 1977 — 88.00%

There are several points to make about these figures. They still 'fall off' during
each term and gradually over the year. They are not easy to sustain and we are
already 'missing' our extra 'on site' social worker. A further problem arises
from our 'success' — we are under pressure from the welfare and social
services to take on girls transferring from other schools, mostly girls with bad
attendance records. The hope is, presumably, that we have the attitudes and
the resources to help these girls make a new start. Unfortunately, it is much
more difficult to change an established pattern of attendance failure with
transferred girls in mid-adolescence. We are becoming concerned about this
phenomenon, which is in danger of overstretching our resources. It also
distorts our attendance figures, since some of these girls never come after the
first time they are brought in. We feel our first duty is to the girls we already
have; we further feel that our main purpose is to be a school and not a
repository for assorted truants. We certainly cannot perform miracles when all
else has already failed.

However, we are certainly proud of our overall progress. Most important,
this improvement in attendance has not come about through any gimmick or
extras. It is the result of a whole-school attitude and approach, with the main
emphasis being on the quality of the learning offered and the overall ethos in
the school. Our experience at Vauxhall Manor is borne out by other research
studies (Carroll, 1977). As long as school is compulsory, there will always be
some pupils who reject it, as well as some who cannot come for good reasons
or reasons beyond their control. If schools have done their best to encourage
pupils to come, and if they have checked that it is not the atmosphere of the
school itself which is putting the pupils off, then they should stop worrying
unduly about non-attendance and concentrate on the quality and nature of
what they offer the pupils who do come. I suspect that this in itself might bring
a few more pupils in!

GENERAL CONCLUSIONS

As far as future educational policy is concerned, I believe that we should lower the school leaving age to 14. From the age of 14 young people need opportunities to find out what work is like, as well as opportunities for further study. Those opportunities for further study continue throughout their lifetime. However, in the current economic situation there would be no jobs for young people if the school leaving age were lowered. Indeed there is a danger that the school leaving age might be raised in order to help solve the unemployment problem. What is needed is a more fundamental and radical solution which would involve persuading the nation's work force to share the available work, and for us all to work fewer hours (a three-day week for all?). Such a revolution would not only largely eliminate that unpleasant divide between the employed and the unemployed, but it would also expand the opportunities for adults (from the age of 14) to go on learning all their lives. Furthermore, it would save the time, energy and resources now poured into the problem of making pupils go to school. Those of us who work in this field could then concentrate on pupils we really *can* help. This would seem to me to be a more constructive use of the nation's resources.

SUMMARY

In this chapter, I have identified various aspects of school life which need work if we are to improve attendance rates in schools. Whilst recognizing the importance of background factors in both conditions and attitudes which militate against good attendance, I have attempted to analyse some of the factors in schools which discourage borderline attenders. These I have identified as teachers' expectations and attitudes, confusion about the main task of the secondary school, role confusion among teachers, insufficient recognition of pupils' adultness, insufficient challenge to pupils in their role as pupils, 'splitting' between pastoral and academic aspects of school, too much emphasis on curriculum as opposed to method, too much organized pastoral care and not enough actual pastoral care (i.e. knowing the pupils and listening to them).

I have given examples from my own school of measures which did in fact improve attendance: a special programme for first years; measures to help pupils identify with the school; a positive attempt to include parents in their daughters' learning; special provisions such as a counsellor, a school social worker, and two special units; and a close working relationship with the Education Welfare Service. However, my belief is that none of these measures works unless the overall ethos of a school is positive, challenging and geared towards learning. Schools need to reaffirm their belief in themselves: most pupils are ready and willing to learn, given a challenge and a chance.

REFERENCES

BBC (1977). *Life Lines*. Programme 8: The transition from school to life after school.

Carroll, H. M. C. (1977). *Absenteeism in South Wales' Studies of Pupils, Their Homes, and Their Secondary Schools.* The Faculty of Education, University College of Swansea.

Department of Education and Science (1974). Results of school absence survey. *Press Notice,* 25th July.

Grubb Institute (1977). *Education for Mature Responsibility: Countering Some of the Ill-effects of the Present Educational Process in Secondary Schools.* The Grubb Institute, London.

Inner London Educational Authority (1975). *Non-Attendance and Truancy.* Report of the Schools Sub-Committee to the Education Committee.

Jones, A. (1976). Coping in the school situation. *The Disruptive Pupil in the Secondary School.* In (Eds.) Jones-Davies, C., and Cave, R. C. Ward Lock Educational, London.

Jones, (1977). *Counselling Adolescents in School.* Kogan Page, London.

Venables, E. (1971). *Teachers and Youth Workers: A Study of Their Roles.* Evans/ Methuen Educational, London.

Out of School
Edited by L. Hersov and I. Berg
© 1980, John Wiley & Sons, Ltd.

Chapter 10

Childhood Fears in
Developmental Perspective

David Bauer

Since the turn of the twentieth century children's fears have been the object of widely scattered investigations. Past studies, for example, focused on issues as diverse as the psychodynamic origin of fears (Freud, 1962; Rheingold, 1967), the evolutionary ground of fears (Jung, 1964), conditioning and systematic desensitization of emotional responses (Watson and Rayner, 1920; Wolpe, 1962), classification of fears experienced by children of different chronological ages (Jersild and Holmes, 1935; Miller, Barrett, and Hampe, 1974), as well as examination of children's fear of going to, and failure to progress in, school (Eisenberg, 1958; Jersild, Goldman, and Loftus, 1940; Johnson, Falstein, Szurek, and Svendsen, 1941; Hersov, 1960; Hill and Sarason, 1966; Pintner and Lev, 1940; Sarason, Davidson, Lighthall, Waite, and Ruebush, 1960; Zeligs, 1939).

Regardless of content, however, fears are products of conceptions of reality created by children from perceptual and mental processes typical of their age and developmental level. In the case of childhood phobias, for instance, Miller *et al.* (1974) concluded that: 'the phobic child sees as dangerous a stimulus that most children disregard even though there may be some potential unpleasantness or low probability of danger (e.g. wind noise and thunderstorms).' Accordingly, it follows that understanding the evolution of children's fears in relation to their emerging views of reality, is fundamental to prevent the development of, and help children cope with, fears which either may actively contravene attendance at school or be associated with school refusal and truancy.

Unfortunately, 'the role of the subject's interpretation of a feared stimulus has had little attention in the literature on the etiology of phobias (Miller *et al.*, 1974)' and few empirical studies have examined the development of children's fears in relation to maturational changes in their emerging perceptions of the physical and social environments (Bauer, 1976). In this chapter, results of past research regarding children's fears are discussed within the context of trends in mental development known to affect the child's subjective view of reality. In addition, findings of a recently completed investigation charting the course of growth in elementary school children's school-related fears and perceptions are reported.

CHANGING FEARS AND VIEWS OF REALITY

From birth to death, human experience is built upon a developing sense of space, time, and causality. Indeed, studies conducted by such pioneering researchers as Piaget (1954; 1955; 1962) and Werner (1940; 1957) not only show that children generate a personal reality by abstracting spatial, temporal, and causal dimensions from their concrete experiences with people, places, and things, but also that the course of growth in those conceptions is predictable as well. For example, Piaget (1954), and more recently Clark (1973), demonstrated that when organizing their experience, children order space before they structure time. Other investigators, moreover, discovered that prior to the emergence of any highly abstract or visualized space, conceptions of space are derived from the way things are handled physically (Piaget and Inhelder, 1956; Werner, 1957; Werner and Kaplan, 1964). Not surprisingly, this direction of growth from concrete, personal conceptions of reality to more abstract, objective ones manifests itself in the fears expressed by children of increasing chronological age.

FEAR OF UNFAMILIAR AND UNPREDICTABLE STIMULI

Take, for instance, the fact that research reported by Jersild and Holmes (1935) and by Miller *et al.*, (1974) shows that while fears experienced by children during the first six months of life are largely confined to primitive emotional responses elicited by loud noises and loss of support, by the ninth month, fears in response to more abstract stimuli (e.g. faces of unfamiliar people) have emerged. Bronson (1972) discovered, moreover, that whether or not infants fear an unfamiliar stimulus, such as the face of a stranger, is dependent on whether or not they experience the actions of the stimulus as being predictable — that is, as being constant, cyclical, or contingent upon the child's own directed acts. Interestingly, findings of the Bronson investigation were consistent with those of Watson (1972), who discovered that infants take great delight in events that are contingent upon their own motor responses, and of Lewis and Goldberg (1969), who reported that an environment characterized by recurrent noncontingent events can produce a chronic sense of fearfulness in children.

Evidently, when actions of caretakers such as parents, nursery personnel, physicians, and teachers as well as of inanimate elements in the environment are consistently made in response to children's behaviour, children learn that their actions have consequences and that they can affect their environment. As a result, even unfamiliar people and objects are perceived as being somewhat responsive, predictable, and safe. Conversely, when children do not experience regularities in the operation of stimuli and cannot form reliable expectations about the consequences of their actions on the physical and social environments, they fail to learn that a causal connection exists between their own actions and the responses of the environment. Hence, unknown persons and things tend to be perceived as being unpredictable and frightening. Obviously, some children may carry this apprehensive response set to new stimuli into school contexts encountered later on in childhood. Bauer (1975), for instance, discovered that ten-year-old children who feared failure on school tasks also perceived themselves as being less in control of their academic successes and failures and more controlled by forces outside themselves, as represented by parents, teachers, and chance happenings.

Even when the actions of unfamiliar stimuli are constant and cyclical, however, '. . . the childish conception according to which moving objects are endowed with an activity (life) of their own . . . (Piaget, 1955)' may create in the child's reality what surrounding adults consider to be unrealistic fears. Further, along with the predisposition to confuse movement with life, younger children tend to attribute human qualities and motivations to the form and action of animate and inanimate stimuli as well as to natural events. This characteristic of the young child's thinking termed *anthropomorphism*, has the capability of turning even rigid, lifeless objects into fearful entities for the child. Speaking on this magical quality in the young child's thinking, Werner (1940) offered the following illustrative anecdote drawn from results of his descriptive study of the children's fears: 'today we found our boy (a two-year-old) in the twilight of the bedroom, sitting on his bed, his eyes staring fixedly at the stove. "Look, the stove is sticking out his tongue!" '

Unmistakably, from this toddler's perspective, an object that was viewed by surrounding adults as innocuous, harmless, and ordinary became a dramatically animated and scary creature. While animation of totally inert objects, such as a stove, is most likely to occur among two- and three-year-olds, children four to six years of age are inclined toward animistic and anthropomorphic symbolism in their mental constructions of reality as well (Piaget, 1955; Werner, 1940), and that inclination seems to be manifest in their fears. Specifically, at younger ages, rather than fearing things that are an actual source of danger in external reality, children tend to represent their own inner experience symbolically by externalizing it in the form of relatively harmless objects such as cats and dogs, or other animals, like lions and tigers, which they seldom find in their environment.

Jones and Jones (1928) found, for example, that when exposed to a living snake under experimental conditions, children up to the age of two showed no fear of snakes; by three or three and a half, caution reactions were common, with close attention paid to movement; definite fear behaviour occurred more often after four years. That this fear of snakes emerged from a complex interaction between perceptual and emotional processes, rather than from simple conditioning, was indicated by the fact that children in the Jones and Jones study were developing in a common environment in an institution where they 'had no opportunity to be conditioned against snakes, either through pictures, stories, or from encounters with live specimens (p. 142).' In short, many times children's fears cannot be traced to actual life experiences.

Thus, MacFarlane, Allen, and Honzik (1954) discovered that a commonly expressed fear at age two was of imaginary creatures, while Jersild and Holmes (1935) discovered that fear of dogs and other animals predominated at age three. At ages four and five, on the other hand, Bauer (1976) and Maurer (1965) observed that fear of animals of varying types persisted and that fear of the dark emerged as a significant source of fear. At slightly older ages, Waldfogel, Coolidge, and Hahn (1957) found this same type of fear, stemming from externalization of feelings, to be connected with morbid dread of some aspect of the school situation and children's refusal to attend school. Similarly, Marks (1971) discovered that while most situational and social phobias begin after puberty, animal phobias tend to arise in early childhood. Generally, however, research carried out by Agras *et al.* (1972), Hampe *et al.* (1973), Hellman (1962), indicated that the types of fears and phobias arising in children under 10 years of age dissipate rapidly.

In any case, at the same time that animism and anthropomorphism colour the young child's perceptions and fears, difficulty in forming a clear visual image of space, and therefore, in conceptualizing the location of objects in abstract space, may be instrumental in the development of fear about being spatially separated from objects with which the child has established an emotional attachment.

FEAR OF SEPARATION

Consider, for example, that Laurendeau and Pinard (1970) experimentally substantiated Piaget's (1954) earlier observation that prior to about age two, children's understandings of space are based largely on their concrete sensory and motor experiences, so that the location of objects removed from their immediate tactual, visual, and auditory perceptions is obscure. As a result, when parents leave a one-or two-year-old with someone else, or when the child must leave to explore on his or her own, fear of separation emerges. Miller *et al.* (1974) observed, for instance, that fear of separation reaches its most acute phase at age two, when patterns of attachment behaviour between mothers and their children are firmly established (Bowlby, 1969), but when children are just beginning to conceive of objects as existing beyond their sensory experience in abstract space (Piaget, 1954). That concrete cognitive awareness of space is a factor in the child's fear of separation was further substantiated by Littenberg, Tulkin, and Kagan (1971), who conducted an experimental investigation in which each of 24 11-month-old infants watched its mother leave it from an exit in the home that was either normally or rarely used by the mother. The incidents of crying, staring, and crawling to the exit was greater when the mother left by the unfamiliar exit. At age four, on the other hand, when most children are cognitively capable of conceptualizing the location of objects in abstract space, studies show that fear of separation exhibits a corresponding marked decline (Miller et al., 1974).

Nonetheless, separation from significant adults and from familiar home environments made necessary by entry into unfamiliar school settings has been found to generate, if not abnormal fear of separation, at least some degree of emotional conflict.

FEAR OF GOING TO SCHOOL

Van Leewen and Tuma (1972) reported, for example, that at the time of nursery school entry the majority of young children show signs of apprehension which may be aggravated by caretaker's lack of awareness of, and responsiveness to, children's attachment needs. Similarly, Klein and Ross (1958) discovered the prevalence of such temporary behavioural disturbances as increased dependence, exaggerated uncooperativeness or hostility, and regressive behaviours (e.g. crying, vomiting, bed-wetting, and thumbsucking) during the first two months of kindergarten, while Kellam and Schiff (1967) found that 70 per cent of first graders they studied were rated by their teachers as maladapted, as evidenced in behaviours such as timidity, thumbsucking, fidgeting and obstinacy. Almost 10 per cent were discovered to have significant symptoms of psychiatric disturbance.

Despite the fact that entry into the school's complex bureaucratic institutional structure was found to be an emotionally upsetting experience for many children and traumatic for a few, each year increasing numbers are introduced to the institutional context of school at younger and younger age levels. Reports indicate, for example, that in the United States preschool enrollments increased 30 per cent between 1965 and 1970, and as of March 1972 the proportions of three-, four-, and five-year-olds attending school were 15.5 per cent, 33.5 per cent, and 76 per cent respectively (Almy, 1975; Steinfels, 1973).

Unfortunately, ethological field studies suggest that the transition from home environments to unfamiliar school contexts may be complicated by parents' and children's handling of the network of social relationships existing in the school. Specifically, Leach (1972) found that children having trouble entering into school activities directed less behaviour toward, and were less responsive to, other three-, four-, and five-year-olds in their nursery school. Correspondingly, the other children interacted less with them than they did with other children. The paradoxical situation also existed, however, in which even though the troubled children remained close to their mothers, they were less responsive to them than was normal, while the mothers themselves tended to avoid interactions with their children. Furthermore, a similar configuration in mother–child relationships was observed by White and Watts (1973) who suggested that one of the distinguishing characteristics of competent, compared with less competent, kindergarteners is the tendency of mothers of more competent children to accept the initial strivings for autonomy by their infants in the realms of movement in the space, communication and personality. Some mothers allow for, and even encourage, their children's transition to walking and talking, while others cannot accept easily such transformations in their children.

At any rate, as they grow into the elementary school years (6- to 12-year-olds), fears stemming originally from concrete sensory and motor perceptions of reality seem to be replaced by others associated with more abstract conceptions of space, time, and causality. Studies conducted by Klingberg (1957), Piaget (1955), and Werner (1940), revealed, for instance, that movement in space is sufficient condition for the young child to regard objects as being alive. Conversely, Anthony (1971) more recently discovered that young children conceptualize death as a state of immobility. Hence, when a situation arises in which by chance the motion of an object is accidentally interrupted, it is looked upon as causing death. Before age nine, however, the concept of chance causality seems not to exist in the child's thought. As a result, in the young child's conception of things, death is inexplicable. It is the fortuitous and mysterious phenomenon *par excellence*.

FEAR OF DEATH

In one study, for example, Bauer (1976) discovered that four- to six-year-olds living in the United States personified the thing which they regarded as 'most frightening' in the form of ghosts, monsters, and other mythical creations representing death in American culture. In addition, research studies conducted over the last four decades demonstrated consistently that one of the most frequent worries of 12-year-olds is about the health and welfare of family members (Bauer, 1976; Pintner and Lev, 1940; Zeligs, 1939). Moreover, while some authorities (e.g. Coolidge, Hahn and Peck, 1957; Kennedy, 1965) argue that children's refusal to attend school stems primarily from disturbed family relations, and others (e.g. Eisenberg, 1958; Johnson *et al.*, 1941;) believe that fear of separation from the mother is the core problem in school refusal, many clinicians are of the opinion that a recurrent theme underlying some children's refusal to attend school is concern about the permanent loss (death) of a parent when they are away from home at school (See Chapter 14).

Regrettably, even though apprehension about death was found to be reflected in children's refusal to attend school, in their most significant fears, as well as in their psychological adjustments to the actual death of a parent (Furman, 1974), knowledge about children's understandings of death remains strikingly limited (Koocher *et al.* 1976). In a recent review, for example, Bauer (1978) noted that investigations show unmistakably that even professionals charged with the care of terminally ill children seldom take into consideration, or fully appreciate the child's view of death and dying.

FEAR OF FAILURE IN SCHOOL

Not only may development of abstract perceptions of reality create fears through recognition of human finiteness. Research carried out by Clark (1973), Klineberg (1967), and Kluckhohn and Strodtbeck (1961), for instance, shows that with each advancing year of life, children construct increasingly articulate views of themselves as objects located in a space through which they are projected on a linear course, and that by age 11 or 12, children begin to perceive their future adult life as a point toward which their self (object) is propelled in its linear trajectory. Moreover, in the United States at least, social scientists (Weisskopf, 1973) tell us that this perceived motion occurs in a cultural matrix in which judgment of social worth is heavily based on intellect, academic credentials, and level of school attained. Hence, parents expect, and children aspire to, scholastic excellence, while schools insist that every student achieves the same result by studying the same thing in a lock-step system anchored to chronological age. As a result, children are pressured constantly to achieve, and failure to progress leads not only to social-devaluation but ultimately to self-depreciation as well. Thus, many children live under the prolonged stress created by fear of failure to progress in academic-achievement situations at a rate expected by self and significant others, such as parents and teachers.

Not surprisingly, therefore, in a study of parents' ratings of children's fears, Miller, Barrett, Hampe, and Noble (1972) identified a factor indicative of long term psychic and social stress. Among the specific fears contributing to the stress factor were fears of examinations, school, social events, and being criticized. Likewise, research carried out by Angelino, Dollins, and Mech (1956), Bauer (1977), Jersild *et al.* (1940), Pintner and Lev (1940), Sarason, *et al.* (1960), and Zeligs (1939) uncovered a cluster of fears expressed by the majority of 11- and 12-year-olds focusing on facets of school entailing evaluation of their academic progress — facets such as promotion to the next grade, school marks and reports, reciting in class, and tests of academic aptitude and achievement. Moreover, while Jersild *et al.* (1940) found in their early study that the most frequent worry of fourth- and fifth-graders was about 'failing a test' and 'getting a poor report card', Hill and Sarason (1966) more recently discovered that this fear of failure to perform in academic-achievement situations (termed *test*, or *school anxiety*) begins to develop in both boys as well as girls as early as age six and is resistant to change once developed. Maccoby and Jacklin (1974) reported that, while between the ages of 8 and 13, girls in England and America were found to express greater amounts of school anxiety than boys, by mid-adolescence boys manifest as much of that anxiety as girls.

Prior to adolescence, however, since Minuchin, Biber, Shapiro, and Zimiles (1969) discovered that children's conceptions of the remote future when they are grown up tend to be, '. . . prestructured by social convention, adultlike in orientation, and essentially irrelevant to their current interests and activities', fear of failure to perform in school should not be presumed to stem simply from children's perceptions of progress toward a distant future in adulthood. Specifically, Klineberg (1967) found that although the sense of the relatively near future is well established in 10- to 12-year-olds, for they have developed the ability to delay gratification, awareness of the future beyond childhood is endowed with little reality. Consequently, rather than orientation to the remote future, what seems to generate the school anxiety observed in children of preadolescent age is the presence of a conflict between students' affect for school activities and their perceptions of the value of the material to be learned at school. Dunn (1968), for instance, theorized that: 'A child who considers academics important but dislikes them (is) in an approach–avoidance situation and hence presumably under a good deal of stress in precisely those situations calling for a high level and quality of academic performance.' Even though the simplest defence in such a situation is either psychological withdrawal *via* daydreaming and/or rationalization, or physical withdrawal *via* truancy and/or school dropout, neither is typically possible. Consequently, heightened levels of school anxiety, hostility, and affect may be expected to be found.

In that regard, Dunn discovered in his cross-sectional study that children in the United States increasingly dislike academic and social aspects of school as they grow from the fifth to the ninth grades. Furthermore, despite the fact that children from lower socioeconomic communities develop dislike for school, they continue to value academic aspects of school and give evidence of being anxious about doing well in school. Likewise, just as Hill and Sarason (1969) observed increased levels of school anxiety from the first to the sixth grades, so did Neale and Proshek (1967) discover that children's evaluations of phrases such as 'my school books', 'my teacher', and 'me' become more negative with each advancing year from the fourth to the sixth grades, and Yamamoto, Thomas, and Karnes (1969) find that students' ratings of teachers, of curriculum, and of themselves get to be less favourable from the sixth to the ninth grades.

In sum, then, past research regarding children's fears and the emergence of their views of reality suggests that concrete perceptions of space lead naturally to apprehensions about unfamiliar people, places, and things as well as about separation from familiar ones. Further, because these normal fears may be aggravated by the dynamics of parent–child relations and by the social climate of the school, transition from home to school contexts during the formative years tends to be an emotionally upsetting experience for many children. In the course of growth through the elementary school years, moreover, the emergence of increasingly articulate views of abstract space and time makes possible the recognition of human finiteness (death). And, that dawning awareness introduces fears which may be aggravated by emotional stress generated by constant fear of failure to achieve scholastic aspirations.

Regrettably, even though research indicates that with advancing age children are exposed to increasing sources of emotional stress resulting from school transition, fear of failure in school, and death awareness, few investigators have attempted to chart developmental changes in the amount of emotional conflict and character of school-related fears and perceptions normally experienced by children. That such normative data pertain to the emergence of pathological fear of school was suggested by Miller *et al.* (1974) who argued that: 'Phobias are exaggerated developmental fears, or a continuation of such fears past their expected decay point, or fears of stimuli other than those associated with the developmental period.'

DEVELOPMENTAL CHANGES IN SCHOOL-RELATED FEARS AND PERCEPTIONS

The research project described in the following brief report used a cross-sectional design to investigate developmental changes in the amount of emotional conflict and fear of failure in school (school anxiety) normally experienced by children and to describe the course of growth in children's orientations to life-stages. Specifically, since research suggested that children are subjected to increasing sources of psychological stress as they progress in school, the study investigated the prediction that older grade-school children would display greater amounts of emotional conflict as well as school anxiety than younger ones. Because sex-typing is known to affect emotional development through socialization of sex roles, however, growth trends were expected to differ in boys and girls. Moreover, as a consequence of emergence of progressively more articulate perception of time, greater numbers of older than younger children were anticipated to be oriented to the distant future represented by the life-stage designated 'adulthood'.

A total sample of 62 children were randomly selected from the first (6- and 7-year-olds), third (8- and 9-year-olds), and sixth (11- and 12-year-olds) grades of two elementary schools situated in middle-socioeconomic communities in northern California. Subsequently, individual interviews were conducted to obtain information regarding amounts of emotional conflict and school anxiety as well as orientation to life-stages (childhood *vs.* adulthood). Indices of emotional conflict and orientation to life-stages were obtained from a slightly modified version of Sarason *et al.*'s (1960) Test Anxiety Scale for Children (TASC), from Human Figure Drawings (HFD's) in which emotional indicators were identified following criteria established by Koppitz (1968), and from a Stick Figure Scale (SFS) previously used by Minuchin *et al.* (1969).

Change in level of emotional conflict and school anxiety

Levels of emotional conflict (mean number of emotional indicators) and school anxiety (mean scores on the TASC) expressed by first, third, and sixth grade boys and girls are reported in Table 1. Results of 2 × 3 (sex × grade)

Table 1. Mean number of emotional indicators and school anxiety scores obtained by first, third, and sixth grade boys and girls

		Grade Level							
Sex	Scale	First	*n*	Third	*n*	Sixth	*n*	Grade total	*n*
Boys	Emotional indicator	1.80	10	1.00	10	2.88	8	1.82	28
	School anxiety	7.30	10	9.00	10	11.55	9	9.21	29
Girls	Emotional indicator	2.09	11	1.22	9	1.25	12	1.53	32
	School anxiety	7.64	11	12.00	10	11.58	12	10.39	33
Sex total	Emotional indicator	1.95	21	1.10	19	1.90	20	1.67	60
	School anxiety	7.48	21	10.50	20	11.57	21	9.84	62

analyses of variance (method of unweighted means) revealed that level of school anxiety was reliably higher in third- and sixth-graders than in first graders ($F = 2.43$, $p < 0.10$, df 2/56) and that amount of emotional conflict in boys compared with girls varied depending on grade level ($F = 3.30$, $p < 0.05$, df 2/54). Further, contrasts between pairs of means showed that whereas first grade children experienced significantly more conflict than third-graders, sixth grade boys expressed dramatically more conflict than girls in that grade. This interaction between grade and sex becomes considerably more clear when portrayed graphically in Figure 1.

Results of the study only partially confirmed the predictions that older children would evidence greater amounts of emotional distress than younger ones, and that developmental trends would differ in boys and girls. Specifically, just as Kellam and Schiff (1967) found behavioural indications of emotional disturbance in 70 per cent of the first-graders they studied, so did the data in this investigation reveal that the children experienced heightened levels of conflict on entry into the first year of primary school. For boys as well as girls, this apprehension was significantly diminished at the third grade. On the other hand, just as Hill and Sarason (1966) uncovered increased levels of school anxiety with each advancing year of elementary school, so too in this investigation, internalization of the prevailing academic-achievement value structure led to heightened fear of failure which was expressed in anxiety test scores obtained by third-graders.

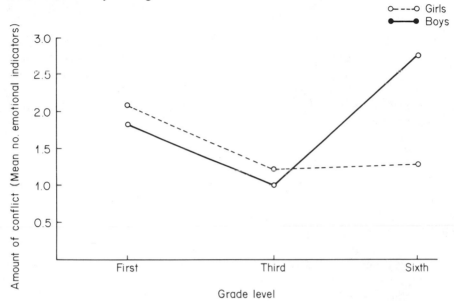

Figure 1. Graphic representation showing mean number of emotional indicators in HFDs drawn by first, third, and sixth grade boys and girls

With the onset of the transition from childhood to adolescence at the sixth grade, however, boys seemed to encounter greater amounts of emotional conflict than girls, suggesting that identification with masculine sex roles generated excessive aspiration stress among the preadolescent boys. More precisely, McCandless (1967), pointed out that American culture, '. . . emphasizes independence, initiative and success "on one's own" more for boys than girls. Girls are expected to be conforming, obedient, and responsible. Boys are expected to *stand out.*' Hence, sixth-grade boys may have experienced emotional conflict stemming from personal aspiration to stand out socially by successfully competing against peers on school academic tasks, while simultaneously remaining acceptable to members of the competing reference group. The emotional distress created by this conflict is called *aspiration stress*, and though sixth grade girls experienced as much specific fear of failure to progress in school as did boys, less pressure to attain scholastic and social superiority may have resulted in lower aspiration stress, and therefore, fewer indications of emotional conflict as well. Indeed, the fact that the correlation between school anxiety scores and number of emotional indicators in this study was positive in boys ($r = +0.32$, $p < 0.10$) and negative in girls ($r = -0.23$, $p < 0.10$) lends additional empirical justification to this aspiration stress interpretation of results.

Change in orientation to life-stages

Indications of differences in children's orientation to life-stages was ascertained first from responses given to the following item on the SFS:

> 'Here's a boy (girl) who thinks *versus* 'Here's a boy (girl) who thinks
> it will be wonderful to be all   it was really best when he was
> grown up — that will be the   a little kid.'
> best time.'
>   'Which one is more like you?'

Contrary to this author's thesis that larger proportions of older than younger children would be oriented toward the distant future represented by adulthood, significantly ($p < 0.05$) greater numbers of first (67%) and third (50%) grade children expressed orientations toward adulthood than sixth-graders (29%). Evidently, the majority of sixth-graders in this study did not hold optimistic perceptions of their life in the distant future, for only the minority felt that adulthood was the best time of life. The overwhelming majority preferred their life as children!

Not only were these findings comparable to those obtained by Minuchin, *et al.* (1969), who reported that only 25% of the fourth-graders they studied felt it would be 'wonderful to be all grown up', but they also were indicative of a general developmental trend outlined by Keniston (1960) and Mead (1970). According to Mead and Keniston, the tendency in modern industrial societies is toward enculturation of alienation and aimlessness rather than of commitment and devotion to the future. Further, Keniston argued that because the existing adult world denies the human qualities of childhood in which work, play, love, and fantasy are closely intertwined, children hesitate to choose adulthood when faced with the transition into adult roles. Since roles in the adult world are not viewed as being exciting and fulfilling, the world of childhood is romanticized, and the prospect of 'growing up' is seen in an even darker light.

In that regard, what seemed to differentiate children choosing adulthood as the best time of life from those electing childhood in the present study was the quality of vagueness and fantasy in perceptions of adult roles in society. More precisely, to supplement information regarding life-stage orientations provided by the SFS item, children were asked at the close of each interview the following series of questions concerning their aspirations for adult life: *Do you ever think about being grown up? What do you think you'll be or do?*

Why would you like to be a (doctor; fireman; etc.)? Reported below are verbatim transcriptions of representative answers to these questions given by younger (first-graders) and older (sixth-graders) children choosing either adulthood or childhood as their favoured life-stage.

Generally, conceptions of life in adulthood held by children electing adulthood as well as by those preferring childhood tended to be prestructured by social convention and stereotyped with respect to sex-roles. Perceptions of adulthood exhibited by children identifying that stage as 'the best time', however, seemed less constrained by realistic considerations and more undifferentiated with respect to work, play, and fantasy than perceptions displayed by children identifying childhood. First-graders choosing adulthood as the best time of life, for example, gave such reasons as the following for aspirations to be a marine, a fireman, a mailman, a nurse, and a teacher: 'Cause it's fun to go in the boat.' 'It would be fun.' 'Because I get to drive around and stop and put mail in the mailbox.' 'Fix people and do things for the doctor.' 'Tell the kids to be quiet.' Those first grade children indicating a preference for childhood, on the other hand, appeared less inclined to consider future goals and more realistic in conceptualizations of past, present, and future experience. Consider, for instance, these comments about the future made by the few first-graders feeling that it was better to be a child than an adult:

I don't think about what I'll be.

I wish I was in kindergarten. That would be more fun than the first grade. 'Cause you could paint and stuff.

'Cause I'll just work and work and work all day.

Indeed, one first grade girl touchingly expressed her disenchantment with life in adulthood when she said: 'I think I'll be like my Mom — just ordinary. Because I don't want to be all over the place like my Dad. Because then I have to work and have no time for my children.'

Just as was the case with first-graders, perceptions of adult life expressed by sixth-graders choosing adulthood as the best time were permeated with fantasy and wish-fulfilment. Take, for example, the following comments made about aspirations and the reasons for having them: 'Be a stewardess on an aeroplane. I like flying and I like to give people food.' 'Yes, a nurse. I don't know. I've been reading a book.' 'I'll be a veterinarian. I like animals.' 'A policeman — I want to be a policeman more than anything. I just like it because they know everybody and stuff. I like to be somebody.' 'A football player. Can I say everything I want to be? I think many people want to be many things. I guess because I like sports, I guess.' Conversely, though remarks about aspirations for adulthood made by sixth-graders preferring childhood were somewhat wish-fulfilling, they were generally less imaginative and more indicative of an emerging conflict between personal desires and social realities. Listen, for instance, to a few of those children speaking:

> Yea, I think like in the future what is going to happen, and what I'm going to be. I want to be a cartoonist or a football player. Well, in football a lot of guys do a lot of catches, and I like to be good at a lot of things. Like I watch Monday Night Football. My Dad watches it really. I watch and see these guys doing everything spectacular. A cartoonist? Well, I don't really know what to say. I want to be a cartoonist because I really like it a lot. I do it at home all the time. I draw all the time and stuff. I like drawing a lot.

> Yea, sometimes, although I wish I could still stay small. I think it's fun being a kid. I like to be an astronomer. Well, I like to study, and I like to be a scientist. I think it's interesting. I think that's what I want to be.

> Yes, a teacher, or an airline stewardess, or a waitress. I want to be an airline stewardess because you can see so many places. And, I want to be a waitress because my Mom's a waitress. I want to be a school teacher because I like being around kids.

> Sometimes. I know. I'll be a mother. Maybe a nurse. A mother would be tak'n after my Mom and a nurse would be tak'n after my sister.

> No. I would like to travel. Maybe a waitress. My mother's a waitress.

Conflicting feelings about growing up pervade statements of sixth-graders opting for childhood as the most desirable time of life. In fact, in the case of a youngster in conflict about whether or not to pursue his own unique artistic talents and interests by becoming a cartoonist, or to stand out ('be spectacular' in his words) by becoming a football player, identification of five emotional indicators on his HFD placed him more than two standard deviations above the mean number of indicators present in drawings of sixth-graders. Similarly, his school anxiety score was more than half a standard unit above the mean anxiety score obtained by his reference group of sixth-graders.

CONCLUSIONS AND PRACTICAL IMPLICATIONS

Results of this study of developmental changes in school-related fears and perceptions of elementary school students indicated that the children experienced heightened levels of emotional distress on entry into the first year of primary school, but that this apprehension diminished significantly by the third grade. With the transition from childhood to adolescence at the sixth grade, however, boys seemed to encounter greater amounts of emotional conflict than girls. For children of both sexes, while the course of growth through elementary school led to increased fear of failure to progress toward goals established by the school, it resulted as well in rejection of the distant future in adulthood as a desirable goal toward which their own life was directed.

In general, these findings were reminiscent of those of Lichter, Rapien, Seibert, and Sklansky (1962) who concluded, from a study of 105 intellectually capable students on the verge of dropping out of high school, that the primary motivation for leaving was to reduce the stressfulness in their lives and that the adolescents were running away from a disagreeable situation, but not toward any positive or definite goal. After receiving counselling help in coping with stress, of all the youth about to drop out when counselling was initiated, 77% of the boys and 44% of the girls were able to continue instead. Hence, helping children construct coping strategies for handling stress becomes central to counteracting possible school refusal and truancy.

Regrettably, few careful studies have been made of styles of coping with environmental demands. Nevertheless, Torrance (1965) analysed Murphy's (1957, 1962) description of eight types of strategies naturally used by children in coping with stress and suggested several ways to aid them in mastering more effective ways of handling common pressures encountered at school. The following conceptualization, summarized from Torrance (1965, pp. 205–207, reproduced by permission of Wadsworth Publishing Company, Inc.) could be used to guide students in making curricular and career choices, in adapting to the pressures of peer culture and of school itself, as well as in changing patterns of absconding from school.

Permitting Risk. For some children anything new is so threatening that they tend to rely on counselors, teachers, or parents to decide their fates for them. Since it is often difficult for surrounding adults to withstand the temptation of protecting such individuals by making choices for them, counselors need to take special care to encourage children to make their own decisions and to recognize and accept the seriousness of their situation. One of the most dangerous features of behavior under stress is the tendency to resist acceptance of the danger by denying its seriousness. Thus, the problem is one of helping students achieve cognitive insight into, and personal awareness of, their own circumstances by permitting risk. At times, this may mean confronting the possibility of failure.

Developing Skills of Mastery. Fear of the unknown is one of the reasons students avoid risks, resist learning and making changes, and are anxious about new experiences. One of the ways of coping with this difficulty is by structuring the situation through actual experience under the careful guidance of an experienced comrade. While it is not always possible to provide such experiences even in safe situations, role playing, and other types of practice in prestructuring forthcoming experiences can be helpful. For example, helping the child find out what to expect in the new situation, by becoming acquainted with its requirements through surveying and appraising it, puts the child in a position to start developing strategies and skills for coping with it. Knowing the requirements helps the child assess his own resources in terms of environmental demands. Critical skills to be developed include restructuring situations too big or too difficult to handle, developing interpersonal skills for coping with the problem, developing patterns of mutual support and encouragement, and decision making.

Helping Unload. Before students are able to recognize the seriousness of their situation, plan ahead, overcompensate and the like, they need to unload accumulated or overwhelming tensions. Counselors should permit this. Students often are in need of a relationship in which they can feel safe and in which they can relieve tensions by 'spilling all of their woes'. In short, they need someone in whom to confide.

Encouraging the Continued Fight. One of the most valuable social conditions that assists people of all ages in maintaining a continued fight, as opposed to submitting to stress through resignation (truancy) and apathy, is one of mutual support from fellow students, teachers, parents, and counselors. Counselors might carefully solicit the help of these significant others in children's life. Conversely, the student may bolster his own will to continue the struggle by giving support to others. Generally, children ought to be guided toward acceptance of stress and learn to live and cope with it by exploiting it strategically and bending it to their own advantage. This means that counselors should help students in working out a plan of action that will give them a fighting chance by keeping them busy integrating meaning into their lives.

In closing, perhaps the most disconcerting finding of the present study was that, when contrasted with younger children, the majority of older ones appeared to be alienated from adulthood and reluctant to use the distant future for fulfilment in imagination of personal wishes and desires. While the course of growth in human life is directed normally toward increased separation of inner wishes, desires, and fantasy from outer reality, planned action for coping with environmental demands requires the connection of inner guidelines with the real world of people and objects. Though space precludes extended discussion of this topic, Weisskopf-Joelson (1968) suggested that endeavours such as friendship, art, myth, and creativity can assist individuals in achieving integration of imaginary with material realms and developing a sense of relatedness to the world. Similarly, Bettelheim (1976) argued persuasively for the importance of incorporating hopeful images of the future into the life of children in order to aid them in conquering their fears.

ACKNOWLEDGEMENTS

The author wishes to gratefully acknowledge the assistance of Miss Maryam Abedi, Mrs. Teresa Anderson, Mr. Myron Curtis, and Dr. Beatrice Wynants, M.D., in conducting interviews and of Miss Vicki Ross in processing data for the investigation reported in this chapter.

REFERENCES

Agras, W. S., Chapin, H. N., and Oliveau, D. C. (1972). The natural history of phobia. *Archives of General Psychology*, **26**, 315–317.
Almy, M. (1975). *The Early Childhood Educator at Work*. McGraw-Hill, New York.

Angelino, H., Dollins, J., and Mech, E. V. (1956). Trends in the fears and worries of school children as related to socioeconomic status and age. *Journal of Psychology*, **89**, 263–276.

Anthony, S. (1971). *The Discovery of Death in Childhood and After*. Basic Books, New York.

Bauer, D. H. (1975). The effect of test instructions, test anxiety and locus of control on scores on an intelligence test. *Measurement and Evaluation in Guidance*, **8**, 12–19.

Bauer, D. H. (1976). An exploratory study of developmental changes in children's fears. *Journal of Child Psychology and Psychiatry*, **17**, 69–74.

Bauer, D. H. (1977). Motivation of aptitude and achievement test performance. *Elementary School Guidance and Counselling*, **12**, 77–86.

Bauer, D. H. (1978). What of the Dying Child? In (Ed.) Yamamoto, K., *Death in the Life of Children*, Kappa Delta Pi, West Lafayette, Indiana, 83–113.

Bettelheim, B. (1976) *The Uses of Enchantment: The Meaning and Importance of Fairy Tales*. Alfred A. Knopf, New York.

Bowlby, J. (1969). *Attachment and Loss*, Volume I. *Attachment*. Basic Books, New York.

Bronson, G. W. (1972). Infants' reactions to unfamiliar persons and novel objects. *Monographs of the Society for Research in Child Development*, **37**, (3, Whole No. 148).

Clark, H. H. (1973). Space, time, semantics and the child. In *Cognitive Development and the Acquisition of Language*. In (Ed.) Moore, T. E., Academic Press, New York, 27–63.

Coolidge, J. C., Hahn, P. B., and Peck, A. L. (1957). School phobia: Neurotic crisis or way of life. *American Journal of Orthopsychiatry*, **27**, 296–306.

Dunn, J. A. (1968). The approach-avoidance paradigm as a model for the analysis of school anxiety. *Journal of Educational Psychology*, **59**, 388–394.

Eisenberg, L. (1958). School phobia: A study of communication anxiety. *American Journal of Psychiatry*, **114**, 712–718.

Freud, S. (1962). Analysis of a phobia in a five-year-old boy. *Complete Psychological Works*. Vol. 10. Hogarth Press, London, 101–147.

Furman, E. (1974). *A Child's Parent Dies*. Yale University Press, New Haven.

Hampe, E., Noble, H., Miller, L. C., and Barrett, C. L. (1973). Phobic children one and two years posttreatment. *Journal of Abnormal Psychology*, **82**, 446–453.

Hellman, I. (1962). Hampstead nursery follow-up studies: Sudden separation and its effects followed over twenty years. *Psychoanalytic Study of the Child*, **17**, 159–174.

Hersov, L. A. (1960). Refusal to go to school. *Journal of Child Psychology and Psychiatry*, **1**, 137–145.

Hill, K. T., and Sarason, S. B. (1966). The relation of test anxiety and defensiveness to test and school performance over the elementary school years. *Monographs of the Society for Research in Child Development*, **31** (2, Whole No. 104).

Jersild, A. T., and Holmes, F. B. (1935). *Children's Fears*. Teachers College, Columbia University, New York.

Jersild, A. T., Goldman, B., and Loftus, J. J. (1940). A comparative study of the worries of children in two school situations. *Journal of Experimental Education*, **9**, 323–326.

Johnson, A. M., Falstein, E. I., Szurek, S. A., and Svendsen, M. (1941). School phobia. *American Journal of Orthopsychiatry*, **11**, 702–711.

Jones, H. E., and Jones, M. C. (1928). Fear. *Childhood Education*, **5**, 136–143.

Jung, C. G. (1964). *Man and His Symbols*. Aldus Books Ltd., London.

Kellam, S. G., and Schiff, S. K. (1967). Adaptation and mental illness in the first grade classrooms of an urban community. *Psychiatry Research Reports*, **21**, 79–91.

Keniston, K. (1960). Alienation and the decline of utopia. *The American Scholar*, **29** (2), 161–200.

Kennedy, W. A. (1965). School phobia: Rapid treatment of fifty cases. *Journal of Abnormal Psychology*, **70**, 285–289.

Klein, D. C., and Ross, A. (1958). Kindergarten entry: A study in role transition. In *Orthopsychiatry and the School*. In (Ed.) Krugman, M. American Orthopsychiatric Association, New York, 60–69.

Klineberg, S. L. (1967). Changes in outlook on the future between childhood and adolescence. *Journal of Personality and Social Psychology*, **7**, 185–193.

Klingberg, G. (1957). The distinction between living and not living among 7–10 year-old children, with some remarks concerning the so-called animism controversy. *Journal of Genetic Psychology*, **90**, 227–238.

Kluckhohn, F. R., and Strodtbeck, F. L. (1961). *Variations in Value Orientations*. Greenwood Publishers, Westport, Connecticut.

Koocher, G. P., O'Malley, J. E., Foster D., and Gogan, J. L. (1976). Death anxiety in normal children and adolescents. *Psychiatria Clinica*, **9**, 220–229.

Koppitz, E. M. (1968). *Psychological Evaluation of Children's Human Figure Drawings*. Grune and Stratton, New York.

Laurendeau, M., and Pinard, A. (1970). *The Development of the Concept of Space in the Child*. International Universities Press, New York.

Leach, G. M. (1972). A comparison of the social behaviour of some normal and problem children. *Ethological Studies of Child Behaviour*. In (Ed.) Jones, N. B., Cambridge University Press, Cambridge, 249–481.

Lewis, M., and Goldberg, S. (1969). Perceptual-cognitive development in infancy: A generalized expectancy model as a function of the mother-infant interaction. *Merrill-Palmer Quarterly*, **15**, 81–100.

Lichter, S. O., Rapien, E. B., Seibert, F. M., and Sklansky, M. S. (1962). *The Drop-Outs*. Free Press of Glencoe, New York.

Lindquist, E. F. (1953). *Design and Analysis of Experiments in Psychology and Education*. Houghton-Mifflin Company, Boston.

Littenberg, R., Tulkin, S. R., and Kagan, J. (1971). Cognitive components of separation anxiety. *Developmental Psychology*, **4**, 387–388.

Maccoby, E. E., and Jacklin, C. N. (1974). *The Psychology of Sex Differences*. Stanford University Press, Stanford, California.

MacFarlane, J. W., Allen, L., and Honzik, M. P. (1954). A developmental study of the behaviour problems of normal children between twenty-one months and fourteen years. In *University of California Publications in Child Development*. Volume 2. University of California Press, Berkeley.

Marks, I. M. (1971). Phobic disorders four years after treatment: A prospective follow-up. *British Journal of Psychiatry*, **118**, 683–688.

Maurer, A. (1965). What children fear. *The Journal of Genetic Psychology*, **106**, 265–277.

McCandless, B. R. (1967). *Children: Behavior and Development*. (Second Ed.) Holt, Rinehart, and Winston, New York.

Mead, M. (1970). *Culture and Commitment: A Study of the Generation Gap*. Doubleday and Company, Garden City, New York.

Miller, L. C., Barrett, C. L., and Hampe, E. (1974). Phobias of childhood in a prescientific era. In (Ed.) Davids, A. *Child Personality and Psychopathology*. John Wiley and Sons, New York, 89–134.

Miller, L. C., Barrett, C. L., Hampe, E., and Noble, H. (1972). Factor structure of childhood fears. *Journal of Consulting and Clinical Psychology*, **39**, 264-268.

Minuchin, P., Biber, B., Shapiro, R., and Zimiles, H. (1969). *The Psychological Impact of School Experience*. Basic Books, New York.

Murphy, L. B. (1957). Psychoanalysis and child development, Part II. *Bulletin of the Menninger Clinic*, **21**, 248-258.

Murphy, L. B. (1962). *The Widening World of Childhood*. Basic Books, New York.

Neale, D. C., and Proshek, J. M. (1967). School-related attitudes of culturally disadvantaged elementary school children. *Journal of Educational Psychology*, **58**, 238-244.

Piaget, J. (1954). *The Construction of Reality in the Child*. Basic Books, New York.

Piaget, J. (1955). *The Language and Thought of the Child*. Meridian Books, New York.

Piaget, J. (1962). *Play, Dreams and Imitation in Childhood*. W. W. Norton, New York.

Piaget, J., and Inhelder, B. (1956). *The Child's Conception of Space*. Routledge and Kegan Paul Ltd., London.

Pintner, R., and Lev, J. (1940). Worries of school children. *Journal of Genetic Psychology*, **56**, 67-76.

Rheingold, J. C. (1967). *The Mother, Anxiety, and Death*. Little, Brown, and Company, Boston.

Sarason, S. B., Davidson, K. S., Lighthall, F. F., Waite, R. R., and Ruebush, B. K. (1960). *Anxiety in Elementary School Children*. John Wiley and Sons, New York.

Steinfels, M. O. (1973). *Who's Minding the Children?* Simon and Schuster, New York.

Torrance, E. P. (1965). *Constructive Behavior: Stress, Personality and Mental Health*. Wadsworth Publishing Company, Belmont, California.

Van Leewen, K., and Tuma, J. M. (1972). Attachment and exploration: A systematic approach to the study of separation–adaptation phenomena in response to nursery school entry. *Journal of the American Academy of Child Psychiatry*, **11**, 314-340.

Waldfogel, S., Coolidge, J. C., and Hahn, P. B. (1957). The development, meaning and management of school phobia. *American Journal of Orthopsychiatry*, **27**, 754-780.

Watson, J. S. (1972). Smiling, cooing, and 'the game'. *Merrill-Palmer Quarterly*, **18**, 323-340.

Watson, J., and Rayner, R. (1920). Conditioned emotional reactions. *Journal of Experimental Psychology*, **3**, 1-14.

Weisskopf-Joelson, E. (1968). Meaning as an integrating factor. In *The Course of Human Life* (Ed.) Buhler, C., and Massarik, F. Springer Publishing Company, New York, 359-383.

Weisskopf, W. A. (1973). The dialectics of equality. *The Annals of the American Academy of Political and Social Science*, **409**, 163-173.

Werner, H. (1940). *Comparative Psychology of Mental Development*. Harper and Brothers Publishers, New York.

Werner, H. (1957). The concept of development from a comparative and organismic point of view. In (Ed.) Harris, D. B. *The Concept of Development*. University of Minnesota Press, Minneapolis, 125-148.

Werner, H., and Kaplan, B. (1964). *Symbol Formation: An Organismic-Developmental Approach to Language and Expression of Thought*. John Wiley and Sons, New York.

White, B. L., and Watts, J. C. (1973). *Experience and Environment*. Volume I. Prentice-Hall, Englewood Cliffs, New Jersey.

Wolpe, J. (1962). The experimental foundations of some new psychotherapeutic methods. In *Experimental Foundations of Clinical Psychology* (Edited by Bachrach, A. J.), Basic Books, New York, 554–575.

Yamamoto, K., Thomas, E., and Karnes, E. (1969). School-related attitudes of middle school age students. *American Educational Research Journal*, **6**, 191–206.

Zeligs, R. (1939). Children's worries. *Sociology and Social Research*, **24**, 22–32.

Chapter 11

School Refusal in Childhood —
a psychiatric–paediatric perspective

David Waller and Leon Eisenberg

Going to school is part of growing up in Western society. The path leading from the relatively dependent, protected state of childhood to the state of responsible independence that characterizes the adult is a path that goes through the school building. Acquiring a formal education is crucial if a child is to be able eventually to provide for himself or herself, but formal education *per se* is only a part of what school attendance provides along the route from dependence to independence. Of equal importance is a gradual 'extension of relationships from within the family to relationships within the community', (Kahn and Nursten, 1962) as the primary attachments to parents and home are gradually attenuated by separation and supplemented by increasingly important ties to others.

In the Western world, the school-aged child is expected to tread this path five or six days a week — indeed laws often require it, making school attendance one of the few aspects of human development legally enforcible. The only exception is the child who is ill, for whom school absence is sanctioned, so long as the child is deemed too sick to attend. It is assumed that an ill child is in need of a temporary return to the extra care and protection of home, in order to gather once again the necessary resources to continue along the path toward school and maturity. A thread emerges with three distinct strands: a biological strand, having to do with health or disease; a psychological strand, characterized by development toward maturity or regression toward dependence; and a behavioural strand, described simply by school attendance or school absence. The manner in which these three strands intertwine may be relatively straightforward or quite complex. A paediatric–psychiatric team may be needed to unravel the complexities of the most challenging cases.

This chapter will focus on problems of school attendance in children for whom the behavioural common denominators are: (1) the child is at home and (2) the parents know it (Rutter, 1975). Besides their problem in school attenance, these children are similar in that they are located at the dependence end of the psychological developmental continuum referred to above (Berg *et al.*, 1969). Their inability to separate from their home environment in order to attend school is an overt manifestation of their state of increased dependency. Equally characteristic is the fact that the parents are well informed as to where the child is, inasmuch as anxious 'touching base' characterizes abnormally close attachment.

Before considering these problems in more detail, it is instructive to contrast the so-called truant from the same perspectives. At one time truancy was defined simply as 'absence from school without proper leave'. The term is now used for a particular kind of unsanctioned school absence, in which the child is neither at school nor at home; usually the parents have no idea where their child is. Indeed, the word truant derives from the French term for a vagrant or wanderer. Truant children are in a sense at the opposite end of the developmental spectrum from the children whose school problems are to be considered in this chapter. The truant role can be viewed as a kind of perversion of the adult, post-school role, whereas the children to be discussed here are more like pre-schoolers. The truant child, attached less to home than is appropriate rather than more, takes on an 'independent' role for which he is not prepared, and more importantly, which society does not permit. His 'decision' not to attend school, along with decisions to engage in other delinquent, anti-social activity, is in marked contrast to the exceptionally 'well-behaved' quality, outside the home, of the children we will discuss in this chapter. Truancy is considered in detail elsewhere in this book.

INAPPROPRIATE 'HOME-BOUND' SCHOOL ABSENCE

We use this terminology, cumbersome though it is, because it provides a straightforward behavioural description without causal assumptions. It permits us to step back for a moment and examine the evolution of professional concepts of this behaviour syndrome, an evolution which is mirrored in the changing terminology employed as diagnositc labels. What makes this group of problems in school attendance so fascinating is that through the years, there has been a progressive 'unmasking' of the underlying difficulties which the 'absent-from-school behaviour' effectively disguised, and continues to disguise, despite all that has been written to encourage physicians to detect their presence.

The first key discovery in this saga was made by Broadwin (1932), when he reported that there was a group of children whose 'truant' behaviour concealed an underlying 'obsessional neurosis' or 'obsessional character disorder' that prevented them from attending school. The children were obsessed with ideas that their mother might be injured or even killed if they were away from home. Seven years later, Partridge (1939) gave this disorder the label 'psychoneurotic truancy', and further characterized it as a form of the 'mother-following syndrome', and a kind of 'stay-at-home neurosis'.

In a classic article, Johnson and associates (1941) called attention to the terror school attendance sometimes aroused in such children and designated the problem a 'school phobia'. The exciting part of their detective work lay in the discovery that whatever anxieties the child had were matched by equally significant anxieties in the mother, a crucial emphasis that the previous focus on the child alone had obscured. Thus, behind the child's 'school phobia' lay anxieties in the child, anxieties in the mother, and a problem in their relationship, having to do with 'poorly resolved early dependency'. In a follow-up study fifteen years later, Estes, Haylett, and Johnson (1956) coined the term 'separation anxiety' in an attempt to provide a diagnostic label that more accurately reflected the true locus of pathology in this group of problems. The child's fear of school masked what was in large part his anxiety over leaving his mother, as well as his mother's anxieties over letting him go.

It should be emphasized that neither mother nor child recognizes the attitudes concealed behind the child's inability to attend school. The child knows simply that he does not want to go; his mother states that she wants her child to be in school; neither is aware of the difficulty they are having separating from one another, and both will tend to deny it if asked about it.

How can we know that this separation anxiety exists, and how is it communicated? Once again, careful clinical observation provides the answers. Utilizing an opportunity to observe mothers and children directly at moments of separation and gathering data from other observers at a special nursery school and at a psychiatric out-patient clinic, Eisenberg (1958) documented the subtle manner in which a mother's difficulty with separation might be communicated to her child, even at a time when her words might state the opposite, concealing her true feelings from herself as well as unwary observers:

'One mother bid her twins goodbye with many reassurances of her early return. They played on unconcerned. She stopped again at the door to assure them they had nothing to fear. They glanced up but played on. Having gotten her coat, she made a third curtain speech in a tremulous voice, "Don't be afraid. Mommy will be back. Please don't cry." This time one of the twins got the cue and cried till she left.'

Perhaps the most common 'disguise' of school phobia, familiar in every paediatric practice, is the phenomenon of 'week-day morning-sickness' (such as headaches, abdominal pain, or vomiting), the symptoms of which magically disappear once the child is declared 'ill', so that school attendance is no longer necessary.

With all of this information available, it might be expected that physicians would be quite adept at recognizing, and properly interpreting the meaning of inappropriate 'home-bound' school absence. However, recent literature suggests, and our own experience confirms, that the various disguises of this problem have only begun to be identified, and that the complexities of the matter are only beginning to be appreciated. We suggest that these additional phenomena constitute an entity that might be called a 'Masquerade Syndrome', (a term first suggested to us by Professor Mary Ellen Avery).

THE 'MASQUERADE SYNDROME'

(A) A paediatrician serving dependents in a busy military paediatric out-patient clinic was asked to evaluate an eight-year old boy for a 'persistent cold'. His mother was concerned that, although his fever had remitted after the first twenty-four hours, he still had a 'runny nose' ten days later. The paediatrician was struck by how well the child appeared — at that moment there was only a small amount of watery nasal discharge — but after an appropriate examination, he reassured the mother along the lines of her concerns — no evidence of 'strep throat' or other dire disease.

(B) A twelve-year old girl was admitted to a large referral children's hospital to evaluate hypersomnia. The number of hours she slept had increased in recent months to about twenty hours per day. An occult brain lesion was suspected, even though initial diagnostic studies were negative or normal. Psychiatric consultation was requested to evaluate the possibility of 'psychiatric overlay', after all tests were negative.

(C) A ten-year old girl was admitted for evaluation of severe abdominal pain, accompanied at times by diffuse abdominal tenderness. The pain could occur at any time, and was incapacitating while it lasted. Diagnostic studies were unrevealing, and psychiatric consultation was requested to determine if her pain might be related to stress.

Other examples of the phenomenon to be described included a child recovering from a case of infectious mononucleosis that had possibly been complicated by mild meningoencephalitis; a child admitted with a two-week history of fever, the latest of several episodes of fever of undetermined etiology; and a child admitted for evaluation of headaches so severe as to awaken her at night.

The common thread that linked this diverse group of children was that they had all missed days, weeks, or in some instances, months of school, altogether out of proportion to that required for their medical needs. Yet in no case was the diagnostic significance of this fact initially appreciated, and in some, the history of school absence was not even obtained. It seemed that once a sick role had been legitimatized, the possibility of the dimension of school phobia was not even entertained, despite its key role in the persistence of symptoms. These children exemplified a variant of school phobia it is convenient to designate a 'Masquerade Syndrome', children whose medical problems masquerade their difficulty in leaving home to go to school. To detect this syndrome, the paediatrician must ask the parent specifically how much school the child's medical symptoms have caused him to miss, and examine the relationship between school absence and the illness.

In the first case cited, as the child and his mother were about to leave, it belatedly occurred to the doctor that it was 10.15 in the morning — was it fair to assume that the child was simply missing school that day in order to see a physician? Subsequent inquiry revealed that the child had been out of school for the entire ten days; no effort had been made for medical help until the day of the clinic visit. Mother noted that her child's illness had been especially difficult for her 'inasmuch as her husband had just gone away for combat duty'. After a brief conversation about how hard it is when one parent is left alone, the importance of the child's prompt return to school was stressed, and provision was made for another outpatient paediatric visit — *after* school hours — if the 'runny nose' persisted.

The crucial respect in which such children differ from those more commonly described as having school refusal is that the physician is not presented with an *identified* problem in school attendance. Rather, the following sequence of events occurs: Parents request that a paediatrician evaluate and treat their child's medical illness. The paediatrician proceeds to do this, bringing to bear the best methods available to diagnose the illness. If a psychological component is suspected, a consulting psychiatrist may be asked to evaluate the signs and symptoms. The matter of school attendance escapes surveillance, because whatever decisions the child and his parents have made about going to school are seen by the child and his parents as totally appropriate to the child's illness. The child is not refusing school — he is seen as 'too sick to go'. The paediatrician does not initiate enquiry into school attendance, because the medical problems preempt centre stage, and behavioural aspects recede into the background.

A child with a persistent problem of intermittent abdominal pain was evaluated and treated symptomatically as an out-patient over a period of three months. Psychiatric consultation was sought only when a passing remark by the mother led to the discovery that the child had been out of school for the entire three months.

It is tempting to dismiss such an episode as merely an example of 'poor paediatric practice'. However, to do so misses the essential point: the extent to which the parent unwittingly *misleads* the physician in this situation. For example, one mother, when specifically asked whether her child's illness had interfered much with school, replied 'Oh no — he loves school and has maintained a straight A average despite being sick'. She neglected to say that all of his recent instruction had been at home with a tutor!

It is separation that is anxiety-producing for these parents and children, not the fact that the child's attendance at school has been interrupted or curtailed. The positive developmental consequences of the child's leaving home and going to school are ignored in favour of exclusive focus on academic aspects — 'keeping up with school work'. Regret may be expressed that the child's illness has prevented him from going to school, but this is not seen as a serious problem by either parent or child. Indeed, when a parent brings a child for medical evaluation, if both parent and child appear upset about the amount of school being missed, one can be confident that that child does not have the 'Masquerade Syndrome'.

In an important article published in *Paediatrics* (1971), and subsequently reviewed in the *Year Book of Paediatrics* (Gellis, 1973), Schmitt began the delineation of this syndrome, yet the impact upon the intended paediatric audience has been far from optimal. In our recent experience, the diagnosis was overlooked at least nine times in a four-month period, amidst extensive in-patient and out-patient evaluations. The major obstacle preventing paediatricians from incorporating this information into their work appears to be the failure of psychiatrists and behavioural paediatricians to place sufficient emphasis on the medical manifestations of the 'Masquerade Syndrome'.

When the possibility of a significant school phobia dimension was called to the attention of paediatricians in these cases, they frequently protested, on grounds that the child's symptoms were 'real', since in some instances specific illnesses had been documented. The Cartesian mind–body dichotomy continues to plague medical practice (Eisenberg, 1976). The identification of organic pathology is taken as sufficient explanation of the ill behaviour. In other cases, there was a persistent fear, despite the fact that tests had so far ruled out serious illness, that 'something was being missed'.

Comments like these suggest the notion that when medical symptoms accompany school phobia, the symptoms themselves are less worthy of careful evaluation and follow-up; the child does not have a 'real' illness. Re-consideration of some of the cases alluded to will clarify this problem.

The small amount of watery nasal discharge present in the child in the first case was quite real, as was the upper respiratory infection from which he was recovering.

The child whose abdominal pain appeared to be related to stress had no less 'real' pain than if it were from an ulcer; indeed, both ulcer disease (Millar, 1965) and colitis (Sperling, 1950) have been reported in children with school phobia; there is no reason to assume that a problem in school attendance will 'protect' a child from concurrent 'organic' disease.

The child sleeping twenty hours a day had a very worrisome symptom, despite negative tests. No physician at that moment could in good conscience give the parents an unequivocal 'clean bill of health' for their child.

How, then, is the physician to diagnose and manage the underlying school phobia in the 'Masquerade Syndrome', in a manner that properly addresses the medical aspects? The physician must consider objectively and separately the appropriate evaluation and follow-up for the child's medical problems and for the problems with school attendance. In the cases described, the families had been unable to do this. The first child had undoubtedly been well enough to return to school a number of days earlier. His mother's concern that he might have a 'strep throat' is appropriate perhaps, but not her delay in seeking medical clarification of the issue. The child with hypersomnia might have had an occult brain tumour, but further absence from school after all studies were negative would not lead to earlier diagnosis, nor does school absence constitute 'treatment' for cancer — diagnosed or undiagnosed. On the other hand, it was necessary to stress to parents, children, and physicians that return to school would in no way diminish the carefulness of medical follow-up; the latter would simply be arranged so as not to interfere with the former.

When it was first proposed to the paediatrician that the child with hypersomnia return to school, he asked, 'What if she has a brain tumour?' The uncertainty was apparently making it as difficult for the paediatrician to 'let the child go' as it was for the parent. Once an appropriate medical out-patient plan was formulated, he could see that there was no medical indication for further school absence.

The paediatricians in these cases were generally sceptical that the issue of school attendance had any real significance. After all, all of the children were in some sense sick, and all professed to enjoy school — how then could one diagnose any form of 'school refusal'? It was fascinating to watch the more typical and recognizable features of the school refusal syndrome, namely separation anxiety, begin to emerge *once an appropriate medical plan was formulated and return to school was advised.* Plans for school return are invariably resisted. Mother and child maintain that the physical symptom makes it impossible for the child to attend. Or they predict it is certain to recur at school, making it necessary for the child to return home. Or it is suggested that since the child has missed so much school already, a further period at home would be useful to help the child 'catch-up', perhaps with the assistance of a home tutor.

Results of tests, and plans for out-patient follow-up, were presented to the child who had been admitted for evaluation of severe abdominal pain, and to her parents. When prompt return to school was addressed, both mother and child seemed shocked. The father, a busy professional whose work had permitted him little time at home in recent months, thought return to school was quite appropriate, and was amazed at the interchange that ensued between mother and child. The mother asked her daughter 'Do you think you will be able to go back to school Monday?' The daughter smiled and said 'No, I'm sure my stomach will be hurting'. Mother then turned to the paediatrician and said, 'See? She can't go.'

Unfortunately, it was not possible to follow all of these cases systematically. For those children on whom follow-up data were available, an interesting pattern began to emerge. The plan for return to school took into account the physical symptom, but in a way that kept the child in the school building for the duration of the school day. For example, the child with abdominal pain was allowed to leave the classroom and rest in the nurse's office until she 'felt better'. A similar plan was arranged for the child with hypersomnia. The boy recovering from mononucleosis was temporarily excused from physical education. These children (and others) initially had to spend time out of the classroom; but they did not return home. They were gradually able to engage in all of the activities of a normal school day.

The child with hypersomnia slept a little less each day, once she returned to school. Two years later, in response to our inquiry about outcome, her mother reported that although her daughter had been initially very 'sluggish' and difficult to return to school, nevertheless they had followed the paediatrician's orders, and the results had been dramatic. Gradually over a period of several months, she had returned to her full range of normal activity, and she has had no hypersomnia since. In retrospect, her mother believed that several antecedent viral illnesses, and her doctor's instructions to 'let her daughter rest' as much as she wanted to in order to recuperate, had contributed to her daughter's state at the time of admission. Her daughter's subsequent return to school, rather than continuing with the home tutor that had been advised, seemed to have had a remarkably beneficial effect, and occasional viral illnesses in the intervening two years had not resulted in any significant interruption to her daughter's activities.

THE 'MASQUERADE SYNDROME' AND CHRONIC ILLNESS

The 'Masquerade Syndrome' will be recognized only if the paediatrician and/or consulting psychiatrist recognize the potential significance of, and evaluate properly, the matter of school attendance for *every* ill school-aged child. This applies as well to the child who is already known to have a specific chronic illness. Interest in this subject has increased recently, but an interesting study by Wallace and associates (1955) over twenty years ago may be relevant. In a paper titled *The Homebound Child*, these authors reported that the two major groups of handicapped children in New York City receiving home instruction from teachers provided by the New York City Board of Education were 800 children with a primary diagnosis of an orthopaedic handicap and 300 children with a primary diagnosis of rheumatic fever or heart disease. The authors evaluated the seventy-four children who comprised practically all of the orthopaedic homebound school-aged children in the borough of Manhattan. Only one child was under no medical care. 'The most outstanding observation . . . was the recommendation that one-half of the homebound children were considered by the evaluation team as physically capable of returning to school immediately'. In their discussion, the authors limit themselves to the inadequacy of out-patient follow-up for these children, but one is tempted to speculate that mother–child separation and dependency issues may have played a contributing role. Several months later, only about half of the children recommended for return to school were attending.

When the illness is life-threatening, special problems are created. In defining a 'Vulnerable Child Syndrome', among children who were expected to die but recovered, Green and Solnit (1964) listed as presenting symptoms: (1) difficulty with separation including school phobia; (2) infantilization; (3) bodily overconcerns; and (4) school underachievement. The child who actually has a chronic, life-threatening illness appears to be at greatest risk for developing what we suggest calling the 'Masquerade Syndrome'. Lansky and associates (1975) looked for school phobia in children with malignant neoplasms by direct questioning of the parents and child on each clinic visit. The incidence was high, representing at least 10% of the total number of children with malignant neoplasms under their care. Typical for the 'Masquerade Syndrome' was the fact that the problematic school attendance was not an 'identified problem'. In fact, parents often responded to enquiries about school attendance with evasive answers or even hostility.

'Mothers of children with a neoplasm tend to 'give up' after a few early-morning scenes. They express it as follows: "Why should I go through this hassle every day? It upsets the child and me and furthermore, this child is not going to benefit from an education, so why bother!" '

Also typical of the 'Masquerade Syndrome' is the way in which the medical symptoms of these children posed an especially difficult problem. Vague physical complaints were the presenting features of these children's school phobia dimension, but in a child with leukemia one must always consider the possibility that the symptom is part of the malignancy. Nevertheless, the authors were usually able to tell whether a child was really 'too sick to go to school', once the clues to school phobia and separation anxiety were watched for.

Our own experience with chronic, life-threatening illness and the 'Masquerade Syndrome' has centred on children with cystic fibrosis. In some ways this is a problem even more perplexing than the situation in leukemia. States of remission and relapse, of relative health *vs.* illness are poorly defined in cystic fibrosis, especially as the pulmonary disease progresses. Imperceptibly, the child slips into a pattern of school absence; ostensibly because of being 'too sick to go', and neither child nor parent protest the interruption to this normally important routine, by immediately contacting the physician, pressing for a way to allow the child to continue in school, etc. In the case of cystic fibrosis, the question of just how much school attendance a child *is* capable of may be difficult to answer, especially in the late stages.

A more fundamental question arises as well. We would agree in general with the principle espoused by Lansky and associates (1975), that:

'when the child withdraws from school, he misses one of the most important opportunities for socialization and independence . . . It is important . . . to maintain a normal life style, including school attendance, in order to prevent emotional deterioration'.

But what of the child whose illness, as in the case of end-stage cystic fibrosis, produces a sense of isolation from peers (Boyle *et al.*, 1976) whether he goes to school or not, the child for whom education for the future no longer has real meaning, the child who in this context, with his parents' approval, elects to spend the final months at home?

A 12-year old girl with end-stage cystic fibrosis stopped attending school with her mother's approval and without notifying the clinic physician who followed her. Although she and her mother believed that she had now reached the point of being 'too sick to go', it was clear during a subsequent hospitalization that much of the time she had recently spent sitting at home could have been spent sitting in school. Mother and daughter developed an intense relationship that by its nature excluded almost everyone else. Much of their time was spent writing poetry together, including the following poem that mother shared with the hospital staff when her daughter died a few months later:

'Dear Lord we thank you for the times we had together. For the joy and tears, the hard times and the good. And most of all, Dear Lord, we thank you for holding our hand and leading us to peace.'

The mother said that her daughter had called this her 'lean against' poem, and that it had made both her and her daughter feel very safe and comforted.

The negative aspects of such a 'housebound dyad' have been described, including the feelings of mutual hostility that such a relationship may engender (Lansky *et al.*, 1975). Indeed the mother in the case above spoke of the sense of relief she felt when her child finally died. We can only speculate whether her daughter at times experienced similar resentment over what under ordinary circumstances would certainly be considered a pathological degree of intrusion on the part of mother and child into each other's life. But these are no ordinary circumstances, and it would appear prudent to evaluate each case carefully and individually rather than assuming that one course of behaviour or another, related to school attendance or anything else, is necessarily best. To paraphrase Futterman (1970), when the threat of the ultimate separation, death, is real rather than fantasied, separation anxiety may be seen as normal rather than pathological, and regression may have an adaptive value, bringing partial relief at moments of severe distress.

Levy's study of 'maternal overprotection', (1943) is relevant to this discussion. A majority of the twenty cases he described of the 'pure phenomenon' of maternal overprotection showed evidence of mother–child separation problems related to school, though not necessarily outright school refusal. One mother stood out among other parents by the way she escorted her child to school every morning, personally escorted him home, and gave specific instructions to school officials as to what he should eat for lunch. Another mother moved to a particular house so that she could watch her child from her window while he walked to school. One mother went to the school frequently to protect her child against supposed discrimination. Finally, there was a mother who delayed her child's schooling until he was 7 because she did not like him to leave her. At an older age, when he was sent to camp, mother visited him on the second day, found that 'his feet were wet', and took him home.

Levy noted that in eight of the 20 cases, the child had received prolonged nursing care because of illness. Indeed the incidence of illnesses in the 'overprotected group' was 3.1 per child, versus 1.4 in a control group. The possibility was considered that the overprotective mothers were giving more complete and accurate histories of illness. Nevertheless, it appeared that for many of these children, illness had resulted in an intensification of normal maternal protectiveness and mother-child closeness. Levy's assumption was that 'given a high or even an average maternal woman, a number of experiences may reinforce maternal behavior, without assuming that the explanation must necessarily and primarily be a psychoneurosis'. One additional interesting consequence of this behaviour was an apparently significantly lower rate of accidents among the 'overprotected' children as compared to controls.

In a study of the 'ordinary child adjusting to primary school', Moore (1966) found that some degree of reluctance to go to school was the rule rather than the exception at 6 years of age, decreasing at 7, rising to a secondary peak at 8, then dwindling steadily to 11. A negative attitude to school was shown consistently by more boys than girls at every age. This study, and the one referred to above, raise a number of questions: What constitutes the 'norm' in terms of mother–child attachment, dependency, and school attendance when the child has a lethal illness? Should we expect a change over time in the direction of increasing separation anxiety or increasing psychological growth towards independence and maturity as the threat of death looms larger and larger? And are the 'norms' to be accepted, or should we be directing our efforts toward changing them?

THE 'MASQUERADE SYNDROME' AND FACTITIOUS ILLNESS

There is one additional phenomenon that merits mention, though it is undoubtedly rare; namely, reports of the paediatric equivalent of 'Munchausen's Syndrome' in children whose illness is the result of factitious 'disease' produced by parents or children.

Sneed and Bell (1976) describe a 10-year old boy with a history of intermittent, colic-like pains in the right abdomen for the previous 24 hours and passage of red blood in the urine the previous night. Urinalysis showed moderate occult blood. His mother had a history of passing a 'dark kidney stone' 14 years previously. When the child reported passing 'black specks' in his urine, one of them was identified as the leg of a small insect. He and his mother were encouraged to collect any passed stones. One day mother reported that the child had had fever and colicky abdominal pain the previous night and had passed a stone from his penis. She had been able to feel the stone in the ventral surface of his penis prior to its passage into their gauze urine screen. Representative stones were analysed and found to be water-worn pebbles, of quartz and iron oxide, small enough to have been inserted into the urethra. It was learned that the child had been outdoors immediately prior to passage of these stones.

The intriguing aspect of this case for the study of school refusal is that the incident with factitious renal stones was preceded by threats from the school authorities to take legal action if this child's attendance record did not change. The child's teacher stated that the patient did satisfactory work, but due to extremely poor attendance, he was far behind his age group in all subjects. When the principal called his mother, and warned of legal action based on compulsory school attendance laws, the mother thought the school was placing the child under undue and unreasonable pressure to perform, and was quite angry at the school personnel, even though he had missed 44 out of 89 school days during the school term. It was in this context that the passage of bloody urine was reported. Personality evaluation of the child revealed 'almost complete dependence upon others, particularly his mother, to take care of his needs', along with difficulty in interpersonal relationships.

This case constitutes a form of the 'Masquerade Syndrome' in which the medical 'illness' masking the problem in school attendance was factitiously produced. The mother continued to deny knowledge of the origin of her child's 'stones' after the facts were made known to her, suggesting to the authors of this report that there was some collusion, either active or passive, on her part; an observation not surprising in view of the mutual involvement of parents and children in separation difficulties. Issues of over-dependence and over-protection may play a role in cases like those described by Meadow (1977), in which the parents, who seemed intensely involved with their children during hospitalization, were found to have caused the 'illnesses' that made hospitalization necessary — 'Munchausen Syndrome by Proxy'.

Cases of the Masquerade Syndrome and factitious illness form a striking contrast to those in which the medical component includes a chronic, life-threatening disease. In the latter situation, separation anxiety and school refusal may sometimes be a normal mother–child response to the circumstances of the disease, whereas in the former, dependency needs may be so pathological that illness has to be 'produced' in order to avoid separation. Some of the mothers described in the 'Vulnerable Child Syndrome' (Green and Solnit, 1964) seemed to have a 'psychologic need to find something physically wrong with the patient'. Apparently a mother and/or child may in some instances make this need a reality, one consequence being an interruption in school attendance 'because the child is too sick to go'.

MANAGEMENT

Three dimensions are important in the understanding of the child who is having difficulty leaving home and going to school: the actual behaviour of school attendance or absence; the developmental issue of separation and progression toward maturity *versus* regression and dependence; and a biological or constitutional dimension. The management of inappropriate homebound school absence is best discussed in relation to each of these three important dimensions.

1. School attendance behaviour

It has been repeatedly stressed in the past, but bears re-emphasis, that bringing about school attendance as quickly as possible is the cornerstone of effective treatment. The presence of the child within the school building is almost invariably therapeutic and growth-producing; every minute spent inappropriately at home is quite the opposite. So-called school phobia appears to be like other phobias in the respect that this behavioural aspect of treatment is crucial; it is followed by decreasing anxiety, as the new behaviour is maintained. Steps in arranging a rapid return to school have been outlined (Eisenberg, 1959, and Lassers *et al.*, 1973); school officials need to be involved in planning. Provisions should be made for managing problems that arise at school in a way other than having the child leave school early and returning home. It is particularly important, especially at the beginning, that the child actually remain *at school* for the entire school day, whatever special arrangements have to be made at the school for the child to be excused from some particular learning or recreational activity temporarily, during the school day.

2. Psychological developmental issues

Experience has shown that certain specific, identifiable factors contribute to mother–child separation difficulties (Johnson *et al.*, 1941; Klein, 1945; Warren, 1948; Waldfogel *et al.*, 1957; Glaser, 1959; Messer, 1964; Malmquist, 1965; Crumley, 1974; and Waldron *et al.*, 1975). If the role that one or more of these factors is playing in a particular case can be ascertained, it may be possible to find an alternative way for mother and child to deal with the feelings involved, rather than through inappropriate home-bound school absence. For the convenience of the reader, we have listed these factors, grouped somewhat arbitrarily as factors relating primarily to the child, to the mother and father, and to the school:

(A) Factors relating to the child

1. Normal children often show reluctance to attend school in the early school years.
2. The child may have had a recent illness that caused anxiety.
3. The child may be anxious over the recent birth of a sib, or over a conflict with a sib.
4. The child may be anxious over the illness or death of a parent.
5. The child may be anxious about recent promotion in school, or change to a new school, or both.
6. The child may have been denied the opportunity to master situations on his own, and thereby find it difficult to cope with the challenges of school.

(B) Factors relating to the mother

1. The mother may value especially highly and hence overprotect the child because of previous sterility, previous loss of a child, threatened pregnancy with the child, or previous serious illness in the child.
2. The mother may wish to give the child the caring she feels she missed out on as a child herself, and in such circumstances provides inappropriate 'care'.
3. The mother may have a significant illness herself, increasing her anxiety.
4. The mother may be under stress because of recent family economic difficulties.
5. The mother may feel ignored by a husband who is insufficiently involved with her; the result is that the child becomes more important to her than her husband.
6. The mother may have unresolved separation issues with her own mother, or even her grandmother; issues which she 'repeats' with her child.
7. The mother may, for whatever reason, need the child to gratify in some manner unmet dependency, narcissistic, or sexual needs.
8. The mother may feel very inadequate as a mother.
9. The mother may have hostile feelings toward the child which must be compensated for.

(C) Factors related to the father

1. Any of the factors relating to the mother.
2. The father may be passive and dependent, and unable to provide support for the mother.
3. The father may be reliving his own anxieties as a child.
4. The father may be inadequately involved with his family because of work demands or marital discord.

(D) Factors relating to school

1. An especially strict teacher may be frightening to a child who displaces other fears and anxieties onto the teacher.
2. A pupil who is a 'bully' may intimidate the child.
3. The experience of school may be that of enormous, undue pressure to achieve and succeed, to be 'perfect'.
4. There may be some particular aspect of the school day that is especially upsetting for the child.

5.   Absence from school makes it difficult to go to school; the longer the absence, the more difficult the return.

One should not accept complaints about school at face value in evaluating school phobia. Other children in the same class with a 'strict teacher' do not respond with school avoidance, and attempts to deal with the problem in school attendance merely by altering the school environment are notoriously unsuccessful. The final common path by which school factors, like other contributing factors, interfere with school attendance is *via* increased mother-child dependency and separation anxiety. Nevertheless as a means of supporting therapeutic efforts aimed at the separation problem, correction of palpable school problems is appropriate.

3. Biological, constitutional factors

The relationship between medical illness and inappropriate, homebound school absence has been discussed in delineating the 'Masquerade Syndrome'. Being alert to school–attendance difficulty should be part of the paediatric management of every ill school-aged child. If the situation warrants, medical evaluation and follow-up need not be cut short once the child is encouraged to return to school; one aspect of management need not interfere with the other. In cases of perplexing symptomatology and/or known chronic illness, the paediatrician can provide the child, parents, and school officials with the necessary expertise and support in helping to decide on a given morning whether it is appropriate for the child to attend school that day. Evaluation of the situation by telephone and by an office visit if necessary should be available, early enough in the day to permit school attendance for the remainder of that day if it is deemed appropriate. Parents and school officials cannot, and should not be expected to shoulder alone the responsibility for encouraging school attendance when the child does not have a 'clean bill of health'. Once the physician makes his services available in this manner, he may be surprised to find that the parent and child have difficulty making use of them; this highlights the separation issue and sharpens the opportunity to deal with it.

In some instances there may be severe psychiatric factors that bear on school attendance problems. The occasional child whose difficulty attending school is due to incipient or frank psychosis and the threat of ego disintegration obviously needs specific attention to that problem; in such instances, school attendance *per se* offers little by itself, and may be detrimental (Kahn and Nursten, 1962).

The question of endogenous depression in school phobia is currently a controversial issue. Some observers view breakdown in school attendance as a behavioural manifestation of what is fundamentally an affective disorder, which may exhibit familial patterns (Campbell, 1955; Agras, 1959; Hersov, 1960; and Davidson, 1960). Episodes of 'school phobia' correlate with episodes of depression, and both may respond to anti-depressant medication (Gittelman-Klein, and Klein, 1971; Gittelman-Klein and Klein, 1973; and Weinberg *et al.*, 1973). In our experience, the typical child with inappropriate homebound school absence does not appear particularly depressed or distressed so long as the separation from home imposed by school attendance is avoided. But in some cases, specific attention to depression, including the use of anti-depressant medication, may provide a useful adjunct to management.

Even when 'biological' depression is present, a behavioural focus on the separation issue may be effective, as the following case illustrates:

A child with recent infectious mononucleosis was admitted because of weakness and a possibly ataxic gait. All studies were negative except for spinal fluid examination, the results of which were equivocal: there appeared to be a slight increase in mononuclear white cell count, raising the possibility of a subsiding mild meningoencephalitis. Psychiatric consultation was requested because he seemed so depressed. His mental faculties were intact; his recent physical complaints, vague. But he had been out of school for two months, spending his time at home with his mother, 'recovering'. We decided that, despite the diagnostic uncertainties, it was no longer appropriate that he be out of school. His lassitude and depression appeared attributable in part to the sometimes prolonged recuperation phase of mononucleosis, seen also in other viral illnesses. But it was hypothesized that a dependency-related, separation problem between mother and child had supervened during the course of his illness and was now interfering with appropriate school attendance. A plan for immediate school return was devised which allowed for periodic rest periods *at school* in response to initial fatigue. Outpatient paediatric follow-up was arranged as well, until such time as medical findings were either normal or at least clarified.

His mother reported a dramatic improvement in her child's mental and physical state once this plan was implemented. Within a short period, he was able to participate fully at school, and could subsequently be given a 'clean bill of health' by his paediatrician.

OUTCOME AND PREVENTION

It is of interest to look forward and ask what becomes of children with school phobia, and to look backward and ask what preventive measures might have been taken. Rodriguez and associates (1959) evaluated the academic and social adjustment of 41 children with school phobia at a mean (and median) interval of 3 years following their treatment by a programme of prompt return. Of the 27 children younger than 11, 89% were attending school regularly, and most of these children were found to be making an adequate social adjustment as well. Coolidge and associates (1964 and 1976) have reported 10-year and recently, 21-year follow-up studies of 66 children referred for school phobia. The purpose of the 10-year follow-up study was to examine the quality of their adolescence. While 13 of the 49 children were doing well, a second group of 20 children showed definite limitations in developmental maturation, characterized by a 'stifling of achievement' or 'constriction' in one or many important areas of adolescence. The third group of 14 children were 'at a severe impasse in all areas of their lives or had given up realistic attempts to move into psychological adulthood'. Almost half of the children re-evaluated were performing below what would have been expected on the basis of prior performance and elementary school IQ test results, suggesting to the authors that a shift may have occurred from the school-phobic symptom to increased difficulties in learning.

The 21-year follow-up 'continues to emphasize the consequent limitations to a rich, full, and varied life that have ensued for many of the subjects'. Separation difficulties and dependency issues now seem to emerge in the form of difficulty in assertiveness, an overly cautious obsessional approach to life, lack of mobility, and perhaps even a decreased divorce rate compared to the general population, even though this seemed to reflect not marital happiness but the 'lifelong pattern of fear of separation'. The authors acknowledge the limitations of their study resulting from the absence of a control group and the fact that the amount of available data is now considerably less than it was at the time of the first follow-up. Nor was treatment administered according to a research design. Nonetheless, these studies suggest that the fundamental developmental difficulties that underly school phobia behaviour may persist well into adult life if not beyond, though clothed in different behavioural guises at different ages.

The results of these and other studies have led several authors to consider the precursors of school phobia, in the hope that some preventive measures might be taken. It is useful once again to focus the discussion around behavioural, medical, and psychological developmental issues.

In his discussion of the prevention of school phobia, Schmitt (1971) suggests that there are certain enquiries about parent–child behaviour in a paediatric workup that provide clues to the possibility of a future school phobia. Are the parents of a young child finding time to spend with each other, allowing the child to master being with others? Is the child developing self-care skills appropriately? Anticipatory guidance regarding these behaviours may foster appropriate development toward greater independence. Medical illness, especially if serious or chronic, poses a particular threat. The physician must manage the case with a view toward preventing the child from begin seen by parents and others as more 'vulnerable' than he really is. The parent's understandable tendency toward overprotection must be countered by the paediatrician's concern for mastery of normal developmental tasks for child and family insofar as this is possible. In particular, he must enquire about school attendance and evaluate it carefully, if inappropriate school absence is to be avoided.

Lansky and associates (1975), finding the treatment of school phobia to be especially difficult in children with malignant neoplasms, devised a prevention programme involving close co-operation with schools and group sessions for parents. In the 18 months following institution of this programme, there were no new cases of school phobia. The authors found that:

> 'families who cope with the neoplasms by working to maintain a normal life for themselves and their sick child — which certainly includes school attendance — tend to manage better both during the illness — especially the critical periods — and after the child dies. Their grieving period is more clearly defined and they are able to get back into the mainstream of life sooner. The more fortunate children with longer survivals become fairly indistinguishable in a population of average children — certainly a desirable goal.'

The consulting psychiatrist too may have a role to play in the prevention of school phobia, by devoting some attention in every case to the important psychological developmental issues that underly this behaviour. When 'vertical bonds', those running between parents and children, are seen to be overly intense, with a corresponding failure in the child to develop 'horizontal', peer-group bonds (Skynner, 1974), the stage for school phobia is set. Careful attention to these issues, with a watchful eye on the specific behavioural indicator of school attendance, and with active paediatric participation where indicated, may avert school phobia, and help maintain the child on the path to adulthood.

REFERENCES

Agras, S. (1959). The relationship of school phobia to childhood depression. *American Journal of Psychiatry*, **116**, 533–536.

Berg, I., Nichols, K., and Pritchard, C. (1969). School phobia — its classification and relationship to dependency. *Journal of Child Psychology and Psychiatry*, **10**, 123–141.

Boyle, I. R., di Sant'Agnese, P. A., Sack, S., Millican, F., and Kulczycki, L. L. (1976). Emotional adjustment of adolescents and young adults with cystic fibrosis. *Journal of Pediatrics*, **88**, 318–326.

Broadwin, I. T. (1932). A contribution to the study of truancy. *American Journal of Orthopsychiatry*, **2**, 253–259.

Campbell, J. D. (1955). Manic-depressive disease in children. *Journal of the American Medical Association*, **158**, 154–157.

Coolidge, J. C., and Brodie, R. D. (1976). A 21-year follow-up study of 66 school-phobic children. *Unpublished manuscript.*

Coolidge, J. C., Brodie, R. D., and Feeney, B. (1964). A ten-year follow-up study of sixty-six school-phobic children. *American Journal of Orthopsychiatry.* **34**, 675–684.

Crumley, F. E. (1974). A school phobia in a three-generational family conflict. *Journal of the American Academy of Child Psychiatry*, **13**, 536–550.

Davidson, S. (1960). School phobia as a manifestation of family disturbance: its structure and treatment. *Journal of Child Psychology and Psychiatry*, **1**, 270–287.

Eisenberg, L. (1958). School phobia: a study in the communication of anxiety. *American Journal of Psychiatry*, **114**, 712–718.

Eisenberg, L. (1959). The pediatric management of school phobia. *Journal of Pediatrics*, **55**, 758–766.

Eisenberg, L. (1976). Delineation of clinical conditions: conceptual models of 'physical' and 'mental' disorders. In *Research and Medical Practice: their interaction.* Ciba Foundation Symposium 44, Elsevier, New York.

Estes, H. R., Haylett, C. H., and Johnson, A. M. (1956). Separation anxiety. *American Journal of Psychotherapy*, **10**, 682–695.

Futterman, E. H., and Hoffman, I. (1970). Transient school phobia in a leukemic child. *Journal of the American Academy of Child Psychiatry*, **9**, 477–494.

Gellis, S. S. (Ed.) (1973). *The Year Book of Pediatrics*, Yearbook Medical Publishers, Chicago.

Gittelman-Klein, R., and Klein, D. F. (1971). Controlled imipramine treatment of school phobia. *Archives of General Psychiatry*, **25**, 204–207.

Gittelman-Klein, R., and Klein, D. F. (1973). School phobia: diagnostic considerations in the light of imipramine effects. *Journal of Nervous and Mental Diseases*, **156**, 199–215.

Glaser, K. (1959). Problems in school attendance. School phobia and related conditions. *Pediatrics*, **23**, 371–383.

Green, M., and Solnit, A. J. (1964). Reactions to the threatened loss of a child: a vulnerable child syndrome. *Pediatrics*, **34**, 58–66.

Hersov, L. A. (1960). Refusal to go to school. *Journal of Child Psychology and Psychiatry*, **1**, 137–145.

Johnson, A. M., Falstein, E. I., Szurek, S. A., and Svendsen, M. (1941). School phobia. *American Journal of Orthopsychiatry*, **11**, 702–711.

Kahn, J. H., and Nursten, J. P. (1962). School refusal: a comprehensive view of school phobia and other failure of school attendance. *American Journal of Orthopsychiatry*, **32**, 707–718.

Klein, E. (1945). The reluctance to go to school. *Psychoanalytic Study of the Child*, **1**, 263–279.

Lansky, S. B., Lowman, J. T., Vats, T., and Gyulay, J. E. (1975). School phobia in children with malignant neoplasms. *American Journal of Diseases of Children*, **129**, 42–46.

Lassers, E., Nordan, R., and Bladholm, S. (1973). Steps in the return to school of children with school phobia. *American Journal of Psychiatry*, **130**, 265–268.

Levy, D. M. (1943). *Maternal Overprotection.* Columbia University Press, New York.

Malmquist, C. P. (1965). School phobia. A problem in family neurosis. *Journal of the American Academy of Child Psychiatry*, **4**, 293–319.

Meadow, R. (1977). Munchausen syndrome by proxy. The hinterland of child abuse. *Lancet*, **2**, 343–345.

Millar, T. P. (1965). Peptic ulcers in children. *Canadian Psychiatric Association Journal*, **10**, 43–49.

Moore, T. (1966). Difficulties of the ordinary child in adjusting to primary school. *Journal of Child Psychology and Psychiatry*, **7**, 17–38.

Partridge, J. M. (1939). Truancy. *Journal of Mental Science*, **85**, 45–81.

Rodriguez, A., Rodriguez, M., and Eisenberg, L. (1959). The outcome of school phobia: a follow-up study based on 41 cases. *American Journal of Psychiatry*, **116**, 540–544.

Rutter, M. (1975). *Helping Troubled Children*. Penguin Education, Harmondsworth, Middlesex, England.

Schmitt, B. D. (1971). School phobia — the greater imitator: a pediatrician's viewpoint. *Pediatrics*, **48**, 433–441.

Skynner, A. C. R. (1974). School phobia: a reappraisal. *British Journal of Medical Psychology*, **47**, 1–16.

Sneed, R. C., and Bell, R. F. (1976). The Dauphin of Munchausen: factitious passage of renal stones in a child. *Pediatrics*, **58**, 127–130.

Sperling, M. (1950). Mucous colitis associated with phobias. *Psychoanalytical Quarterly*, **19**, 318–326.

Waldfogel, S., Coolidge, J. C., and Hahn, P. B. (1957). The development, meaning and management of school phobia. *American Journal of Orthopsychiatry*, **27**, 754–780.

Waldron, S., Jr., Shrier, D. K., Stone, B., and Tobin, F. (1975). School phobia and other childhood neurosis: a systematic study of the children and their families. *American Journal of Psychiatry*, **132**, 802–808.

Wallace, H. M., Siffert, R. S., Deaver, G., and Pingitore, E. (1955). The homebound child. *Journal of the American Medical Association*, **158**, 158–160.

Warren, W. (1948). Acute neurotic breakdown in children with refusal to go to school. *Archives of Disease in Childhood*, **23**, 266–272.

Weinberg, W. A., Rutman, J., Sullivan, L., Penick, E. C., and Dietz, S. G. (1973). Depression in children referred to an educational diagnostic center: diagnosis and treatment. *Journal of Pediatrics*, **83**, 1065–1072.

Out of School
Edited by L. Hersov and I. Berg
© 1980, John Wiley & Sons, Ltd.

Chapter 12

School Refusal in Early Adolescence

Ian Berg

INTRODUCTION

This contribution is based on a series of studies carried out by the writer and his colleagues on a group of school phobic youngsters admitted to a psychiatric inpatient unit for boys and girls of secondary school age. (The terms 'school refusal' and 'school phobia' are used interchangeably in this chapter). The number of cases included in each investigation varied according to when it was decided to collect the relevant information and at what point it was decided to begin analysing the data.

Diagnostic Criteria

The diagnostic criteria for school refusal were:

1. *Severe difficulty in attending school* usually amounting to prolonged absence.
2. *Severe emotional upset when faced with the prospect of going to school,* including excessive fearfulness, undue tempers, misery, and complaints of feeling ill without an organic cause being found.
3. *Staying at home* with the knowledge of their parents when they should be at school.
4. *Absence of significant anti-social disorders*, such as stealing, lying, wandering, and destructiveness.

It will be appreciated that the group of children selected for study had some distinctive features. These were the characteristics determined by the place where the work was carried out. Thus their ages ranged between 11 and 15 years inclusively. The problem was of some severity since inpatient management was only arranged when outpatient treatment had failed. Limitations on the nature of the sample were also imposed by the diagnostic criteria. The first of them merely limited the group to school attendance

231

problems. By itself it would have led to the inclusion of truants, and children kept off school unnecessarily by their wayward parents, as well as school phobics. The second criterion was the most important of the four. It was not possible to distinguish between children who were essentially afraid of some aspect of the school situation and those who were only fearful of leaving mother, as has been recommended (Eysenck and Rachman, 1965; Smith, 1970), despite attempts to do so. The failure of this attempt to subdivide school phobia on the basis of distinguishing groups of children who either fear school or are anxious about separating from mother is in keeping with the views of Bowlby (1975). He notes that children faced with an external threat tend to cling to their mothers and children who are unduly attached to their mothers are consequently more likely to perceive stressful situations as fear provoking. The two tendencies, fear of school or some aspect of the school situation, and worries about leaving mother and home, thus tend to go together rather than occurring separately. Nor was it found to be possible to make a clear distinction between emotional disturbance manifested by fearfulness and emotional upset shown by displays of temper and stubborn refusal to attend school. This is a differentiation which has led to the view that some children are truly school phobic in that they show an irrational fear of school, whilst others are better described as manifesting school refusal since they wilfully resist attempts to get them to go to school (Smith, 1970). However, for want of evidence to the contrary, the alternative view is adopted here that some children with school refusal showed obvious signs of anxiety and fearfulness whereas others manifested a similar degree of emotional upset in resisting any attempts to force them into attending school. The third criterion usually applied throughout the duration of the school phobic problem. However, in one or two instances, the youngster came home after seeming to go to school, whilst the parents were out at work. Nevertheless, even when their parents found out about their absence, they continued to stay away from school. In applying this criterion it was necessary to make a judgement about parental collusion. Parents had to have made reasonable efforts either to get the child back to school themselves or to have obtained help from others to do so. The fourth criterion helped to eliminate truants, who often show antisocial behaviour (Tennent, 1970).

Features of the Series

The first hundred cases admitted consisted of 53 boys and 47 girls. Their mean age was 13.0 years (SD = 1.5). Thirty-four were attending grammar schools, which was not an undue proportion. The social class frequencies (Registrar-General, 1960) were I = 4, II = 17, III = 51, IV = 15, and V = 13, which were also not markedly deviant from the general population distribution. Sixty-seven were called 'acute' since they had had at least three years of previous trouble-free attendance at school. The 33 who had not, were classified as 'chronic' (Berg, Nichols and Pritchard, 1969); they presumably came from the 5% of children in the general population who are chronically reluctant to attend school (Mitchell and Shepherd, 1967; Moore, 1966). Clinically, this group of school phobics appeared similar to other British series such as those of Morgan (1959), Hersov (1960b), and Smith (1970). In about a third ($n = 42$), the problem arose around the time of transfer from primary to secondary school at 11 years of age. Most of the youngsters had neurotic problems other than school phobia and showed a variety of obsessional, anxiety, depressive, hysterical, and hypochondriacal symptoms. Anorexia and suicide attempts were occasionally associated. A small number of cases who turned out to have a psychosis were excluded from the series. Some youngsters had persisting difficulties travelling, fears of crowds and anxiety attacks away from home, like adult agoraphobics. Some responded to the threat of being forced to go to school, more by anger and resistiveness than frank fearfulness. Most of them ($n = 80$) had completely refused to go to school, and the others had only continued to attend with great reluctance. Whether or not a youngster stayed away from school completely seemed to depend, in many instances, on the attitudes of schools, medical agencies or parents. In about a fifth of them, complete failure to attend had been finally induced because parents, teachers, or doctors had considered the child too upset emotionally to go to school or because hospital admission had been suggested. Somatic complaints, particularly abdominal pain, were prominent in about half of the cases.

School phobia in childhood and adolescence

School refusal affecting young adolescents may be considered as a problem somewhat distinct from that occurring in younger children in view of differences in possible causative factors, clinical features, response to treatment and outcome. With regard to causation, school phobia was first described as a condition characterized by fear of leaving mother, that is *separation anxiety* (Johnson, Falstein, Szureck, and Svendsen, 1941). This view of the nature of school phobia is less plausible when the problem occurs in early adolescence, as it seems to more often in Britain (Kahn, 1958; Morgan, 1959; Hersov, 1960a and b) than in North America (Eisenberg, 1958). Separation anxiety has been attributed to a state of excessive emotional dependency of the child on mother (Johnson, Falstein, Szureck, and Svendsen, 1941). Presumably dependency on mother declines with age. It is thus difficult to see how the undue dependency with separation anxiety hypothesis could predict a peak incidence of school phobia about age eleven, which appears to be the usual state of affairs (Leventhal and Sills, 1964; Hersov Berg, 1960b, 1970). Maternal attitudes of overprotectiveness, overindulgence, excessive affection and submissiveness to the child which are said to occur in school phobia (Kahn and Nursten, 1962), and which support the idea of undue dependency of the child on mother, have not always been found to exist in the mothers of school phobic children over the age of ten (Morgan, 1959; Hersov, 1960b). Other causative factors must be looked for in school phobic teenagers. The clinical features of school phobia also appear to vary with age and are said to be more severe in adolescence (Eisenberg, 1958). Young children usually show school refusal of acute onset not interfering with general adjustment. Older children, on the other hand, tend to develop a fear of school which comes on more insidiously as part of a more general personality disorder involving, amongst other problems, difficulties in making friendships (Coolidge, Willer, Tessman, and Waldfogel, 1960). Also, unlike the same problem earlier on, it has been found that school refusal in adolescence can represent the beginnings of a psychosis (Markey, 1941; Berg, Hullin, Allsopp, O'Brien, and MacDonald, 1974) or herald a severe phobic state continuing into adult life (Warren, 1960; Berg, Butler, and Hall, 1976). The age of the child also influences the way in which school phobia is treated. The usual method of insisting on return to school, as quickly as possible, as a most important aspect of treatment is much more successful in younger children (Rodriguez, Rodriguez, and Eisenberg, 1959). Older school phobics often require different management techniques. They may need to be admitted to psychiatric inpatient units (Warren, 1948; Hersov, 1960b; Weiss and Cain, 1964; and Barker, 1968) (see Chapter 15). In addition, special educational provisions may be needed when a child cannot cope with the greater demands of secondary schools compared to those of primary education (Coolidge, Willer, Tessman, and Waldfogel, 1960; Capes, Gould, and Townsend, 1971). It is also often necessary for medical, educational, and social agencies, such as school medical services, educational welfare departments, school counsellors, and social services departments, to be more actively involved in the rehabilitation of older school phobic youngsters (Kahn and Nursten, 1968). There are good reasons therefore to look at school refusal in early adolescence as a condition with sufficiently distinctive features to justify special consideration.

Investigations carried out

The group of secondary school phobic children were studied from a variety of points of view. Dependency of child on mother and overprotective attitudes on the part of mother were investigated. Birth order, family size, and maternal psychiatric illness were looked at. Wilfulness in the child and self image were studied. Educational achievement was evaluated. Admission as a method of treatment was examined. The outcome of the condition several years after discharge was assessed and possible links with psychiatric disorders of adult life such as agoraphobia were explored.

DEPENDENCY AND OVERPROTECTION

Clinical descriptions have emphasized the importance of dependency in school refusal. Thus Partridge (1939) described a 'mother-following syndrome' in children with psychoneurotic disorders who were reluctant to go to school. And Johnson, Falstein, Szureck, and Svendsen (1941) who first used the term school phobia claimed that 'a poorly resolved dependency relationship' between child and mother was a central feature of the condition. Excessive attachment of child to mother in cases of reluctance or refusal to go to school was also described by Klein (1945) and Warren (1948). Likewise, Coolidge, Hahn, and Peck (1957) also described marked clinging to mother as a characteristic of school phobia; some cases had shown this all their lives and others developed clinging behaviour after the onset of school refusal. They found that the relationship between child and mother was characterized by companionship rather than by overindulgence. Waldfogel, Coolidge, and Hahn (1957) emphasized the genuineness of the affection between mother and school phobic child, a view which had previously been questioned. They described how the mothers typically subordinated themselves to their children and protected them too much from unpleasant experiences. Similarly, an over-close relationship between child and mother was described by Morgan (1959) as being frequent in school phobia. Kahn (1958) and Nursten (1958) came to the same conclusions. However, Hersov (1960b) found an excessive attachment of this kind in only approximately a third of fifty children who refused to go to school. Coolidge, Willer, Tessman, and Waldfogel (1960) said that an exaggerated dependency on mother, present from an early age, occurred in school phobia at adolescence. Bowlby (1975) did not accept the view of the genuineness of the affection between mother and school phobic child which he referred to as the 'theory of spoiling'. He favoured an alternative hypothesis that over-dependency in school refusal is due to what he called 'anxious attachment'. He believed that this arose as a result of actual experiences of separation from mother or from threats of abandonment. But, little convincing evidence is presented to support this opinion. He did, in fact, admit that one of his main sources of information, a survey of about four hundred preschool children (Sears, Maccoby, and Levin 1957) did not show that a high degree of dependency was related to separation experiences, and even went on to say that one of their findings would support the theory of spoiling. This finding was that a small group of mothers who were excessively demonstrative of affection were more likely to have children rated as quite dependent. To sum up, the clinical literature on school phobia is thus by and large in agreement that most cases, even in early adolescence, manifest an excessive state of dependency in the mother child relationship and that school phobic youngsters differ quantitatively rather than qualitatively from normal in this respect.

Nature of dependency

Dependency has been studied in children from the general population as well as in youngsters attending clinics. This term has been used in these investigations in connection with a child's attachment to, and reliance on, other people. Two sorts of dependency, 'person-orientated' and 'task-orientated' have been described (Bandura and Walters, 1963; Ainsworth, 1969). Attachment between child and mother is shown by physical contact, proximity, affectionate interchanges, and the effects of temporary separations (Berg, 1966; Berg, Stark, and Jameson, 1966; Bowlby, 1966). Reliance on mother is shown by assistance with personal activities such as dressing, washing, or eating and lack of participation in household tasks. Some definitions of dependency include negative attention-seeking behaviour (Bandura and Walters, 1963) but this is probably best excluded because of its associations with aggressiveness and its lack of relationship with other forms of dependency (Sears, Rau, and Alpert, 1966). Cultures vary in the extent to which they encourage independence training and this has been found to influence childhood dependency (Whiting and Child, 1953), but the attitudes and child-rearing practices of mothers have not been shown to influence their children's behaviour in any straightforward way (Sears, Rau, and Alpert, 1966). Age is obviously an important variable affecting dependency. The more passive manifestations, such as staying close to mother, predominate at about two years of age, whereas the more active and verbal forms such as seeking help and reassurance, occur more noticeably at about five years of age (Heathers, 1953). In an assessment of dependency in adolescent boys, physical contact was not asked about at all (Bandura and Walters, 1959). Dependency has been defined (Bandura and Walters, 1963) as behaviour eliciting caring responses in others. It has been studied by direct observations of children in natural (Sears, Rau, and Alpert, 1966) and experimental situations (Heathers, 1953), and by interviews with parents (Sears, Maccoby, and Levin, 1957) and children (Bandura and Walters, 1959). No firm evidence for the existence of a unitary personality trait has emerged (Sears, Rau, and Alpert, 1966). Disturbed dependency behaviour has aroused clinical interest, apart from that concerned with school refusal, among child psychiatrists who are interested in the quality of relationships formed by children suffering from emotional disorders. This applies to the subject of maternal deprivation and its effects on the child (WHO, 1962). It also applies to the emotional disorders occurring in children who are referred to clinics and who always seem to be with their mothers and to have things done for them that they are capable of doing themselves (Levy, 1943).

Measurement of dependency

A self-administered questionnaire was developed by the writer and his colleagues to measure dependency in school children. It is called the self-administered dependency questionnaire (SADQ). This scale was used with mothers of 256 children drawn randomly from the normal school population. The group was stratified according to sex, age, type of school, and social class. The children were aged 8 to 15 inclusively. Although the questionnaire was self-explanatory, some mothers required a little help to complete it properly (Berg, 1974). Using the statistical method of principal components factor analysis (Hope, 1968) it was found that there were four groups of questions which were unrelated and varied independently. One group was concerned with *affection*. Another involved *communication* with mother. The third asked about reliance on mother for household tasks, that is about *assistance* given to the child. The last group was concerned with staying in the house and not *travelling* away from home either in the local neighbourhood or into the nearby town. Thus there were four kinds of dependency which were not significantly intercorrelated. As might be expected, all four sorts of dependency scored more highly in primary than secondary school children. However, neither grammar compared with secondary-modern type of schooling, nor social class, influenced dependency. Boys had higher *assistance* scores than girls. Girls, on the other hand, scored higher on *affection*, *communication*, and (unwillingness to) *travel*. The scale was found to measure dependency reliably.

Dependency in school phobia

Using a preliminary version of the SADQ, which was administered rather than filled in by mothers themselves (Berg, McGuire, and Whelan, 1973), it was found that 42 school phobic secondary school children were more reliant on their mothers, scoring higher on average on *assistance*, than 68 controls from the general population (Berg and McGuire, 1971). Staying home and (not) *travelling* were also more pronounced in school phobics. When the SADQ was used with the mothers of 47 school phobic youngsters, who had also been admitted to hospital, and the results compared with a group of 128 normal controls, it was found that *assistance* scored higher in school phobics of both sexes and (unwillingness to) *travel* was higher in school phobic girls. Fifty eight psychiatrically disordered youngsters, also admitted to the adolescent unit with a variety of neurotic and conduct disorders (Rutter, 1965) were not significantly different from the controls in any of the four sorts of dependency (Berg, 1974). The SADQ was also used with the mothers of 42 conduct disordered boys, 38 boys with other psychiatric problems and 34 controls. The only way in which the antisocial youngsters revealed any abnormality of dependency, was in a low *communication* score (Berg and Sanderson, 1974).

The finding that reliance on mother for material assistance is excessive in secondary school boys and girls, rather than emotional dependency being affected (Maccoby and Masters, 1970), suggests that they are in some way deficient in forms of behaviour and would enable them to cope more successfully in the secondary school situation (Murphy, 1962). Difficulties travelling probably reflect emotional problems in coping with situations outside the home, where mother and other members of the family are not there to help. Clinical impressions suggest that excessive reliance on mother and difficulties travelling from home may affect school phobic youngsters long before the onset of the clinical conditions. The staying home excessively becomes more pronounced with the onset of school phobia. This is possibly analogous to the way in which agoraphobic symptoms affecting adults may be made worse or appear for the first time in the course of an affective illness (Schapira, Kerr, and Roth, 1970).

Measurement of overprotection

The SADQ is filled in by mothers in two different ways. They are first of all asked to complete the questionnaire, for what was actually the existing situation in the recent past. When all the questions have been answered in this manner, they are requested to answer them once more from the point of view of what they would like to have been the case. The first set of responses produce the *actual* scores. The second set of answers produce the *preference* scores. Using these preference scores and comparing them to the actual scores it is possible to get a measure of overprotection, that is the extent to which mothers prefer their children to be more dependent than would normally be expected. When 38 secondary school phobic youngsters were examined from this point of view, it was found that their mothers in fact did tend to be over protective. *Preference* scores for *affection* and *communication* were higher in school phobics than controls (Berg and McGuire, 1974). This confirmed the view that mothers of school phobic youngsters do encourage *affection* and *communication* to an excessive extent. Although mean *preference* scores for *assistance* and lack of independence *travelling* were not raised, the fact that they were not lower than the *actual* scores, on average, suggests that the mothers of school phobics tended to condone excessive levels of actual dependency in these respects. Three levels of actual scores were looked at separately and the results were the same for all three. As in the case of the *actual* scores, non-school-phobic cases tended to come somewhere between school phobics and normal controls as far as their preference scores were concerned. Within the group of normal controls, mothers preferred their children to be more affectionate and communicative, whereas they preferred their youngsters to be less reliant and more independent with regard to travelling.

FAMILY FACTORS

Birth Order

A study of 63 school phobic youngsters (Smith, 1970), a group comparable to that reported here, showed an excess of youngest children. An excess of youngest members of a sibship was also found in a group of boys, who disliked school, taken from a random sample of 6,000 children of school age from the general population in Britain (Mitchell and Shepherd, 1967). Slater's index is an elegant way of expressing birth order. It is $(m-1)/(n-1)$, where m is the ordinal position in the sibship and n is the family size (Slater, 1962). The value of this index ranges between 0 and 1. The mean in a group of individuals should tend towards 0.5. Slater's index was used to investigate birth order in 100 school phobic youngsters, 91 non-school-phobic neurotic and 127 secondary school controls from the general population (Berg, Butler, and McGuire, 1972). The mean index of the school phobic group was 0.59 which indicated a significant tendency for them to come late in birth order. This was found to apply only to sibship sizes greater than two. In contrast to these findings, a previous study of boys with severe antisocial problems, a group quite different from school phobic youngsters (Berg, Fearnly, Paterson, Pollock, and Vallance, 1967), showed an excess of individuals coming early in birth order. The mean age of mothers of the school phobic group was higher than that of the general population. It could be that the child's position in the family and the mother's age were partly responsible for the excessive dependency and overprotection of school phobic children.

Family size

Only children have not been found to occur more frequently in the families of school phobics (Hersov, 1960b; Smith, 1970). This was confirmed by the writer and his colleagues. The proportion of only children was 11% in the 100 secondary school phobics, a similar percentage to that found in normal controls (Berg, Butler, and McGuire, 1972). Family size otherwise was not found to differ between the school phobics (mean = 2.9) and normal controls (mean = 2.6). Conduct disordered youngsters tend to come from somewhat larger families. Hersov 1960a.

Maternal psychiatric illness

Information was obtained by the writer on psychiatric illness affecting mothers of the group of secondary school phobic children by writing to their family physicians (Berg, Butler, and Pritchard, 1974). Maternal psychiatric illness was considered to be an affective disorder when it was characterized by anxiety, depression, and/or phobias. Defining psychiatric illness in terms of attendance at a hospital clinic, the overall incidence in school phobic mothers was 22%. This is a higher prevalence than would be expected in the normal population and is similar to that found previously in a group of disturbed children (Rutter, 1966). The same can be said about the predominance of mentally ill mothers over fathers that was found in the school phobics. However, a similarly high incidence of psychiatric disorder was found in non-school-phobic cases. Half the psychiatrically ill mothers, in both groups of cases, had an affective disorder which is in general agreement with previous investigations that have usually failed to find any association between the type of childhood disorder and the sort of parental illness which may occur (Rutter, 1966). Intactness of home was also investigated. School phobic girls were more likely to have intact homes, not broken by parental divorce, separation or death, than non-school-phobic cases. This finding is in keeping with other similar studies (Hersov, 1960b). Out of 100 school phobic teenagers, 79 were living with both parents and 19 with mother but without father.

SELF-IMAGE AND WILFULNESS

Self-image

It has been suggested that school phobic children have an inflated self-image (Leventhal and Sills, 1964). Self image is a term used for the way an individual perceives himself (Snagg and Combs, 1949). Its measurement presents considerable difficulties (Marshal-Lowe, 1961). The semantic differential technique (Osgood, Svei, and Tannenbaum, 1957) which has been used with children (DiVesta and Dick, 1966) can be employed. The method was used on 25 school phobic and 23 other cases (Nichols and Berg, 1970). The results were in keeping with the school phobic children having a lowered self-image rather than a raised one. This finding runs counter to the Leventhal–Sills hypothesis and is in line with studies of self evaluation in normal children. Thus it has been found that the child from the general population with a high level of self-evaluation rates low on anxiety, low on sensitivity to criticism and low on maternal overprotection (Cooper Smith, 1967).

Wilfulness

School phobic youngsters have sometimes been considered to be unusually wilful and stubborn, especially in the home (Hersov, 1960b). This tendency has been invoked as an explanation of the increased incidence of school phobia in early adolescence (Leventhal and Sills, 1964). It also has been used to distinguish those youngsters possibly better described as school refusal problems than school phobic ones, since they react by anger, defiance, and temper rather than fearfulness when faced with the prospect of going to school (Smith, 1970). The fact that, in the general population, dislike of school is only reflected in actual absence when the secondary school years are reached (Mitchell and Shepherd, 1967) supports the view that assertiveness, which presumably becomes more effective as the child gets older, plays some part in school refusal. An investigation into opposition and resistance to parental wishes shown by school phobic teenagers was carried out (Berg and Collins, 1974) to see if they had more of these characteristics than other emotionally disturbed young people. A rating scale was devised which was administered to mothers. It covered various sorts of oppositional behaviour shown by children. They were asked to indicate how many days in the previous week their child had gone against what they knew to be expected of them. Twelve activities were covered. Forty-three school-phobic and 37 non-school-phobic cases were studied. The results were not in keeping with excessive wilfulness as a feature of school phobia in early adolescence.

EDUCATIONAL FACTORS

There is little evidence that educational difficulties are at all common in school phobia although some youngsters with this condition undoubtedly have problems with school work (Klein, 1945; Green, 1959; Hersov, 1972). However, there are some reports suggesting that such difficulties may not be as uncommon as previously supposed. Thus, Chazan (1962) stated that half the school phobic children in his series not attending grammar schools had serious educational problems. It has, also, often been found to be necessary to arrange for a change of school to a less demanding educational setting in treating school phobic teenagers (Berg, 1970; Capes, Gould, and Townsend, 1971). It is obviously important to investigate educational attainment in school phobia (Eysenck and Rachman, 1965). A hundred school phobic youngsters of secondary school age were compared with 100 non school phobic cases of similar severity of disturbance (Berg, Collins, McGuire, and O'Melia, 1975). The full scale IQ distribution (mean 106, standard deviation 14) of these school phobics was virtually the same as that found in Hersov's (1960b) comparable study of 50 cases and in Chazan's (1962) investigation of 33 school phobic children. The grammar school group (mean full scale IQ 117) were similar to the grammar group of Chazan (mean full scale IQ 121) in the lack of educational problems. The secondary modern school cases (mean full scale IQ 100) were also similar to Chazan's secondary modern cases in so far as half of both series had educational problems as judged by teachers. However, when the school phobics and controls were compared on the Schonell Graded Word Reading Test (GWRT) looking at older and younger children and three levels of IQ separately, the school phobics had higher reading quotients (RQs) on average than other cases, except for younger children of above average intelligence.

Using the statistical technique of multiple regression (Hope, 1968) in predicting RQ from IQ, sex, type of school and the existence of an educational problem as judged by the teacher, it was found that the addition of school phobia as an additional predictor variable did not improve the prediction. This was further evidence that educational achievement was not impaired in school phobics. Further multiple regression estimations using equations derived from other psychiatric cases (Fransella and Gerver, 1966) and children from the general population (Yule, Rutter, Berger, and Thompson, 1974) also failed to show any evidence of educational backwardness in school phobics.

OUTCOME AND RESPONSE TO TREATMENT

Outcome

There have been several follow–up studies of school phobic children. Forty–one school phobic children treated as outpatients were reviewed about three years after first attendance at the clinic. Only about a third of the 14 cases aged 11 or more had been able to go back to school. Younger children had returned much more often. Overall adjustment was found to be best in those successfully resuming normal school attendance. Prompt return to school had been emphasized in treatment (Rodriguez, Rodriguez, and Eisenberg, 1959). In another study, 50 school phobic children were investigated, 42 of whom were aged 10 to 16 years (Hersov, 1960b). Twenty-nine had been admitted to hospital. About two thirds of the group eventually returned to school and 29 who were followed up from 6 to 18 months after discharge were all attending school regularly. A third enquiry described 16 school phobic children, 12 of whom were aged 12 to 16, who were admitted to hospital and reviewed after an unspecified period (Weiss and Cain, 1964). Thirteen were later found to be in regular schooling. Three had both substantial neurotic symptoms and peer group problems, 8 had neurotic symptoms but adequate relationships with other young people and only 2 had no residual problems. In a follow up study of adolescent psychiatric inpatients seen six or more years after discharge, there were 16 school phobic youngsters, 7 boys and 9 girls (Warren, 1960 and 1965). Four were found to be seriously handicapped by phobic states, 3 lived rather limited lives because of minor phobic difficulties, 3 had other kinds of neurotic difficulties and 6 were quite well.

The writer and colleagues successfully followed–up 100 school phobic youngsters on average three years after discharge from hospital (Berg, Butler, and Hall, 1976). A third of them had improved very little. They had persistently severe symptoms of emotional disturbance and continuing social impairment. Another third had improved to a considerable extent. They were found to be suffering from neurotic symptoms rather than being handicapped by social impairment. The last third had improved to such an extent that they were quite better or almost completely free from problems. In about half of all cases, school attendance difficulties had persisted. Later problems going to work were less frequently reported. Clinical state on discharge was a good predictor of outcome, since half of the children did not change in this respect during the period of follow up. High intelligence was correlated with a poor outcome. This finding runs counter to the conclusions reached when educational attainment was investigated since it suggests that less bright children were particularly disturbed whilst they were still at school because of academic pressures. Five girls and a boy had already developed severe agoraphobic symptoms and nine others had received further psychiatric treatment. The investigation thus provided evidence for the view that school phobia in early adolescence is likely to lead to psychiatric problems in later life. The outcome of the group studied was similar to that of affective disorders in adult life, using the term to include all disturbances in which there is a mood change and anxiety or depression are predominant (Kerr, Roth, Schapira, and Gurney, 1972). These disorders include acute conditions in which agoraphobic symptoms may appear for the first time, only to disappear when the illness clears up. They also include more chronic disturbances in which acute affective disorders are superimposed on otherwise persistent symptoms of anxiety and agoraphobia (Kerr, Schapira, Roth, and Garside, 1970). School phobia in early adolescence, severe enough to warrant hospital admission, appears to follow a similar pattern. Some of those affected having relatively circumscribed illnesses which appear to recover completely and others manifesting acute school phobic difficulties superimposed on longstanding neurotic problems and social withdrawal. It has been found that neurotic disorders in early adolescence, other than those associated with school refusal, also tend to persist and cause severe problems of adjustment several years later (Waldron, 1976; Gersten, Langner, Eisenberg, Simcha-Fagan, and MacCarthy, 1976).

Response to treatment

There have been few controlled trials of methods of management in school phobia, especially when the problem occurs in early adolescence. A group of 35 school phobic children of mean age 10.8 years, which must have included a reasonable proportion of young teenagers, was used in a double-blind placebo-controlled study of the drug imipramine (Gittleman-Klein and Klein, 1971). This drug was given in doses ranging from 100 to 200 mg per day over a six week period. Those children receiving it were more likely to return to school and to score higher on ratings of overall improvement. Another controlled trial was carried out on 67 school phobic children, 40 of whom were aged 10 or more (Miller, Barrett, Hampe, and Noble, 1972). Psychotherapy and a behaviour modification technique, reciprocal inhibition, were evaluated using a sophisticated design. Neither method of treatment was found to be any more effective than being left on a waiting list.

In an evaluation of hospital inpatient management of school phobia affecting adolescents (Berg and Fielding, 1978), 32 school phobic youngsters of mean age 13 were randomly allocated to two treatment groups after ensuring that there were equal numbers of boys and girls in each. One group was admitted for three months' treatment and the other for six. It seemed likely that a longer length of inpatient management improved the outcome in girls assessed in terms of attendance, psychiatric symptoms and adjustment. No difference was found as far as the boys were concerned. In hospital the main forms of treatment were supportive psychotherapy, milieu therapy and social skills training.

SCHOOL PHOBIA AND AGORAPHOBIA

A group of nearly 800 women under the age of 60, who were members of a nationwide correspondence club for people who suffer from agoraphobia, completed a questionnaire which included questions about any previous school phobia (Berg, Marks, McGuire, and Lipsedge, 1974). About 60 non-agoraphobic psychiatric outpatients were used as controls. School phobia was assumed to have been present when the following question was answered in the affirmative: 'Did you ever stay away from school for at least two weeks with a great reluctance or fear of going back?' Approximately a fifth, that is 173 out of 786 women answered yes to this question. Most had had school phobia in secondary school ($n = 80$) or in both primary and secondary school ($n = 50$). It seemed to be a valid criterion of school phobia to use since scores on this question correlated with scores on other questions asking about fears of the school situation, worries about leaving parents and staying home a lot. A doctor had been consulted in about a third of cases. When school phobia had been present, the agoraphobic condition came on earlier and more severely. There was a similarly high incidence of previous school phobia in the non-agoraphobic psychiatric cases. School phobia thus appears to be related to adult neurotic illness in general rather than agoraphobia in particular. Tyrer and Tyrer (1974) reported comparable frequencies of previous school phobia in agoraphobic adults and other neurotic cases, which were greater than the frequency of school phobia previously affecting non–psychiatric controls.

The questionnaire sent to the agoraphobic women of the club included items concerned with school phobic difficulties in their children. School phobia was assumed to have been present in a child when the mother answered the following question in the affirmative: 'Has your child ever completely refused to go to school for longer than one or two days since starting Junior School at seven?' (Berg 1976). Five hundred and eighty three of the women had at least one child. Two hundred and ninety nine had at least one child aged 7 to 15.

The overall incidence of school phobia was 7% (boys 5%, girls 9%). From 11 to 15 years the overall incidence of school phobia was 14% (boys 11%, girls 16%), the highest percentage of 19% was at age 12. In sibships of two, the number of school phobic girls exceeded the number of school phobic boys. This finding is in keeping with several other investigations that have shown the daughters of women suffering from neurotic conditions to be more neurotic than the sons (Rutter, 1972). School phobia was associated with other indicators of school phobic difficulties in children of agoraphobic mothers. Women who had a school phobic child were more likely to have had school phobia themselves. Many of the features of agoraphobia occurring in adult life, especially a preference for remaining in familiar surroundings, are also highly characteristic of school phobia when it affects young adolescents (Leader, 1974). In both conditions there are anxiety symptoms more marked away from home, staying in the home a lot, limited social contacts and reluctance to enter situations where performance is required, escape is difficult and movement is confined. Difficulties travelling and going to crowded places occur in both. Personality traits of immaturity and overdependence are also typical of both (Kerr, Roth, Schapira, and Gurney, 1972).

PREVALENCE

School refusal is a relatively uncommon clinical problem forming about 5% of child psychiatric referrals (Kahn and Nursten, 1962; Chazan, 1962; Smith, 1970). It affects boys and girls equally without any definite social class bias (Berg, 1970). In a survey of about 2,200 ten and eleven year old children from the general population 118 psychiatric disorders were identified of which only three had a clinically significant fear of school (Rutter, Tizard, and Whitmore, 1970). The same group of children produced 15 cases of school phobia at age 14 (Rutter, Graham, Chadwick, and Yule, 1976). In a random sample of 6,000 school children from the general population, 5% were said to dislike going to school and this aversion was associated with actually missing school only when the secondary school stage was reached (Mitchell and Shepherd, 1967). In another survey (Miller, Barrett, Hampe, and Noble 1971), fear of school was reported in about one per cent of the general population in contrast to some other fears which occurred in as many as 20%. Despite this, two thirds of 67 phobic children coming to clinics for treatment were suffering from school phobia. In adults, agoraphobic fears were commoner in phobic cases seen at clinics than in individuals selected from the general population (Agras, Sylvester, and Oliveau, 1969). It seems not unlikely from the available literature that the period prevalence rate of school phobia in early adolescence is about one per cent.

CONCLUSIONS

School phobia in early adolescence would thus appear to be a neurotic condition characterized by undue reliance on mother and a tendency to stay home excessively. Affected youngsters tend to be overprotected by their mothers and to be younger members of a family. Like other young people with emotional disorders their mothers are more prone to affective psychiatric disorders than those in the general population. The problem is not explicable in terms of an inflated self-image or excessive wilfulness. There are no significant educational problems to account for school refusal. About a third of cases continue to show neurotic symptoms and difficulties in adjustment to a severe degree several years after onset. Some seem to go on to develop adult agoraphobia and others to get other psychiatric problems in adult life to a greater extent than would otherwise be expected. Hospital admission over a six months period appears to produce better long term results in girls than a stay of half that duration.

REFERENCES

Agras, S., Sylvester, D., and Oliveau, D. (1969). The epidemiology of common fears and phobias. *Comprehensive Psychiatry*, **10**, 151–156.

Ainsworth, M. D. S. (1969). Object relations, dependency, and attachment: a theoretical review of the infant-mother relationship. *Child Development*. **40**, 969–1025.

Bandura, A., and Walters, R. H. (1959). *Adolescent Aggression*. Ronald Press, New York.

Bandura, A., and Walters, R. H. (1963). *Social Learning and Personality of Development*, Holt, Reinhart, and Winston, New York.

Barker, P. (1968). The inpatient treatment of school refusal. *British Journal of Medical Psychology*, **41**, 381–387.

Berg, I. (1966). A note on observations of young children with their mothers in a child psychiatric clinic. *Journal of Child Psychology and Psychiatry*, **7**, 69–73.

Berg, I. (1970). A follow up study of school phobic adolescents admitted to an inpatient unit. *Journal of Child Psychology Psychiatry*, **11**, 37–47.

Berg, I. (1974). A self administered dependency questionnaire (SADQ) for use with the mothers of school children. *British Journal of Psychiatry*, **124**, 1–9.

Berg, I. (1976). School phobia in the children of agoraphobic women. *British Journal of Psychiatry*, **126**.

Berg, I., and Collins, A. (1974). Wilfulness in school phobic adolescents. *British Journal of Psychiatry*, **125**, 468–469.

Berg, I., and Fielding, D. (1978). An evaluation of hospital inpatient treatment in adolescent school phobia. *British Journal of Psychiatry*, **131**, 500–505.

Berg, I., and McGuire, R. (1971). Are school phobic adolescents overdependent? *British Journal of Psychiatry*, **119**, 167–168.

Berg, I., and McGuire, R. (1974). Are mothers of school phobic adolescents overprotective? *British Journal of Psychiatry*, **124**, 10–13.

Berg, I., and Sanderson, H. (1974). Correspondence. *British Journal of Psychiatry*, **124**, 505.

Berg, I., Butler, A., and Hall, G. (1976). The outcome of adolescent school phobia. *British Journal of Psychiatry*, **128**, 80–85.

Berg, I., Butler, A., and McGuire, R. (1972). Birth order and family size of school phobic adolescents. *British Journal of Psychiatry*, **121**, 509–514.

Berg, I., Butler, A., and Pritchard, J. (1974). Psychiatric illness in the mothers of school phobic adolescents. *British Journal of Psychiatry*, **125**.

Berg, I., McGuire, R., and Whelan, E. (1973). The High Lands Dependency Questionnaire (HDQ): an administered version for use with the mothers of school children. *Journal of Child Psychology and Psychiatry*, **14**, 107–111.

Berg, I., Nichols, K., and Pritchard, C. (1969). School Phobia — its classification and relationship to dependency. *Journal of Child Psychology and Psychiatry*, **10**, 123–141.

Berg, I., Stark, G., and Jameson, S. (1966). Measurement of a stranger's influence on the behaviour of young children with their mothers. *Journal of Child Psychology and Psychiatry*, **7**, 243–250.

Berg, I., Collins, T., McGuire, R., and O'Melia, J. (1975). Educational attainment in adolescent school phobia. *British Journal of Psychiatry*, **125**, 435–438.

Berg, I., Marks, I., McGuire, R., and Lipsedge, M. (1974). School phobia and agoraphobia. *Psychological Medicine*, **4**, 428–434.

Berg, I., Fearnley, W., Paterson, M., Pollock, G., and Vallance, R. (1967). Birth order and family size of approved school boys. *British Journal of Psychiatry*, **113**, 793–800.

Berg, I., Hullin, R., Allsopp, M., O'Brien, P., and MacDonald, R. (1974). Bipolar manic-depressive psychosis in early adolescence: a case report *British Journal of Psychiatry*, **125**, 416–417.

Bowlby, J. (1969). *Attachment and Loss. Vol 1 Attachment*, Hogarth, London.

Capes, M., Gould, E., and Townsend, M. (1971). *Stress in Youth*. London.

Chazan, M. (1962). School phobia. *British Journal of Educational Psychology*, **32**, 200–217.

Coolidge, J. C., Hahn, P. B., and Peck, A. L. (1957). School phobia: neurotic crisis or way of life. *American Journal of Orthopsychiatry*, **27**, 296–306.

Coolidge, J. C., Willer, M. L., Tessman, E., and Waldfogel, S. (1960). School phobia in adolescence: a manifestation of severe character disturbance. *American Journal of Orthopsychiatry*, **30**, 599–607.

Coopersmith, S. (1967). *The Antecedents of Self-esteem*, Freeman, London.

DiVesta, F. J., and Dick, W. (1966). Test-retest reliability of children's on the semantic differential. *Educational Psychol. Measurement*, **26**, 605–616.

Eysenck, H. J., and Rachman, S. J. (1965). The application of learning theory to child psychiatry. In Howells, J. (Ed.), *Modern Perspectives in Child Psychiatry*. Edinburgh.

Eisenberg, L. (1958). School phobia: a study in the communication of anxiety. *American Journal of Psychiatry*, **114**, 712–718.

Fransella, F., and Gerver, D. (1966). Multiple regression equations for predicting reading age from chronological age and WISC verbal IQ. *British Journal of Educational Psychology*, **35**, 86–89.

Gersten, J., Langner, T., Eisenberg, J., Simcha-Fagan, O., and MacCarthy, E. D. (1976). Stability and change in types of behavioural disturbance in children and adolescents. *Journal of Abnormal Child Psychology*, **4**, 111–127.

Gittelman-Klein, R., and Klein, D. F. (1971). Controlled imipramine treatment of school phobia. *Archives of General Psychiatry*, **25**, 204–207.

Green, J. L. (1959). Truancy or School Phobia. In *Truancy or School Phobia?* N.A.N.H., London.

Heathers, G. (1953). Emotional dependence and independence in a physical threat situation. *Child Development*, **24**, 169–179.

Hersov, L. A. (1960a). Persistent non-attendance at school. *Journal of Child Psychology and Psychiatry*, 1, 130–136.

Hersov, L. A. (1960b). Refusal to go to school. *Journal of Child Psychology and Psychiatry*, 1, 137–145.

Hersov, L. A. (1972). School refusal. *British Medical Journal*, 3, 102–104.

Hope, L. (1968). *Methods of Multivariate Analysis*. University of London Press, London.

Johnson, A. M., Falstein, E. I., Szureck, S. A., and Svendsen, M. (1941). School Phobia. *American Journal of Orthopsychiatry*, 11, 702–711.

Kahn, J. H. (1958). School refusal — some clinical and cultural aspects. *Medical Officer*, 100, 137.

Kahn, J. H., and Nursten, J. P. (1962). School refusal: a comprehensive view of school phobia and other failures of school attendance. *American Journal of Orthopsychiatry*, 32, 707–718.

Kerr, T. A., Schapira, K., Roth, M., and Garside, R. F. (1970). The relationship between the Maudsley Personality Inventory and the course of affective disorders. *British Journal of Psychiatry*, 116, 11–19.

Kerr, T. A., Roth, M., Schapira, K., and Gurney, C. (1972). The assessment and prediction of outcome in affective disorders. *British Journal of Psychiatry*, 121, 167–174.

Klein, E. (1945). The reluctance to go to school. *Psychoanalytical Study of the Child*, 1, 263–279.

Leader, (1974). Agoraphobia. *British Medical Journal*, 2, 177–178.

Leventhal, T., and Sills, M. (1964). Self-image in school phobia. *American Journal of Orthopsychiatry*, 34, 685–695.

Levy, D. M. (1943). *Maternal Overprotection*. Columbia, New York.

Maccoby, E. E., and Masters, J. C. (1970). Attachment and dependency in *Carmichael's Manual of Child Psychology* (Edited by Mussen, P.) 3rd Edn. Vol. 2, Wiley, London.

Markey, O. B. (1941). Discussion of school phobia. *American Journal of Orthopsychiatry*, 11, 708–711.

Marshal-Lowe, C. (1961). Self concept, factor or artifact. *Psychological Bulletin*, 58, 325–336.

Miller, L. C., Barrett, C. L., Hampe, E., and Noble, H. (1971). Children's deviant behaviour within the general population. *Journal of Consulting and Clinical Psychology*, 37, 16–22.

Mitchell, S., and Shepherd, M. (1967). The child who dislikes going to school. *British Journal of Educational Psychology*, 37, 32–40.

Moore, T. (1966). Difficulties of the ordinary child in adjusting to primary school. *Journal of Child Psychology and Psychiatry*, 7, 17–38.

Morgan, G. A. V. (1959). Children who refuse to go to school. *Medical Officer*, 102, 221–224.

Murphy, L. B. (1962). *The Widening World of Childhood*. Basic Books, New York.

Nichols, K., and Berg, I. (1970). School phobia and self-evaluation. *Journal of Child Psychology and Psychiatry*, 11, 133–141.

Nursten, J. P. (1958). The background to children with school phobia. *Medical Officer*, 100, 340–342.

Osgood, C. E., Svei, G. J., and Tannenbaum, P. H. (1957). *The Measurement of Meaning*. University of Illinois Press, Urbana.

Partridge, J. M. (1939). Truancy. *Journal of Mental Science*, 85, 45–81.

Registrar General (1960). *Classification of Occupations*. H.M.S.O., London.

Rodriguez, A., Rodriguez, M., and Eisenberg, L. (1959). The outcome of school phobia. *American Journal of Psychiatry*, **116**, 540–544.

Rutter, M. (1966). *Children of Sick Parents*. Oxford University Press, London.

Rutter, M. (1972). Relationships between child and adult psychiatric disorders. *Acta Psychiatrica Scandinavica*, **48**, 3–21.

Rutter, M., Tizard, J., and Whitmore, K. (1970). *Education, Health, and Behaviour*. Longman, London.

Rutter, M., Graham, P., Chadwick, O. F. D., and Yule, W. (1976). Adolescent turmoil: fact or fiction. *Journal of child Psychology and Psychiatry*. **17**, 35–56.

Schapira, K., Kerr, T. A., and Roth, M. (1970). Phobias and affective illness. *British Journal of Psychiatry*, **117**, 25–32.

Sears, R. R., Maccoby, E. E., and Levin, H. (1957). *Patterns of Child Rearing*, Harper and Row, New York.

Sears, R. R., Rau, L., and Alpert, R. (1966). *Identification and Child Rearing*, Tavistock, London.

Slater, E. (1962). Birth order and maternal age of homosexuals. *Lancet*, **i**, 69–71.

Smith, S. L. (1970). School refusal with anxiety: a review of sixty-three cases. *Canadian Psychiatric Association Journal*, **15**, 257–264.

Snagg, D., and Combs, A. W. (1949). *Individual Behaviour: A New Frame of Reference for Psychology*, Harper, New York.

Tennent, T. G. (1970). Truancy and stealing. *British Journal of Psychiatry*, **116**, 587–592.

Tyrer, P., and Tyrer, S. (1974). School refusal, truancy, and adult neurotic illness. Psychological Medicine, **4**, 416–421.

Waldfogel, S. J. C., Coolidge, J. C., and Hahn, P. B. (1957). The development, meaning and management of school phobia. *American Journal of Orthopsychiatry*, **27**, 754–776.

Waldron, S. (1976). The significance of childhood neuroses for adult mental health: a follow up study. *American Journal of Psychiatry*, **133**, 532–538.

Warren, W. (1948). Acute neurotic breakdown in children with refusal to go to school. *Archives of Disease in Childhood*, **23**, 266–272.

Warren, W. (1960). Some relationships between the psychiatry of children and of adults. *Journal of Mental Science*, **106**, 815–826.

Warren, W. (1965). A study of adolescent psychiatric inpatients and the outcomes six or more years later. *Journal of Child Psychology and Psychiatry*, **6**, 1–17, 141–160.

Weiss, M., and Cain, B. (1964). The residential treatment of children and adolescents with school phobia. *American Journal of Orthopsychiatry*, **34**, 103–112.

Whiting, J. W. M., and Child, I. L. (1953). *Child Training and Personality*. Yale University Press, New Haven.

World Health Organization (1962). *Deprivation of Maternal Care*. WHO, Geneva.

Yule, W., Rutter, M., Berger, M., and Thompson, J. (1974). Over- and Under-achievement in reading: distribution in the general population. *British Journal of Educational Psychology*, **44**, 1–12.

Out of School
Edited by L. Hersov and I. Berg
© 1980, John Wiley & Sons, Ltd.

Chapter 13

Psychotherapeutic Treatment in School Refusal

Melvin Lewis

DIAGNOSIS

The choice of treatments in school refusal depends in part upon the diagnosis. The criteria for a diagnosis of school phobia according to Berg *et al.* (1969) are: '(1) severe difficulty in attending school often amounting to prolonged absence; (2) severe emotional upset shown by such symptoms as excessive fearfulness, undue tempers, misery, or complaints of feeling ill without obvious organic cause on being faced with the prospect of going to school; (3) staying at home when they should be at school with the knowledge of the parents at some stage in the course of the disorder; (4) absence of significant antisocial disorder, such as stealing, lying, wandering, destructiveness, or sexual misbehaviour.'

The diagnostic evaluation must include an assessment of the relative importance of causes in the family, causes in the child, and causes in the school. In each case the causes have multiple, biopsychosocial components, necessitating a pluralistic approach to treatment.

Approximately one fifth of the parents of all children with school phobia have a history of psychiatric disorder (Berg and Pritchard, 1974). The family may be structured in such a way that mutual, hostile-dependent relationships exist, particularly between parent and child, and most often between mother and son, leading to an acute separation anxiety (Johnson *et al.*, 1941; Coolidge *et al.*, 1957; Waldfogel *et al.*, 1957). Sometimes the child is responding specifically to anxiety transmitted by the mother (Eisenberg, 1958). The child's anxiety about losing the mother may become linked to the school through a conditioned response (Garvey and Hegrenes, 1966). Separation anxiety from other causes (Sperling, 1951; Robinson *et al.*, 1955; Bowlby, 1960) and secondary anticipatory anxiety in the child may be present (Gittelman-Klein and Klein, 1973). Occasionally, transient school refusal may occur from sudden acute separation anxiety associated with impending death (Futterman and Hoffman,

1970). Anxiety leading to school refusal may result from unresolved sexual and aggressive feelings toward either parent (Klein, 1945). The father may contribute to the child's difficulties (Skynner, 1976). School phobia may be associated with schizophrenia (Millman, 1961), depression (Campbell, 1955; Agras, 1959), decompensating obsessive compulsive disorders, or a wide range of family disturbances (Malmquist, 1965). Fear of loss or fear of school failure, whether due to real or imagined perceptual, intellectual, or physical handicaps or fear in the child, may contribute to the refusal to attend school, as may anxiety associated with a threat to the child's inflated self-image (Leventhal and Sills, 1964). Lastly, the fear, real or imagined, of a tyrannical teacher or school bully may add to the child's anxiety (Klein, 1945; Hersov, 1960). The choice of treatment method also depends in part upon the severity of the condition.

MANAGEMENT

Supportive measures

Mild, uncomplicated cases can usually be managed with supportive measures alone. For example, the child with transient whining or reluctance to go to school on Monday mornings or after vacations will usually respond to gentle but firm reassurance (Lewis and Lewis, 1973). Indeed, this may constitute the most common form of school avoidance. Other supportive measures include the use of a friendly peer, relative, or family friend to call for the child to accompany him or her to school, and the active participation of the father in encouraging the child's return to school. Berryman (1959) has extended this list into a series of graduated steps.

Sometimes this approach can be supplemented by a paediatrician who knows the child and family, offering telephone time when the child is about to go to school. The paediatrician can also help by providing supportive paediatric interviews with the parents and child (Cohen and Leonard, 1963). (See Chapter 11)

The school may assist by providing a school social worker to bring the child, or by alerting the teacher to help the child 'plug in' rapidly on arrival with school work or some other classroom duty. Home teaching should be avoided because it encourages secondary gain.

Medication

Mild to moderate cases may be helped to respond to the above regimen through the judicious use of medication. For example, imipramine may be used in the following manner: 25 mg for the first 3 days; 50 mg for the next 4 days; 75 mg daily during the second week; adjusted dosage (100–200 mg daily) for the succeeding 4 weeks to a total of 6 weeks (Gittelman-Klein and Klein, 1973). ECG monitoring is required when the dose of imipramine exceeds 3.5 mg/kg (Saraf et al., 1978). Other medications used include sulpride, 100 mg before breakfast for children aged 10–14 years (Abe, 1975), or maprotiline, starting with 10 mg and increasing cautiously to adult doses of 75–150 mg/day (Kuhn-Gebhardt, 1972). A more comprehensive account of the use of imipramine is described elsewhere (See Chapter 16).

Family therapy and individual psychotherapy

When the condition is more severe or more complicated and these simple methods fail, other interventions are required. Attention must be paid to the family as a whole, since the most common psychopathological interaction usually involves all members of the family, often extending back two or three generations (Crumley, 1974). All members of the family must be evaluated, as a family group and individually (Malmquist, 1965).

Family therapists view the symptom of school refusal as a product of the family system or, more accurately, the symptom of school refusal is seen as one symptom among many that arise when a family functions in a particular manner. Family members other than the child who has the presenting symptom often have symptoms of their own.

In each of the members of the family of a child who refuses to attend school, needs are not met satisfactorily, joint solutions to problems are not achieved, and the family tends to turn inwards rather than to seek outside help. The family consequently becomes dysfunctional, and the child is exhibited or labelled as the pathological member, when in fact the child's behaviour is induced by pathological family patterns of behaviour. Specifically, the families of children who refuse to attend school have dependency needs that are unmet, aggression that is poorly dealt with, and an approach to relief in which each family member continuously seeks gratification but experiences disappointment and anger in relation to other members. Each member seems to have an investment in maintaining this homeostasis, usually for fear of worse consequences if changes occurred. Frequently, there is passivity in the father, hostile-dependency or somatization in the mother, and parallel inter-generational symptoms in the grandparents.

At first sight it might seem that the logical approach would be to see the whole family as a unit, together at one time in one place. Thus one may first try to identify individual needs and how they are expressed and responded to by each family member. One may also try to clarify what is appropriate, and one may suggest better responses.

If the response fails to occur, one must look for the causes of the failure. Sometimes the therapist has not sufficiently perceived the force of unconscious motivations, particularly the role of aggression and anxiety. A next stage, therefore, is for the therapist to respond to what he or she perceives to be the more powerful and basic unconscious messages being sent and received. The therapist infers these unconscious messages from the verbal and nonverbal behaviour, and interprets the unconscious communication to all the family members. The family will use the therapist as a 'member' of the family who is instrumental in changing the communication patterns, expectations, and motives for achieving expression and gratification of growth needs.

The individual member, particularly the child, may still need the opportunity for individual exploration and working through of unconscious fantasies. At this point individual psychotherapy for the child, and possibly one or both parents, is indicated. Combined individual and group therapy has been used, particularly for latency-aged children (Coolidge *et al.*, 1957).

Family therapy may be contraindicated when the process itself appears to intensify the pathological patterns (Malone, 1979). This may occur particularly when there is a severe psychiatric disturbance such as a massive depression or schizophrenia in one or both parents, when there is no motivation to give up entrenched sadomasochistic behaviour, or when pathological dependency or symbiotic ties in an adolescent are fostered rather than diminished by the family therapy process. Family therapy is also contra-indicated when the parents are moving firmly toward divorce and are in an active, hostile phase. Such parents may react with an intensification of their mutual hostility when they are brought together. Lastly, the developmental thrust of older adolescents who are struggling to disengage themselves from their families may be hampered when the family is artificially kept 'together'.

Behaviour therapy

Lastly, the principles and techniques of behaviour therapy have been applied to the treatment of families (Werry, 1979). Ayllon *et al.* (1970), for example, described an 8-year-old girl with severe school refusal who was treated purely on the basis of observed behaviour, using a behavioural approach that included a progressive, positive reinforcement approach to school attendance and removal of any reinforcement for non-attendance, and introducing an aversive consequence for the mother if the child did not attend school (See Chapter 14).

In summary, the available treatment choices now include family therapy (Skynner, 1976), behaviour therapy (Ross, 1972; Garvey and Hegrenes, 1966), medication (Frommer, 1967; Gittelman-Klein and Klein, 1973), psychotherapy (Davidson, 1960), and residential treatment (Hersov, 1974). Hersov (1977) reviewed all treatments and concluded that the outcome is good whatever the treatment. Berg *et al.* (1976) and more recently Baker and Wills (1978) reported good or fair outcome in the majority of cases.

The following cases illustrate the selective use of some of the multiple approaches just outlined.

CASE NO. 1. KENNETH B.

Kenneth B., six years of age, was referred to the paediatric clinic by his harassed, thin, tired, and worried mother. Kenneth had suddenly refused to attend school and had also bewildered the school personnel with the increase in severity of his temper tantrums and nightmares, which had been present for the previous six months. Four weeks prior to the clinic visit, the family had moved into a housing project, which had necessitated a change of school for Kenneth and his older sister Evelyn.

The developmental history of the child was normal. There had been no previous illnesses.

Mrs. B., who was in her mid-thirties, had had ten pregnancies, resulting in four stillbirths and six live children, during her thirteen years of marriage. Kenneth was her second oldest living child.

Mrs. B. described her fear that she might not be able to provide a home for her children. The family had moved quite precipitously into a housing project after eviction proceedings had been instituted against them. There had been talk between the parents about what would happen, particularly to the children, if they did not find a place to live — the children would have to be sent to various relatives or institutionalized until the family could be reunited. The possibility of institutionalizing the children had been very threatening to the mother, as she had experienced separation from her own parents when she was a child. Her parents had been poor and had quarrelled continually about money. There had been nine children in her family. Her parents had eventually separated, leaving Mrs. B. to spend the greater part of her own childhood, from five years of age until sixteen, in a large institution. She had always hoped she could provide a better life for her own children.

During her last pregnancy, Mrs. B.'s husband, a 35-year-old semiskilled labourer who had been employed continuously for 17 years in one factory, had threatened to leave her, apparently overwhelmed by the numerous bills for obstetrical care, hospitalization, and furniture payments. Mr. B. had begun to drink increasingly during the preceding year or two, and Mrs. B. understood her husband's drinking as a way of escape from the constant demands of creditors. Mr. B. had also been threatened at that time with the loss of his job because of the many attachments on his salary made by his creditors. His take-home pay had been decreasing while the size of his family had been increasing.

Soon after moving to the new apartment, Mrs. B. had left for the hospital to have her tenth child. The maternal grandmother and aunt had come to stay with the children. Kenneth had been difficult for them to manage; not only had he had temper tantrums, but his speech had regressed to the level of baby talk, and he had wanted to be treated as a baby.

The family as a unit was disrupted by both external and internal stresses, having the most noticeable effect on the second oldest child, Kenneth. Kenneth was evidently experiencing acute anxiety in relation to fears of abandonment, manifesting his need for attention in the temper tantrums.

The family

The family was in a state of crisis. In the course of family interviews, it could be seen that each family member was reacting to the failure of the others to meet his or her needs, with the result that the family group was threatened with dissolution; the threat of dissolution lead to further anxiety and defensive attempts to deal with it. The aim of treatment by cotherapists in the family therapy was to help each family member deal with his or her own anxiety, and help each other to meet each other's particular needs as far as possible. A combined family therapy and individual therapy approach was used.

The child

The individual therapist's approach was to learn what Kenneth himself was experiencing and to help him feel more comfortable. Kenneth said that school was 'okay' and that his reason for not going to school was 'a secret'. Kenneth readily formed an attachment to the therapist and began a play activity that persisted for many interviews. Kenneth would repeatedly 'move house' and act out in a play situation several related fantasies. He feared someone would break into the house, rob the family, and perhaps harm or kidnap his mother. He also feared his mother and father might move away without telling him, leaving him abandoned. Linked to these fears was a fantasy that if a robbery occurred, there would not be enough money for food and the parents would have to get rid of the children.

Although Kenneth experienced some relief, his fears persisted, preventing him from leaving the house to go to school. Then one day Mrs. B. called for an immediate appointment. Her husband had left home, and Kenneth was adamant about not leaving the house. The 'secret' was now in the open, as Kenneth's fears were partially realized.

The father

Mr. B. was an immature person who reacted to stress with flight. The therapist used a task-oriented approach (Berlin, 1978) to help Mr. B. cope more effectively with the problems he and his family were experiencing. Mr. B. used the Legal Aid Society to institute bankruptcy proceedings, and the welfare department provided temporary financial assistance until Mr. B. could return to work.

The mother

Some of the specific factors that contributed to Mrs. B.'s depression were tackled directly. The threat of family separation was averted. The therapist provided direct support and coordinated all the treatment. Mrs. B.'s health problems, due to a poor nutritional state and anaemia, were treated in the medical clinic of the hospital. Visiting nurse and homemaker services were furnished to help Mrs. B. during her convalescence.

Whereas in a more stable family a parent might plan thus to meet the family's needs, the state of disorganization in the B. family required outside support until the family could regain its equilibrium and function more adequately. Increasingly, the therapists performed this function, both in individual therapy and in family therapy.

The family was told that Kenneth's inability to return to school was partly related to his preoccupation with the family disorganization and his worry about what would happen next to himself and his family. Mr. B. was encouraged to take Kenneth to school and stay with him initially — a plan that could not have been accomplished earlier. Kenneth then was able to return to school and work through his crisis.

The child and family

The events that appeared significant for Kenneth were the birth of the sibling, the partial loss of love through the depression and withdrawal of the mother, the ineffectiveness of the father, and the violence between the parents. Other fantasies that were present included the fear of losing the love of the mother and an earlier anxiety that the mother would desert the child, leaving him alone in a threatening situation. Kenneth had the compensating fantasy that he was big, calling the doctor's attention to his 'big muscles'. The intense anxiety that was aroused resulted in a number of defensive attempts, e.g. regression ('baby talk'); anxiety dreams (nightmares); and acting-out behaviour (temper tantrums). These manifestations occurred when a demand for performance was made that exceeded the boy's capacities.

After resolving these developmental crises, Kenneth was better prepared for the developmental tasks ahead. A follow-up report two years after the initial visit showed him to be a happy, intelligent boy leading a full and active life.

In this case, the therapists functioned in part as a coordinating and restitutive agency for the family. Each member was helped to master his or her anxieties more effectively and cope with the repeated family crises more appropriately.

CASE No. 2. MICHAEL, AGED 14 YEARS

Mr. and Mrs. D., concerned and interested parents, were particularly worried about Michael's acute reluctance to attend school for two weeks' duration, his insecurity, and his withdrawal from his friends. Mrs. D. did most of the talking. She was somewhat controlling and somewhat obsessive-compulsive in her need to fill in every detail. She also tended to control her husband and correct anything he had to say. Mr. D. was quite passive and accepting of anything that was said.

Mrs. D. was functioning under some degree of tension. She was clearly very concerned about her own state of health. Mrs. D. had a serious cardiac disorder which was life-threatening at times. She had undergone open heart surgery. At the same time, once one got beyond her defences and her anxiety, she was a woman who was deeply committed to her family and to her son. She made good use of the interviews and understood well some of the difficulties that Michael was experiencing. Mr. D. tended to be more passive and to deny his own anxiety. He was less perceptive about Michael's problems, yet had a genuine concern for his son.

There was an atmosphere of mutual affection in the relationship between each parent and Michael.

Michael's birth history was normal. Developmental history was unremarkable. Appetite, sleep, bladder, and bowel control were all normal. The only significant previous illness was that of croup at the age of 6 and a scalp laceration from a toboggan accident at the age of 9. The school history had been satisfactory up until the onset of his present symptoms. He had always done well in school academically, and had also presented no behaviour problems. He had excellent relationships with his peers and usually enjoyed playing games such as hockey and football. The D.'s lived in a house and Michael had a room of his own.

Michael appeared as a sturdy, attractive young boy who was somewhat reluctant at first to separate from his father. He did not express any clear complaint, other than the fact that he did not want to go to school. During the interviews he did not indicate what precipitating factors he might be aware of, but it soon emerged that there was considerable anxiety within the family about the mother's state of health. It is significant in the history that there had been several occasions in which the mother had to be rushed to the hospital in the middle of the night because of her heart condition. This caused acute anxiety in the family.

Michael was anxious during the initial part of the first interview. He seemed uncomfortable, and giggled. He described how he was alone in his house with his mother before school, and was reluctant to leave. Indeed, one of his three wishes was that there would be no school. The other wishes were that he would have all the fishing tackle that he would need and three more wishes. He drew the following sequence of Squiggles: a hammerhead shark, then a rather large rat eating cheese, a dog being tickled by the cat's tail, and a drawing that he called Mr. Jaws. The aggressive elements in these Squiggles was clearly evident.

In his drawing of a person, he did a somewhat stereotyped drawing to which he then added various graffiti. The crux of the graffiti was that the person wanted to kill off people. There was a great pleasure in killing and destroying.

Figure 1

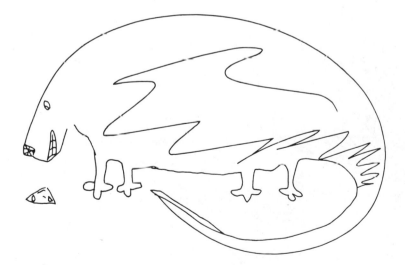

Figure 2

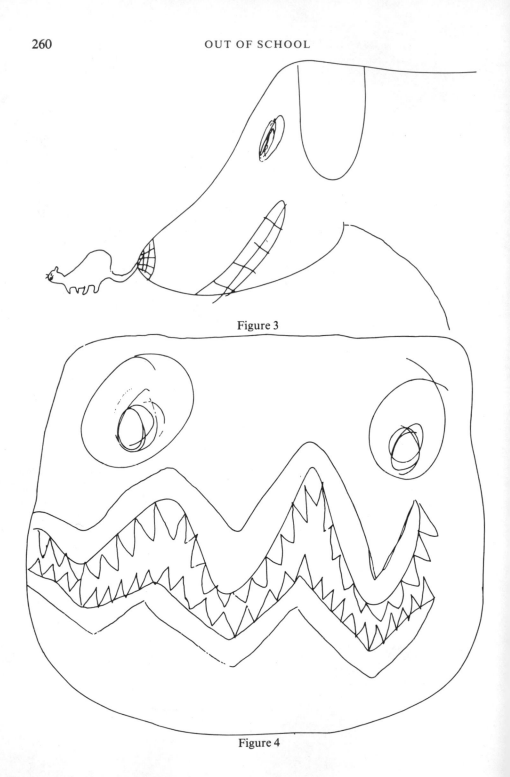

Figure 3

Figure 4

Figure 5

Michael brought a magazine showing a photo of himself and a huge fish he had caught. What was striking was his pleasure as he described in detail his struggle with the fish. He had to 'hit the fish on the head with a baseball bat' and kick the fish. All this was described with great gusto and pleasure.

At the same time, he was very reluctant to talk about any feelings he might have for his parents or about his difficulty in going to school. What became clear was that he had experienced acute anxiety and conflict around his aggression, and that for the most part his aggression was directed toward his mother. As the evaluation proceeded, there was some relief of this anxiety, not only in Michael but also in his mother. This permitted him to begin to return to school, a course of events that happened during the evaluation. Indeed, Michael was quite affable and friendly on leaving after the second interview and the mother reported that he was much better in every way and that they were very pleased.

In an interview with the parents, a very moving and profound sense of entering into the family was experienced. Mrs. D. had made a slip which led to her talking of her atrial fibrillation and her fear that she might die. This had become acute in August, about the time Michael was getting ready to start school at the beginning of September. It was clear that as the mother had become increasingly anxious, so the whole family had become anxious, and Michael experienced his own anxiety and difficulty in dealing with his aggressive feelings. This led to a wish to stay close to the mother and not leave her when it was time to go to school in the morning.

The most significant problem within the family was the handling of aggression and aggressive conflicts within the family, and particularly within Michael. A heightened anxiety around the serious, life-threatening cardiac illness of the mother precipitated a high level of anxiety and a fear of expressing aggression within the family. This lead to an exacerbation of individual characteristics within each of the members of the family: the mother became more obsessive-compulsive and controlling; the father appeared more passive, compliant, and unassertive; and the boy developed acute anxiety about his aggression and separating from his mother. When these dynamics were clarified and presented to the family individually and as a group, and when each individual member had an opportunity to talk alone with the therapist, the anxiety in the family subsided, realistic steps could be taken, and Michael was able to return to school.

COMMENT

In each of these cases, the child experienced a difficulty in controlling aggression. The difficulty arose in the first place from the threat of realization of feared external events such as separation, loss, harm, and family dissolution, albeit from different causes and for different reasons.

In each case there was some need, partly conscious and partly unconscious, on the child's part to avoid or deny the anxiety and the threat to the internal control of aggression. This led to a mobilization of defences, the nature of which was partly determined by developmental factors; regression, acting-out, somatization, and displacement were some of the mechanisms used. In each case secondary, restitutive attachment behaviours occurred, all of which had proximity to the mother as their immediate goal. When this was achieved, increased binding of aggression was possible and anxiety abated. When these environmental and intrapsychic factors could be recognized and accepted by the child and the parents, return to school could take place. Binding of aggression therefore appears to be an important factor in the etiology of school phobia, and is a key to the multiple approaches used in the treatment.

The approaches that may be used include a combination of family interviews and individual psychotherapy. However, it is important also to note the ecological context of the child, the family, and the therapy (Minuchin, 1970). School, peers, and other agencies are some of the areas into which interventions may extend. Interventions in these areas, while at different levels, must be coordinated and linked. Even within a subsystem, such as the family in part or as a whole, interventions by the therapist change the ecological context of the family behaviour patterns. This was particularly clearly experienced when the therapist had the very moving and profound sense of entering into the family and becoming part of the family at the moment. The focus may change from the individual member to any dyad through to the family as a whole, and still further to the extended family and the family's social environment. This flexibility of approach requires a broader therapeutic armamentarium than child psychiatrists have hitherto been accustomed to use.

REFERENCES

Abe, K. (1975). Sulpride in school phobia. *Psychiatria Clinica*, **8**, 95–98.
Agras, S. (1959). The relationship of school phobia to childhood depression. *American Journal of Psychiatry*, **116**, 533–536.
Ayllon, T., Smith, D., and Rogers, M. (1970). Behavioural management of school phobia. *Journal of Behaviour Therapy and Experimental Psychiatry*, **1**, 125–138.
Baker, H. and Wills, U. (1978). School phobia: Classification and treatment. *British Journal of Psychiatry*, **132**, 492–499.
Berg, I., Butler, A., and Hall, G. (1976). The outcome of adolescent school phobia. *British Journal of Psychiatry*, **128**, 80–85.
Berg, I., Nichols, K., and Pritchard, C. (1969). School phobia, its classification and relationship to dependency. *Journal of Child Psychology and Psychiatry*, **10**, 123–141.
Berg, I., and Pritchard, J. (1974). Psychiatric illness in the mothers of school phobic adolescents. *British Journal of Psychiatry*, **125**, 466–467.
Berlin, I. N. (1978). A developmental approach to work with disorganized families. *Journal of the American Academy of Child Psychiatry*, **18**, 354–365.
Berryman, E. (1959). School phobia: management problems in private practice. *Psychological Reports*, **5**, 19–25.
Bowlby, J. (1960). Separation anxiety. *International Journal of Psycho-Analysis*, **41**, 89–113.
Campbell, J. D. (1955). Manic-depressive disease in children. *Journal of the American Medical Association*, **158**, 154–157.
Cohen, N. J., and Leonard, M. F. (1963). Early pediatric management of acute school avoidance. In: *Modern Perspectives in Child Development*. Solnit, A. J., and Provence, S. A. (Eds.). International Universities Press, New York, pp. 419–441.

Coolidge, J. C., Hahn, P. B., and Peck, A. L. (1957). School phobia: neurotic crisis or way of life. *American Journal of Orthopsychiatry*, **27**, 296–306.

Crumley, F. E. (1974). A school phobia in a three-generational family conflict. *Journal of the American Academy of Child Psychiatry*, **13**, 536–550.

Davidson, S. (1960). School phobia as a manifestation of family disturbance: its structure and treatment. *Journal of Child Psychology and Psychiatry*, **1**, 270–287.

Eisenberg, L. (1958). School phobia: a study in the communication of anxiety. *American Journal of Psychiatry*, **114**, 712–718.

Frommer, E. (1967). Treatment of childhood depression with antidepressant drugs. *British Medical Journal*, **1**, 729–732.

Futterman, E. H. and Hoffman, I. (1970). Transient school phobia in a leukemic child. *Journal of the American Academy of Child Psychiatry*, **9**, 477–494.

Garvey, W. P. and Hegrenes, J. R. (1966). Desensitization techniques in the treatment of school phobia. *American Journal of Orthopsychiatry*, **36**, 147–152.

Gittelman-Klein, R., and Klein, D. G. (1973). School phobia: diagnostic considerations in the light of imipramine effects. *Journal of Nervous Mental Disease*, **156**, 199–215.

Hersov, L. A. (1960). Refusal to go to school. *Journal of Child Psychology and Psychiatry*, **1**, 137–145.

Hersov, L. A. (1974). Neurotic disorders with special reference to school refusal. In *The Residential Psychiatric Treatment of Children*. Barker, P. (Ed.). Crosby, Lockwood Staples, London, pp. 104–151.

Hersov, L. A. (1977). School refusal. In Rutter, M. and Hersov, L. (Eds.), *Child Psychiatry: Modern Approaches*. Blackwell, Oxford, pp. 455–486.

Johnson, A. M., Falstein, E. L., Szurek, S. A., and Svendsen, M. (1941). School phobia. *American Journal of Orthopsychiatry*, **11**, 702–711.

Klein, E. (1945). The reluctance to go to school. *The Psychoanalytic Study of the Child*, **1**, 263–279.

Kuhn-Gebhardt, V. (1972). Results obtained with a new antidepressant in children with depressive illness. In Annell, A. (Ed.) *Depressive States in Childhood and Adolescence*.

Leventhal, T., and Sills, M. (1964). Self-image in school phobia. *American Journal of Orthopsychiatry*, **34**, 685–695.

Lewis, M., and Lewis, D. O. (1973). Pediatric management of psychologic crises. *Current Problems in Pediatrics*, **3(12)**, 1–48.

Malmquist, C. P. (1965). School phobia: a problem of family neurosis. *Journal of the American Academy of Child Psychiatry*, **4**, 293–319.

Malone, C. A. (1979), Child psychiatry and family therapy. *Journal of the American Academy of Child Psychiatry*, **18**, 4–21.

Minuchin, S. (1970). The use of an ecological framework in the treatment of a child. In Anthony, E. J. and Koupernik, C., (Eds.) *The Child in His Family*. Wiley-Interscience, New York, pp. 41–57.

Millman, D. H. (1961), School phobia in older children and adolescents: diagnostic applications and prognosis. *Paediatrics*, **28**, 462–471.

Robinson, D. B., Duncan, G. M. and Johnson, A. M. (1955). Psychotherapy of a mother and daughter with a problem of separation anxiety. *Proc. Staff Meetings Mayo Clinic*, **30**, 141–148.

Ross, A. O. (1972). Behaviour therapy. In Quay, H. C. and Werry, J. S. (Eds.) *Psychopathological Disorders of Childhood*. Wiley, New York, pp. 273–315.

Saraf, K. R., Klein, D. F., Gittelman-Klein, R., Gootman, N., and Greenhill, P. (1978), EKG effects of imipramine treatment of children. *Journal of the American Academy of Child Psychiatry*, **17**, 60–69.

Skynner, A. C. R. (1976), *Systems of Family and Marital Psychotherapy*. Brunner/ Mazel, Chap. 16, pp. 306–327.

Sperling, M. (1951). The neurotic child and his mother. *American Journal of Orthopsychiatry*, **21**, 351–362.

Waldfogel, S., Coolidge, J. C., and Hahn, P. B. (1957). The development, meaning, and management of school phobia. *American Journal of Orthopsychiatry*, **27**, 754–776.

Werry, J. S. (1979). Family therapy behavioral approaches. *Journal of the American Academy of Child Psychiatry*, **18**, 91–102.

Out of School
Edited by L. Hersov and I. Berg
© 1980, John Wiley & Sons, Ltd.

Chapter 14

Behavioural Treatments of School Refusal

William Yule, Lionel Hersov, and Judy Treseder

INTRODUCTION

School refusal is not a unitary syndrome, nor is behavioural treatment a single therapy. The behavioural approach to treating children's disorders is a problem-solving one (Yule, 1977). The presenting problem is described carefully and objectively, hypotheses are set up to account for the observations and other clinical data, they are tested by introducing a deliberate therapeutic intervention, and, most of all, the outcome is carefully evaluated. We will show the type and breadth of information needed to understand the presenting problem and suggest a treatment plan. A wide range of interventions involving the child, his family, and school may need consideration. In evaluating the response to treatment, full-time school attendance is usually the major goal but there may be subsidiary goals to therapy, and additional information on the child's overall social and emotional adjustment is also gathered.

We will review the growing literature on behaviour therapy in school refusal, and illustrate the behavioural approach with recent clinical cases. Attention will be drawn to important factors in the onset and maintenance of school refusal related to the choice of this method of treatment.

Review of the Literature

In their excellent review of 'Phobias of childhood in a prescientific era', Miller, Barrett, and Hampe (1974) claim that whereas school refusal probably occurs in less than 1% of the school population, non-attendance at school arouses such concern that the ratio of papers on school phobia to other phobias is at least 25 to 1.

The earliest reported case explicitly treated by behaviour therapy (Lazarus, 1960), has a familiar ring. A 9½ year old girl was healthy and well adjusted until two months after her ninth birthday. Then, in quick succession, she had three traumatic experiences of death: a school friend drowned; her next door playmate died suddenly of meningitis; and she witnessed a man killed in a motor accident. She became enuretic, afraid of the dark, had night terrors and developed such abdominal pains at school that she was excused classes and her mother was sent for. Unfortunately, her mother had recently read that it was wrong to show overt affection to nine-year-old girls, so the child's natural anxieties were not relieved.

During a three week holiday, her fears vanished, only to reappear intensified on return to school. As her mother put it: 'The child won't let me out of her sight.' Discussions with the girl confirmed the therapist's view that she was really most afraid of the possibility of her mother's death. She was given training in muscle relaxation, and asked to imagine being separated from her mother for five minutes. A hierarchy of seven lengthening periods of separation was worked through. Therapy began on a Tuesday, and the girl went willingly to school the following Friday. In all, a total of 5 sessions were given, spread over a ten-day period. Once she was back at school, all her other symptoms disappeared. Follow-up 15 months later showed that all was well, apart from occasional wetting.

This study is interesting as one of the clearest examples of the use of systematic 'desensitization in imagination', with a child's phobia. The precipitants seemed clear, and the school refusal was treated as separation anxiety. The writer gave no details on how the actual return to school was effected, nor whether school personnel were involved.

One of the problems in treating phobic behaviour is to identify a behaviour which is both antagonistic (that is, 'reciprocally inhibiting') and can be controlled by the child at the request of the therapist (Jones, 1924; Yule, 1977). Many therapists claim that it is difficult to get children to relax; whether this reflects the ability of the child or the skill of the therapist, is a moot point.

Lazarus and Abramowitz (1962) report the use of 'emotive imagery' in desensitizing young children. They describe an 8 year old girl with persistent nocturnal enuresis and a fear of going to school, which had been precipitated by a series of classroom emotional upsets. She avoided going to school by throwing temper tantrums at home or complaining of pains. The authors do not say explicitly that she found it difficult to relax, but they decided to ask her to imagine her favourite fictional hero, Enid Blyton's 'Noddy', as a truant and responding fearfully to school. She was encouraged to protect Noddy by active reassurance. In only four sessions, her school phobia was eliminated, and she continued to improve during an unspecified follow-up period despite some additional classroom upsets. This was an important example of the therapeutic value of confronting the feared situation in imagination. Relaxation, *per se*, was not necessary.

Scherman and Grover (1962) report the treatment of a ten year old boy by pairing relaxation with discussions of going to school. He had been out of school for four weeks following one week's absence with legitimate illness. A verbally bright, tense, and anxious boy, he had recently shown a preoccupation with brutality, death, and revenge in his written stories. He was trained in a simplified form of relaxation and encouraged to practice his exercises at home last thing at night and first thing in the morning and whenever he felt tense. He was also told that he would not have to go back to school for a few days; then, he would return in easy stages. An eight stage hierarchy was contructed, ranging from going to school by car, sitting inside the car with his mother, to complete return. After practising each step in the natural setting, he returned to the clinic where, after relaxing, he discussed his achievement with the therapist and planned the next day's step. In six weeks, he was fully back at school. His mother reported that his previous tantrums associated with school attendance disappeared early in treatment. Although no follow-up is reported, this case is interesting in that the authors discuss modified relaxation training and combine an *in vivo* graded approach with clinic-based sessions.

Eysenck and Rachman (1965) point out that much of the literature on school phobia stresses separation anxiety rather than difficulties experienced at school because there has often been insufficient examination of adjustment to all aspects of school life. They conclude that the term 'school phobia' should be retained, but should be differentiated from 'separation anxiety in a school situation', as each requires a different therapeutic approach. They describe their approach to 'school phobia' in a thirteen year old boy who had been off school for a whole year.

The onset coincided with starting at his new secondary school when due to a tooth infection, he could not go on the first day. He attended on the fifth day of term, but was injured in a rugby game, losing two teeth. He was unable to return to school after the week-end, and his over-solicitous mother and grandparents initially let him stay at home, and then could not get him to return. By the time he was referred, he would not even come to outpatients and so was admitted as an inpatient. From the ward, he was initially able to attend his school, but stopped when his therapist left.

A more intense behavioural programme was initiated which involved a graded reintroduction to school in the mornings, paralleled by training in relaxation and working through a hierarchy of feared situations, in imagination, in the afternoons. Within five days, he was spending more time in his classroom; he spent most of the ninth day at school, having gone there on his own. Treatment was continued for two weeks, followed by discharge home.

He was re-admitted for one week's planned 'booster' treatment immediately prior to the start of the new school term. After experiencing a little difficulty in the first two or three days, he attended well for two months. He had one slight relapse requiring more treatment, and after a further three months he was attending well.

This case illustrates one of the many forms of school refusal where, at a crucial stage in a child's life — i.e. at transfer from primary to secondary school — a series of otherwise minor trauma can lead to school refusal.

However understandable the initial school refusal may be, the family are later unable, on their own, to support the entry back into the now feared situation. The therapists and a psychiatric social worker discussed the treatment with the boy's mother and grandparents, but unhappily the content of their conversation is not recorded. Of interest is the attempt to understand the problem within a clear learning theory framework. Treatment involved elements of *in vivo* graded reintroduction, with careful attention to details of school procedures, together with systematic desensitization in imagination. The use of 'booster' treatments at critical times — usually after school holidays — is also noteworthy. However, it is not possible to isolate which elements of the treatment package were essential and most effective.

Patterson (1965) accepted that separation anxiety lay behind the behaviour of a 7 year old school refuser. The boy had always found separation from mother difficult, and during his second week of first grade would only remain in the classroom if one of his parents were present. Patterson argued that a variety of stimuli connected with separation elicited an anxiety reaction which in turn led to escape or avoidance behaviour. The task of the therapist was therefore to link other, anti-anxiety reactions to the eliciting stimuli.

He worked with the boy four days a week for 23 sessions of only 15 minutes each using a form of doll play to simulate a variety of separation situations. This allowed discussion of how it felt to leave mother and go into school. Since behavioural testing had shown that he was much less responsive to social rewards than others of his age, tangible reinforcers in the shape of chocolate drops were given, contingent on his making appropriate non-anxious replies to questions. Anyone who doubts the warmth involved in behaviour therapy with children should read the vivid account of the tenth treatment session.

After 11 clinic sessions he went to school with his special teacher, staying longer and longer each day. After a week he announced that he would go to school by himself and stay an hour. Complete return to school was effected in 23 sessions — a total of 10 hours of therapist's time plus two bags of chocolate sweets! A follow-up three months later showed a dramatic improvement in all round adjustment. Patterson deliberately involved both parents as co-therapists in the treatment, carefully instructing them to look out for and reinforce new, independent, coping behaviours, to maintain improvement.

Lazarus, Davison, and Polefka (1965) report an over-determined case of school phobia in a nine-year-old boy, with a long history of difficulty in separating in school situations. He survived until the end of his third grade, despite being dragged screaming to school on advice from a psychologist consulted about an earlier incident. Then he had a serious appendectomy with critical complications, was left with post-operation pain, and in this state witnessed a drowning. Coincidental with his entry to the fourth grade, a close friend of his elder sister died suddenly.

They attempted to treat the problem using systematic desensitization, but the boy could not imagine situations in the hierarchies, so an *in vivo* approach was adopted. Initially, a therapist accompanied the boy to school, out of school hours. Gradually, he was reintroduced to his classroom with more and more pupils there, and encouraged to stay longer. At first the therapist used his relationship to reduce the anxieties; later, he used it to reinforce the boy for achievements. There were numerous setbacks during 4½ months of treatment, giving rise to an important theoretical and practical point — how should the therapist react when the boy says he cannot stay in the classroom any longer? Should he sympathize and allow him to go home, thereby reinforcing his avoidance behaviour? Or, should he make him stay until the anxiety habituates?

They conclude that the therapist's estimate of the degree of the anxiety should determine the decision. If the anxiety level is clearly high, then this is dealt with within a classical paradigm and the therapist should reassure and allow the boy to go home. If the level of anxiety is relatively low, the avoidance behaviour should be ignored and attempts to stay should be reinforced.

Here, the boy's parents were minimally involved in the first instance, and given a list of 'do's' and 'don'ts' later on. Historically, and practically the case is important both for its detailed description of the *in vivo* treatment and for its attempt to relate the therapist's decisions on intervention to the level of anxiety.

The largest series of cases of school phobia treated behaviourally was first published by Kennedy (1965) and slightly elaborated later (Kennedy, 1971). He differentiated clearly between Type I or 'neurotic crisis' phobias and Type II or 'way of life' phobias. From 1957 to 1964 his students treated 50 cases of Type I phobia. Unfortunately, in neither paper are details given about length of school absence. He claims that good liaison with schools will enable them to refer cases within two or three days, and that only 5 of the 50 cases had been untreated for some time, or had been unsuccessfully treated elsewhere.

As Kennedy (1965) describes it: 'The treatment involved the application of broad learning theory concepts by blocking the escape of the child and preventing secondary gains from occurring. In addition, the child was reinforced for going to school without complaint.' All fifty cases received rapid treatment which took only three days and were followed up regularly. They all returned successfully to school.

The major contribution in this paper is clear description of overall strategy. This involves six components: (1) Good professional public relations; (2) Avoidance of emphasis on somatic complaints; (3) Forced school attendance; (4) Structured interview with the parents; (5) Brief interview with the child; (6) Follow-up. In the parent's interview the therapist anticipates the parent's questions, and thereby demonstrates that he knows all about this puzzling condition. The parents are given detailed instructions on what to say to the child in a variety of common circumstances.

He does not, unfortunately, give any longer follow-up data. He states that the treatment plan is less successful with Type II cases, but it appears that the 6 cases of this type that he saw in the same 8 year period were given only supportive therapy. It is therefore not clear whether he really ever used his rapid treatment with more difficult cases.

Garvey and Hegrenes (1966) report a case study of a ten-year-old boy which brings in other aetiological elements commented on in the wider literature. Their patient had failed to return to school after six months in traditional psychotherapy. His earlier refusal was precipitated by a bronchial infection, but he had always been a sensitive boy 'preoccupied with high level performance.', and so reminiscent of cases described by Leventhal and Sills (1964). By the time his second treatment was started, secondary problems of avoidance of friends and peers were evident. As Garvey and Hegrenes (1966) put it: 'Apparently, Jimmy could not find adequate excuses for being out of school, and as his friends telephoned or visited the home, he became quite anxious and finally refused any contact with peers at all.' The problem was further complicated by his mother's insensitive handling of his concern for her safety. They adopted an *in vivo* systematic densensitization approach. A careful hierarchy was constructed, and was worked through on twenty consecutive days. Each session lasted 20–40 minutes, and a total of 10–12 hours of therapist time was needed before Jimmy was back in school. His father took him on the twentieth day, and progress was maintained over the following two years.

This interesting paper shows the therapist's awareness of balancing their positive, anxiety-reducing effect against the strength of their patient's avoidance reaction. They deal with the inevitable setbacks by working simultaneously along parallel hierarchies. When Jimmy was unable to go closer towards the school, he was encouraged to spend a longer time at the point previously attained. Thus, a simple manoeuvre results in the patient feeling that he is constantly making some progress. It also appears important that the therapist must never push the child beyond the sub-goal which they have previously agreed. Characteristically, the child will suddenly pluck up courage on an unexpected occasion and volunteer to attempt a more difficult step than agreed. The therapist must respond positively but may have to temper the patient's enthusiasm with some realism and effect a compromise.

Chapel (1967) also sees separation anxiety as the main component of school refusal. He reports a moderately severe school phobia in an eleven-year-old boy who had failed to respond to conventional one-to-one therapy as an outpatient. The boy was taken on to a ward as a day-patient where hypnosis was used to help relaxation, and he was then desensitized to a hierarchy of his fears of separation. Eighteen sessions of 20–30 minutes each enabled the boy to return to school after six weeks. He again had difficulty going back to a new class after the summer vacation, but responded well to a further set of 15 sessions of desensitization. This case again demonstrates that some children are at high risk of further breakdown on changing classes or after long vacation, but that quick intervention can prevent secondary problems arising.

Olsen and Coleman (1967) also subscribe to the view that separation anxiety is the underlying problem in school phobia, and describe a 6-year-old boy who refused to stay in first-grade class without a member of his family. His father brought him to a clinic where he was separated from his father for very brief periods which were systematically increased until he could walk out with the psychologist for 30 minutes. On the first day back at school, he was taken by his therapist who waited in his new classroom for twenty minutes before leaving. He never looked back and made very good academic progress.

It is not clear whether the method of Leventhal, Weinberger, Stander, and Stearns (1967) should be categorized as 'behavioural'. Elaborating on an earlier paper (Leventhal and Sills, 1964) they see one of main problems as that of aiding the children to reappraise their unrealistic and omnipotent self-image. This is done by forcing a confrontation over attendance between the parents and the child, and helping the parents win the ensuing battle. In both cases they describe, as soon as the children saw that the parents were firm in their resolve over-attendance, the children not only 'gave in', but positively enjoyed having firm control from their parents.

Ney (1967) reports another case of a 13-year-old girl who feared she would vomit if she was not with her parents. The whole family were highly sensitive to vomiting so both parents and daughter were treated. All were taught to relax and were desensitized to vomiting. Half the session was given over to insight-oriented psychotherapy. Since the girl had a variety of other fears, some of which were connected with school, the family role-played what she would say to her friend on her return. The total programme took some 22 hours and at the end she was attending 'quite regularly'. At follow-up, one year later, her attendance was 100%. The ingenuity of the therapist in combining different approaches precludes any conclusions regarding which were the effective therapeutic elements.

Hersen (1968) reports the complex case study of a twelve year old boy who was absent for 30 to 60 days a term. His mother received ten weekly discussions on behavioural management. She was made aware of the need to reinforce behaviour appropriate to going to school and alerted against inadvertently reinforcing school avoidance. Six months after treatment, the boy's attendance was normal and his social functioning was improved. The study is important not only as an account of training a parent in differential reinforcement techniques, but it acknowledges and discusses the mother's overt resistance to behavioural treatment.

Cantrell, Cantrell, Huddleston, and Woolridge (1969) briefly illustrate their use of contingency contracting with school problems with a case of a girl (of unspecified age) diagnosed as school phobic, showing how detailed each step in treatment must be to incur a reward.

Ayllon, Smith, and Rogers (1970) present a detailed example of the value of careful behaviour analysis in the treatment of school refusal. Their eight-year-old girl patient had shown increasing absences during her second grade and stopped attending before she was due to enter the third grade. She only attended on four occasions in the third grade, and threw tantrums when her mother tried to get her to go. Traditional psychological and psychiatric diagnostic work up did not produce any relevant information which would guide treatment, so it was decided to observe the girl at home for thirteen days. This direct observation revealed that she stayed very close to her mother and had little interaction with her father. When her mother went out to work, Val tried to follow her, but then stayed at the neighbour's home, where no demands were made on her. It seemed clear to Ayllon that the girl was being heavily reinforced for staying at home.

A graded intervention plan was drawn up. School related materials were given to Val to play with while at the neighbour's home. She was then taken by one of two therapists to school, but at the end of the school day. Gradually, over a seven day period, she went earlier and therefore spent longer at school. It was assumed that leaving school each day is a strong natural reinforcer for most children. Thus, a backward chaining paradigm was being employed.

Pressure was taken off Val for 5 days. During this reversal phase, she did not attend school. By now, it was clear from observations made during therapy that the timing of mother's departure for work was a complicating factor. For the next 12 days, mother left for work at the same time as the children left for school, instead of later as previously was the case. Then, for the next 10 days, mother took the children to school. All the children were by now placed on a star system, whereby attendance at school was rewarded at home. In the final phase, the therapist decided to push mother a little harder. They got her to leave for the school ten minutes *before* the children. If they arrived within 15 minutes of mother, they received their tokens. If Val didn't arrive, mother had to walk the mile back home and then accompany her back to school. This extra walking was mildly aversive to mother, and she only tolerated it twice. Thereafter, Val attended school regularly. The star system was faded out after one month. Follow-up 9 months later showed that not only was the girl's attendance perfect, her work was markedly improved, her social skills had improved, and she had survived her parents divorce without any effect on her schooling.

Wahler and Cormier (1970) also describe a detailed approach to behavioural analysis with the case of 10 year old Willie, who was refusing to go to school. Having obtained detailed information from the parents, the teacher and the boy himself, all were asked to keep records of relevant aspects of the boy's behaviour. '. . . teacher and mother were trained to reinforce differentially, behaviours competing with Willie's problem behaviour and Willie was encouraged to produce some of these competing behaviours when he observed himself "worrying".' The authors claim that their data indicated improvement without details or adequate follow-up being given.

In the second of his contributions Hersen (1970a) reports the case of 12½ year old Bruce whose five elder siblings had all refused school at one point or another. His parents and the school counsellor all inadvertently reinforced his school avoidance behaviour. For example, when he cried in class, he was immediately sent to the counsellor's room where he stayed for 1 to 3 hours.

Hersen mounted a three-pronged attack on the problem. The mother was first seen on her own for 15 weekly sessions. These focused on getting her to identify occasions when she reinforced maladaptive behaviour, finding ways of altering her pattern of reinforcement, and dealing with her overt resistance to the behavioural approach. She was helped to be firm and resolute on school attendance, and to reinforce Bruce for any appropriate, coping behaviour. She aimed to regain control over the boy in minor areas of altercation before tackling the school refusal directly. Meanwhile, since Bruce was not altogether refusing to attend, his elder brother took him to school. In six months, his pattern of attendance was normal, and a further two months follow-up showed no relapse.

Meanwhile, the counsellor was advised to return Bruce firmly to the classroom after no more than 5 minutes if he should complain of feeling uneasy in class. Bruce, himself, was seen for 15 half-hour sessions during which the therapist reinforced him for any coping response reported. He was also given an opportunity to vent any hostile feelings concerning the treatment programme. It is not clear whether the boy availed himself of this opportunity.

For the purposes of the present review, we should note that the mother and boy were worked with separately, apparently by the same therapist. Responsibility for getting the boy to school was taken away from the mother who was helped to re-establish her authority over the boy in relatively minor areas of conflict whilst simultaneously reinforcing him for coping with his difficulties. Hersen again acknowledges that some parents find the behavioural approach difficult to accept, and he elaborates on this in some of his other publications (Hersen, 1970b, 1971).

A very different approach is introduced by Smith and Sharpe (1970). Their patient, thirteen-year-old Billy, had been off school for seven weeks following a three week illness. His many previous illnesses had resulted in his mother becoming overprotective. He was perfectionist and prior to his illness he had transferred to a large junior high school where he experienced increased academic competition and a comparative lowering of achievement. He was asked to recount his school day minute by minute. This revealed that he was most anxious in two particular classes, and feared being ridiculed by the teacher for giving an incorrect answer. Thus, Smith and Sharpe formulated the main cause of his problem as being fear of '. . . achievement failure and resultant peer and adult disapproval within the school situation.'

They decided to use implosive therapy based on the classical extinction model. In practical terms, this involved getting the boy to imagine the most feared situation until his subjective feeling of anxiety began to wane. It also required co-operation from the parents and teachers to remove all sources of secondary reinforcement and to prepare for his re-entering school. He had a total of six consecutive daily sessions of implosion therapy. After the first session, he was required to go to his maths class the next day. After session four, he had to attend for a whole day. Despite being made very anxious by the first session, Billy was perfectly well the next morning and attended his maths class without difficulty. He was in school full-time from the fourth day of treatment and thirteen weeks later, he was attending regularly, showing no anxiety and attaining better grades. As with adult phobias, anxiety can be managed either by a graded, reciprocal inhibition approach or by sudden, implosion approach. Both can work in particular cases, the problem is to know before hand which approach to try first with which cases.

Welch and Carpenter (1970) describe treatment modelled on the Cantrell *et al.* (1969) report. An eight-year-old boy, began complaining of not wanting to go to school during the second week in September. He had been out of school completely for over a week when referred. His mother was interviewed, and an analysis was made of available reinforcers and punishers. The same hierarchy as that developed by Cantrell *et al.* (1969) was followed. His parents were given a detailed contract and recording sheets. After the first day, the boy returned to school, and the programme was stopped after three weeks. No follow-up data are reported. For the present purposes it is important to note that the parents carried out this treatment programme without the boy being seen by the therapist using fairly straight-forward methods.

Tahmisian and McReynolds (1971) also report a case in which a major therapeutic role was given to the parents. Their thirteen-year-old girl patient first showed signs of separation anxiety when attending a summer camp. She was home-sick, and on returning home became unusually clinging. She began to resist going to school, and early in the autumn term her parents were called on several occasions to take her home. Once home, the anxiety disappeared.

The most interesting point about this case is that the girl was taken through most of a twelve-step hierarchy during desensitization therapy. Although she could tolerate all the scenes in imagination, there were no signs of her returning to school. Therefore, a more direct instrumental approach was tried instead. By then, she had missed 80 days of school.

It had been noted that her parents consistently gave in to her when she was upset. They were introduced to behaviour modification techniques. The first task they were set was to walk round the school with their daughter for 15 minutes after the end of classes. The second step was for the girl to repeat this on her own. In three weeks, they went through a 15-step programme, rewarding her co-operative behaviour and not giving in to any emotional outbursts. At the end of three weeks, she was attending regularly and in four weeks follow-up found that progress was maintained. Apart from assessment and the unsuccessful trial of desensitization, the final programme required only two hours of therapist time.

The authors do not say why they thought the desensitization alone did not work. Perhaps, by separating off the clinic treatment component from *in vivo* practice, desensitization was not effective. On the other hand, one cannot conclude that it was not necessary for the girl to go through the imaginal desensitization before she was prepared to go along to school with her parents. As always, one cannot readily tease out the relative contributions of different components in an uncontrolled single case.

Miller (1972) reports on a ten-year-old boy of average intelligence but poor scholastic attainment who presented with a number of fears. He had been demoted academically, and after being criticized by his teacher he stopped attending, some eight weeks before referral. He also had an extreme fear of separating from his mother, he had difficulty in getting to sleep at night because he feared he might die, and he was enuretic. All three aspects of the problem were treated simultaneously.

The fear of separation from his mother was dealt with by systematic imaginal desensitization. After training in muscle relaxation, the boy was asked to imagine being separated from his mother by longer and longer distances. The fear soon diminished. This was reflected in a sudden drop in the number of times he telephoned his mother each day to seek reassurance. By the ninth week of treatment, the phone calls had ceased. His difficulty in sleeping, in contrast, was overcome by encouraging him to telephone the therapist when he could not get to sleep. The therapist then went over the instructions for relaxation (by telephone), and in six weeks, the sleeping difficulties disappeared. So did the enuresis, although it was never specifically treated.

The boy's fear of school attendance was first tackled in imagination, and he was instructed to employ his relaxation exercises *in vivo* whenever he experienced anxiety. Full-time attendance was achieved after 5 weeks treatment and no days were missed for the remaining 3½ months of the school year. Follow-up 18 months later showed that all gains, including attendance and improved academic achievement, had been maintained, and no new problems had emerged. This case is interesting in that it shows a number of problems being dealt with simultaneously, as well as illustrating Miller's ingenuity in utilizing the telephone calls as an index of the boy's anxiety level. For our present purposes, we should also note that the relaxation exercises were deliberately commended to the patient as a new way of coping with his anxiety level.

Blackham and Eden (1973) stress the need to gain complete control of the reinforcers in the environment in dealing with a long-standing school phobia in a thirteen-year-old boy.

Rines (1973) challenges Kennedy's (1965) views in a report of a 12-year-old girl who, at the time of referral, showed 7 or 8 of the 10 Type II, or 'way of life' features which Kennedy did not consider appropriate for his rapid behavioural approach to school phobia. The parents were reluctantly seeking hospital admission for their daughter, but equally reluctantly agreed to try a behavioural approach which they considered overly simplistic and so co-operated with difficulty. He gained the co-operation of the school, and impressed on the parents the need to reinforce their daughter's appropriate behaviour in the manner suggested by Kennedy (1965). At the end of the school year, the girl was attending regularly and getting good academic grades, although the family pathology remained untouched.

Vaal (1973) reports another case in which contingency contracting was successfully employed. This time, a thirteen year old boy who had been out of school for over six months during which traditional psychotherapy had failed, was the subject of the report. Interviews with the parents, the school and the boy failed to reveal any significant pathology. A simple set of targets was presented to the boy — go to school on time without tantrums, attended all classes, and remain at school till dismissed! If he achieved his targets, he was allowed to go to basketball, bowling, visiting. These privileges were withheld if he failed to meet the targets. In the six months before the contract was implemented, he attended on 6% of the occasions. For the next 3 months, his attendance was 100%. After the summer break, he returned without problems, and missed only 1½ days of the next 85. Vaal argues that the contract had shifted the balance of reinforcers sufficiently to bring about the dramatic change — all the more dramatic when it is realized that the contract was in force for only six weeks.

Weinberger, Leventhal, and Beckman (1973) follow Leventhal and Sills (1964) in viewing the underlying problems as one of a power struggle between the child and the parents, so that it is important to get the child back into school as soon as possible.

They illustrate their planned-confrontation approach with the case of a 15 year old girl, Type II school phobia, with a long record of poor attendance. Although very bright, she had not attended at all during eighth grade, and was showing very poor attendance in the 10th grade. The girl and her mother were seen by the psychologist on neutral territory, where he presented a clear ultimatum to the girl — return to school or face the consequences of court appearance and probable removal to a children's home. The girl went to school for the following 5 days. She then stayed off a few days with a foot injury which may have been self-inflicted. Father was recruited to the therapy team, and he also confronted his daughter — he was going to take her to school, dressed or not. She went, and the father is reported to have said that he felt like the man of the house for the first time ever. Three months later, the girl's attendance was very satisfactory. It's difficult to appreciate in what sense the reported confrontations were planned step by step, but there can be little doubt that in this case the tough, uncompromising line was instrumental in returning the girl to school.

In his short paper, Blagg (1977) gives one of the most detailed accounts of an overall strategy which involves taking into account information from the child, the parents and the school, and tailoring the precise details of the treatment plan to the information obtained. One novel aspect of his approach is to have the preliminary interview with the parents and the child on the school premises. He illustrates his approach with the case of 14 year old Robert who had been off school for at least six weeks. In this case, the boy showed a marked reluctance to leave his father, whilst his mother had a long history of agoraphobia. Robert's problems with attendance seemed to relate to an incident 18 months earlier when he feared that his parents might have been involved in a car crash. This coincided with a change of school. Robert was of average intelligence, somewhat introverted and neurotic, and lacking in self-confidence. He was overweight and disliked changing for games.

At the diagnostic meeting, it was agreed that a teacher would collect Robert each morning and take him to school. As a special privilege, he would, initially, be excused games. Since he was already in school, the plan was implemented immediately and his parents were asked to go home. Robert protested strongly, and it took two teachers to hold him. However, he calmed down very quickly after his parents left and several months later, he was attending regularly without fear. This is one case study in a longer series which will be published in future.

McAuley and McAuley (1977) report the case of a 12-year-old boy of average intelligence but below average attainment whose attendance had been deteriorating until he was absent on all but one or two days per month. He disliked separating from his mother who worried excessively. His father was little involved with the family. The boy was treated by a nurse therapist who tackled two aspects of the problem — (a) a gradual return to school and (b) his relationship with his mother and his peers. The former was accomplished by inducing relaxation by drugs and muscle relaxation training and then having him spend progressively longer time in school. His progress was reinforced at home. In addition, his mother was helped to foster his greater independence by helping him to join a boy's club. The progress was continued over the next term and the boy returned to school after the long summer holiday. Alas, just before Christmas, his maternal grandmother died, his mother got depressed, his father's drinking landed him in hospital, and the family moved from the area. No follow-up was possible. Even so, the case illustrates that even in the face of enormous odds, a nurse therapist can implement a successful programme for a boy with a lengthy history of school refusal.

Galloway and Miller (1978) report the case of 11-year-old Harry who refused to attend school on certain mornings. Interviews revealed that he disliked undressing for showers following games or swimming. He was an unpopular boy with a mother who could not be firm. He was desensitized to taking showers. Imaginal presentation was followed by *in vivo* exercises, and after four sessions of 40 minutes duration and 3 sessions of 15 minutes duration, Harry was not only having showers with the other boys, he also showed no further attendance problem over the following 5 weeks. This paper is interesting in that fear of or embarrassment at undressing in front of other children often features in the children's complaints of school activities. Here, a direct attack on that underlying fear produced changes in the pattern of school attendance which was not the direct target of treatment.

COMMENTS

This review serves to underline our opening remarks that a wide variety of behavioural techniques have been used to treat, for the most part successfully, a wide variety of school refusal problems. What general indications for choice of treatment approach can be drawn from these studies?

In the first place, most authorities in the field agree that the child should be returned to school 'as soon as possible', to avoid the behaviour becoming entrenched, with secondary consequences of falling behind in school-work. The clinical problem is how to judge 'as soon as possible', when to take the pressures off (Scherman and Grover, 1962), when to return the child abruptly (Blagg, 1977), when to force a confrontation (Leventhal, Weinberger, Stander, and Stearns, 1967; Weinberger, Leventhal, and Beckman, 1973)? The review suggests that the decision may be more determined by the authors' prior theoretical approach to treatment than an individual appraisal of each child's needs.

Secondly, different therapists have reported success with different techniques. Those who stress separation anxiety in their formulations tend to use relaxation and a gradual confrontation with the school situation either in imagination or *in vivo*, or to work on prolonging separation from the mother, whereas those who stress the secondary gains of remaining at home place more emphasis on some variety of contingency management. Few authors report on a variety of cases where different approaches have been combined to meet unique needs.

Despite the paucity of descriptive data in some reports, it is possible to draw one inference from this review. Where children have been out of school for only two or three days, simple, directive methods will work well. Thus Kennedy's (1965) rapid method, and Cantrell *et al.*'s (1969) and Vaal's (1973) use of contingency contracting demonstrate relatively direct and simple techniques for use with less severe cases. It is perhaps worth noting in passing that others have also studied the use of behavioural approaches to encourage better school attendance. In an experimental study, Morgan (1975) found that whilst any form of reinforcement contingent on attendance was better than no treatment, the most effective reinforcement involved material reinforcers and peer social reinforcers. The effects of social reinforcement delivered by the teacher extinguished more quickly. Parker and McCoy (1977) showed that whilst praise of children for attendance had an initial effect, better results were obtained when the school made direct contact with the parents and showed disapproval at their child's absence or approval at their child's attendance.

The other point to emerge from this lengthy review is that most behaviour therapists attempt to take account of a wide range of factors — in the child, in the family, and in the school. A number of papers (Ayllon, Smith and Roger, 1970; Wahler and Cormier, 1970; Blagg, 1977) describe detailed strategies for obtaining information relevant to making a full behavioural analysis of the presenting problems.

CASE ILLUSTRATIONS

The following cases have been selected to illustrate particular problems in treatment. They are not a random selection of or even a consecutive series of school refusals. Since we work in a teaching hospital setting, many cases referred to us are seen by inexperienced students under our supervision and they cannot be summed to show the percentage success rate of behavioural approaches in the treatment of school refusal.

Case No. 1: 'Richard'

Richard aged 12 years was referred by his family doctor and seen as an outpatient one June. Following a period of ill-health and unexplained pyrexia for which he had been admitted to hospital in February, Richard had become increasingly tense and anxious at school. He could not concentrate and complained of feeling weak. At the beginning of March, he walked out of school and refused to return. His parents were totally puzzled by this reaction and quickly arranged for him to be seen by a child psychiatrist. They attended for six sessions, but did not continue.

They were advised to take Richard back to school, without any practical guidance on how to do this. They tried to do so on two occasions but the attempts ended in failure. At this point they were referred to us by their GP.

By the time of first attendance he had been out of school almost continuously for five months, doing some studying at home, and able to play with some former friends from his primary school, but becoming very anxious even thinking about his present school. He had difficulty falling asleep at night and had to go through a series of checking rituals before going to bed. He was afraid of the dark and intruders getting into his bedroom. Psychometric testing showed that he had a WISC Full Scale IQ of 139. His reading and spelling attainments were in keeping with his high IQ. He appeared very concerned about falling behind in his academic work.

From his parents, we learned that he had an uneventful early childhood. He was a friendly boy who coped with new situations well, but was always very competitive and a poor loser. In his primary school (i.e. 5–11 years) he was easily top of his class, and his ambition is always to be so. After transfer to secondary school he enjoyed the first term, and showed considerable ability, enthusiasm, confidence, and interest. He had many friends among the other boys, and never any difficulties over attendance prior to his illness.

His parents were in their late forties. His father, a scientist was often away from home, very little involved with his family, and recently had been very worried about work. His mother had worked part-time, gave it up when Richard's difficulties emerged, and appeared very anxious. Both parents were extremely puzzled by Richard's behaviour and their self-confidence in handling him had been shattered by their unsuccessful attempts to help him back to school. They were very worried that Richard's promising academic career was now in jeopardy. Richard had one sister, a year younger, who was average at her work. She presented no problems and attended school regularly.

Richard's problem was formulated as an Emotional Disorder with School Refusal in a prepubertal boy of very superior intelligence, following an undiagnosed pyrexial illness and enforced absence from school. His increasing anxiety had been shown in fatigue and poor concentration on return to school, with a gradual emergence of compulsive rituals and phobic avoidance of lessons, school friends, and school buildings. His previous personality traits of perfectionism, competitiveness, and high drive sustained him through his first term in his secondary school, and he met his parent's expectations of conformity and success. However, he now felt anxious and threatened by increased competition from his peers, who were equally highly selected on intellectual prowess, as well as by the prospect of academic failure according to his own high standards. Previous attempts at psychotherapy and attempts to return him to school had not been successful because his phobic avoidance had not been effectively treated, and his parents' own anxiety had been too high to permit them to provide effective support. Separation anxiety was not a major problem. His parents were anxious and uncertain and unable to manage him. Our treatment plan was to use systematic desensitization with the boy (to deal with his phobic avoidance) whilst his parents were seen independently by a psychiatric social worker to explain the method and goals of treatment and their own role in this.

There were only six weeks before the end of the school year. If we could not get Richard at least partly back to school in that time, there was a real possibility that his anxiety would build up so much toward the end of the long summer vacation that it would be even more difficult to return to school in September.

Immediate discussions were held with the school to ascertain what options were open. Should he repeat the first year, should he proceed to the second year, and if so, should he remain in the highest academic class or should he drop into the second 'stream'?

He was seen again two days after our diagnostic conference, to discuss the various options open to him when he returns to school, and agreed to think them over. We then obtained a very detailed description of how he felt from waking up first thing in the morning to arriving in school. Recently, he had been driven to school, a 20 minute journey, throughout which he felt very tense and sick although he sat back and tried to relax. When he arrived and saw the school buildings, he felt even worse. He found it very uncomfortable even to think about going into the school playground, more so if any other boys were around. In other words, he described a classic phobic response which increased as he approached the school.

We explained that he was quite right to try to counteract his anxiety by relaxing. This was precisely what we would help him to do. The difference would be that we would teach him how to relax and would not ask him to approach the school until we felt he could cope with it.

Preliminary instruction in muscle relaxation was given. We asked him to practice tensing and relaxing his muscles for a few minutes each day, and again just before going to sleep.

Three days later, Richard returned for his second treatment session, this time accompanied by his distraught father who feared that we didn't realize how serious Richard's problem was and that we were going too quickly in treatment. Since the father had been relatively reserved at the time of the initial interviews, it seemed important to provide psychotherapeutic help now that he had brought his own problems into the open. He readily agreed to discuss these with the psychiatrist in the clinical team.

Richard himself was then seen for about half-an-hour. He had been practising his relaxation exercises and these were continued, using more muscle groups, followed by some imaginal desensitization. He was asked to imagine three scenes in succession: (1) getting up on a school morning (this had to be presented three times before he was able to relax sufficiently); (2) putting on his school uniform; (3) walking, in his uniform, towards the car at the end of the driveway. He reported feeling a little tense initially each time, but quickly relaxed.

Three days later, he reported that he was still practising his relaxation exercises at home and these helped him to get to sleep more quickly, although he still went through some checking rituals first. We discussed his views about the next year's schooling. He said he would prefer to move on to the second year rather than repeat the first year, but to move in to a lower stream. We then practiced some more relaxation. Once he was judged to be sufficiently relaxed, we repeated the same three scenes as in the second treatment session. Since by now there were only about two weeks of the school term left, we decided to speed things up a little. We suggested that we drive him to school and sit outside, but not go in. He was agreeable to that so we immediately drove to school and sat outside in view of the buildings, talking in a comfortable, relaxed fashion for ten minutes.

Even though the school visit was sprung upon him, the limits of what we hoped to accomplish were clearly spelled out, and no time was given for anxiety to build up.

Four days later, after a brief relaxation practice in the clinic, we drove to the school and sat outside the entrance which he normally used. It was a hot day and it was very stuffy in the car so he found it a bit difficult to relax. When the therapist suggested that we walk round the school, Richard wanted to go into the building and look at a noticeboard. We stayed there at the board for two to three minutes, seeing no one. Richard was both very relieved and very jubilant. When we got back to the clinic, he told his mother who did not react with any sign of pleasure.

The next day, while his parents saw the social worker, Richard was again taken to school. He said that he was much more tense because he was not sure what the next step would be. He had asked his mother and she had suggested that it might be to talk to the headmaster! Richard was assured that this was not to be, unless of course we bumped into him accidentally when, of course, it would be only courteous to say something. We walked around the school buildings and Richard said that they did not worry him. At one point, we saw some boys in uniform in the distance, and Richard tensed noticeably. This allowed us to discuss his fear of meeting boys he knows, although he could go quite easily into an empty classroom.

At this point, we discussed breaking any problem into smaller, attainable goals. He was most worried about explaining to his peers why he had been off school. We rehearsed, on the spot, in the middle of the street, talking about feeling depressed after 'flu, and also what to say about the particular treatment he was now having. It was agreed that one way of breaking the confrontation into steps would be to meet school friends, one at a time, in his own home during the holiday.

We then went into the school. At this point, he rated his anxiety level as 8 to 9 on a 10-point scale, 10 being most anxious. He was scared of meeting boys in the building. Our luck held, and he stayed at the same noticeboard for 5 minutes. His anxiety rapidly dropped — to a rating of 5 as we read the notice-board, down to 1 as we walked back to the car. When we got back to the clinic, his parents, having seen the social worker, were fulsome in their praise for his achievement.

Three days later, at his sixth treatment session, we drove to the school after much less preamble. We went into the building, and climbed up the stairs to the corridor outside his classroom. He was obviously scared — hanging behind the therapist, clinging to the rails, jumping every time a door banged. We encountered no one, since we had timed our visit when everyone should be in class. Again, we stayed in the building for five minutes.

The seventh session was held five days later. By now, the school was on holiday, so there were no boys around. He was very relaxed.

Thus, we had achieved our first objective in six treatment sessions spread over a two and a half week period. We had got the boy back into the school grounds and buildings. Moreover, we had clarified that he was really afraid of meeting his former classmates and didn't know what to say to them. We had discussed practical arrangements with the school and negotiated his placement for the next year. In addition, his parents had received considerable support with their anxieties and instruction in their roles, as will be described later.

At this stage, the treatment plans were to boost his academic attainment during the holidays so that he wouldn't start the new term too far behind, to increase his contacts with school friends, and to create opportunities for him to practise giving his explanations to them, to maintain visits to school, and to continue some imaginal sessions to prepare him for the beginning of the autumn term. It was decided that the psychologist would accompany him to school for the first few days, thereby reducing his parents' anxiety about having this responsibility.

At this point, we reviewed the considerable progress he has made and discussed what steps were left. He still had to face going into a crowded playground, to meet other boys, and to deal with his school work. We also had to prepare him for returning to school should he experience a further illness or accident.

One week later, we went through a whole series of desensitization scenes. On a 1 to 10 point scale, he rated them as follows:—

Getting up on a school day	3
Up, and having breakfast	1
Putting on uniform	1
Getting in to car; mother driving	2–3
In car, half-way to school	2
At gate, early, no other boys around	3 (Presented twice)
At gate, lots of boys in the playground	6
At gate, only one boy (his friend) there	2
Into playground with only his friend	1
Talking to friend, joined by one other	3
New boy asks: 'What's been wrong with you?'	4, 2
Going into school assembly	3
Going into classroom with everyone there	4

The tenth session was held a few days before school re-opened. He had had a good holiday, but was feeling terrible about the week to come. He said he would prefer his mother to take him to school, but this was immediately vetoed since it might prove too difficult for both of them. His mother later reported that she was very relieved.

Richard said that he wanted to arrive at school before anyone else so that the other boys could join him in stages rather than his joining a whole group of them. This was agreed to as a very constructive way of coping with his worries. He said that he had worked out what to say to boys — 'I've had this illness — a bad case of 'flu — and was depressed for a long time afterwards. During the summer, I've been getting some help to get to school again'. At this point, the psychologist drove Richard home and from there practised driving to school.

The next session occurred the day before school was due to re-open. To be as realistic as possible, the drive to school was undertaken at the time which would be normal for school days. Richard was collected at 8 a.m. He was not in his uniform. We sat in the car, outside the school, watching all the new, first year boys arrive one day earlier than the others. Although Richard was a bit anxious, we discussed how all the new boys might be feeling, as well as going over the plans for the next day.

D-Day came with this twelfth session. Richard was ready at 8 a.m. He was more anxious than previously, but not completely terrified. (Later, his mother told the psychologist (when he telephoned her to let her know all was well) that he had been crying and had not eaten much breakfast). At the school, the therapist watched him go into the playground, meet up with other boys and get involved in a game of football. He remained outside in the car until all the boys went in to school. Richard telephoned his mother at lunch-time, not for reassurance, but to ask her to take in his games kit so that he could stay behind at the end of school to go to a football trial.

The next day, Richard was less anxious. When we arrived at school, he went straight in to the playground whilst the therapist remained in the car until the boys were called to class. On the third day of term, Richard ate a good breakfast. He said he didn't want the therapist to stay outside the school after we arrived. The following day, his father drove him to school. Richard continued to go on his own after that.

Six weeks later, Richard reported that everything was going very well. He was top in his class occasionally and had made lots of friends whom he saw at week-ends. He was elected captain of his class. He has no problems getting to sleep, although he still had some checking rituals.

At the end of the school year, his sleep was still good but he still had minor, non-intrusive checking habits. Looking back to the previous year, he regarded the whole incident as stupid and silly. He occasionally worried that it might happen again, but quickly agreed that he now knew how to cope if he was off school unexpectedly. He had had no days off school throughout the academic year.

Whilst all this work was going on with Richard, his parents were seen regularly by the psychiatric social worker. Richard's progress and practical details were kept under constant review. The question of his strong drive to succeed was discussed, with both parents expressing uncertainty why this had so developed. They recognized why he might have difficulties coping with increased competition at school but felt unable to help him over these. They were encouraged to praise Richard for each step he mastered, and they were very relieved when told that our team would take responsibility for taking him to school for the first few days.

At an early stage, they expressed considerable anger over the failure of previous treatment. In particular they resented not being included actively in the treatment plan. They also discussed their personal anxieties, particularly father's work worries. During the holidays, at the point that Richard complained to the psychologist that his parents were pushing him too hard, they expressed irritation at the slow progress. They discussed their disagreement over how hard to push him — mother wanting to go more slowly, saying that she would have to cope when father was at work. The PSW pointed out the distinction between helping the boy over his anxiety and 'forcing' him, and looked at the need for the parents to establish with Richard that he needs help with the first move, as after this he can usually cope. His mother was concerned about what to do if Richard got cross with her.

The parents were next seen shortly after Richard had returned to school. They were cautiously optimistic about his progress. His mother had been able to support him over the first few days and encouraged him to talk about his worries. He now did so much more openly. Two weeks later, they were extremely pleased with his progress. Richard had been attending every day without hesitation, and coped with boys' questions about his absence. They, themselves, were far more relaxed and less anxious, and felt there was much less tension at home. The PSW discussed possible problem times such as returning to school after breaks; illnesses or holidays. The parents said they would have no hesitation in contacting our team for advice, because they still feared that their son had a psychiatric disorder which would recur under future stress.

The parents were seen at the beginning of the following term, four months after Richard went back to school. He was still attending regularly, was making excellent academic progress and had made many more friends. They were still uncertain as to how to cope with his return to a more academic class the following school year. They wanted to keep a link with the hospital, although Richard had made it clear that he wanted to forget about coming to the hospital. At a further follow-up, three months later, all the progress was being maintained, as it was a further three months later.

Early in the autumn term, two years after Richard went back to school, Richard's father was seen at his request. The father was very tense and anxious. His worry centred around an incident of shoplifting. Richard and a friend were going to a disco dance and stole a half-bottle of spirits each. The police were not preferring charges. Even so, the parents were concerned over Richard's general attitude at home, where he is much more argumentative. Despite additional strain on the whole family associated with the deaths of both grandfathers within the previous year, Richard's academic progress was excellent. He had come second in the whole year, and there were no attendance problems. Apart from the isolated antisocial act, his overall social adjustment was excellent.

We have given a rather length account of treatment reasons in order to convey in some detail how we approach a case of school refusal from a predominantly behavioural viewpoint. As can be seen, we pay attention to factors in the child, the home and the school. We spend considerable time ensuring that all major parties to treatment are fully aware of progress and problems, and try to anticipate difficulties by exploring all options open to us at any one point in time.

The face-to-face behavioural work with the child begins with the explicitly stated premise that our job is to get him back to school. There is never any attempt to disguise this aim. In conversation, we talk about '*When* you are back at school . . . ', never 'If you get back . . . '. We try to show the child that we understand, in broad outline, the difficulties he is facing. We talk about the sorts of problems that other children have faced — children whom we have helped back to school. We recognize that it may be difficult for him to put in to words what aspects of the situation worry him most, so we try to set up a therapeutic contract wherein he will tell us at any time if he feels uncomfortable. We discuss the rationale of desensitization and graded re-entry, and agree that we will not push him beyond sub-goals which have been previously agreed. Equally, during treatment, we seize on any opportunity to move at a faster pace, particularly when, as often happens, the patient plucks up his courage and attempts to do more than was planned. Such initiative is reinforced, although the therapist has to try to ensure that the patient's enthusiasm doesn't result in painful failure.

In this first case, the situation had been complicated by a previous unsuccessful attempt at treatment and by the time, at the end of term, when he was first seen. The school was a very academic one and this made for difficulty, not because they were unco-operative, but rather that the whole ethos of the school was one of academic achievement so as to have a scholarship boy demoted to the lower stream was unheard of.

Richard's case illustrates the use of relaxation training, imaginal and *in vivo* desensitization. As with the adult literature on the treatment of phobias, it is far from clear that relaxation is a *necessary* component, but we believe that it provides sufficient mystique as to allow the patient to 'save face'. It is much easier to confront the feared stimulus after you have been 'treated' for it, such is the medical model to which our patients seem to adhere! In addition, we stress the value of relaxation as a mechanism for coping with future anxiety, but the stress is on the *patient's* coping.

A final point to emphasize on this case is that the *in vivo* sessions were invaluable in clarifying that Richard was really most afraid of confronting the other boys. Once he started to talk about this, we provided him with an acceptable explanation which he could use and constructed a graded hierarchy from role-playing through talking to one boy at home to talking to boys in school. This particular fear features in many of the cases we have seen.

In this case, we have more than two year's follow-up on Richard. Apart from the isolated incident of anti-social behaviour as he entered adolescence, he has maintained his academic progress, extended his social relationships and school attendance have been regular.

Case No. 2: 'Keith'

Keith aged 11 years was referred by his family doctor, with the presenting problem of fears about the welfare and safety of his parents, particularly his mother. His greatest fear was that she would be killed in a car crash. The fears were first noticeable and intrusive nine months before referral, following his first separation from his parents when he went to a Wolf Cub camp. He had numerous panic attacks after that, precipitated by his mother going out alone. His parents insisted that he attended school, but difficulties were beginning in that area. He had to be brought home on occasions to check that his mother is well, and he often telephones her to reassure himself. Effectively, his mother was trapped at home.

Keith was of average intelligence, and read well. He was well-liked by his school who were puzzled by his bouts of uncontrollable crying, which were dealt with by letting him telephone home. His parents were very concerned that they would shortly be unable to get him to go to school.

Treatment was focussed on Keith's anxiety over separation from his mother. In the first session details of his separation fears were elicited and hierarchies varying along distance of separation, length of time separated and uncertainty of mother's whereabouts or return, were constructed. Keith was taught to relax, but then had difficulty visualizing the scenes. Therefore, an *in vivo* approach was adopted. In brief, he was separated from his mother in the clinic for very short times whilst she was sent out in her car on prescribed routes. Once he could cope with her going off for unspecified times over unspecified routes, the next major target was tackled. This consisted of his coping with arriving home to find his mother out. Initially, he knew that she would return 5 minutes after he got home, and gradually the period became longer and less predictable. (His mother hid in the garage for up to 30 minutes so that she could 'arrive back' on time.) These home exercises were carried out between weekly visits to the clinic.

His parents were very encouraged by Keith's progress. A few weeks after the start of treatment, he went out to a youth club one evening. His parents took the opportunity to visit a neighbour, making sure they were back before he returned. The next day they told him what they had done, and the following week he refused to go to his club in the evening. The parents were reminded of the need to stick to agreed steps in the programme.

At this point, the youth club leader proposed to take the boys to a week-end camp. With trepidation, we agreed to Keith's going, but made careful plans with the leader that he would take Keith home at the first signs of difficulty. Keith's parents agreed to stay home all week-end. In the event, Keith went to the camp, was slightly injured at a nearby fairground, enjoyed his weekend and did not feel homesick. The fact that he coped so well was a great morale booster for all his family.

Keith was not seen for any sessions during the summer holidays. He moved to his secondary school and apart from normal anxiety on the first day attended daily afterwards and his parents reported no remaining problems. Treatment contact amounted in all to 10 hours.

We feel justified in including this case in a chapter on School Refusal because all the indications were that Keith was on the point of ceasing to attend school. It is very unlikely that he would have managed the transfer to secondary school without help. The boy was unable to visualize scenes on his hierarchies, so an *in vivo* approach was used. Mother and boy were given exercises to carry out at home between clinic sessions. The parents jumped a few steps and set back the programme. On the other hand, the prospect of attending a week-end camp came earlier than the therapists would have liked. Fortunately, it passed off well. In summary, an *in vivo* desensitization programme was helpful in treating a clear case of Separation Anxiety in which School Refusal was imminent.

[Ms. Margaret Ballard was the primary therapist in this case. Fuller details are contained in M. Ballard and W. Yule (in preparation) A case of separation anxiety treated by *in vivo* systematic desensitization.]

Case No. 3: 'Norman'

Norman aged 11 years was referred by his G.P. His school reported that his academic work was seriously hindered by frequent absences, having been off 36 sessions in 12 weeks of the current term. He often complained of headaches and of feeling sick.

Norman's father had died when he was four. His mother had not remarried, and was still, seven years later, on antidepressants and tranquilizers. She found it very difficult to be firm and consistent with Norman who was of average intelligence, but specifically retarded in reading and spelling. He expressed a number of anxieties related to school and examinations, and was clearly worrying about the transfer to secondary school the following academic year. He also expressed fears for his mother's health.

The formulation was of School Refusal, part of an Emotional Disorder, the clinical picture being complicated by his poor scholastic attainment and consequent lowering of self-esteem. Consequently, we arranged for him to have extra remedial teaching at school. At our clinic an operant reading approach (see Hayes and Yule, in press) was followed. Although the focus was on academic improvement, the therapist made it clear that he was also interested in Norman's progress and attendance at school, and discussion on these topics featured in every lesson. His mother was seen regularly by a Social Worker to help with her depression over her husband's death.

In the following three months, Norman made good progress with his reading. He was off school with influenza, but had no difficulty returning. During this time, his mother was given the opportunity to discuss her own illnesses and widowhood. During the Easter holiday, Norman and his sister spent time at a relative's house without difficulty. In the summer term, despite the impending change of school, he continued to attend without difficulty. He was seen at fortnightly intervals for reading teaching and counselling until the end of term and then twice after he transferred to his new school. They had been alerted to continue with some remedial help. During the seven months of remedial help, he improved by 23 months of reading age on comprehension of reading. He transferred to his new school without difficulty, and his attendance was exemplary, and his case was closed six weeks after he transferred.

It was very clear to us that Norman was not truanting. By providing systematic casework for his mother, we were able to help her with her depression, to take some of the burden off Norman and to reinforce him for his better attendance. Norman himself was helped with his poor reading, which had caused him considerable embarrassment. He transferred to his secondary school with renewed self-confidence that was non-existent nine months earlier.

Mother was seen weekly while Norman was in treatment. She was a very fearful, anxious person, who was handicapped by severe spelling problems. She identified closely with Norman and was very worried that he would pick up her fears and grow up with similar handicaps. She needed help in separating him out from herself and we worked out ways of gradually increasing Norman's independence. Mother herself needed to mourn for her husband and to discuss ways of adjusting to widowhood as she had always been well-looked after by her husband and her own father. She also used the sessions to discuss her considerable worries about her physical health and she was encouraged to obtain proper medical attention. This freed Norman from the burden of worrying about his mother's illnesses. Mother needed help in recognizing the progress which Norman was making educationally. Her considerable anxiety about him made it hard for her to envisage that progress could be made.

In this case, as in many others, the aetiology of the school refusal was over-determined. A behavioural approach to his reading difficulties, combined with a casework approach to mother's problems proved helpful. This case underlines the finding that whereas *on average* school refusers may be above average with respect to their academic attainment, school failure can, at times, be associated with anxieties over school attendance.

Case No. 4: 'Mavis'

Girls also refuse to go to school. Mavis was referred aged 13 years by the school doctor. She was an intelligent, only child with a fear of facing people and over the previous year or two, she had become gradually more nervous of going outside to meet people. After a week's absence from school with influenza, she was unable to return to school and now had not been outside the house for nine weeks.

A social worker visited the home within a few days of the referral, to find a socially isolated family with few friends and no relatives. Mavis had been born with a cleft palate, and still showed a facial disfigurement of which she was acutely aware. She was depressed and refused to attend the clinic so it was decided that the social worker would act as primary therapist in the girl's own home.

Visits were arranged weekly. After gaining a measure of trust, it was agreed to institute a very gradual programme to get Mavis out of the home. Taking the milk in from the front door-step was too threatening, but working in the kitchen with the back door open was an acceptable first step. By the sixth visit a clear hierarchy was worked out. In the meantime, the therapeutic relationship had been strengthened by the therapist telling 'the facts of life' to Mavis who had been woefully ignorant. This led on to her relating a harmless incident with a boy, which had left her guilty and afraid to tell her parents. By the eighth visit, Mavis had been introduced to systematic muscle relaxation, and she was able to venture out into the back garden. From this point on, half of each visit was spent in counselling and half in systematic desensitization *in vivo*.

By the end of the third month of treatment, Mavis was able to accompany the social worker to the nearby park for a walk. She went out on her own for a short walk each day thereafter. Over the Easter holidays, she re-established contact with friends and went out shopping. A planned visit to the school during the holidays had to be cancelled when the therapist was ill. Therefore, Mavis started straight back to school on the first day of term after the holiday without the benefit of a graded re-entry.

She was very anxious that first morning and delayed setting off for school, running through a whole repertoire of excuses. The therapist telephoned her twice. Initially, the girl wanted to go on her own, but after the second 'phone call, agreed to the therapist's accompanying her. Although sobbing quietly, she was dressed for school when the therapist arrived. After a short discussion, they set off together by car. She was quite relaxed when they arrived and went off to class happily. The next day, she went to school on her own without difficulty. One week later, Mavis made it clear that she did not want to continue seeing the therapist on a regular basis. After one more interview, the case was closed.

Initially, this seemed an impossible case. However, the social worker felt that she had made a slight relationship with the girl at the initial home visit, and with Mavis's refusal to attend the clinic that was where we began. The counselling aspects have not been done full justice in the above account. The case is presented here as an example of using a combined approach with the girl herself as the major focus of intervention.

[The primary therapist in this case was Ms. M. Jacques.]

Case No. 5: 'Ronald'

Not all our cases are unqualified successes. Ronald was referred aged 12 years by his school. He had started at his secondary school the previous September, but by Christmas he was complaining of stomachaches and not getting to school. His form tutor arranged for him to transfer from classes which he said he disliked, but after only ten days attendance, he complained of bullying and stopped going to school. He had been absent for three months.

He had poor peer relationships, responded poorly to teasing, but disliked fighting. He was much more comfortable in the company of adults, and had been helping out at a local garage while not at school. There had been a previous episode of school refusal at the age of 9, associated with difficulties between the parents at home.

At the initial interview, Ronald's parents seemed very pleasant and co-operative. Ronald was of average intelligence and attainment although somewhat introverted and neurotic on testing. Although a hierarchy of anxiety provoking items was established, he could not sit still for very long and found it difficult to imagine any scenes. However, he reacted strongly by blushing and fidgetting whenever a difficult scene was discussed so discussions of difficult and pleasant scenes were alternated. After six sessions in the clinic, an *in vivo* session was held. He reacted very strongly to all school related cues, becoming extremely anxious when he saw boys from his school in the far distance.

It was noticeable that Ronald was less anxious in father's presence and would spend longer outside the school when father was there. Despite this encouraging sign, the end of the summer term was reached without Ronald being back in school. At the beginning of the autumn term, he was able to drive up to the school with the therapist and go into the building. However, the school personnel were growing increasingly sceptical that this gradual approach would work. We agreed to set a deadline for November, and when that was reached without significant progress, a place was found for Ronald in an 'Educational Guidance Centre' — a small facility for difficult children.

He attended regularly for 5 half-days a week. The aim was to use this as a base to get him back to his ordinary school. The teachers from the centre carried out the re-introduction programme under the psychologist's supervision. Within three months, he was also attending some classes at his ordinary school. In the summer term, the number of sessions he was to spend in his ordinary school was gradually increased, but when an ultimatum was presented after the summer vacation that he should attend his own school full-time, the parents withdrew the boy from school.

In retrospect, the parents were the key to our failure. After their initial co-operation, they made it impossible for the social worker to meet with them. They both worked in their own separate businesses, and both refused to take time off during the day to visit the clinic. Home visits were made late in the evening, but it was difficult to use them in therapeutic terms. The unsuspected presence of a non-attending model in the form of his elder sister, must also be considered an important factor in the failure of treatment.

Since Ronald arranged to attend the small, special centre soon after it was suggested, one may well ask why a change of school was not arranged earlier. Two points should be made. First, sufficient, if minimal, progress occurred to make us believe that return to school was imminent; secondly, we broke all conventions in managing to arrange Ronald's entry into the particular facility. Previously, it had only accepted aggressive, acting-out children.

Case No. 6: 'Simon'

Wherever possible, we try to treat the children as outpatients, but if the parents cannot cope or, for some other reason (see Section on Hospital Treatment) hospital admission is arranged. Such a case was Simon, referred to us at the age of 10 years by his mother.

Briefly, he had first had an episode of school refusal at the age of 7½ years following a series of deaths and illnesses among neighbours. He was seen at a local child guidance clinic, but they failed to help. Some time later, Simon cut his hand badly, and on recovery returned to school using the injury as an excuse for absence. His mother never understood his long absence and was continually worried that he would refuse again. Nearly two years later, after a bout of influenza, she couldn't get him to return to school and he was seen two months later.

He was described as a very bright boy who couldn't tolerate failure at school. Normally, he was an easy boy, but recently he had been extremely demanding and impossible to manage. Neither of his parents could stand up to him. When first seen, mother was in a state of near panic and Simon was in control of the family. He would issue orders to them from his bedroom and his parents were very afraid, both of the possible effect on him, of his panic attacks, and of his aggression towards them.

Both parents were seen regularly in joint sessions by a psychologist and psychiatric social worker. The aim was to give them techniques of controlling Simon's demanding behaviour, emphasizing the need for each to back the other up. In particular, the father's role was stressed and his tentative efforts at asserting himself were reinforced. The parents were given 'Living with Children' (Patterson and Gullion, 1968) to read, and helped to devise small programmes for Simon. However, it was a slow business. Although the parents felt more confident, and indeed were able to bring Simon to sessions after two months, it was getting to the end of the school year and there was no sign of his return. One of our difficulties in working out a programme with them was father's rigidity and obsessive pre-occupation with detail. We helped the parents to back one another in their handling, but their fears were so great that they needed the concrete evidence of seeing Simon managed by staff on the children's ward before they were convinced that no harm would come to him through firm handling.

We set a deadline — either Simon was back in school on the first day of the autumn term or else we took him into the ward. We worked with them on how to support Simon but, in the event, he began to cry on his way to school on the first morning and their resolve crumpled. He was admitted to the ward the next day.

Details of ward management are given in Chapter 15 (Case 2). A pattern of regular attendance at his ordinary school was established by having nursing staff taking him daily. Then, very gradually, he was allowed home for increasing periods and his parents had to take him to school. By the end of term, he was back home and attending regularly.

Six months later, his parents wrote saying: ' . . . All in all, things are going rather well. There have been absolutely no problems about going to school . . . .' They recognized that the meetings we had with both parents had been very important in resolving their differences over how to manage their son. During the period of Simon's school refusal, his mother's own activities had been curtailed as he insisted on checking her every movement. She gained a great deal of confidence as she was enabled to build up her own social life again and to share the responsibility for the family with father.

IMPLICATIONS

Readers who have treated school refusers will, hopefully, have recognized many of the factors involved in the cases, yet all six are very different. Within the limitations of our waiting list, we try always to react to cases of school refusal as quickly as possible. In addition to obtaining a full history of the problem, of the child's development and of family structure and life, we interview the child very fully and assess his level of intelligence and academic attainment. From the start, we emphasize that our job is to help get the boy (or girl) back to school. We are prepared to negotiate with the school to get some lessons changed, and offer ourselves as mediators. We try to establish the various aetiological factors which preceded the school refusal, and to anticipate difficulties the child will face on re-entry. Where appropriate, we explain the rationale of systematic desensitization, laying stress on the value of relaxation in coping with future difficulties. Unlike Blagg (1977) we do not interview the parents and child at school. Apart from that, our overall strategy is fairly close to his.

It is clear that many behavioural techniques have proved of value in some cases. The problem remains of indications for each technique and when to switch to a different approach? There are as yet no comparative studies to answer these practical questions, and approximate answers must be inferred from the earlier evidence.

In our view, there are many different sub-types of school refusal. The following crude classification has treatment implications:

(1) Where the school refusal shows at first school entry, then one is probably dealing with a manifestation of separation anxiety. This may well be complicated by the parent's inability to handle their child firmly and consistently. In such cases, some form of *in vivo* desensitization exercises such as described by Montenegro (1968) seems the most appropriate initial approach. It is noticeable that in the literature review above, in three of the five youngest cases — i.e. 6 to 8 years old — separation problems were prominent and treated (Olsen and Coleman, 1967; Patterson, 1965; Ayllon, Smith, and Rogers, 1970). Separation difficulties are not mentioned in the other two cases (Lazarus and Abramovitz, 1962; Cantrell *et al.*, 1969).

(2) Many cases of school refusal occur shortly after a major change of schooling (Hersov, 1960). Often, a critical change is from the smaller, more child-centred form of primary schooling to the larger, less personal secondary school at around 12 years of age. In our experience, some vulnerable children are able to cope with the demands of schooling in the protected environment of the primary school, but are under greater pressure at transfer. This pressure may take the form of, for example, the bright child coming up against real competition for the first time. The transition from being the eldest in the primary setting to being the youngest in the rougher secondary setting can also be threatening. Whatever the particular school stress experienced, the addition of any extraneous threat such as personal experience of illness, or illness or death of a family member, or the loss of close friends, may be sufficient to

spark off an episode of refusal. In such cases, systematic desensitization, paying attention to details of the physical and social environment, is the approach of choice. A graded re-entry to school should be effected relatively quickly.

(3) It is worth mentioning school refusal in older children. Where a child has managed to attend school regularly for 9 to 10 years, the non-attendance may well be associated with the onset of a depressive illness or even an early onset schizophrenia. In all cases treatment must involve the child more individually than is often necessary with younger patients. The therapist may have to respect the adolescent's reasons for non-attendance at a school whose academic programme appears irrelevant. However, before accepting the situation, the therapist may argue that difficult situations cannot always be avoided and so he will offer his patient the opportunity of learning better coping skills.

(4) Where children of any age have been out of school for a very short time — a matter of less than two weeks, say — then it is clear from the review that a variety of simple, straightforward techniques are likely to be successful very quickly. Kennedy (1965) gets his 50 cases back in under a week. Contingency contracting was used successfully by Cantrell et al. (1969). Welch and Carpenter (1970) and Vaal (1973). Clearly, it must be the aim of all services to encourage schools to recognize school refusal early. Such secondary preventive work makes for easier therapeutic intervention.

(5) Implicitly, we have adopted an additive stress model. Whilst this appears to lead to more breakdowns in attendance at the time of school transfer, it can happen at any time. Specific incidents of bullying or of ridicule at school which are shrugged off by most children are taken to heart by children who already are afraid of separating from home. It seems to us to be no coincidence that fears of death figure prominently in the 10 to 13 years olds. (See Chapter 10). Although the literature on children's awareness of death is pitifully small, it is clear that it is in this developmental stage that most children are beginning to realize that death is both universal and irreversible (Childers and Wimmer, 1971; Koocher, 1974; Wolff, 1969). Should there be a reality based incident, their fear may well be exacerbated. If the parents mishandle the situation, then the child may well stay at home to be near them. Thus, whatever the age of the child, when school refusal is recognized, we enquire into the child's history of separations and his recent experiences of death (in family, friends, or even pets) in more detail than usual, as well as whether a parent has threatened to leave home or commit suicide or whether such behaviour has occurred.

It will be obvious from our account, that we pay careful attention to details in the school and in the family. We involved the parents wherever possible and we try to maintain them in the principal role of being responsible for their child's attendance. Where we judge it necessary to remove that responsibility, we do so on the basis that it would be damaging for them to experience (more) failure in helping their child back to school. Even so, we hand the responsibility back to them as soon as is possible. We use a combination of methods. As cotherapists in implementing the behaviour programme, parents need to understand the rationale and the principles of the approach. They take part in planning each stage of the treatment and are fully conversant with the reasons underlying each suggested step. At the same time parents are offered casework help with other family problems. Very often the child is caught up in anxieties about a parent's own depression or severe illness in a family member as is illustrated in Norman's case. We aim to free the child from this responsibility by offering the parents an opportunity to discuss their concerns and to work on problems in the family. However, as we are mainly concerned in this chapter to describe behavioural methods in working with school refusers we have concentrated on this aspect of our work with parents.

At the point when we first meet families, parents are often feeling bewildered by changes of behaviour in the child. A child who has formerly been conforming and quiet has often become irritable, sullen, and aggressive when school is mentioned. Parents may not be used to having to exert control over the child. They can misinterpret panic as anger directed against themselves and can feel at a loss to know how to handle it. We therefore think it is essential to work with both parents. It can be a source of great relief to both mother and child if father can be helped to exert his authority in the family and take an active part in the treatment programme. Parents need to be able to explore their differences of opinion in handling the child in other areas of his behaviour, and to gain understanding when the child is fulfilling their own needs by remaining at home. These situations often seem entrenched and there are strong resistances to the child returning to school. The therapists need to look for the parents' feelings of dissatisfaction with the situation, e.g. that they are being controlled by the child, that their own activities are being curtailed by his insistence on checking every detail of their daily activities. We have seen how this operated in Simon's case. It is only when these dissatisfactions can be tapped that the therapist can form a good working partnership with the parents.

Before setting up a behaviour programme we explore possible areas of resistance in the parents. Very commonly they had been frightened by seeing the child in a state of panic and there is often a fear that actual physical damage may occur if pressure is put on the child. At this stage we sometimes take the responsibility away from the parents by taking the child to school ourselves. It is always made clear that this is a temporary measure and the demonstration that nothing harmful happens to the child can give parents the confidence to take over the management themselves. Identification between parents and child is sometimes so strong that the parents continue to suffer vicariously when in fact their child is happily occupied at school. Parents need to be helped to separate out their own feelings from those of the child and to be assured that they are not being too harsh.

When parents take on the handling of the programme they often need help in pacing it correctly either because they are anxious about moving on to the next step or because they tend to rush each step. This was true in Richard's case when we were helping the parents to encourage him to have a friend visit him at home. Their immediate response was to suggest that a large group of boys from Richard's school should be invited to spend a day with him. We encouraged parents to praise the child for achievement. This can present difficulties if the step seems trivial to the parents as we have seen in Norman's case. When the child begins to improve there is sometimes bewilderment that the problem cannot be mastered immediately so that parents need help in recognizing what is being achieved. When the child is back at school we anticipate with the parents possible danger points in the future such as absence from school for illness or holidays. To begin with we try to meet with the parents at these times and always ensure that they have easy access to us if problems do recur.

We are aware that families can sabotage treatment plans. When things are going unexpectedly slowly, we look around for parental collusion or the presence of an as-yet-unidentified model for non-attendance. Above all, we try to be flexible so as to change plans as the changing situation dictates. New facts emerge during treatment, and in particular we clarify any situations which produce the fear reaction in the child. Once they are more clearly delineated, then we can help the child confront them more openly. Our approach is predominantly behavioural yet with close attention to other personal and family factors. In a similar way to Miller, Barrett and Hampe (1974) we agree that there are four steps in an overall treatment approach: (i) establishing a good, trusting relationship with the child and his family; (ii) clarifying the stimulus situations which give rise to anxiety; (iii) desensitizing the child to the feared situations by using imagination, relaxation or merely talking, whichever is appropriate; and (iv) confronting the feared situations. We prefer, when we have a choice, to adopt a gradual rather than a sudden approach to the latter. Nevertheless, we try to remain firm and we have learned that in most cases the fears and tantrums which destroy the resolve of many parents soon subside when the child makes progress. The art is to know what is progress in the eyes of the child.

REFERENCES

Ayllon, T., Smith, D., and Rogers, M. (1970). Behavioral management of school phobia. *Journal of Behavior Therapy and Experimental Psychiatry*, **1**, 125–138.

Blackham, G. J. and Eden, B. F. (1973). Effective re-entry in a long-standing case of school phobia. *Devereaux Forum*, **8**, 42–48.

Blagg, N. (1977). A detailed strategy for the rapid treatment of school phobics. *Bulletin of the British Association of Behavioural Psychotherapy*, **5**, 70–75.

Cantrell, R. P., Cantrell, M. L., Huddleston, C. M., and Woolridge, R. L. (1969).

Application of contingency contracts to four school attendance problems. *Journal of Applied Behavioral Analysis*, 2, 215–220.

Chapel, J. L. (1967). Treatment of a case of school phobia by reciprocal inhibition. *Canadian Psychiatric Association Journal*, 12, 25–28.

Childers, P. and Wimmer, M. (1971). The concept of death in early childhood. *Child Development*, 42, 1299–1301.

Eysenck, H. J., and Rachman, S. (1965). *The Causes and Cure of Neurosis*. Routledge and Kegan Paul.

Galloway, D., and Miller, A. (1978). The use of graded *in vivo* flooding in the extinction of children's phobias. *Behavioural Psychotherapy*, 6, 7–10.

Garvey, W. P., and Hegrenes, J. R. (1966). Desensitization techniques in the treatment of school phobia. *American Journal Orthopsychiatry*, 36, 147–152.

Hayes, C. J. A., and Yule, W. (1980). Operant reading programmes (in preparation).

Hersen, M. (1968). Treatment of a compulsive and phobic disorder through a total behavior therapy program: A case study. *Psychotherapy*, 5, 220–225.

Hersen, M. (1970a). Behavior modification approach to a school-phobia case. *Journal of Clinical Psychology*, 26, 128–132.

Hersen, M. (1970b). The complementary use of behavior therapy and psychotherapy: some comments. *Psychology Record*, 20, 395–403.

Hersen, M. (1971). The behavioural treatment of school phobia. *Journal of Nervous and Mental Diseases*, 153, 99–107.

Hersen, M. (1971). Resistance to direction in behavior therapy: some comments. *Journal of Genetic Psychology*, 118 121–127.

Hersov, L. (1960). Refusal to go to school. *Journal of Child Psychology and Psychiatry*, 1, 137–145.

Jones, M. C. (1924). The elimination of children's fears. *Journal of Experimental Psychology*, 7, 383–390.

Kennedy, W. A. (1965). School phobia: Rapid treatment of fifty cases. *Journal of Abnormal Psychology*, 70, 285–289.

Kennedy, W. A. (1971). A behavioristic community-oriented approach to school phobia and other disorders. In Richards, H. C. (Ed.), *Behavioral Intervention in Human Problems*. Pergamon, Oxford.

Koocher, G. P. (1974). Talking with children about death. *American Journal of Orthopsychiatry*, 44, 404–411.

Lazarus, A. A. (1960). The elimination of children's phobias by deconditioning. In Eysenck, H. J. (Ed.), *Behaviour Therapy and the Neuroses*. Pergamon, Oxford, pp. 114–122.

Lazarus, A. A., and Abramowitz, A. (1962). The use of 'emotive imagery' in the treatment of children's phobias. *Journal of Mental Science*, 108, 191–195.

Lazarus, A. A., Davison, G. G., and Polefka, D. A. (1965). Classical and operant factors in the treatment of school phobia. *Journal of Abnormal Psychology*, 70, 225–229.

Leventhal, T., and Sills, M. (1964). Self-image in school phobia. *American Journal of Orthopsychiatry*, 34, 685–695.

Leventhal, T., Weinberger, G., Stander, R. J., and Stearns, R. P. (1967). Therapeutic strategies with school phobias. *American Journal of Orthopsychiatry*, 37, 64–70.

McAuley, R. and McAuley, P. (1977). *Child Behaviour Problems: An empirical approach to management*. Methuen, London.

Miller, L. C., Barrett, C. L. and Hampe, E. (1974). Phobias of childhood in a pre-scientific era. In (Ed.), Davies, A. *Child Personality and Psychopathology: Current Topics, Vol. I*. Wiley, New York, pp. 89–134.

Miller, P. M. (1972). The use of visual imagery and muscle relaxation in the counter-conditioning of a phobic child: A case study. *Journal of Nervous and Mental Diseases*, **154**, 457–459.

Montenegro, H. (1968). Severe separation anxiety in two pre-school children: successfully treated by reciprocal inhibition. *Journal of Child Psychology and Psychiatry*, **9**, 93–108.

Morgan, R. R. (1975). An exploratory study of three procedures to encourage school attendance. *Psychology in the School*, **12**, 209–215.

Ney, P. G. (1967). Combined Therapies in a family group. *Canadian Psychiatric Association Journal*, **12**, 379–385.

Olsen, I. A. and Coleman, H. S. (1967). Treatment of school phobia as a case of separation anxiety. *Psychology in the School*, **4**, 151–154.

Parker, F. C., and McCoy, J. F. (1977). School-based intervention for the modification of excessive absenteeism. *Psychology in the School*, **4**, 84–88.

Patterson, G. R. (1965). A learning theory approach to the treatment of the school phobic child. In (Eds.) Ullman, L. P., and Krasner, L., *Case Studies in Behavior Modification*. Rinehart and Winston, New York. pp. 279–285.

Patterson, G. R. and Gullion, M. E. (1968). *Living with children: new methods for parents and children*. Research Press, Champaign, Illinois.

Rines, W. B. (1973). Behavior therapy before institutionalization. *Psychotherapy: Theory, Research and Practice*, **10**, 281–283.

Scherman, A. and Grover, V. M. (1962). Treatment of children's behavior disorders: A method of re-education. *Medical Proceedings*, **8**, 151–154.

Smith, R. E. and Sharpe, T. M. (1970). Treatment of a school phobia with implosive therapy. *Journal of Consultative Clinical Psychology*, **35**, 239–243.

Tahmisian, J. A. and McReynolds, W. T. (1971). Use of parents as behavioral engineers in the treatment of a school phobic girl. *Journal of Counselling Psychology*,

Vaal, J. J. (1973). Applying contingency contracting to a school phobic: A case study. *Journal of Behavior Therapy and Experimental Psychiatry*, **4**, 371–373.

Wahler, R. G. and Cormier, W. H. (1970). The ecological interview: A first step in outpatient child behavior therapy. *Journal of Behavior Therapy and Experimental Psychiatry*, **1**, 279–289.

Weinberger, G., Leventhal, T., and Beckman, G. (1973). The management of a chronic school phobic through the use of consultation with school personnel. *Psychology in the School*, **10**, 83–88.

Welch, M. W., and Carpenter, C. (1970). Solution of a school phobia by contingency contracting. *School Applications of Learning Theory*, **2**, 11–17.

Wolff, S. (1969). *Children under Stress*. Penguin, Harmondsworth.

Yule, W. (1977). Behavioural approaches. In (Eds.) Rutter, M. and Hersov, L. *Child Psychiatry: Modern Approaches*. Blackwell, Oxford, pp. 923–948.

Chapter 15

Hospital Inpatient and Day-patient Treatment of School Refusal

Lionel Hersov

The descriptions of treatment so far have dealt with methods used in out-patient settings with or without the help of community services. This section is concerned with hospital treatment, either in-patient or day-patient, and aims to delineate the indications, describe the most important elements with illustrative case studies, and discuss the outcome of this type of treatment.

Warren (1948) in one of the early papers on School Refusal states that outpatient treatment 'is difficult, prolonged and in many ways unsatisfactory' often failing to solve the impasse that had arisen at home. Three of his group of eight children were admitted to the Children's Inpatient Unit at The Maudsley Hospital. There had been no mention of such measures in earlier reports of school refusal and Warren (1948) found that they helped in recovery, including a saving in treatment time, through a quicker return to school in suitable cases. In his opinion, this line of treatment depended on parental cooperation and the child's willingness to come into hospital. However, once achieved it saved the child much anxiety and misery and made for easier psychotherapy in a neutral emotional atmosphere away from home. Warren (1948) did not describe the elements of treatment in hospital other than psychotherapy and participation in ward group activities for the child while a psychiatric social worker treated the mother. He laid stress on the child going to school each day from hospital unobtrusively escorted by a nurse until this support became unnecessary. This occurred in all three children admitted to hospital. However, a relapse in the one case is attributed to the absence of concomitant change in the mother's attitude and behaviour, with a return to the earlier situation of avoidance of school once the patient returned home, thus emphasizing the importance of work with parents and family even with hospital admissions.

Weiss and Cain (1964) describe a group of sixteen older more chronically ill children and adolescents, resistant to community efforts and psychotherapy who failed to return to school in spite of these forms of treatment. They

303

delineated two distinct dynamic patterns of behaviour and relationships amongst their total group although separation anxiety was present in both. They noted further differences during direct observation of the children and their families at the time of hospital admission. In the group where 'symbiotic' parent–child relationships dominated the clinical picture, admission was dramatically resisted with tears, last-ditch offers and promises to conform, quite unlike the second group where the children were 'parasitically' dependent on the parents and also limited in their capacity to form meaningful relationships. Here there was a conspicuous lack of affect at the time of admission without clinging or pleading but a willingness to turn too early to a substitute mother among the ward staff. They considered the second group to be less accessible to treatment yet follow-up five to ten years later showed no differences in adaptation between the two groups (Weiss and Burke, 1967).

The first study (Weiss and Cain, 1964) is of particular interest because it drew attention to the need for an individualized treatment plan to meet the needs of a particular child. It also described those aspects of the therapeutic milieu which benefited children displaying this particular problem of school refusal in a setting of deviant development and family relationships. Important elements in treatment included close observation of overall behaviour and attempts at manipulation at the time of separation and admission to hospital, followed by a consistent response to the child's manipulative demands for family contact which had proved so successful at home. A policy of planned hospital visits by parents allowed the child to face the issue over separation and the fact that the problem lay at home and not at school. These authors stress the therapeutic value of the hospital school. Immediate successful attendance is experienced as a tangible gain as well as the beginning of an end to worries about falling behind at school and the loss of peer relationships. They remark on the remarkable ease with which the children attended school, proving to be conscientious students so that school soon became the area of best adjustment. This also helped the child to see that his problem was around separation from home and not about going to school.

The therapeutic milieu included a host of activities often successfully avoided by the child in the past or withheld by the parents because of overprotection or social isolation. Clumsy unskilled children lacking experience in team games learned to enter into mandatory activities including various sports leading to fuller social participation and increased self-esteem. The experience of group living and shared activities was particularly important often showing up avoidance of peers and efforts to achieve a 'special' role in relation to nurses, and also attempts to form 'exclusive' friendships with other children. It is of interest that during the follow-up study the milieu aspect of treatment was later recalled as most helpful particularly the chance it offered for new peer group relationships and social experiences (Weiss and Burke, 1967).

Barker (1968) describes six cases of school refusal under the age of 12 years admitted to a hospital inpatient unit. Here, the major psychopathology appeared to be an unresolved dependency situation with overprotection and excessive maternal care. Treatment was essentially physical separation of child and parents after the child had earlier established a relationship with his therapist. This usually meant delaying admission until a relationship with the family had been built up while a trial of the efficacy of outpatient treatment was in progress. This author mentions that a full programme of daily activities helps the children to stop thinking about home and separation from parents while the therapeutic milieu accepts their regressed state at first, and then gradually increases demands upon the child and exposes him to increasing stress. Barker (1968) encourages frequent, even daily visiting by parents, particularly in the early stages of treatment when separation anxiety is marked, insists on school attendance and provides occupational therapy for constructive activities to re-establish self-esteem. Return to school is *via* gradually lengthening weekends at home and making contact with the school in the community although there is no mention of attendance at such schools while still in hospital. Involvement of a single case-worker with parents before, during and after admission is considered desirable because of evidence of strain and depression in a parent and also to give support and deal with psychopathological material which is more accessible during these phases of treatment. He concludes that inpatient psychiatric care is a valuable treatment measure, in some of the most severe school refusers, with an appropriate therapeutic milieu able to meet these children's needs better than other treatment measures.

These reports of treatment are of interest in that they all emphasize the importance of the therapeutic milieu, while giving less importance to individual psychotherapy (see Chapter 13). This reflects the altered place of psychotherapy in keeping with the structural and functional changes in modern therapeutic hospital environments. Noshspitz (1962) has described how the earlier 'holding' role of residential institutions has changed so that treatment strategies now encompass all members of staff, not only the child's psychotherapist, while others (Greenwood, 1955; Redl, 1959) find that psychotherapeutic methods are not the only therapeutic means of psychiatric intervention. Weiss and Cain (1964) describe the difficulties encountered by psychotherapists in treating youngsters with school phobia in hospital, including the reluctance to talk and silent opposition to exploration of fantasy. This they felt arose, as much from an inability to relate and lack of fantasy life, as from unwillingness to take part in psychotherapy. Barker (1968) also found that psychotherapy played a relatively small part in the treatment of his cases and was supportive rather than interpretative in nature with discussion of family relationships in some cases.

Berg (1970) describes an inpatient unit run along therapeutic community lines dealing mainly with neurotic problems for youngsters aged 10–16 years.

All relevant staff and patients are included where possible in daily policy decisions. Child social therapists are given particular responsibility for an individual child. Decision-taking is delegated to social therapists and patients within a framework of frequent staff and staff-patient meetings and a minimum of rules which are constantly reviewed. Patients return home every weekend from Friday afternoon to Sunday and are expected to be in the unit school every morning. Otherwise they are mostly free to please themselves what they do with encouragement to join in organized games, group meetings and to mix socially with other children. There appears to be no formal psychotherapy provided but patients are encouraged to talk to their social therapists. Berg (1970) describes problems among half his school phobic patients in accepting their stay in hospital shown as severe emotional upset on admission, running home, refusal to return from weekends, constant requests to return home and communicate with parents and reluctance to mix with other children. Management of these difficulties requires a firm consistent approach, with special attention by social therapists, and sometimes special eating and medication arrangements and help for parents in bringing their child back to the unit. During the process of attempting the return to school, emphasis is given to liaison with the particular school, support for the family and the aid of a social therapist in accompanying the youngster to school for a few days every morning when necessary. Several attempts are made before achieving success or admitting failure and no child is discharged from hospital until there is a good chance of successful regular attendance.

INDICATIONS FOR INPATIENT AND DAY-PATIENT TREATMENT

Clinical experience and scrutiny of the literature shows the following to be the common reasons for admitting a child or adolescent with school refusal to a hospital inpatient or day-patient unit as the treatment of choice.

(a)   The onset of school refusal early in the child's school career interspersed with short periods of regular attendance culminating in complete break-down of school attendance after the child has entered secondary school. Nowadays the trend is to start with outpatient treatment but the chronicity of the problem should signal the need for inpatient treatment in the first instance.

(b)   Parents' inability to exercise any effective control over a child or adolescent so that physical force is needed to get the child to school leading often to violent struggles with 'hysterical' behaviour by the child. Parental over-involvement with the child is usually so marked that each episode arouses strong guilt feelings, and compensatory overprotection in parents with increased anxiety about separation. Parents and child become locked in a struggle for dominance which cannot be resolved without external help, including planned separation of parents and child.

(c) Where outpatient treatment is increasingly hampered by the child and parent's inability to separate from each other or to carry out a systematic programme of graded return to school (see Chapter 14). This may be also associated with the parent's inability to make use of social case-work, or where parent and child are locked into a maladaptive interaction which interferes with the child's normal emotional development and wish to become independent of the family.

(d) Increasing social isolation and withdrawal on the child's or adolescent's part which may be part of a depressive disorder or a psychotic illness. In the latter case, the non-attendance has a bizarre quality to it and is associated with other grossly abnormal behaviour.

(e) Where a lengthy period of thoughtful well-planned treatment has proved ineffective because of strong manipulative tendencies in the patient which parents are unable to withstand and where an enforced separation of patient and family is considered necessary to begin and maintain an effective treatment plan.

(f) Less severely disturbed children, whose families are still able to make decisions and exercise some control, can be helped to overcome their phobic avoidance of school by attending as day-patients. They master their fears initially by entry into the hospital school. Separation problems are usually less evident in these cases and social relationships can be re-established through membership of the children's group in hospital before attempting the return back to ordinary school.

(g) In those circumstances where one or both parents are so psychiatrically or physically ill that they cannot manage to carry out a treatment plan, admission to hospital is indicated sometimes for both child and one or other parent at the same time. Whole family admission and treatment has been advocated, but in the author's experience, admission to separate wards of the same hospital has advantages.

MILIEU THERAPY FOR SCHOOL REFUSAL

The 'therapeutic milieu' in inpatient and day-patient treatment implies that the physical and social surroundings are themselves part of the treatment process. It is a setting where different therapeutic experiences can be provided for the youngsters during most, if not all of, their day. These experiences go beyond the daily routine and require careful consideration of the individual child's needs, abilities or lack of them, tolerance of stress, handicaps either physical, emotional, or educational, quality of interpersonal relationships and social experience. The fact that the other children and adolescents in a hospital inpatient or day-patient unit make up a peer group is important for children with school refusal for they so often have experienced faulty or inappropriate social learning in their own family or in school. They may have problems in relating to other children comfortably or may even fear the normal manifestations of active competitive behaviour in youngsters of their own age.

A pre-admission home visit is carried out by two or three members of the inpatient treatment team, usually psychiatrist, social worker, and the 'special' nurse who will be most closely involved with the child's treatment. This allows the whole family to meet the team on their home ground, thus reducing somewhat the sense of distance and disparity they must inevitably feel at the beginning. The visit is also a continuation of the process of negotiating admission which is a very significant experience for a family in which a child is refusing school. The nurse makes particular contact with the child, if possible, gets to know his interests and hobbies, sees his pets, visits his bedroom, discusses his toys, and what he might like to bring into hospital. This initial contact will be used at the time of admission to ease the difficulties of separation and diminish some of the anxiety, by providing a person who now knows the child and his family and can become the focal point for later enquiries, discussion about weekend leave and progress in treatment.

Hospital admission in school refusal often lays bare the stresses and divisions within a family or reveals an impending marriage breakdown. Hence, the importance of a family approach to treatment usually including the patient. It is our experience that families are more cooperative and more satisfied if they are actively involved in the treatment plan from the beginning.

In hospital the children are involved in peer group interaction supported all the while by a nurse therapist who can regulate the amount of exposure within the child's tolerance. The aim is to keep the youngster engaged in group activities so he cannot resort to the avoidance behaviour he may have displayed prior to admission. Programmes of independence training or training in social assertiveness and social skills can be set up aimed at bringing them up to the level appropriate for their age. Where educational attainments are retarded for age and intelligence, remedial teaching as well as experience in classroom work can be provided. For many school refusers, the classroom is often the area of greatest achievement and success but in others, frequent absence or a lack of basic groundwork may have led to increasing retardation which, in turn, becomes a potent factor in the maintenance of symptoms.

The problems of psychotherapy with school refusers have been mentioned above. Where the child can make use of this form of individual and group treatment, it can be extremely helpful in dealing with anxieties about feelings of anger and guilt and anxieties about separation. Far more often the personality of the youngster and the difficulty in eliciting significant therapeutic material means that the goal of conflict resolution has to be replaced by goals of improvement in behaviour in relation to school attendance and social relationships (Sand and Golub, 1974).

ILLUSTRATIVE CASE STUDIES

The case studies will illustrate this treatment approach and demonstrate several ways of using hospital resources in different types of school refusal.

Case I

An 11-year-old boy referred from a London Child Guidance Unit with one year's duration of known school refusal preceded by a long history of poor attendance for a variety of reasons. He was the younger of two children with a 13-year-old brother who had also been periodically anxious about attending school. The patient was born six weeks prematurely, weighing 4lbs 10ozs and put in special care for three weeks. His mother was told he only had a 50/50 chance of survival and this knowledge profoundly influenced her later handling of his anger, any moves toward independence, and response to illness. She also controlled her own negative feelings aroused by his behaviour by never displaying overt anger to him. He was a difficult, demanding infant with normal development in all respects apart from unusual dependence on his mother as he grew older. He was at home for two weeks when two years old while his mother was in hospital, but had no other separations.

He was bullied at primary school needing constant pressure to attend and so had a record of chronically poor attendance. However, he liked his teacher and his work was good. After one Easter holiday, he refused to return to school for no apparent reason. If persuaded by mother to return and accompanied by her, he would later run out of school and come home. Pressure by an Educational Welfare Officer only resulted in a fortnight's attendance. When first seen at the Child Guidance Unit six weeks later he was described as showing severe separation anxiety during the assessment and at home in relation to school.

Treatment was begun using outpatient psychotherapy but he only attended one session. His parents were unable to engage in planned joint treatment interviews and were reluctant throughout to accept help with the difficulties over separation. They persisted in viewing the problem as entirely that of fear of boys at school. Both parents were in their mid-forties with father presenting as an apparently emotionally stable migraine sufferer who was over-attached to his own father, ineffectual and unassertive with his sons, and obsessionally concerned wtih stamp collecting. Mother was anxious and overprotective, and had herself been a school refuser with minimal attendance after the age of 12 years.

Treatment was unsuccessful in that the patient was mute and motionless for 30 minutes during psychotherapy, wrapping himself around the staircase banisters to avoid going into sessions alternating with violent outbursts of rage when he threw objects about. Medication had no effect and the picture emerged of an anxious manipulating home-bound child unable to assert himself or form relationships with peers at home and at school, gradually withdrawing from the outside world into the safety of the family while his parents, especially his mother, were overprotective and unable to control him. The family, as a whole, were assessed for possible admission to the 'family unit' of a hospital for neurotic disorders but he was regarded as unsuitable.

Treatment as an out-patient under these circumstances was clearly not feasible so he was referred to the Children's Inpatient Unit at the Maudsley Hospital. At the assessment interview, the picture was identical with that above and the boy produced a temper tantrum in which he broke a window while his parents remained powerless in the face of his fear and anger. We departed from our usual practice of making a pre-admission home visit because we felt he should be admitted there and then as his parents were unlikely to be able to bring him back again. It was decided that his separation anxiety and manipulative control of the family could only be dealt with by immediate separation from the family in spite of his protests and his parents' distress. He was therefore taken directly up to the ward by a nurse, introduced to the other children and taken straight into school. The farewell was limited to the minimum time to avoid emotional upset and bargaining, and parents were told that there would be no visiting for two weeks but telephone conversations were encouraged.

The goals of 'milieu therapy' were: (1) Immediate regular attendance at the hospital school with the long-term goal of regular school attendance from home; (2) Independence training by nursing staff so that he could master social situations away from home e.g. travelling alone, attending a Youth Club; (3) To bring his level of school attainment up to the appropriate level for his age and IQ. (He was in the dull normal range of intelligence with a reading age slightly below that predicted for Age and IQ); (4) Psychotherapy to encourage ventilation of feelings, to deal with separation fears, and to help with control of anger towards parents when frustrated; (5) Family interviews and then conjoint family therapy to deal with sibling rivalry, parental overprotection, excessive involvement of mother with patient, father's lack of participation and assertion, and the general social isolation of the family.

During the family interviews the patient's sibling was quiet and unsure while the patient himself showed the earlier angry defiant refusal to participate. There was underlying fear that he would drive his mother away, and anxiety about her leaving him. After some time, mother could face her fear that any expression of anger would lead to family break-up bringing back her own experience as a child, and could see why she placated all the males in the family, especially the patient, and so could not deal with his tantrums and manipulation.

After seven months' treatment, there had been considerable change in that the parents could allow the boy much more independence at home, could value the social skills he had acquired on the ward, and perceived him as more competent and confident. Mother was thinking about getting a job and parents had become closer to each other. However, the family remained inhibited in the expression of feelings and too socially isolated for comfort.

Return to school was begun from the ward initially. There was meticulous preparation for re-entry but the patient's extreme fear of school returned soon after beginning school in spite of support from an accompanying staff member. Phobic avoidance of aspects of the school situation such as games, PE and swimming were negotiated rather than confronted and a programme to try and overcome these was set up on the ward. Diazepam was administered to reduce morning anxiety prior to school but a long period of support to attend was needed before he could return home and continue attendance from there. Much of his earlier stubbornness in the face of therapeutic and parental demands returned but parents could now cope more effectively.

Follow-up

Attendance continued to be fairly regular but the boy still related very poorly with other youngsters and still had the handicap of social anxieties. Further treatment was attempted at home by the team from the referring Child Guidance Unit. The boy avoided these sessions by being late or refusing to join the therapists and his parents who were also thought to be colluding with his behaviour. Finally, the case was closed with the prediction that further breakdown and recurrence of school refusal was highly likely.

Case II

A 10-year-old boy referred to the Hospital Children's Department by his mother *via* a Clinical Psychologist to whom she had written following a newspaper article on the treatment of 'school phobia'. The first episode of school refusal occurred at the age of 7½ years following the unexpected death of a neighbour at Christmas. On the way back to school next term, he and his mother heard of another sudden death. Mother was then suffering with a bleeding angioma of the tongue and this was coupled in the boy's mind with gossip about who, among neighbours and friends, would be the next to die. He refused to go into school and became increasingly anxious with hyperventilation symptoms over the next week. A single attendance at a local Child Guidance Unit achieved no change and he became irritable, demanding, and destructive if crossed while also clinging anxiously to his mother.

He appeared to resolve the situation by himself with his mother's help following cutting his hand badly. This gave him a face-saving excuse for being off school and his mother gradually reintroduced him to school *via* attendance at sports day, school football matches and then visits to his classroom. After two terms absence, he made a shaky re-entry to school settling down after three weeks to his usual level of competent work of a high standard. He was an extremely intelligent lad and two years ahead of his predicted level in reading.

There were no further school problems in the next two and a half years but in the New Year term he suffered with influenza and was at home for three days just prior to the half-term holiday. He was unable to get back to school although recovered and would not return after the half-term holiday. Diazepam did not relieve his anxiety and he became irritable and aggressive, refused to discuss his school refusal, remaining moody, and excitable at home and would not leave home during school hours.

He was healthy, would never eat breakfast, and came home from school for lunch. He was normally a placid, charming, well-spoken lad, who enjoyed the company of adults, liked to get his own way, and worried about doing well at school. His peer and sibling relationships were good and he showed no anti-social behaviour.

His mother, in her late forties, had not worked since marriage and appeared as an anxious person carrying the burden of her son's problems as well as the neighbours' problems without she maintained, the help of her husband who had opted out because of his failure to exert any control over the boy. There was constant marital conflict and the father appeared to invest all his energies in his work. The patient's early development had been quite normal with some difficulty in separating at the time of entry to a play group at three and a half years, when he refused to remain after three days and did not return. There were no apparent problems at school entry.

The patient refused to attend the outpatients' department and so was visited at home. He became panicky and angry refusing to talk. His mother was unable to control him and it was left that we would still try and treat him on an out-patient basis with the participation of both parents. The formulation was of severe separation anxiety underlying both the present and the first episode of school refusal in a sensitive intelligent boy with high standards of school work and behaviour. The important model in the family was his father but he had apparently opted out leaving his wife to deal with the problem. The boy was holding his mother to ransom by his refusal to cooperate in any treatment.

The initial attempts to provide outpatient treatment led to the emergence in parental interviews of marked differences between the parents on how to handle the boy. It appeared that father could handle his aggressive outbursts very effectively provided he was not undermined by his wife. It was constant reiteration of his ineffectiveness which originally had led to his withdrawal from the contest. The treatment plan had strongly emphasized the need for both parents to work out a plan of consistent management at home in which each took part according to defined and agreed tasks (see Chapter 14, Case 6).

After four interviews with no apparent progress, it was made explicit to all concerned that if the lad did not return to school at the beginning of the September term, he would be admitted to hospital. This was agreed for, by this time, the parents had been helped to learn methods of controlling his demanding behaviour, backed each other up and father was now becoming more assertive, constructive, and involved in managing the boy. Parents were now able to bring the boy to sessions and so could stand firm on the issue of hospital admission. This was arranged after the failure to return in spite of his promises to do so and attempts to bargain in the face of parents' determination to keep their side of the contract.

Initially, the boy was upset about being parted from his parents and again made promises to go back to school. The treatment plan involved regular meetings with the boy and weekly sessions with parents to discuss handling during the weekends at home which, although limited at first, were gradually increased in frequency. The treatment goal was to help the boy return to school from the ward not later than mid-term, if possible, and to establish his attendance on a firm basis.

The ward staff worked closely with the parents and the school and he was successfully reintegrated there. Control of school-going situations was gradually returned to the parents and he returned finally to school from home at the beginning of the January term. His attendance remained regular, he made the transition to Secondary School without any problems and a year later was still attending regularly and showing no reluctance to attend even when feeling off-colour. He continued to worry about homework but after discussing a routine to complete it early, overcame this, and so could devote his time to his hobbies. He was able to go on a school visit lasting one week plus day trips and was planning to visit France with a school party.

Tensions remain in the home but parents continued to act consistently and to deal with their differences in a more effective fashion. Both admitted how important their disagreements had been in adding to the problem of school refusal and were grateful for the help given them.

Follow-up

Eighteen months later, his parents reported that he had just completed his first year at secondary school with very little absence, apart from a day or two off with minor illness. He had taken up philately and collected cacti. He had been on trips in England and abroad with his school lasting one week without upset, had friends to play with and was generally happy. His parents were aware how family tensions affected him and could now avert problems in a more effective fashion. They appeared very pleased with the results of treatment.

Case III

An 11-year-old referred by her family doctor in January 1975 at the request of an Educational Welfare Officer for school refusal of four months' duration coupled with severe backwardness in reading. This the girl attributed to bullying at school and being called a dunce. She also complained of numerous somatic symptoms when under pressure to go to school such as limb weakness, toothache, headache, and dizzy spells and would become pale, sweaty, and clinging at such times. She became very anxious when she did not know where her mother was but had easily been able to leave the house to enjoy riding lessons. At first she refused to attend the hospital but was persuaded by her father. She at first refused to be interviewed but then responded to firm insistence.

She was the youngest of four children with an eight-year age gap between her and her brother aged 19 years who was living at home. Father aged 55 years was an intelligent competent man running his own successful business and able to exert authority in the family. He spent most of his time at work or running a football club because he was irritated and embarrassed by his less intelligent wife. She was 51 years old, very house-proud, menopausal, anxious, lacking in confidence, and very caught up in her daughter's problems. She had been required to care for her own ill mother when a schoolgirl and so missed a lot of school. She felt angry and martyred by her daughter's demands, unable to cope with her somatic complaints, adopting a nurse's role, and keeping her at home for minor illnesses with family doctor support.

The patient was unexpectedly conceived but was apparently a wanted child. There were no problems during pregnancy or at delivery but she spent much of her first two months in hospital while mother visited twice daily. There were three further hospital admissions for tonsillectomy at four years, head injury at six years and abdominal pain for one day at seven years. She began nursery school at four years but refused to go after two months and never went again.

During her interview, she described herself as a very nervous person: 'I come over dizzy sometimes and me dad knows there is something wrong'. She appreciated her severe backwardness in reading, writing, and spelling, and wished to be able to learn but said she was so bullied and shamed by other girls that she would never return to her old school again. She likened herself to her mother in enjoying caring for each other when ill and in their shared dislike of crowded places, and was a breezy and coquettish pre-pubertal girl with a wish to have her own horse to ride.

Psychological Assessment WISC. Full Scale IQ 80. Verbal Scale 81. Performance Scale 83. Neale Test of Reading; Rate, below basal reading age. Accuracy, six years two months. Comprehension, six years six months. She did not know the sounds of 18 letters of the alphabet and her Arithmetic sub-test score was very low.

The formulation was of school refusal in a pre-pubertal girl of dull normal intelligence with gross retardation in all attainments. This, together with the reported bullying, was regarded as an important but not necessarily sufficient explanation of school avoidance. Her ordinal position in the family, over-dependent and manipulative relationship with her mother and her account of somatic symptoms around some separation and sress situations were considered more important. This hypothesis could be tested by a treatment plan which would deal with: (a) Academic retardation with remedial teaching help; (b) Peer group difficulties and phobic avoidance in a school situation by introduction to the hospital school; (c) Separation anxiety by day-patient attendance; (d) Contacting family doctor to short-cut school avoidance on the basis of somatic complaints and sick notes excusing the non-attendance.

Day-patient treatment was thought likely to meet these requirements and this was arranged. However, during the first four weeks, her attendance was too sporadic to be of any use and there were frequent absences due to minor illnesses with her parents colluding with her manipulative demands to stay at home and not come to hospital. She also complained of teasing by the other children and had great difficulty in settling to any school work. It became clear that inpatient treatment was necessary to intervene in the collusive parent–child relationship and to ensure reasonable exposure to schooling and her peer group. This required careful negotiation with parents by the Social Worker who was seeing them together weekly for case work. Mother became very anxious at the thought of her daughter existing independently away from home and the interviews brought into the open mother's own dependent needs and her feeling that her daughter should be at home to meet her own needs for company and care as she had provided for her own mother.

The girl precipitated admission a week earlier than planned to hospital by cutting her wrists. We took this as a communication by her that she was in need of help to separate from her family and gain our support and her parents who, up till then, had been unable to accept her need for psychiatric treatment, began to change their views and became very supportive of our treatment plan. There were two episodes of running away from hospital to home but she gradually settled into the ward routine and made excellent use of the experience, mixing happily with the other patients and maturing physically and emotionally. She was well-motivated toward her remedial teaching and was reading at the nine year old level after 11 months teaching — a gain of four years. She also progressed in Arithmetic and became skilful in swimming and netball with great strides in her self-esteem.

She and her parents were helped to work through their mutual separation anxieties by family case-work and increasing periods of time at home. She managed a camping holiday with the ward group during the summer, began to attend a Youth Club from the ward and started at her secondary school approximately one year after her first attendance at hospital.

Follow-up

September 1978 — two and a half years after discharge, she appeared to be happily settled at school, made friends with other girls and was willing to work hard at her reading which continued to improve. There were occasional absences on grounds of illness often coinciding with lessons she disliked. Her parents were very positive about her happy state at school. Her mother was now working and therefore allowing her daughter much more freedom and independence.

COMMENTARY

These three cases all had a successful outcome if the criterion is return to school and regular attendance. However, only cases, 2 and 3, showed a commensurate change and improvement in social and emotional development appropriate to age. In both, the parents were able to make use of social case-work and to play an important part in the total treatment programme after initial difficulties. In both, the fathers needed to be brought actively into the programme to play an effective part. The families in cases 2 and 3, although different in structure and outlook, had in common personal resources and family strengths which meant they could independently generate their own plans to deal with problems over attendance following cessation of hospital treatment.

The family in case 1 remained constricted, socially isolated and unable to facilitate their son's growth to independence and social maturity. They were very diffident to engage in treatment and there was a strong likelihood of the patient showing further school refusal in later adolescence. The prognosis is worse in this lad than in the other two cases because of the lack of normal social and emotional development commensurate with improvement in school attendance, which was shown by the other two children.

There are some aspects of inpatient treatment which deserve further discussion particularly those relating to the successful outcome of treatment. Several mechanisms seem to be working at the same time. Separating patient and family brings the problems of pathological attachments painfully into focus and unless patient and parents are helped to understand their origins and how to cope with them, their persistence will undermine the treatment plan. Some parents may then withdraw the child from hospital. Admission brings the family hard up against the precise situation which they were avoiding in a way which is similar to the exposure to feared situations in the treatment of circumscribed phobias. The early stages of the process are very painful to deal with as the suffering of child and parents is obvious. Experienced staff can help the process to continue with the knowledge that neither party will actually be harmed by the experience of mastering separation anxiety. Child and parents find they can be apart without their fears of loss, harm, or damage being realized. Both experience the freedom of independence from each other and the loosening or dissolution of pathological bonds of closeness. The child in the therapeutic milieu is helped to feel competent and self-sufficient and is rewarded for his independence while the parents are helped to re-establish their own relationship and the mothers are encouraged to look for satisfaction outside the home in work or other social relationships. This is harder to do when parents, particularly mother, have become fixed in an over-protective role feeling that this is the only way in which they can justify themselves and maintain self-esteem. It is also difficult in elderly parents with a relatively young child; a situation often found in school refusal, because patterns are more fixed and harder to alter and families are likely to slip back into old ways, once treatment is ended.

The phases of treatment are illustrated by the case histories. They are (a) reducing or overcoming separation anxiety through actual experience allied to understanding of the origins of the anxiety and the reasons why it persists (b) helping the child to feel socially competent by learning new skills in the setting of a peer group while supported by adults (c) making it clear from the outset that the goal is return to school and paying great attention to the minute details of the re-introduction to school by gradual stages. This often generates much anxiety, sometimes of the same intensity as that displayed on admission. Graded re-entry in stages usually overcomes this and the child has the advantage of a cover story of hospital treatment to explain his absence, an important factor in many cases, (d) a change of school may be necessary or merely a change of class and teacher to give the chance of a fresh start. This should not be just in response to family demands but for valid reasons such as a need for a smaller school, a school with less stringent academic demands or the need for a school where psychiatric supervision is provided. Boarding school placement is necessary where a child needs the continuing experience of independence away from home because living at home will mean a return to pathological closeness, opportunities for manipulation and recrudescence of separation anxiety. A family may be able to accept the value of boarding school experience after they have realized what their child has gained from being in hospital away from home.

OUTCOME OF TREATMENT

There are very few reports on the outcome of hospital treatment. Samples are small, treatment methods are not compared and in only one study (Berg and Fielding, 1978) is length of treatment evaluated using comparison groups. Weiss and Cain (1964) reported on sixteen youngsters (ten girls and six boys) aged 8–16 years of age whose average period in hospital was nine months with all but two discharged within one year. Of the 14 youngsters, eight were placed in a residential group setting or boarding school for one to two years, six returned home, five attending their community day school, one remained as a day attender at the hospital school and two were in hospital at the time of the report. Criteria for improvement were ability to return to school, quality of peer group relationships and nature and intensity of remaining symptoms. Two were considered greatly improved in all these respects, eight still showed overt neurotic symptoms while otherwise functioning well and were considered moderately improved. Three maintained regular school attendance with difficulty in peer relationships and a significant number of neurotic symptoms and were noted as mildly improved. Only one child showed no improvement relapsing back into school refusal after six months. Thirteen children were therefore able to return to school, attend regularly and maintain above average academic progress.

A longer term follow-up five to ten years later of the same sixteen children was reported by Weiss and Burke (1967). All but one graduated from high school and were reliable workers, becoming economically independent. About half still showed social difficulties with restricted relationships, hesitancy about heterosexual ties, and avoidance of social activities. Some still clung to parents for emotional direction and support and about one-third of the total group of fourteen still retained some phobic or other neurotic symptoms while over half were constricted, inhibited, and compulsive in their make-up. The majority saw their earlier problems in terms of security at home or concern for their mothers.

Berg *et al.* (1976) reviewed 100 adolescents treated in hospital for school phobia using a standard interview form covering psychiatric symptoms and overall adjustment. Four grades of improvement were established related to proportion of time that patient was incapacitated by symptoms and degree of social adjustment. There were 17 in the most severely ill group and this included five agoraphobics and two patients with severe depressive illnesses, two with severe schizoid personality traits, one schizophrenic, and one severe obsessional illness. Twenty-seven were rated as well, but seven of these still retained depressive features, anxiety symptoms and obsessional difficulties to some degree. The authors found just over 10% of those categorized as ill remained so over the four years after discharge but that those who reached school-leaving age had less difficulty in going to work than they had going to school. Overall, the outcome was worse in the more intelligent children. They found that school phobia is likely to lead to psychiatric illness in later life in that six were severe and persistent agoraphobics at follow-up, while one third of the total group had severe emotional disturbance and social impairment. In a more recent study, Berg and Fielding (1978) randomly allocated 32 school phobics treated in hospital to two treatment groups. The mean age was 13 years, the groups were stratified for sex and also compared on a variety of clinical features so that reasonable matching was achieved. One group received three months inpatient treatment and the other six months and the total group was followed up six months, one year and two years after discharge. The total sample was not followed up on each occasion although some children were seen two or three times. The question arises of the effect that those not followed up might have on the reported findings, given that they may have been the more seriously disturbed members of the clinical sample. The results showed that neurotic disorders in adolescence do persist in later life contrary to some beliefs; that length of stay in hospital made no difference to outcome in boys but that longer stay was marginally more effective in girls.

The authors point out the problems of evaluating different forms of treatment in residential or hospital settings because of the number of influences and staff to which the patient is exposed. As has been described above, 'milieu therapy' includes a range of relationships and experiences which could well benefit a child or adolescent's development quite apart from a treatment focus on the major problem of return to school. However, it is clear from the material in this whole section on treatment, that a comparative evaluation of different treatment methods, psychotherapeutic, behavioural, drug, and milieu therapy is needed to establish what is the most appropriate in each type of clinical problem.

REFERENCES

Barker, P. (1968). The inpatient treatment of school refusal. *British Journal of Medical Psychology*, **41**, 381–387.

Berg, I. (1970). A follow-up study of school phobic adolescents admitted to an inpatient unit. *Journal of Child Psychology and Psychiatry*, **11**, 37–47.

Berg, I., Butler, A., and Hall, G. (1976). The outcome of adolescent school phobia. *British Journal of Psychiatry*, **128**, 80–85.

Berg, I., and Fielding, D. (1978). An evaluation of hospital inpatient treatment in adolescent school phobia. *British Journal of Psychiatry*, **132**, 500–505.

Greenwood, E. C. (1955). The role of psychotherapy in residential treatment. *American Journal of Orthopsychiatry*, **25**, 692–698.

Hersov, L., and Bentovim, A. (1977). Inpatient units and day hospitals. In (Eds.) Rutter, M., and Hersov, L. *Child Psychiatry: Modern Approaches*. Blackwell Scientific Oxford. pp. 880–900.

Montenegro, H. (1968). Severe separation anxiety in two pre-school children successfully treated by reciprocal inhibition. *Journal of Child Psychology and Psychiatry*, **9**, 93–108.

Noshpitz, J. (1962). Notes on the theory of residential treatment. *Journal of the American Academy of Child Psychiatry*, **1**, 284–296.

Redl, F. (1959). The life space interview: I. Strategies and techniques of the life space interview. *American Journal of Orthopsychiatry*, **29**, 1–18.

Sand, R. M., and Golub, S. (1974). Breaking the bonds of tradition. A reassessment of group treatment of latency-age children. *American Journal of Psychiatry*, **131**, 662–665.

Warren, W. (1948). Acute neurotic breakdown in children with refusal to go to school. *Archive of Diseases in Childhood*, **23**, 226–272.

Weiss, M., and Cain, B. (1964). The residential treatment of children and adolescents with school phobia. *American Journal of Orthopsychiatry*, **34**, 10–114.

Weiss, M., and Burke, G. B. (1967). A five–ten year follow-up of hospitalized school phobic children and adolescents. *American Journal of Orthopsychiatry*, **37**, 294–295.

Out of School
Edited by L. Hersov and I. Berg
© 1980, John Wiley & Sons, Ltd.

Chapter 16

Separation Anxiety in School Refusal and its Treatment with Drugs

Rachel Gittelman-Klein and Donald Klein

School attendance is one of the important social demands placed on a child, to the point that its implementation is not left to the exclusive discretion of parents, but is regulated by law. Failure to comply with the expectation that a child will attend school is viewed with alarm, and referral of the child to a mental health clinic is often a consequence.

The first diagnostic step in evaluating refusal to go to school is ruling out truancy. There is ample evidence that school absence because of truancy differs in a number of respects from school absence stemming from fear or anxiety. The two have different antecedents and different associated behaviour disturbances and prognoses, and distinguishing between them does not present a difficult diagnostic challenge. This issue is discussed fully elsewhere in this volume (Introduction and Chapter 12).

For purposes of the present discussion, which focuses on the pharmacological management of children who refuse to go to school, truancy can be dismissed with the emphatic assertion that, at present, there is no known drug treatment for this condition *per se*, though if truancy is secondary to hyperkinesis, stimulant pharmacotherapy may improve the child's general level of functioning and alter the behaviour of which truancy is a part. But in this case, truancy is not the target symptom to which stimulant treatment is specifically directed.

Our discussion of pharmacotherapy is restricted to children who refuse to go to school because of reasons other than those that motivate the truant, who typically has a dislike for school and a predilection for nonschool-related activities. Our concern is children who are fearful of attending school or anxious while in school. Unlike truants, these children have an episodic disorder; and when symptom free, they like school and are conscientious students who derive considerable enjoyment from school.

It is important to distinguish between the refusal to go to school itself and its psychological antecedent — anxiety — lest the erroneous impression be fostered that there is a drug treatment for the former. There is not; rather, there is a pharmacological treatment for the severe anxiety children who refuse to go to school experience. Careful attention to the diagnostic characteristics of this anxiety is essential to the proper management of these children.

Children who are called 'school phobic', or 'school refusers', typically suffer from marked separation anxiety. Attending school is often only one of the many independent ventures such a child resists; therefore the symptoms associated with school are usually a limited aspect of a pattern of difficulties that interferes with the child's ability to function comfortably when away from his parents or his home. The key difficulty is separation anxiety.

SEPARATION ANXIETY

The distress experienced by a child when separated from the person who cares for him (or her) is a normal developmental phenomenon. At some time after the age of six to eight months, most children occasionally display some negative affect when separation from the mothering figure occurs. The first observations of such a reaction follow temporally the development of object constancy in the infant. This is quite understandable since the level of cognitive functioning of the child must allow for an internal representation of the mother for the child to be affected negatively by the mother's absence (See Chapter 10).

Most of the investigations regarding the impact of separation on children have dealt with reactions to major life-disrupting events, such as total removal of the child, or the parent, from home. In animal studies as well, experimentally induced separation between offspring and parent typically has consisted of marked alterations of the mother–child relationship. In such cases it is difficult to relate the reaction of the youngster to the parent's absence exclusively, without regard for the contribution other factors, such as greatly modified life circumstances or social deprivation, might make to the observed behavioural changes in the child. In a comprehensive review of the effects of separation on children's behaviour, Rutter (1977) notes that the type of care given during separation, contact with people familiar and close to the child during the separation period, and the parents' reactions to the child upon being reunited may mitigate the severity of the child's immediate and extended reaction to separation.

Some data are available concerning children's responses of distress to nontraumatic separation from their mother. Ainsworth, who has conducted intensive observations of infants and toddlers up to two years of age in West Africa, has noted a great deal of variability among children in the intensity of distress they exhibit at normal separation experiences, i.e. the mother's stepping out of a room and thus leaving the child's visual field, or the child's being left in the care of someone else for brief periods (Ainsworth, 1967). It is clear from these and others' observations that children may have strong negative reactions to seemingly ordinary separation events.

Bowlby and Robertson have termed the overt distress the 'protest phase' of the separation reaction. In some cases, when separation continues, protest is followed by withdrawal and sadness, referred to as the 'despair phase', and finally, by indifference to the reappearance of the person whose departure provoked the reaction, (though the child displays active interest in new caretakers), the 'detachment phase' (for a review of this work, see Bowlby, 1969).

The first part of the emotional sequence, the protest phase, is the psychological state known as separation anxiety.

The fact that separation anxiety can be considered part of children's normal social development may lead to some ambiguity as to when it should be considered deviant or pathological.

The problem of defining the boundaries of pathology is an issue that pervades psychiatric classification and is especially salient in child psychiatry. In some instances there is no confusion regarding the pathological nature of behaviours. For example, delusions and hallucinations are considered indicative of mental dysfunction even if they are transient or cause only minor distress and disorganization of behaviour. But, symptoms such as delusions or hallucinations are the exception, not the rule. Much of the time, children for whom psychiatric services are sought present with behaviour that in mild form would be considered unremarkable and undeserving of costly professional attention. However, severe manifestations of the same behaviours understandably call for knowledgeable intervention. Though separation anxiety is a common childhood characteristic, it may assume forms that render the child dysfunctional.

Moreover, not only is consideration of the severity of behaviours a key criterion in defining abnormality in children but so is the timing of certain behaviours. Some characteristics are of no psychodiagnostic relevance whatever early in life, but may be viewed as symptoms later on. An obvious example is enuresis, which is defined as a symptom only if it occurs beyond a certain age. Similarly, it may be argued that, although separation anxiety is an appropriate developmental response in early childhood, it may be considered abnormal, even if not severe, when it occurs in middle childhood and beyond.

The key concern for the child with separation anxiety is easy access to the mother. The situations that are interpreted as interfering with the feasibility of reaching the mother differ in both type and in intensity from child to child. The specific behavioural outcomes of pathological separation anxiety vary with age.

By the time the child is of school age, he may retain behaviours associated with early childhood and the protest phase, such as crying and clinging and, moreover, beg the parent to stay with him and refuse to venture away from the parent. The child's reluctance to be separated from the parent may assume various forms. For instance, the child may resist leaving home without the parent, or may experience discomfort only when he ventures beyond a delineated perimeter close to home. Sometimes the child refuses to allow the parent to leave the home. Alternatively, the child may be unable to stay in a room by himself within the house. Frequently the child 'shadows' the mother, following her through the house, or on errands. Some children are quite able to go out by themselves, though typically not far from home, provided the mother is home.

Most commonly children with separation anxiety experience discomfort when away from their parents, though sometimes, in exceptional cases, the child will tolerate being away from the parent, but become anxious when he himself is away from home. In the latter instance, if the child remains home, he easily tolerates the parent's departure, but is uncomfortable when he himself is away from the house, even if accompanied by the parent. Enquiries about the thought content in such children typically reveal a concern about getting lost and not finding one's way home.

In addition to distress upon separation, morbid worries also emerge with age. Thoughts about death are common (See Chapter 10). While away from the mother, or even in her presence, children with separation anxiety often harbour the fear that something dangerous may happen to the mother. Events portending a threat to the integrity of the family are common fantasies. The child may be plagued with thoughts about the possibility of never being reunited with the parent or the home. There is no worry about a parent's losing her or his job, being unable to make ends meet, or other life experiences clearly unpleasant to the parents, even if these are frequent subjects of conversation in the home. Therefore, the child's anxiety cannot be construed as reflecting a nonspecific concern about the parents' well-being; rather, it is a morbid worry about their potential disappearance.

Any object of a child's attachment, such as a pet, may become the centre of the child's morbid thoughts.

Sometimes children worry about some harm befalling themselves rather than those close to them. They may fear being abducted or getting killed and, as a consequence, not being able to get back to their family.

Pathological separation anxiety may have behavioural consequences that at times do not seem obviously related to it. For instance, some children have nightmares revolving about the death of their parents, but no other symptom; but an in-depth interview will reveal morbid concerns about the family.

It is also possible, on occasion, for a youngster with separation anxiety to show no overt evidence of being unable to separate from his parent(s). The child may move freely outside and yet, while doing so, be plagued by severe morbid preoccupations regarding the welfare of the parent. Thus, it is possible for a child to attend school regularly but, while doing so, to feel miserable and anguished. In such cases separation anxiety is detectable only in the mental ent of the child, but not in his overt behaviour.

Our clinical impression, not empirically documented, is that this situation is more likely to occur when parents force the child to separate and refuse to allow the behavioural expression of the child's anxiety. The child's response becomes one of a 'stiff upper lip'; but the subjective psychic pain remains, and the child may appear unhappy and socially reticent. Careful interviewing is required, in such cases, to elicit these concerns.

We view separation anxiety as manifesting itself in three ways. Most obvious is distress on separation, which, in the severe form of the disorder, becomes panic. Second, morbid worries about potential dangers that threaten the integrity of the family are also pathognomonic of the disorder. Finally, homesickness involving missing the home or family members and a yearning to be reunited to a degree which goes beyond usual reactions is a sign of the disorder. These key characteristics of separation anxiety can occur concurrently or independently. They are considered symptoms when they restrict the child's activities or interfere markedly with his emotional well-being.

Unlike many disorders of childhood that tend to follow a chronic course, without a clear-cut age of onset (i.e. conduct disorders, psychotic or pervasive developmental disorders, hyperactive impulse disorder), pathological separation anxiety often appears suddenly, in a previously well-functioning child who has shown no premorbid signs of unusual separation anxiety. Pathological forms of separation anxiety may occur also in children with histories of chronic separation anxiety, often of subclinical severity. In contrast to the other childhood disorders, separation anxiety may remit spontaneously, leaving the youngster without residual difficulties.

The school situation is especially difficult for, and threatening to, many children with severe separation anxiety because they find themselves constricted in their movement by school schedules. If the child experiences an overwhelming desire to return home while in school, he is automatically prevented from doing so. Other separation situations, in which the child feels he is free to gain access to the mother and has control over his movement, are less likely to be avoided by the child. Thus, children who cannot tolerate staying in school will readily go out to play in the neighbourhood if they know their mothers are accessible at home. This seeming contradiction in the child's ability to function independently often makes a parent think that the child is trying 'to get away with something' by refusing to go to school.

In our experience with children of all ages who refuse to go to school, in about 80 per cent of the cases the onset of school avoidance is associated with a change in the child's life. The typical precipitating events are moves (either from home or school), a relative's death, or illness. These are all events in which a loss is actually experienced, or at least threatened.

We think it is erroneous to assume that separation anxiety plays a crucial role only in young children who refuse to go to school: it is also a common phenomenon among young adolescents. According to the criteria for separation anxiety mentioned above, in 45 'school refusers', the rate of separation anxiety did not differ significantly between 7- to 12-year-olds ($N = 29$) and 13- to 15-year-olds ($N = 16$), being 89 per cent and 87 per cent, respectively.

The possibility of separation anxiety should not be excluded if it is not observed in all situations that entail removal from the parent. The variety of separation event that evoke distress in the child reflects the pervasiveness of the reaction, not its presence or absence. It is possible for a child to have pervasive but mild anxiety, or clearly focal but severe anxiety in response to separation.

Pathological separation anxiety is not restricted to children; it can also occur in adults. We have not observed overt protest on separation among adults (except in some agoraphobes who do not tolerate staying alone for fear of experiencing a panic attack while unattended). Rather, the other two manifestations of separation anxiety, morbid worries about threats to loved ones and acute homesickness, are typical of adults suffering from excessive separation anxiety.

Associated Difficulties

Children who display severe separation anxiety usually develop a variety of secondary difficulties. Among those who refuse to go to school there often are marked diurnal fluctuations in the level of anxiety. The children feel much worse in the morning and at night.

In the morning these children dread the thought of going to school and may develop a variety of somatic complaints. In young children these are typically gastrointestinal symptoms, such as stomachaches or nausea. Older and adolescent children may report sore throats, headaches, cold symptoms, cardiovascular symptoms, such as a fast heartbeat or dizziness. These symptoms vanish if the child is allowed to remain home, and are not reported on school holidays or weekends.

At night, anxiety is also exacerbated. It may be that sleeping alone, which most Western children do, is a mildly stressful form of separation causing a slight sense of isolation and abandonment, even for many children who do not have marked separation anxiety. In addition to this putative normal separation experience at nighttime, children who resist going to school are concerned about having to attend school the next day; and these concerns may interfere with their ability to fall asleep.

The child not only feels anxious when separation is attempted but also when it is anticipated. The degree of secondary anticipatory anxiety is variable but is experienced by most children who resist going to school. The greater such anticipatory anxiety, the more difficult it is to treat the condition.

Frequently, school refusers become socially withdrawn. Their social reticence probably results from two factors: first, because closeness to the her or the home is so important, the attractiveness of social contacts away from home palls; second, these anxious children are often intensely self-conscious and ashamed of their disability and consequently avoid their friends for fear of being embarrassed by questions regarding their school absence. Avoidance of previously well-established peer relationships outside the family is not considered a sign of more serious pathology, as schizoid tendencies might be, if it coincides with the onset of severe separation anxietey.

Since children with severe separation anxiety can become extremely uncomfortable, they often use secondary manipulative manœuvres to protect themselves from potentially painful situations. They are therefore frequently angrily demanding, and may even become physically violent when forced into what they experience as an intolerably distressing situation. They are often ambivalent about their need for the parent's presence because, although they yearn for it, they recognize the unreasonableness of their need, and hence may become easily irritable and short-tempered. Temper outbursts and other manipulative tactics should not be viewed as indications of a grave underlying personality disorder, but rather as secondary complications.

Children with separation anxiety often have specific fears. Prominent is fear of the dark — a situation that probably triggers fantasies of vulnerability and danger, to which these children are particularly susceptible.

In rare instances children report experiences that may appear bizarre, such as feeling eyes staring at them, or seeing monsters while trying to fall asleep. These can be differentiated from hallucinations reported by psychotic people in that, in children with separation anxiety, these experiences disappear if the child is no longer in the dark or alone. Thrcfore, these seemingly bizarre experiences differ from psychotic ones in their responsivity to simple environmental alterations, and may be viewed as visual imaginary experiences reflecting heightened anxiety.

The secondary difficulties in children who refuse to go to school are often related to family pressures on them. In homes in which a serious effort is made to return the child to school, the youngster may complain that no one loves him or cares about him, that he wishes he were dead. Such behaviour may have obvious manipulative intent, but may also reflect the child's despair at convincing his parents of the reality of the intolerable pain he feels. It is also possible to interpret such remarks as indicating a primary depressive disorder. It has been our experience, however, that these complaints disappear if demands for school attendance are lifted, indicating a responsivity to external events and lack of autonomy of mood that are very atypical of severe depression (See also the section on differential diagnosis below).

Some writers do not attribute an important role to separation anxiety in refusal to attend school (for a review of this issue see Hersov, 1977). This clinical conclusion is at variance with the results we have obtained through systematic enquiry regarding possible manifestations of separation anxiety among such children. In a sample of 45 children between ages of 7 and 15, 40

(88 per cent) reported symptoms that, according to our criteria, seemed clearly to reflect separation anxiety. Therefore, we believe that separation anxiety is not one of many equally important psychological determinants of refusal to attend school, but the major one.

There are probably differences in the criteria used by investigators for positive identification of separation anxiety. Those who minimize the relationship between refusal to attend school and separation anxiety usually fail to include the content of the child's ideation as a consideration in determining the presence of separation anxiety.

It is important to obtain consensus on the clinical signs of separation anxiety, since different criteria for making a diagnosis of the disorder will yield different estimates of its presence among children who resist going to school and result in differing clinical concepts that might be artifacts of contrasting definitions. We think this problem of construct variance is an important issue in studies of separation anxiety in children who resist going to school.

Differential diagnosis

A controversy revolves around the diagnosis of severe separation anxiety. Some argue that it is a childhood expression of depressive illness as it is known in adults. Frommer (1968) refers to it as 'phobic depression'.

If depression is conceptualized as an autonomous mood state impervious to environmental manipulations and as a pervasive reduction in hedonic experience coupled with severe pessimism regarding one's chances for recovery, then most children who resist attending school cannot be considered depressed.

Most of these children with separation anxiety recognize the irrationality of their feelings and make hardly any attempt to justify their symptoms. Because of this objectivity and insight, many of these children feel miserable about their behaviour; they can generally recall their symptom-free life, and feel they are 'different' from their previous selves as well as from their normal peers.

As a result, by the time they are seen in a mental health facility, the youngsters frequently are demoralized and look depressed. Their affect may be limited; their speech, slow and weak. They cry readily when questioned about their morbid preoccupations. Of crucial diagnostic importance is that when no demands for separation are made, these children are capable of engaging in a variety of activities, from which they clearly derive enjoyment. Further, the generalized pessimism characteristic of depressed adults is strikingly absent in them.

Separation anxiety can occur in conjunction with other psychiatric disorders. Hyperkinetic children occasionally present similar symptoms. Th___ pathological separation anxiety has been observed in schizophrenic ___nts, treatment of the psychosis naturally takes precedence over inter- to combat separation anxiety.

PHARMACOLOGICAL TREATMENT

Theoretical considerations

If one were to retrace the genesis of pharmacotherapy in children with behaviour disorders, one would identify two clear and independent patterns. The first would be the completely serendipitous discovery of the effects of drugs on children's behaviour. This is true of the psychostimulant treatment of hyperactive children. The second would be a direct, uncritical transfer of established practice from adult psychopharmacotherapy to children's psychiatric disorders. The use of neuroleptics in treating 'psychotic' children is a case in point.

Investigation of the efficacy of impramine in childhood pathological separation anxiety is thus far a unique instance in pediatric psychopharmacology to which neither the serendipitous nor the purely empirical adult–child transfer model applies. The historical events that led to a trial of imipramine in children who resisted attending school are summarized briefly since they are relevant to some of the issues associated with the disorder, such as, for instance, its relationship to adult psychiatric disorders, or its contribution to a theoretical understanding of the nature of anxiety states in children.

The use of a tricyclic, imipramine, in these children was prompted by a series of clinical observations made by Klein while studying adult agoraphobic patients (Klein, 1964). These patients experience sudden panic attacks, which often occur unpredictably, out of a clear blue sky or under circumstances in which the patient feels entrapped and unable to flee easily, such as in crowded theatres, trains, buses, etc. Consequently, people with spontaneous panic attacks avoid crowded places, taking trains, and so on, and limit their movements in a variety of ways (Klein and Davis, 1969).

Fortuitously, Klein observed that imipramine regularly blocked agoraphobic patients' apparently spontaneous panic attacks. Double–blind, placebo-controlled studies confirmed this clinical finding (Klein, 1964). Klein postulated that these patients suffered from a disruption of biological processes that regulate anxiety triggered by separation. This notion was stimulated by the observation that a large proportion of the patients had a childhood history of severe separation anxiety and that their response to initial panic had been clinging, dependent behaviour.

If Klein's assumption that panic anxiety was a pathological variant of normal separation anxiety was correct, imipramine, which relieved panic anxiety, should be useful in patients whose behavioural difficulties clearly stemmed from inability to separate from significant others. Following this line of reasoning, Klein predicted that imipramine would be effective in children with pathological levels of separation anxiety. School-phobic children were selected for treatment of separation anxiety with imipramine. They were ideal subjects for study, since there is a clear, objectively quantifiable, behavioural sequel to the primary pathological separation anxiety.

Therefore, though the use of imipramine in school-phobic children followed its use in agoraphobic adults, its first application was derived from a particular model of psychopathology rather than from strict therapeutic empiricism.

An initial open clinical trial of imipramine in a group of 28 children who resisted attending school suggested that the drug was possibly effective in such children, since 85 per cent of them retrurned to school (Rabiner and Klein, 1969). These results were considered encouraging enough to warrant study of the drug in controlled trials.

The results of an initial trial on 35 children have been published previously (Gittelman-Klein and Klein, 1971, 1973).

Controlled trial with imipramine

In a placebo-controlled study of imipramine among children who refused to go to school, the drug was found to be significantly more effective than a placebo.

Children between the ages of 7 and 15 who had been absent from school for at least two weeks, or had been attending intermittently under great duress, were considered for the study. Upon referral, a vigorous attempt was made for another two weeks to return the child to school. A multidisciplinary team consisting of a psychiatrist and a social worker worked with the child, the parents, and the school. If after two weeks of continued effort the child was still not attending school regularly, he was entered in the study.

Forty-five children, 24 girls and 21 boys, whose mean age was 10 years 7 months, were randomly assigned to a placebo or imipramine in double-blind fashion for a 6 week period; 25 received the placebo; 20 imipramine. Dosage was fixed for the first two weeks: 25 mg/day for the first 3 days; 50 mg/day for the next 4 days; 75 mg/day during the second week. The dosage was adjusted weekly thereafter, a maximum of 200 mg/day being set. Medication was administered in the morning and in the evening. At the end of the study, the dosage ranged from 100 to 200 mg/day (mean = 159 mg/day).

The patient and the family were seen weekly. At the beginning of treatment they were told to expect an abatement of fear. The case worker instructed the family to maintain a firm attitude promoting school attendance. The treatment programme was also explained to the school personnel, with whom the social worker maintained continuous contact so that no discrepancies occurred between our instructions and the school's expectations. In most ... family member was advised to accompany the child to school and the child's presence there until there was a reduction of the child's ... ry anxiety that severe discomfort might recur while he was in school ... ild could attend school alone. The treatment recommendations varied according to the severity of the anticipatory anxiety and the family's ability to set and enforce limits.

If the child could not tolerate being forced back into the classroom, hierarchy of approach to school was instituted, each step causing some anxiety, but to a degree tolerable to both child and mother. Therefore, the overall results of our study represent the effect of a combination of treatments: persuasive and desensitization techniques coupled with either an active drug or a placebo.

After 6 weeks of the treatment programme, 44 per cent of the placebo-treated children and 70 per cent of the imipramine-treated ones were back in school ($p < 0.05$, Fisher Exact Test). Though the difference in the number of children who were attending school after treatment is significant, a substantial proportion of children on the placebo were able to resume school attendance with continued psychosocial treatment alone.

A different outcome picture emerges when one examines the children's report of improvement. As shown in the Table 1, of the 25 on the placebo, 6 (24 per cent) reported feeling much better; of the 19 on imipramine, 17 (90 per cent) reported a similar degree of symptomatic relief (self rating of 1 subject is missing) ($p < 0.004$, Fisher Exact Test).

Table 1. Children's self ratings of improvement
($N = 44$).[a]

	No change or slightly better	Much improved
Placebo ($N = 25$)	19 (76%)	6 (24%)
Imipramine ($N = 19$)	2 (10%)	17 (90%)

$P < 0.004$, Fisher Exact test.
[a]N of 44 reflects missing ratings of 1 subject on imipramine.

These results suggest that, though some children on the placebo returned to school, they continued to feel uncomfortable. This was indeed the case, as may be observed from Table 2, which presents the relationship between return to school and self-ratings of improvement for the two treatment groups. Of the placebo-treated children, 24 per cent were back in school and feeling well, whereas 74 per cent of the imipramine-treated children had a similar outcome.

Imipramine treatment had a significant positive effect on somatic complaints, which are viewed as secondary symptoms. Of 38 children who reported having difficulties such as stomachaches, nausea, dizziness, headaches, or vague aches and pains, 82 per cent were free of these on imipramine, and 33 per cent on the placebo ($P < 0.004$, Fisher Exact Test), as demonstra   e 3.

Despite th   s, imipramine should not be viewed as a treatment that automatically   o renewed school attendance. Rather, it modifies the child's level of anxiety in response to separation. This alteration in affective state may enable the child to return to the classroom. On the other hand, strong anticipatory anxiety about school attendance may inhibit the child from making the necessary attempts to reenter the school situation.

Table 2. Relationship between school return and self-ratings of improvement
($N = 44$)

	Back to school and feeling better	Back to school but not feeling better	Not back to school but feeling better	Not back to school and not feeling better
Placebo ($N = 25$)	6 (24%)	5 (20%)	0	14 (56%)
Imipramine ($N = 19$)[a]	14 (74%)	0	3 (16%)	2 (11%)

[a]Self-rating of 1 subject missing.

Table 3. Post-treatment reports of physical complaints among children with physical complaints at baseline
($N = 38$)

	Present	Absent
Placebo ($N = 21$)	14 (67%)	7 (33%)
Imipramine ($N = 17$)	3 (18%)	14 (82%)

$P < 0.004$, Fisher Exact Test.

School return is a complex behaviour related to factors independent of the effect of imipramine. Some of these factors probably include the child's level of anticipatory anxiety, the attitude of the school officials toward the child, the nature of the child's relationship to his peers, the parents' effectiveness in dealing with the child, and the nature of the psychotherapeutic effort.

The onset of school phobia in adolescence is often thought to signify the development of a pernicious disease process such as a severe personality disorder or schizophrenia. This contention is unproven. The management of older children is more difficult, since parents exercise less control over adolescents' behaviour than over that of young children. The response to medication, however, is not related to age; and adolescents stand as good a chance as prepuberty children of obtaining relief from their subjective distress. In light of the similar rate of improvement with imipramine in children of different ages, it seems unlikely that young and older children's refusal to attend school represent different underlying psychopathologies.

Clinical management with imipramine

Comments regarding the use of imipramine with chil   who refuse to attend school are not rooted in objectively derived data: they represent impressions derived from clinical experience using imipramine for treatment of severe separation anxiety.

Many children require imipramine doses in the adult range (100–200 mg/day). Nevertheless, a daily dose of 5 mg/kg of body-weight should not be exceeded, in view of the possibility of cardiovascular effects at the upper limit of the adult dose used in depression (Hayes, Panitch, and Barker, 1975; Saraf, Klein, Gittelman-Klein, and Groff, 1974; Saraf, Klein, Gittelman-Klein, Gootman, and Greenhill, 1978).

In our group of school-phobic children treated experimentally, no child between the ages of 6 to 14 responded to less than 75 mg/day. Among other children treated clinically who had marked separation anxiety but no school phobia, low doses, from 25 to 50 mg, were effective in some cases. The age and size of the child were found not to provide clear guidelines for appropriate dose levels.

In good responders, no traces of separation anxiety remain. This is one of the few psychiatric treatments that, when successful, induces complete remission. The change may appear almost immediately after initiation of treatment, but is typically observable within two weeks. Return to school may be delayed for several weeks after separation anxiety has decreased, because of persistence of an anticipatory anxiety that the panic experienced under conditions of separation will recur.

In our experience, if a child shows no detectable sign of response at moderate doses (such as 125 mg per day), increments in doses up to 200 mg do not appear to have any effect. In marked contrast to this pattern, medication increases beyond this level contribute dramatically to further improvement when a positive response has been effected, but residual difficulties remain.

Though we began with administration of the drug twice daily, equally good results are obtainable with a nightly dose. The latter has the advantage of circumventing or minimizing side effects. This effect is in contrast to that in hyperkinetic children, in whom divided doses appear to us clinically more effective than single nightly doses.

Imipramine treatment need not be extended. Children usually respond completely within six to eight weeks. Medication should be continued for at least four weeks after remission, and then gradually withdrawn.

Since withdrawal effects are common — flu-like symptoms such as nausea, abdominal pain, and vomiting — imipramine should not be discontinued suddenly. Dosage may be reduced abruptly, from a high to a low dose (from 200 mg to 50 mg for instance); but the child should remain on a low dose (25 mg or 10 mg) for about one week. Using this procedure, we have encountered no difficulties among children treated with imipramine.

The pattern of pharmacological usage in this patient group (i.e. children who resist going to school) is in marked contrast to that generally observed in other psychiatric disorders, in which extended drug administration is the rule rather than the exception. Even among children with long histories of active symptomatology, length of treatment usually need not exceed three months, since children often maintain the drug-induced improvement after cessation of treatment. Only a minority of children have required continuous medication for six months or more.

With ongoing administration of imipramine, the extent to which psychotherapy, counselling, or a family treatment is necessary varies with the severity of secondary anticipatory anxiety and avoidance maladaptations and with the parents' response to these behaviours.

A return to school should not be anticipated as an automatic sequel to successful psychopharmacology. Complete refusal to attend school is the most extreme form of the disorder and regularly requires a comprehensive treatment programme. In some exceptional cases, relief of separation anxiety leads to immediate disappearance of all secondary symptoms. In almost all cases, however, proper treatment requires both medication and supportive-directive psychotherapeutic interventions.

The pharmacological treatment of school-phobic youngsters cannot be undertaken without the active participation of the school. In addition to the teacher's co-operation, that of other school personnel is usually necessary, since exceptions to school rules are often requested. Also, it is imperative to work with the parents — with both parents, if at all possible.

Children who develop resistance to going to school differ markedly from other psychiatric child patients in the feelings they elicit from their families. Unlike children with other disorders, most of these 'school refusers' function without difficulty and, before their acute anxiety appears, provide their parents with a good deal of satisfaction. When resistance to attending school develops, their ability to function is markedly altered, and they are visibly in pain. It would take a remarkably unfeeling adult to remain unmoved and impervious to the children's anguish. As a result, parents are often over-responsive and accommodating to the children's demands. Since the basic treatment tactic requires parents to force the child to sustain even more anxiety, at least temporarily (for reasons explained below), a great deal of ambivalence and even resistance are to be expected from parents. Many parents respond more co-operatively if they know that the medication is alleviating the basic anxiety and that the child is reacting only to the fear of venturing out.

While receiving imipramine, very young children will usually respond to being brought to school forcibly. The school must be asked to tolerate the child's screaming and tantrums, which rarely last more than a few days if the child is on medication. The forcing-back method can be unnecessarily trying for child, parent, and school; and a more gradual approach is often preferable. Psychotherapy, combined with imipramine treatment, is geared to overcoming the anticipatory anxiety.

We have found a form of contract therapy very helpful. The child, parent(s), and therapist negotiate what the child will try to accomplish before the next office visit. The degree to which the child participates in the decision-making process varies with the child's age. Giving the youngster a voice minimizes his resistance and his feeling of being coerced. Clearly defined goals relieve his fear that unpredictable, capricious, and overwhelming demands will be placed on him. He knows where he stands. If security seems guaranteed to the child, full advantage of the drug-induced improvement becomes easily realized.

Even while the child is on medication, his condition is likely to worsen after school absences, regardless of the cause. Anticipatory anxiety often returns after weekends, vacations, and illnesses.

Many children who attend school may also have very high levels of separation anxiety that compromise their functioning in a number of ways without interfering with school attendance. These youngsters suffer from the same disorder as children who resist or refuse to attend school — what distinguishes them are the secondary or associated symptoms they have developed. Drug therapy in these children, as well as among those who resist attending school is aimed at ameliorating the level of separation anxiety.

The management of children who have significant separation anxiety without attendance problems follows the same mode of drug administration, with gradual institution of independent functioning.

In youngsters who have a clear response to imipramine but whose anticipatory anxiety is unresponsive to the school situation, small doses of a benzodiazepine, such as 5 mg of diazepam, may be useful in enabling the youngster to attempt separation. Thus far we have found the adjunctive use of an antianxiety agent to be necessary only in some adolescents.

Imipramine side effects

Imipramine-associated side effects within doses of up to 5 mg/kg of body-weight are rarely troublesome to the point of necessitating termination of treatment or dosage reduction. Dry mouth, related to the drug's anticholinergic effect, is the most prominent side effect. On extremely rare occasions, orthostatic hypotention, sweating, and mild tremor may occur. A small proportion of children may become constipated, or drowsy after a daytime dose. Some pallor may occur.

In general, it may be difficult, in a clinical situation, to be clear about the causal relationship between the medication and the child's physical complaints, since children with severe separation anxiety frequently report multiple symptoms when not under medication. To evaluate symptoms induced by the drug, clinicians must make a very careful enquiry regarding the presence of these symptoms before treatment is initiated, to enable an accurate estimate of the degree to which they occur *de novo* when imipramine is administered.

Recently, imipramine-induced ECG abnormalities, consisting of T-wave changes, P–R interval lengthening, and QRS widening, have been reported in children (Saraf *et al.*, 1978; Winsberg, Goldstein, Yepes, and Perel, 1975). The significance of these ECG changes is unclear, since they are not associated with clinical cardiac abnormalities. These findings, however, have been the basis on which doses not exceeding 5 mg/kg/day have been recommended (Hayes, Panitch, and Barker, 1975). In view of the ECG findings to date, it is suggested that children placed on 3.5 mg/kg of imipramine received an ECG before the dose reaches this level, with a repeat evaluation two weeks later, and regular monitoring every two months.

Very high doses are to be avoided since they may be dangerous (Saraf *et al.*, 1974).

Use of other compounds

Our discussion has focused on the use of imipramine since it is the drug which we have studied and used clinically. It is possible that other compounds, especially other antidepressants, may be equally effective. As a matter of fact, Frommer (1968) claims that phenelzine is superior to imipramine in phobic children.

Frommer (1967) reported on the effects of phenelzine combined with chlordiazepoxide compared with phenobarbitone in a double-blind crossover study of 32 children described as depressed, 15 of whom had phobic symptoms. The combination of the antidepressant and the antianxiety agent was superior to the sedative in inducing overall improvement, as rated by a psychiatrist, in the children with phobic symptoms. The specific effect of the drugs on the children's phobic symptoms or avoidance behaviour is not described, however. It is also difficult to determine whether the antidepressant or the antianxiety agent was the crucial treatment factor. Frommer (1968) believes that tricyclics are best for enuretic depressives.

Frommer's distinction between the clinical efficacy of tricyclic drugs and of the MAO inhibitors may be an artifact of the different doses recommended for each class of drugs. For children 8 to 10 years old, the recommended dose of phenelzine is proportionately higher than that for amitriptyline (30 mg/day *vs.* 75 mg/day, respectively) (Frommer, 1968).

Reports of therapeutic effects of other agents have also appeared. Chlordiazepoxide has been claimed to have marked beneficial effects in school-phobic chldren (D'Amato, 1962; Kraft, 1962; Skynner, 1961). Diphenhydramine has also been reported of value in young children with 'pure anxiety' (Fish, 1960). In addition, claims have been advanced for the efficacy of amphetamines in school-phobic children (Fish, 1960, 1968). These, however, are anecdotal reports that do not provide an empirical basis for clinical practice.

Unresolved issues

The fact that imipramine is effective for the treatment of 'school refusers', ·
adult agoraphobic patients, and some adult depressives cannot be construed as
unequivocal evidence taht these disorders have a common psychopathological
core. Psychoactive agents have multiple pharmacological properties, and to
assume a single neurobiochemical mechanism for varied behavioural alterations
is simplistic. Other studies examining the relationship between agoraphobic
adult patients and children who resist going to school have yielded inconclusive
results. In an uncontrolled study, Berg (1976) has reported a high prevalence
of school phobia among the children of agoraphobic women. On the other
hand, a retrospective study of self-reported school phobia did not differentiate
between adult agoraphobic women and other 'neurotics' (Berg, Marks,
McGuire, and Lipsedge, 1974). The relationship between early separation
anxiety and depressive illness is moot. We failed to find an increased
prevalence of depressive illness in parents of children who resisted attending
school compared with parents of hyperactive children, but parents and siblings
of the former group of children had a significantly greater prevalence of severe
separation anxiety (Gittelman-Klein, 1975).

Though we have found imipramine to be effective in children with
separation anxiety, it is not possible to claim that the drug has a specific effect
on this disorder. It is conceivable that imipramine would ameliorate all types
of anxiety, whether it be phobic anxiety (such as fear of animals), separation
anxiety, or performance anxiety (such as fear of examinations, etc.). Our
results seem to demonstrate that imipramine does not affect anticipatory
anxiety. However, its impact on the other forms of anxiety in children remains
unknown. Relevant to this issue is recent work by Zitrin, Klein, and Woerner
(1978) indicating that imipramine is ineffective in adults with specific phobias.

Another issue is whether compounds from other drug classes, such as
antianxiety agents, would also be effective in reducing separation anxiety. If
so, no specific imipramine effect could be claimed for treatment of this type of
anxiety.

Given our theoretical model of separation anxiety, which views it as serving
a specific adaptive goal, we should expect anxieties other than separation
anxiety to be unaffected by imipramine or similar drugs; we should also expect
drugs unrelated to imipramine in clinical activity to be of no value in the
treatment of separation anxiety. These contentions await critical testing. If
confirmed, current concepts of anxiety as a unitary psychological phenomenon
and the practice of lumping all childhood anxiety states in a general category
of neurotic or emotional disorders would require some conceptual and
classificatory modifications.

A recent study of Rhesus monkeys treated with imipramine or a placebo
suggests that imipramine may be effective in altering the pattern of behaviour
associated with separation in these animals. After about three weeks of

imipramine treatment, in response to separation the four drug-treated monkeys had less self-directed behaviour and more environmentally oriented behaviour than the four placebo-treated monkeys (Suomi, Seaman, Lewis, DeLizio, and McKinney, 1978). Though response to separation in animals is believed to provide a useful model of clinical depression in humans, we think it has more face validity as a model of response to separation, which we believe has different psychobiological and adaptive characteristics. Therefore, it seems reasonable to interpret drug effects on separated animals as pertinent to an understanding of their reaction to separation.

DISCUSSION

There may be negative attitudes toward pharmacological treatment of a disorder that so often responds to a simple environmental manoeuvre, such as forcing a child back to school. The children we have treated with imipramine had been completely refractory to intensive efforts to return them to school. Most of the children referred to us because of refusal to attend school were not accepted as subjects for the imipramine study, since they responded to a continued, unrelenting push to return them to school. Thus, only a minority received medication, after all else had failed. We recommend that nonpharmacological interventions be used initially in the management of this problem. When they fail, or when the child is still considerably anxious even though attending school, imipramine treatment should be considered.

We have mentioned our nonpharmacological tactics in this summary of drug treatment to emphasize that even though imipramine is frequently remarkably effective, its efficacy has been studied only in conjuction with specific and vigorous psychotherapeutic efforts. It would be misleading, and possibly inaccurate, to attribute the same level of efficacy to the drug without other concomitant treatment. Even when pharmacotherapy is indicated, it is almost always necessary to use other treatments as well.

We are not suggesting, however, that individual psychotherapy, in a generic sense, is indicated in conjunction with drug treatment of refusal to attend school. The treatment plan we followed did not focus on the child's intrapsychic conflicts. The role of the latter in resistance to attending school is conjectural. We are emphasizing therapeutic tactics that provide child and family with firm guidance and support in the framework of a behavioural approach.

The concept of separation anxiety we have used follows the ethological model advanced by Bowlby (1973), in which separation anxiety is conceptualized as an evolutionarily adaptive mechanism whose initial elicitation does not require learning by the infant. When the newly mobile infant separates from its mother, it experiences acute discomfort and emits cries of distress that elicit maternal care. If the infant is lost, its cries guide the mother to the stranded offspring, optimally before biological impairment occurs. In this formulation, it is also assumed that the child's distress provokes retrieval and caretaking behaviour in the parent. Therefore, the most efficient evolutionary relationship would be one in which both the young child and the mother would be subject to separation anxiety. This notion is supported by much animal observation, e.g. the distress of mother cats, dogs, monkeys, etc., when their infants are removed or are heard crying, followed by searching and retrieval behaviour on the mother's part. The extension of this model to human development may have heuristic value. For instance, it would suggest that, in adulthood, women should be more vulnerable to separation anxiety than men. There is no objective information concerning sex differences in frequency of this anxiety. Though agoraphobia, postulated by Klein to be an adult pathological variant of separation anxiety, is much more common in women than men.

The ethological model of pathological separation anxiety implies an autonomous, psychopathological process in children with severe separation anxiety. This view is in sharp contrast to that which holds that the child's anxiety is a response to the mother's neurotic needs (Eisenberg, 1958). In the latter model, the therapeutic effect of imipramine would have to be interpreted as protecting the child from the mother's wish for his overattachment. This would be a most unusual drug effect. If it were the case, contrary to our findings, one would expect most children to relapse when medication was withdrawn. Though the drug effect argues for the presence of a disorder intrinsic to the child who refuses to attend school, it does not follow that environmental influences play no role in the various aspects of the disorder, such as its severity, specific form, and maintenance. Pathological separation anxiety may be the outcome of interaction between a biological predisposition in the child and a family setting that facilitates the expression of the predisposition. In keeping with this formulation, pharmacotherapy of the child is only one aspect of a treatment approach aimed at altering both the child and the family's response to the child.

It is clear from our discussion that we do not believe that imipramine is an antianxiety drug. Regardless of one's theoretical convictions regarding the usefulness of distinguishing separation anxiety from other anxiety states, it is important to note that imipramine has been tested only in children who refuse to attend school. Hence, there is no empirical basis for the use fo the drug in other conditions.

REFERENCES

Ainsworth, M. D. S. (1967). *Infancy in Uganda: Infant care and the growth of love.* Johns Hopkins Press, Baltimore.

Berg, I. (1976). School phobia in the children of agoraphobic women. *British Journal of Psychiatry,* **128**, 86–89.

Berg, I., Marks, I., McGuire, R., and Lipsedge, M. (1974). School phobia and agoraphobia. *Psychological Medicine*, **4**, 428–434.

Bowlby, J. (1969). *Attachment and loss, Vol. 1: Attachment.* Hogarth Press, London.

Bowlby, J. (1973). *Attachment and loss, Vol II: Separation anxiety and anger.* Basic Books, New York.

D'Amato, G. (1962). Chlordiazepoxide in management of school phobia. *Disease of the Nervous System*, **23**, 292–295.

Eisenberg, L. (1958). School phobia: A study in the communication of anxiety. *American Journal of Psychiatry*, **114**, 712–718.

Fish, B. (1960). Drug Therapy in child psychiatry: Pharmacological aspects. *Comprehensive Psychiatry*, **1**, 212–227.

Fish, B. (1968). Drug use in psychiatric disorders of children. *American Journal of Psychiatry*, **124**, 31–36.

Frommer, E. A. (1967). Treatment of childhood depression with antidepressant drugs. *British Medical Journal*, **1**, 729–732.

Frommer, E. A. (1968). Depressive illness in childhood. *British Journal of Psychiatry*, *Special Publication No. 2*, 117–136.

Gittelman-Klein, R. (1975). Psychiatric characteristics of the relatives of school phobic children. In Sankar, D. V. S. *Mental Health in Children Vol. 1.* PJD Publications Ltd., Westbury, New York. pp. 325–334.

Gittelman-Klein, R., and Klein, D. F. (1971). Controlled imipramine treatment of school phobia, *Archives of GEneral Psychiatry*, **25**, *204–207.*

Gittelman-Klein, R., and Klein, D. F. (1973). School phobia: Diagnostic considerations in the light of imipramine effects. *Journal of Nervous and Mental Diseases*, **156**, 199–215.

Hayes, T. A., Panitch, M. L., and Barker, E. 61975). Imipramine dosage in children: A comment on 'imipramine and electrocardiagraphic abnormalities in hyperactive children'. *American Journal of psychiatry*, **132**, 546–547.

Hersov, L. (1977). School refusal. In (Eds.) Rutter, M., and Hersov, L., *Child psychiatry: Modern approaches.* Blackwell Scientific Publications, Oxford, pp. 455–486.

Klein, D. F. (1964). Delineation of two drug responsive anxiety syndromes. *Psychopharmacologia*, **5**, 397–408.

Klein, D. F., and Davis, J. M. (1969). *Diagnosis and drug treatment of psychiatric disorders.* William and Wilkins, Baltimore.

Kraft, I. A. (1962). Treatment of school phobia with chlordiazepoxide. *American Journal of Psychiatry*, **118**, 841–842.

Rabiner, C. J., and Klein, D. F. (1969). Imipramine treatment of school phobia. *Comprehensive Psychiatry*, **10**, 387–390.

Rutter, M. (1977). Separation, loss, and family relationships. In (Eds.) Rutter, M., and Hersov, L., *Child psychiatry: Modern approaches.* Blackwell Scientific Publications, Oxford, pp. 47–73.

Saraf, K. R., Klein, D. F., Gittelman-Klein, R., Gootman, N., and Greenhill, P. (1978). EKG effects of imipramine treatment in children. *Journal of American Academy of Child Psychiatry*, **17**, 60–69.

Saraf, K. R., Klein, D. F., Gittelman-Klein, R., and Groff, S. (1974). Imipramine side effects in children. *Psychopharmoclogia*, **37**, 265–274.

Skynner, A. C. R. (1961). Effects of chlordiazepoxide. *Lancet*, **1**, 110. (letter).

Suomi, S. J., Seaman, S. F., Lewis, J. K., DeLizio, R. D., and McKinney, W. T. (1978). Effects of imipramine treatment of separation-induced social disorders in Rhesus monkeys. *Archives of General Psychiatry*, **35**, 321–327.

Winsberg, B. G., Goldstein, S., Yepes, L. E., and Perel, J. M. (1975). Imipramine and electrocardiographic abnormalities in hyperactive children. *American Journal of Psychiatry*, **132**, 542–545.

Zitrin, C. M., Klein, D. F., and Woerner, M. G., (1978). Behavior therapy, supportive psychotherapy, imipramine, and phobias. *Archives of General Psychiatry*, **35**, 307–316.

Out of School
Edited by L. Hersov and I. Berg
© 1980, John Wiley & Sons, Ltd.

Chapter 17

School Attendance and the First Year of Employment

Grace Gray, Alan Smith, and Michael Rutter

INTRODUCTION

In recent times there has been a growing concern over the rather high proportion of children regularly absenting themselves from secondary school without an acceptable reason (Department of Education and Science, 1978). The rate of unauthorized absence increases during the middle years of secondary schooling to reach a peak during the last year of compulsory education. Thus, in inner London (I.L.E.A., 1976), as in other cities (see Chapter 8), the attendance figures tend to be quite high during the first two years of secondary school, and generally comparable to the rates of over 90 per cent which are usual in primary schools (of the 8 or 9 per cent of absentees many will be away as a result of illness rather than for any unlawful reason). However, non-attendance increases gradually to reach a pinnacle of 20 to 25 per cent in the fifth form of secondary schooling which constitutes the last year that pupils are compelled by law to be at school. Many secondary schools have come to regard a very high rate of non-attendance in the fifth year as an intractable problem over which they have little control. On the other hand, in some areas much energy is expended in trying to achieve better rates of attendance and, as exemplified in other chapters of this volume, a wide range of interventions — judicial, behavioural, clinical, and educational — have been devised.

Moreover, there is a widespread view that the problem of non-attendance is getting worse. Whether this is in fact the case, is less certain as national figures on school attendance over the years are not available. The statistics for London show that attendance rates in primary schools have not changed appreciably over the last few decades but that rates of non-attendance in secondary schools have gone up recently — from 9 or 10 per cent in 1966–7 to 14 per cent in 1978. Even more striking, however, is the observation that the proportion of young people remaining at school after 16 years fell by a third in

343

the year after the school leaving age was raised from 15 to 16 years in 1972–73, and ever since then the rate has remained well below that for the preceding decade (see Rutter, 1979). Consequently, it does seem that there may have been a recent increase in both non-attendance during the last years of compulsory schooling and dropout (see Note 1, p. 370) from education when compulsory schooling ends. But does this matter and should it be a cause for concern?

At first sight it would seem obvious that persistent absenteeism from school must be a serious issue. After all, attendance is legally required and children can scarcely be taught if they fail to turn up to lessons. There are a variety of studies which show important associations between truancy and delinquency and between both of these behaviours and an antisocial and deviant life style during the years after leaving school (see Chapters 3 and 4). On the other hand, it has been argued that the problem is basically social rather than educational, a matter not of deviance or disorder, but rather of disaffected youth no longer interested in school (see Chapter 2). In this connection, it may be relevant that absenteeism rates very markedly between schools (see Chapter 5; also Rutter *et al.*, 1979). Perhaps, in part adolescents are failing to attend school because some schools are offering them little which they feel is relevant or useful to them. As Millham *et al.* (1978) put it, '. . . it is the failure of school to measure up to (their) expectations which produces high levels of truancy among vulnerable adolescents in the year before leaving.'

Of course, no one would suppose that all instances of absenteeism arise for the same reasons and it may be that each of these views has some validity for some individuals. However, the question need not be left in that rather unsatisfactory state. Follow-up studies may throw valuable light on the matter by showing what happens to truants *after* they leave school. The studies by Farrington (Chapter 3) and by Robins and Ratcliff (Chapter 4) are very important in that connection. The investigation discussed in this chapter tackles the same problem by examining possible links between absenteeism and employment after leaving school.

In considering the findings, three crucial distinctions need to be borne in mind. Firstly, it should not be assumed that the causes and consequences of absenteeism that occur only in the final year of compulsory schooling are the same as those of absenteeism which first arises at a much earlier age. Persistent truancy is an uncommon phenomenon in primary school whereas it is quite frequent during the fifth year of secondary school. Thus, the overall average absenteeism rate *triples* over this period. *Persistent* unjustified absenteeism increases ever more — there being, for example, a *six*-fold increase between primary school and secondary school in Galloway's study (Chapter 8). It could be that whereas early truancy is often a reflection of serious personality difficulties, truancy just before leaving school is more often a 'normal' response to an unrewarding situation.

Secondly, it is important to differentiate between correlation and causation.

It could be that poor school attendance leads to a poor work record not because there are any ill-effects of truancy as such, but rather because the same psychosocial adversities and same personality attributes that predispose to truancy, also predispose to occupational difficulties in adult life. In other words, if this were the case, truancy and unsatisfactory employment would be linked only because both were consequences of the same set of causal variables. As Tyerman (1974) suggested: 'most persistent truants are . . . maladjusted children who . . . become unsatisfactory employees instead of being unsatisfactory pupils.' Similarly, the typical school dropout has been described as someone with discipline problems, with a family pattern of school failure, and with poor peer relationships (Schrieber, 1967). In these circumstances, truancy may be but one facet of a much wider problem.

Thirdly, even if truancy itself predisposes to employment problems it may be that it does so because absentees from school fail to acquire essential educational credentials rather than because their irregular school attendance has led to bad work habits. If effective prevention or therapeutic intervention is to be possible, it will be necessary to identify the mediating mechanisms which are involved.

The various background characteristics of absentees are described in other chapters and will not be discussed further here. However, before outlining the findings of our own study, it is appropriate to consider briefly, previous investigations of associations between school absenteeism, dropout, and later employment.

Non-attendance at school and subsequent employment

There have been surprisingly few attempts to examine this issue. Relevant data are provided by some of the longitudinal studies which span the adolescent–adult age period. Thus, Cherry (1976) utilized the British National Survey data to study the antecedents of persistent job changing in the early years at work. She found that poor attendance at school was one of three significant predictors of job instability during the 15 to 18 year period (the other two predictors being teacher ratings of behaviour and general intelligence). Moreover, the tendency to frequent changes of job tended to persist over the next eight years (the follow-up being to age 26 years). Poor school attendance and job instability were also significantly associated with personal problems (such as broken marriages, psychiatric disorder, unemployment, and illegitimate births) during the 18 to 26 year age period. It appeared that there was a somewhat persistent pattern of behaviour which included absenteeism at school, frequent job changing, and personal problems in early adult life. However, it was striking that, although this pattern was associated with some job dissatisfaction, it was *not* associated with lower earnings. Indeed, the adults with personal problems who changed jobs frequently actually earned *more* than those who stayed with the same employer throughout. It is clear that different aspects of employment intercorrelate rather poorly and may well have different origins.

Farrington (Chapter 3) similarly found that truancy was associated with an unstable job record. Truancy also tended to be accompanied and followed by antisocial and deviant life styles. A low job status was a further sequel but earnings were not assessed and low status jobs do not necessarily carry a low wage.

Robins and Ratcliff (Chapter 4) examined the consequences of truancy in a very different sample — black school boys of above average ability born in the early 1930s and educated in St. Louis schools. They found that high school truancy was usually preceded by truancy in elementary school and that both were associated with high school dropout and with lower earnings at the time of follow-up (at age 30 to 36 years). The low incomes of the truants were only in part accounted for by high school dropout as the boys who truanted in high school but nevertheless went on to complete grade 12, had lower incomes than other graduates. Similarly, truants who dropped out of higher school had lower incomes than other school dropouts. Interestingly, this was not so to any appreciable extent in the case of boys who truanted only in elementary school but it did apply to those who only began to truant in high school. The next step was to check whether the associations between truancy and low income were a consequence of the fact that many truants also showed a wide range of other antisocial behaviours. The results showed that this was part of the explanation in that the employment outcomes were much better for truants who did not exhibit other forms of deviance. Nevertheless, among the antisocial boys, truants still tended to earn lower incomes. The conclusion, at least for this American sample, is that truancy is associated with lower incomes in adult life and that this association is only partially explained by high school drop out and by associated antisocial behaviour.

This finding seems to run counter to Cherry's findings in the British sample. It may be that truancy has different effects in different cultures but it could be that Cherry was dealing with less serious and persistent truancy. A further possibility is that the lower incomes of truants only become evident in later life. Cherry's sample were up to 10 years younger and many were in jobs (such as lorry driving and construction work) which provide relatively high incomes immediately after starting but which also provide few opportunities for increasing earnings later.

This possibility received some support from studies of high school dropouts in the United States (of course, dropout is not synonymous with truancy and absenteeism, but it is clear that there is substantial overlap between them). Thus, Coombs and Cooley (1968) compared dropouts and controls with respect to their employment at age 19 years. There was no marked difference in either to the stranded offspring, optimally before biological impairment occurs. In this formulation, it is also assumed that the child's distress provokes retrieval and caretaking behaviour in the parent. Therefore, the most efficient evolutionary relationship would be one in which both the young child and the mother would be subject to separation anxiety. This notion is supported by much animal observation, e.g. the distress of mother cats, dogs, monkeys, etc., when their infants are removed or are heard crying, followed by searching and retrieval behaviour on the mother's part. The extension of this model to human development may have heuristic value. For instance, it would suggest that, in adulthood, women should be more vulnerable to separation anxiety than men. There is no objective information concerning sex differences in frequency of this anxiety. Though agoraphobia, postulated by Klein to be an adult pathological variant of separation anxiety, is much more common in women than men.

The ethological model of pathological separation anxiety implies an autonomous, psychopathological process in children with severe separation anxiety. This view is in sharp contrast to that which holds that the child's anxiety is a response to the mother's neurotic needs (Eisenberg, 1958). In the latter model, the therapeutic effect of imipramine would have to be interpreted as protecting the child from the mother's wish for his overattachment. This would be a most unusual drug effect. If it were the case, contrary to our findings, one would expect most children to relapse when medication was withdrawn. Though the drug effect argues for the presence of a disorder intrinsic to the child who refuses to attend school, it does not follow that environmental influences play no role in the various aspects of the disorder, such as its severity, specific form, and maintenance. Pathological separation anxiety may be the outcome of interaction between a biological predisposition in the child and a family setting that facilitates the expression of the predisposition. In keeping with this formulation, pharmacotherapy of the child is only one aspect of a treatment approach aimed at altering both the child and the family's response to the child.

It is clear from our discussion that we do not believe that imipramine is an antianxiety drug. Regardless of one's theoretical convictions regarding the usefulness of distinguishing separation anxiety from other anxiety states, it is important to note that imipramine has been tested only in children who refuse to attend school. Hence, there is no empirical basis for the use fo the drug in other conditions.

REFERENCES

Ainsworth, M. D. S. (1967). *Infancy in Uganda: Infant care and the growth of love.* Johns Hopkins Press, Baltimore.

Berg, I. (1976). School phobia in the children of agoraphobic women. *British Journal of Psychiatry*, **128**, 86–89.

Berg, I., Marks, I., McGuire, R., and Lipsedge, M. (1974). School phobia and agoraphobia. *Psychological Medicine*, **4**, 428–434.

Bowlby, J. (1969). *Attachment and loss, Vol. 1: Attachment*. Hogarth Press, London.

Bowlby, J. (1973). *Attachment and loss, Vol II: Separation anxiety and anger*. Basic Books, New York.

D'Amato, G. (1962). Chlordiazepoxide in management of school phobia. *Disease of the Nervous System*, **23**, 292–295.

Eisenberg, L. (1958). School phobia: A study in the communication of anxiety. *American Journal of Psychiatry*, **114**, 712–718.

Fish, B. (1960). Drug Therapy in child psychiatry: Pharmacological aspects. *Comprehensive Psychiatry*, **1**, 212–227.

Fish, B. (1968). Drug use in psychiatric disorders of children. *American Journal of Psychiatry*, **124**, 31–36.

Frommer, E. A. (1967). Treatment of childhood depression with antidepressant drugs. *British Medical Journal*, **1**, 729–732.

Frommer, E. A. (1968). Depressive illness in childhood. *British Journal of Psychiatry*, *Special Publication No. 2*, 117–136.

Gittelman-Klein, R. (1975). Psychiatric characteristics of the relatives of school phobic children. In Sankar, D. V. S. *Mental Health in Children Vol. 1*. PJD Publications Ltd., Westbury, New York. pp. 325–334.

Gittelman-Klein, R., and Klein, D. F. (1971). Controlled imipramine treatment of school phobia, *Archives of GEneral Psychiatry*, **25**, *204–207*.

Gittelman-Klein, R., and Klein, D. F. (1973). School phobia: Diagnostic considerations in the light of imipramine effects. Journal of Nervous and Mental Diseases, **156**, 199–215.

Hayes, T. A., Panitch, M. L., and Barker, E. 61975). Imipramine dosage in children: A comment on 'imipramine and electrocardiagraphic abnormalities in hyperactive children'. *American Journal of psychiatry*, **132**, 546–547.

Hersov, L. (1977). School refusal. In (Eds.) Rutter, M., and Hersov, L., *Child psychiatry: Modern approaches*. Blackwell Scientific Publications, Oxford, pp. 455–486.

Klein, D. F. (1964). Delineation of two drug responsive anxiety syndromes. *Psychopharmacologia*, **5**, 397–408.

Klein, D. F., and Davis, J. M. (1969). *Diagnosis and drug treatment of psychiatric disorders*. William and Wilkins, Baltimore.

Kraft, I. A. (1962). Treatment of school phobia with chlordiazepoxide. *American Journal of Psychiatry*, **118**, 841–842.

Rabiner, C. J., and Klein, D. F. (1969). Imipramine treatment of school phobia. *Comprehensive Psychiatry*, **10**, 387–390.

Rutter, M. (1977). Separation, loss, and family relationships. In (Eds.) Rutter, M., and Hersov, L., *Child psychiatry: Modern approaches*. Blackwell Scientific Publications, Oxford, pp. 47–73.

Saraf, K. R., Klein, D. F., Gittelman-Klein, R., Gootman, N., and Greenhill, P. (1978). EKG effects of imipramine treatment in children. *Journal of American Academy of Child Psychiatry*, **17**, 60–69.

Saraf, K. R., Klein, D. F., Gittelman-Klein, R., and Groff, S. (1974). Imipramine side effects in children. *Psychopharmoclogia*, **37**, 265–274.

Skynner, A. C. R. (1961). Effects of chlordiazepoxide. *Lancet*, **1**, 110. (letter).

Suomi, S. J., Seaman, S. F., Lewis, J. K., DeLizio, R. D., and McKinney, W. T. (1978). Effects of imipramine treatment of separation-induced social disorders in Rhesus monkeys. *Archives of General Psychiatry*, **35**, 321–327.

Winsberg, B. G., Goldstein, S., Yepes, L. E., and Perel, J. M. (1975). Imipramine and employment or incomes (male dropouts earned somewhat more than their controls and female dropouts somewhat less). But, more than twice as many of the dropouts had married and fewer had gone on to receive further training. Thus, not only had they taken on family responsibilities at an early age but also perhaps they had jobs which offered fewer opportunities for advancement.

Bachman, Green, and Wirtanen (1971) also studied dropouts from American high schools at age 19 years. Their income and job satisfaction at that age were closely comparable to those of individuals who had completed high school (the dropouts earned marginally more), but their unemployment rate was substantially higher (29% vs. 13%) and they tended to hold slightly lower status jobs. However, it should be noted that much of the difference in unemployment was accounted for by the lower social status background and lesser intellectual abilities of the dropouts. In other words, although dropping out of high school somewhat increased the chances of unemployment, the prior characteristics of the dropouts were at least as important as the fact of dropping out itself.

A longer follow-up into adult life is provided by the study of 1000 high school boys in Minnesota by Hathaway, Reynolds, and Monachesi (1969). At about age 28 years, the dropouts were much less likely to be still studying (3% vs. 11%), much less likely to be in a professional (2% vs. 16%) or skilled clerical occupation (17% vs. 24%) and slightly more likely to be unemployed (5% vs. 2%). Also, far fewer dropouts had received further training after leaving high school (29% vs. 59%). The associations between dropouts and later employment still remained even when dropouts were compared with controls of similar intellectual ability. Altogether, the later lives of dropouts tended to be characterized by low social status, downward social mobility, a higher incidence of criminal activity, and more children. The American census data also show higher levels of unemployment, lower social status, and lower levels of earnings, among high school dropouts (Swanstrom, 1967; Bienstock, 1967), although they do not indicate how far the worse occupational outcomes are a consequence of dropout *per se* rather than of the personal characteristics and social background of those individuals who fail to complete high school.

We may conclude that truancy, absenteeism, and school dropout seem to have few effects on employment or incomes in early adult life, but that there is a substantial association with higher unemployment and lower social status when older. However, most of the findings apply to the United States where the educational and occupational situation is not the same as that in Britian. Moreover, it is not entirely clear how far absenteeism from school has effects on employment which are independent of educational qualifications. The present study was designed to examine these issues and in this chapter we report findings which apply to the employment circumstances one year after leaving school for young people who left school at age 16 years.

OUTLINE OF STUDY: SAMPLE AND METHODS

Our findings are based on a longitudinal study of young people who went to school in inner London during the 1960s and 1970s. The study had its origins in an epidemiological survey of all 10-year-olds attending local authority primary schools in one inner London borough (Rutter *et al.*, 1975). The sample was followed through into secondary school and attention became focused on the pupils attending the 12 non-selective schools which took the bulk of the children in the sample (Rutter *et al.*, 1979). Information was obtained on parental occupation and on ethnic origin; and group tests were used to obtain measures on the children's non-verbal intellectual level. Systematic data were collected on the young people's performance on the national examinations taken at age 16 years, and on the date of their school leaving.

The present findings apply to the sample of children who attended these 12 secondary schools. When the age cohort in the school was 100 children or less, all were included; when the number exceeded 100 a sample of 150 was chosen by random allocation. Thus, the basic sample numbered 1025. These young adults were then individually interviewed, using a standardized interview, one year after they could have left school (i.e. at age 17 + years). Systematic information was obtained on family background, on school attendance during the fifth year at secondary school (i.e. the final year of compulsory education), on careers guidance, and on employment after leaving school.

Description of Sample

Out of the total sample of 1025, 181 could not be traced and interviewed, mainly as a result of moving house. Of these 7 had emigrated and 36 refused to be interviewed. This left a group of 844, all of whom were interviewed at the one year follow-up after the end of compulsory schooling. Out of 844, 247 had remained at school. This latter group is being interviewed currently, one year after school-leaving (at ages 18 and 19 years according to whether they stayed one or two years in the sixth form). The present findings are restricted to the 597 children who left school at 16 years to seek employment (although some comparisons are made with those who continued in full-time education).

As shown in Table 1, the great majority of the children came from a working class background and nearly a third had a father who held an unskilled or semiskilled job or who was out of work. Only 15 per cent had a father with a non-manual occupation. Four-fifths had parents who were born in the British Isles (at the time of the study this meant that in almost all cases they were white). Of the children from non-indigenous families, the largest group were born to parents from the West Indies. However, there was also a fairly sizeable minority of children from Cyprus and a few of Asian background.

Table 1. Parental occupation of fifth form school leavers

Parental Occupation	No.	%
Professional & intermediate	49	8.2
Skilled Non-Manual	42	7.0
Skilled Manual	272	45.6
Semiskilled	103	17.3
Unskilled	64	10.7
Unemployed	15	2.5
Father dead or unknown	52	8.7
Total	597-	

Table 2. Ethnic origin of fifth form school leavers

	No.	%
Both parents born in British Isles	486	81.4
One or both parents born in West Indies[a]	61	10.2
One or both parents born in Asia	8	1.3
Other (mainly European)	40	6.7
Not known	2	0.3
Total	597	

[a]Includes one child of African parentage.

Schools, exams, and absenteeism

The 12 schools which the children attended served a large area of inner London extending outwards from the river Thames (see Rutter *et al.*, 1979 for a fuller description). Much of the area had become rather drab and run down and, especially during the 1960s, there was considerable rebuilding by the local authority. The result was a great heterogeneity of buildings and tremendous variation in housing conditions. Over two-fifths of the population lived in local authority flats or houses with subsidized rents; a similar proportion lived in privately rented accommodation; and only a fifth owned their homes. The conditions of the privately rented housing were particularly poor, with over half not possessing or having to share a bath and inside lavatory.

The schools varied in style from rather gloomy three-deckers left over from Victorian times, to modern purpose-built premises. However, in all cases the provision of equipment and other resources was generous. The schools ranged in size from approximately 450 pupils to just under 2000 and included both co-educational schools and single sex schools for either sex. The period when the sample children went through their schooling was one of exceptional difficulty for London teachers and children. Teacher shortages and industrial disputes led to periods of part-time schooling for some children. Education cuts, although less marked than in many areas, also imposed certain limitations.

Many detailed measures of the characteristics of these schools as social institutions are available as a result of an intensive study of them over a three-year period (see Rutter *et al.*, 1979). Questionnaires were completed by over 2700 pupils, interviews were held with over 200 teachers, detailed quantitative observations were made in more than 500 lessons and a variety of other measures were obtained through both school records and observations about the school. It was found that there were marked differences between schools in terms of a range of different pupil outcomes. Moreover, the differences in outcome were systematically related to their characteristics as social institutions. The key variables included items as varied as the degree of academic emphasis, teacher actions in lessons, the availability of incentives and rewards, good conditions for pupils, and the extent to which children were given responsibilities in the school. These variables were combined into an overall 'school process' score which provided a convenient summary measure of school characteristics. This measure will be used to relate to absenteeism and employment; a high score indicates advantageous school conditions and a low score disadvantageous conditions. The 12 schools attended by the children were allocated into four school process groups according to their score in this overall measure.

Two main types of examinations are taken at 16 years — the General Certificate of Education (GCE) leading to 'O' (ordinary) levels and the less academic Certificate of Secondary Education (CSE). The GCE is the accepted examination for children of above average intelligence, in roughly the top 20 per cent of the ability range. In this examination each subject is tested separately and is marked on a 5-point scale from A to E; many careers demand passes of grade C or better. The CSE is a newer type of examination designed to cover a wider range of ability than the GCE — about a further 40 per cent. It, too, is subject-based with grades ranging from 1 to 5, grade 1 being accepted as equivalent to at least a grade C pass in GCE. For most purposes examination success was considered in terms of a three-way subdivision: (a) No examination passes or CSE grades 4 and 5 only; (b) CSE grades 2 or 3, or 'O' level grades D and E but no passes at a higher level; (c) at least one 'O' level pass of grade C or better or a grade 1 CSE pass. In the sample of fifth form leavers as a whole 47.1 per cent fell in the first group and 25.6 per cent fell in the last.

Compulsory education continued until age 16 years. For those whose birthdays fell before February 1, 1960, there was the option of leaving school at Easter (and therefore before taking the GCE and CSE examinations) or of remaining on until the end of the summer term. Of the 250 children who had this option and who left during the fifth year, nearly half (44.4%) took the option of leaving early. However, there is also the opportunity for pupils to stay on into the sixth form either to take the more advanced 'A' level examinations, to resit GCE or CSE, or simply to extend their general education. Out of the total sample of 844, nearly a third (29.3%) stayed on at school.

Our main measure of attendance was based on the pupils' own reports of how often they had stayed away from school during the fifth year without a justifiable reason. For children who left at Easter the number of days absence was prorated to be equivalent to the whole year rate. For most purposes, the scale was subdivided into three subgroupings: (a) 'good' attendance with less than 10 days unjustified absence; (b) 'intermediate' with 10 to 49 days unjustified absence; and (c) 'poor' attendance, with at least 50 days unjustified absence. In the group of fifth form leavers as a whole three-fifths (61.6%) were good attenders and a quarter (25.6%) were poor attenders.

Employment

During the 1970s, unemployment rates in Britain, in common with those in many other European countries, rose sharply (Bulletin of the European Communities, 1977). Thus, the overall rate went up from 3.1 per cent in 1974 to 6.1 per cent in 1976, the year when the young people studied left school. Unemployment among school leavers in Britain was particularly high at that time. This worsening of the job situation applied to London as well as to the rest of the country. Nevertheless, the unemployment rate in the metropolis was substantially lower than that in northern England and in Scotland. On the other hand, there was a considerable problem of mismatch as a result of industries having moved out of London with a resulting reduction in the opportunities for skilled manual work.

We assessed employment in school leavers in several different ways. Thus, we asked about the time spent obtaining their first job. Perhaps surprisingly, in view of the overall work situation, nearly three-quarters (72.0%) obtained a job in 4 weeks or less and only 6.9 per cent spent 13 weeks or more seeking work. We also enquired about the number of jobs held during the first year after school leaving; nearly two-thirds (64.3%) remained in their initial job throughout the whole of the first 12 months; only 8.2 per cent held 3 or more jobs and one in twenty (5.1%) were unemployed at the one year follow-up. The job level was graded according to jobs requiring 'O' levels for entry (a mere 2.2% held jobs of that kind); craft-skilled jobs (all those with training schemes or apprenticeships were included in this category) — held by 22.6 per cent of the sample (in all analyses these first two groups were combined in view of the tiny number of young people in jobs requiring 'O' levels for entry); semi-skilled jobs (32.7%) and unskilled jobs (42.6%) which was much the commonest variety. In addition we asked the young people about various aspects of job satisfaction. Although only 39 per cent said that they had acquired the sort of job they wanted (42% said they had not and 19% were undecided); nearly two-thirds (65.2%) expressed the intention of staying in their present job (23.5% said they would leave and 11.3% were undecided).

Non-interviewed sample

In most studies it has been found that the individuals for whom information is missing tend to be systematically different from those for whom interviews, questionnaires or tests are obtained (Cox *et al.*, 1977). It is not necessarily that bias is created just by refusal to co-operate but also that the people who cannot be traced are often a rather different group. Accordingly, it was important to consider the characteristics of the non-interviewed individuals in the present study, using information which was available from the earlier schools study.

Table 3. Comparison of interviewed and non-interviewed sample

Characteristics	Interviewed ($n = 597$) %	Non-interviewed ($n = 181$) %	χ^2	d.f.	Statistical significance[a] p.
Sex: % girls	42.0	49.0			N.S.
Social class:					
% non-manual	9.2	11.5			N.S.
% unskilled	6.9	8.8			N.S.
Schools:					
% high 'process' score	25.3	18.4			N.S.
% low 'process' score	17.1	18.4			
Ethnic origin:					
% West Indian	10.0	20.8	24.6	3	<0.001
Exams:					
% none/low CSES	48.4	67.0	20.0	2	<0.001
Non-verbal intelligence:					
IQ below 90	27.1	35.7	8.54	2	<0.02
Attendance:					
poor attenders	35.1	51.2	13.9	2	<0.001

[a]In each case the chi-square is based on the complete table rather than the figures for the extreme groups given here.

The findings are summarized in Table 3. The non-interviewed group did not differ in sex, social class, or school characteristics. However, there was a significant tendency for the young people who were not seen to be of lower non-verbal intelligence, to have less good examination results, and to have a worse attendance record. They also included a higher proportion of individuals of West Indian origin.

It might be expected that the intellectual and educational differences would mean that the non-interviewed group were likely to have a worse employment record. This is possible and it may be that the true unemployment rate was higher than that found with the interviewed sample. Nevertheless, this was not the case with the 84 non-interviewed people for whom information was available from the careers service. Their job level and the proportion receiving further education was almost identical with those in the interviewed group.

RESULTS: CHARACTERISTICS ASSOCIATED WITH ATTENDANCE

Before considering the possible employment consequences of poor school attendance, we need to examine the personal, family, and school characteristics associated with absenteeism. Perhaps surprisingly, poor attendance was not significantly associated with either social class or non-verbal intelligence (although there was a slight trend for the less intelligent children to include more poor attenders). However, poor attendance (meaning frequent unjustified absence) was significantly, but only slightly, more frequent among boys (29.2% vs. 20.7%; $p < 0.02$).

Table 4. Attendance and ethnic origin

Attendance	Indigenous %	Asian/European %	West Indian %
Good	59.7	63.3	75.4
Intermediate	13.0	14.3	9.8
Poor	27.4	22.4	14.8
Total $N = 596$	($n = 486$)	($n = 49$)	($n = 61$)

The overall chi-square on the association between attendance and ethnic origin fell short of statistical significance. However, it was evident that there was a pronounced tendency for children of West Indian origin to be better attenders than all other groups; this comparison was statistically significant ($\chi^2 = 5.5$; 1 d.f.; $p < 0.05$).

It is possible that this result could be an artefact of either the higher proportion of West Indian youngsters for whom data were missing or a tendency for them to overestimate their attendance compared with other pupils. Both these potential sources of bias could be avoided by reference to the data on school attendance obtained as part of the prior study of the 12 secondary schools from which our sample was drawn (Rutter et al., 1979). The school data on attendance were gathered from school attendance records and hence were applicable to the *whole* sample and were independent of pupil reporting. The overall agreement between the pupil reports and school reports of attendance was high ($p < 0.0001$) but the latter gave a somewhat lower rate of good attendance (as expected from the fact that the school attendance data did not differentiate between justified and unjustified absence, whereas the pupil reports did). A re-analysis of the association between attendance and ethnic origin on the school attendance record data confirmed that the pupils of West Indian origin were more likely to be good attenders (64% good attenders vs 44% in the remainder of the samples; $\chi^2 = 8.74$, 1 d.f., $p < 0.01$). We may conclude that the finding is valid.

Table 5. Attendance and school characteristics

| | School Process Score | | | |
| | High % | Medium High % | Medium Low % | Low % |
Attendance				
Good	66.9	66.7	60.3	48.4
Intermediate	13.9	12.9	10.7	14.7
Poor	19.2	20.4	28.4	37.3
Total $N = 597$	($n = 151$)	($n = 147$)	($n = 197$)	($n = 102$)

$\chi^2 = 15.48$, 6 d.f., $p < 0.05$

The only other variable with a relatively strong, and statistically significant association with absenteeism was the school attended (see Table 5). The children attending schools with the highest (most advantageous) 'school process' scores had only about a fifth (19.2%) of poor attenders compared with nearly two-fifths (37.3%) in schools with the lowest scores. Evidently, the possible influence of schools will need to be taken into account when examining the occupational outcome for children with poor school attendance.

ATTENDANCE, SCHOOL LEAVING DATE AND EMPLOYMENT

Attendance and staying on into the sixth form

Table 6. Attendance and staying on into sixth form

| | Attendance | | |
	Good %	Intermediate %	Poor %
5th Form leavers	63.1	73.8	96.8
6th Form leavers	36.9	26.2	3.2
Total N	583.0	103.0	158.0

$\chi^2 = 68.78$, 2 d.f., $p < 0.001$

As already noted, the employment data reported in this chapter are restricted to those which apply to young people leaving school at age 16 years. However, it is necessary to pay brief attention to the group of young people who stayed on into the sixth form in case attendance has effects on employment through prior association with the time of school leaving. This is certainly a possibility in that the sixth form pupils had a strikingly better attendance record than those who left in the fifth form (see Table 6). Indeed, out of the total of 158 poor attenders, only 5 (3.2%) continued at school into the sixth form, compared with over a third (36.9%) of the good attenders — a 10-fold difference!

Table 7. Non-verbal ability and staying on into sixth form

	Non-verbal Score		
	Less than 90 %	90–110 %	110 + %
5th Form leavers	81.4	70.9	58.3
6th Form leavers	18.6	29.1	41.7
Total No.	199	470	175

$\chi^2 = 24.05$, 2 d.f., $p < 0.001$

However, before concluding that this constitutes an *effect* of attendance, it is necessary to consider other characteristics of those children who remained at school after 16 years. They did not differ from the fifth form leavers in social class but the sixth form stayers were more likely to be girls (53.8% of girls were stayers compared with 46.2% of boys; $\chi^2 = 9.34$, 1 d.f., $p < 0.002$). Not surprisingly, the sixth form group were also significantly more intelligent (see Table 7) and had significantly better exam results (see Table 8). In addition, there were significant differences between schools in the proportions of their pupils who stayed on into the sixth form; these differences were associated with the characteristics of the schools as social organizations. However, when considered separately in relation to each of these variables, attendance still predicted staying on into the sixth form. That is, even within a group of above average ability or with superior examination results, attendance was still associated with staying on into the sixth form. The independent effect of attendance in relation to continuing on at school after age 16 years was confirmed, so far as numbers allowed, through a log–linear analysis of the table resulting from the cross classification of all six variables. (*Note.* Throughout the study, the contingency tables resulting from the variety of cross-classifications were analysed by the usual chi-square methods and their extensions for two way tables. Higher order tables were analysed by the log–linear model approach as described in Bishop, Fienberg, and Holland (1975). In this method associations between the sets of variates are included as terms in a model for the cell counts. Initially, the appropriate model or models are chosen by the methods suggested by Aitkin (1978) to assess the significance of terms of the same order of association. Then, the final model is derived by including terms that are significant on deletion and excluding terms that are non-significant on inclusion. The fit of any particular model is assessed by the log likelihood chi-square G^2, and terms or sets of terms by the difference in G^2 statistics with adjusted significance levels when necessary. All complex tables were analysed using the E.C.T.A. computer programme.) We may conclude that one of the potential effects of attendance on future employment lies in its association with finishing school at age 16 years. However, whether staying on at school into the sixth form *in fact* improves employment opportunities has still to be determined through the follow-up currently in progress.

Table 8. Exam performance and staying on into sixth form

	Exam performance		
	No passes higher than CSE Grade 4 %	CSE Grade 2/3 or 'O' levels Grade D/E %	'O' level Grade C or CSE Grade 1 %
5th Form leavers	98.3	70.6	50.2
6th Form stayers	1.7	29.4	49.8
Total No.	238	289	317

$\chi^2 = 152.33$, 2 d.f., $p < 0.001$

Attendance and early leaving

Table 9. Attendance and early leaving

	Attendance		
	Good %	Intermediate %	Poor %
Easter leavers	34.4	32.1	73.8
Summer leavers	65.6	67.9	26.2
Total No.	157	28	65

$\chi^2 = 30.90$, 2 d.f., $p < 0.001$

Another facet of the same issue concerns the possible effects of attendance in relation to early leaving in the fifth form before taking exams. This option was available only to the 250 pupils whose birthdays fell before February 1st, so the analysis was confined to that subgroup. Of the poor attenders among the 250, three-quarters (73.8%) left at Easter compared with only a third (34.4%) of the good attenders (see Table 9).

As might be expected the Easter leavers tended to be of significantly lower intelligence ($p = 0.005$). Thus, of those with a non-verbal score of more than 110 on the group test, only 31.8 per cent were Easter leavers compared with 59.7 per cent of those with a score of less than 90. The association between social class and school leaving date fell short of statistical significance ($p = 0.077$) but there was a tendency for the children of non-manual workers to be less likely to leave at Easter. But the association between attendance and leaving date still held even after taking IQ and social class into account. There was no difference between boys and girls in the proportion who left school early.

Table 10. School characteristics and early leaving

	School Process Score			
	High %	Medium High %	Medium Low %	Low %
Easter leavers	26.0	46.2	49.5	52.3
Summer leavers	74.0	53.8	50.5	47.4
Total No.	50	65	91	44

$\chi^2 = 8.98$, 3 d.f., $p = < 0.05$

However, school leaving date was significantly associated with school characteristics. Thus, only a quarter of the children (26.0%) were Easter leavers in the group of schools with the highest 'school process' scores but in those with the lower score over half (52.3%) left early. An analysis of attendance and leaving date after controlling for school characteristics still showed a significant effect. Similarly, 'school process' scores also retained their association with leaving date after controlling for attendance. We may conclude that both school characteristics and attendance are associated with school leaving date. Because poor attenders in the fifth year of secondary school are more likely to leave school at the first possible opportunity, it may be that attendance has an effect on employment through its association with early leaving. To investigate that possibility we need to look at the later employment of these Easter leavers in comparison with that of the individuals who stayed on to the summer to take the national examinations.

Early leaving and employment

As shown in Table 11, the Easter leavers tended to find work somewhat faster than those who left school in the summer. Evidently, the fact that they lacked scholastic qualifications was no handicap in obtaining jobs. Instead, it

Table 11. Time of leaving school and time getting first job

Time getting first job	Summer leavers %	Easter leavers %
4 weeks or less	80.8	67.3
4 to 13 weeks	13.6	25.2
13 weeks or more	5.6	7.6
Total No.	177	330

$\chi^2 = 10,88$, 2 d.f., $p = 0.01$

may be that seeking work at a time when there were fewer school leavers entering the employment market was an advantage. An analysis of the table formed by attendance, sex, school leaving date, and time spent looking for work showed that the association between leaving date and time spent finding work still held after taking the other variables into account. The model chosen to fit the data showed that boys found jobs more quickly than did girls ($G^2 = 10.11$, 2 d.f.; $p = < 0.01$), and that those with poor attendance were most likely to leave at Easter ($G^2 = 43.71$, 2 d.f., $p = < 0.001$).

Table 12. Time of school leaving and job skill level

Job skill level	Easter leavers %	Summer leavers %
Skilled	15.6	32.4
Semi-skilled	30.5	31.4
Unskilled	53.9	36.2
Total No.	154	312

$\chi^2 = 18.51$, 2 d.f., $p < 0.001$

Table 13. Educational qualifications and job skill level

Job Skill Level	Exam Performance		
	No passes higher than CSE Grade 4 %	CSE Grade 2/3 or 'O' level Grade D/E %	'O' Level Grade C or CSE Grade 1 %
Skilled	17.7	28.9	39.1
Semi-skilled	30.0	32.6	31.3
Unskilled	52.2	38.5	29.7
Total No.	203	135	128

$\chi^2 = 23.82$, 4 d.f., $p < 0.001$

On the other hand, although most Easter leavers obtained jobs very quickly, there was a significant tendency for them to obtain less skilled work. Indeed over half of them obtained jobs of an entirely unskilled type. However, as one might expect, the skill level of jobs was fairly strongly related to scholastic qualifications (see Table 13). The relationship between school leaving date and job skill level was therefore re-examined after taking account of both time spent looking for work and examination success. The analysis showed that *both* Easter leaving ($G^2 = 10.24$, 4 d.f., $p < 0.05$) and lack of examination success ($G^2 = 23.22$, 4 d.f., $p < 0.001$) were associated with less skilled work, although the latter variable had a stronger effect. In other words, Easter leavers obtained less skilled jobs in part just because they left school without educational qualifications, but this did not constitute the whole explanation. Even among those without examination successes, Easter leaving was still associated with lower level jobs.

Time spent looking for work was also significantly associated with school-leaving date and examinations as a second order interaction — that is to say those leaving school at Easter without exams spent less time looking for work. Interview data suggested that this may well be largely a consequence of the fact that many Easter leavers had already obtained jobs while still at school and hence had jobs to go to.

One year after leaving school, 27 young people were still unemployed (12 of these had never held a job and 15 had had a job but lost it or left it without another job to go to). Easter leavers were much more likely than summer leavers to be out of work at the one year follow-up (10.5% vs. 2.8%; $\chi^2 = 11.20$, 1 d.f., $p = 0.008$). However, unemployment was also significantly more common among those who left school without any exam successes better than a CSE grade 4 (77.8% unemployed vs. 11.1% among those with at least one 'O' level equivalent); it was more common among those with lower non-verbal ability scores (55.6% unemployed among those with a score of less than 90 compared with 11.1% among those with a score exceeding 110); and it was more common among poor attenders (10.5% in poor attenders, 4.8% in intermediate attenders, and 3.6% in good attenders). Neither the sex of the young person nor his ethnic origin was related to unemployment; similarly, neither social class nor the school attended was associated with unemployment. Thus, unemployment was significantly more frequent among Easter leavers, those of lower intelligence, and those who lacked exam success. As these three variables overlapped greatly and as the total number of unemployed was only 27, it was not possible to determine how far each variable had an independent effect.

Sixty-one of the young people who were interviewed had been dismissed from at least one job during their first year of employment. Dismissal was over twice as common among Easter leavers (18.9%) as among summer leavers (7.7%), the difference being highly significant ($p < 0.001$). However, this could be a result of the fact that Easter leavers tended to be less intelligent and lacked examination successes. This possibility was examined by considering the children who left school without examination successes, and the children who left in the summer as two quite separate samples for the purposes of further analysis (this was required because Easter leavers necessarily had no examination successes because they left before they could sit examinations). Among the 174 children who left school with no examination successes, both IQ ($G^2 = 11.88$, 2 d.f., $p < 0.01$) and leaving date ($G^2 = 7.33$, 1 d.f., $p < 0.01$) were significantly associated with dismissal. Among the 349 children who left school in the summer, lack of examination success was related to dismissal ($G^2 = 15.07$, 1 d.f., $p < 0.001$), but in this group there was no association between IQ and dismissal. In other words, in a rather complex manner, low IQ, lack of examination success, and Easter leaving were all separately associated with dismissal.

In short, we may conclude that the fact of leaving school at Easter rather than at the end of the summer term meant that young people obtained jobs slightly faster, but conversely it was also associated with some adverse effects on employment. Easter leavers had a generally worse employment record in terms of job level, unemployment, and dismissal. In part this was simply because the young people who left school early differed from summer leavers in other relevant characteristics. Much of the importance of early leaving and (hence of the association between poor attendance and early leaving) lay in the fact that it meant that young people were leaving school without educational qualifications. This mattered most, but even among those young people who lacked examination success, the Easter leavers had a somewhat less good employment record.

ATTENDANCE AND EXAMINATION SUCCESS

Table 14. Attendance and examination success among summer leavers

Examination performance	Attendance		
	Good %	Intermediate %	Poor %
No passes higher than CSE Grade 4	17.5	13.8	36.5
CSE Grade 2/3 or 'O' level Grade D/E	40.5	50.0	36.5
'O' level Grade C or CSE Grade 1	42.0	36.2	27.0
Total No.	274	58	63

$\chi^2 = 15.08$, 4 d.f., $p = < 0.01$

That observation makes it necessary for us to look more closely at the associations between attendance and examination success. Not surprisingly, there was a moderate association between examination passes gained and attendance during the fifth year. This was so even after excluding the group who left school at Easter and therefore were not able to sit the examinations, and also the group who stayed on at school into the sixth form. Of the 395 summer leavers, nearly two-fifths (38.7%) gained at least one 'O' level pass or its CSE equivalent; about the same proportions (41.3%) obtained lower level passes and a fifth left school without any examination successes higher than a grade 4 CSE. But whereas 42.0 per cent of the good attenders achieved 'O' level passes, only 27.0 per cent of the poor attenders did so, this difference being significant at the 0.5 per cent level (see Table 14). It should be noted, however, that the main difference applied to the very poor attenders; the good and intermediate attendance groups were fairly similar.

Once more, before concluding that poor attendance might predispose to poor examination results it was necessary to check whether the association might be the consequence of a relationship between attendance and some other variable. General intellectual abilities were obvious factors in that non-verbal IQ was significantly associated with both attendance and examination passes. A multivariate analysis showed that both IQ ($G^2 = 33.06$, 4 d.f., $p < 0.001$) and attendance ($G^2 = 29.85$, 2 d.f., $p < 0.001$) were signficantly associated with examination success. For the purposes of this analysis the intermediate and poor attendance groups were pooled as both were rather small (this was because such a high proportion of poor attenders had left at Easter and hence were excluded from the analysis). However, it appeared that poor attendance had a rather greater association with low examination passes among the less intelligent children than among those of above average ability.

Further analyses were undertaken to determine whether the association between attendance and examination success was explicable in terms of either school characteristics or the children's social background. The results showed that it was not. The child's sex was also not associated with either attendance or examination passes in this subgroup of summer leavers.

We may conclude that part of the associations between poor attendance and poor examination results was a consequence of the fact that the poor attenders included a slightly higher proportion of less intelligent children. However, there was still a significant association between attendance and scholastic achievement even when intelligence, social class, and other background variables had been taken statistically into account. The results so far may be summarized by stating that poor attendance seemed to predispose most strongly to poor examination results by virtue of its association with early school leaving (children passed no exams because they were no longer at school when the exams were taken). However, even within a group who remained at school to sit the national examinations, poor attendance showed some association with scholastic achievement. It is clear that poor attendance is likely to have important consequences for employment simply by virtue of its association with low levels of examination success.

ATTENDANCE, EXAM SUCCESS, AND EMPLOYMENT

The next question is whether attendance has any effect on employment above and beyond its effect on examination success. This issue is most easily considered by dealing with each aspect of employment separately.

Time spent in obtaining first job

We may begin by considering how attendance influenced the entry into the world of work. Did those young people who attended regularly find it easier than poor attenders to gain jobs when they left school? The results showed that they did not. Indeed, this proved to be a rather unimportant variable both in terms of its lack of association with other background variables and its lack of association with other aspects of employment. Only two factors were significantly associated with the time spent finding a job. As already mentioned, Easter leavers obtained jobs more quickly than summer leavers. Also, boys got work more quickly than girls. Thus, over three-quarters of boys (77.3%) found jobs in under 4 weeks and only one in twenty (5.4%) took longer than 13 weeks; the comparable figures for girls were 64.4% and 9.1%. ($G^2 = 10.11$ with 2 d.f. and $p < 0.01$).

Skill level of job

The analysis of the skill level of jobs held one year after leaving school was based on all those in work at 1 year (i.e. excluding the unemployed and those still in full time education). It also excluded those cases where (because the young people were not traced and interviewed until rather late) the job level at one year was not known with sufficient accuracy for the skill level to be determined. Hence, the analysis is based on a sample of 466. Neither social class nor ethnic origin was associated with skill level. Almost exactly the same proportions of boys and girls held unskilled jobs (42% in both cases), but significantly more boys held skilled jobs (31.8% vs. 19.6%), the overall difference in skill level between the sexes being significant at the 1 per cent level. The two major variables associated with job skill level were non-verbal intelligence and examination success. Of those with an IQ below 90 only 14.0 per cent held skilled jobs compared with 38.3 per cent of those with scores above 110. The proportion in unskilled work followed the reverse trend, the figures being 55.3%, 41.0%, and 27.2% respectively. The association between examination passes and job skill level was of comparable magnitude. A multivariate analysis showed that both IQ and examination success were independently associated with job skill level ($G^2 = 16.32$ and 18.35 respectively with d.f. and $p < 0.001$). In other words, although a young person's general level of ability was significantly associated with the skill level of the job he held one year after leaving school, good scholastic achievements significantly improved his chances of obtaining skilled work.

The person's level of attendance in the fifth year of secondary school bore no relationship to the skill level of his job at the one year follow-up. The school characteristics also showed no significant association with job skill level (although there was a non-significant trend, $p = 0.08$, in the expected direction).

Job satisfaction

Perhaps not surprisingly, there was a strong association ($p < 0.0001$) between the skill level of the job held and job satisfaction. Whereas three-fifths (59.8%) of those in skilled jobs said that they were in the kind of job they wanted, only two-fifths (42.3%) of those in semi-skilled jobs said that, and only a quarter of those in unskilled work reported satisfaction. In keeping with these feelings, there was a significant tendency for more of those in skilled jobs (82.8%) to state that they intended to remain in their present job compared with those in semi-skilled (66.2%) or unskilled jobs (53.3%).

There was no association between fifth form attendance and either of these measures of job satisfaction.

The pattern of findings was closely similar in the case of the number of jobs held during the first year of employment. Only 42 young people had had three or more jobs but over half of these (52.4%) were in unskilled work at one year compared with 39.1 per cent of those still holding down their first job after twelve months. Expressed the other way round, this means that 78 per cent of those in skilled jobs had had only one job, compared with 61 per cent of those in semi-skilled or unskilled jobs (the overall association between skill level and number of jobs was significant at the 1 per cent level).

School attendance was unrelated to the number of jobs held in the first year of employment.

Indeed, the only significant predictor of number of jobs held in the first year of employment was IQ (less intelligent youngsters being somewhat more likely to change jobs). As expected, if school leavers got the sort of job they wanted on leaving school they were less likely to change jobs. However, there was only a non-significant trend for the number of jobs held to be related to the reported intention of remaining in the present job.

Dismissal from work

Interestingly, there was no significant association, either, between school attendance and dismissal from jobs. Ethnic origin, sex, school characteristics, and social class also showed no significance associations with job dismissal. However, IQ was significantly associated with dismissal ($p = 0.0282$). Of those with a non-verbal score of less than 90, 17.6 per cent had been dismissed from at least one job, compared with 10.0 per cent of those with a score in the 90 to 110 range and 7.5 per cent of those with a score exceeding 110. Similarly, a lack of examination success was significantly associated with job dismissal. Of those dismissed from jobs, only 8.2 per cent had any 'O' level passes, compared with 25.7 per cent in the group as a whole. As already noted, Easter leaving was also associated with job dismissal among those who left school without examination successes.

Unemployment

Table 15. Attendance and unemployment at one year

| | Attendance | | |
	Good %	Intermediate %	Poor %
Employed	96.4	95.2	89.5
Unemployed	3.6	4.8	10.5
Total No. = 492	306	62	124

$\chi^2 = 8.13, 2$ d.f., $p = <0.05$

As shown in Table 15, poor attendance was signficiantly associated ($p = 0.017$) with unemployment at the one year follow-up. Ten per cent (10.5%) of the poor attenders were without jobs when compared with 3.6 per cent of good attenders. This association applied similarly to the young people who had had jobs but lost them and to those who never obtained work in that first year after school leaving. Unemployment showed no significant association with sex, ethnicity, social class, or school attended. However, unemployment was much more frequent in the young people with lower IQ scores ($p = 0.0015$), without exam success ($p = 0.0001$) and who left school at Easter ($p = 0.0008$). The small number of unemployed did not justify multivariate analyses.

Jobs with further training

Of the 597 young people who left school at 16 years of age, 57 had apprentice type jobs which included further training such as day release or block release to a College of Technology. Non-verbal intelligence, ethnic origin, social class, school characteristics, and fifth year attendance all showed no association with the likelihood of the young person being in a job which involved further training. On the other hand, boys were very much likely than girls to be in such a job (16.4% vs. 1.8%; $p < 0.0001$). This difference is probably due, at least in part, to the fact that traditionally male jobs (such as engineering) tend to be more likely to involve apprenticeship. Easter leavers were also much less likely than summer leavers to be in jobs with further training (3.1% vs. 14.5%; $p <$ 0.001), and as one might expect, young people who had some 'O' level passes were more likely to be in jobs with training than those with only lower level passes or without exam successes (17.2%, 13.1%, and 5.5% respectively; $p =$ 0.0008). A multivariate analysis, taking all the significant variables into account, showed that both sex and examination success had independent significant associations with further training, but that the effect of Easter leaving disappeared once exam success had been taken statistically into account. In short, the young people who do relatively well in the national school examinations at age 16 years are the ones most likely to continue their education in the form of jobs with further training. Absenteeism in the fifth year is not of any direct importance in this connection, but it does have indirect effects insofar as it contributes to early leaving from school and to less good exam results.

The young people in jobs with further training were much more likely to report having got the job they wanted (68% compared with 36% of those in other jobs); were more likely to be in the same job that they obtained on leaving school (96% vs. 64%); and were more likely to say that they intended remaining in that job (86% vs. 62%).

College education

Out of the total group of fifth form leavers, 43 went on to colleges of further education to continue with either academic or vocational subjects. These young people did not differ from those in work (or seeking work) with respect to intelligence, social class, or school attended. On the other hand, there was a sex difference with 10.8 per cent of the girls going on to college compared with 4.6 per cent of the boys ($p = 0.0069$). Interestingly too, there was a strong and significant tendency for more children from immigrant families to continue in further education (20.7% vs. 4.1%; $p < 0.001$).

As with jobs involving further training, further education was significantly less likely in Easter leavers than summer leavers, (2.0% vs. 9.9%; $p = 0.0008$); and significantly more likely in those with at least one 'O' level grade C pass than in those with no exam success or only lower level passes (13.8% vs. 2.2%; $p < 0.0001$).

Attendance was also significantly associated ($p = < 0.0134$) with continuing in full time education. Thus, 9.2 per cent of good attenders went on to college, compared with 7.9 per cent of intermediate attenders and 2.0 per cent of poor attenders. However, this association was almost entirely mediated through the prior association between attendance and examination success. Once examination success was taken into account, the link between attendance and further education ceased to be statistically significant.

CONCLUSIONS

The long-term employment consequences of a higher rate of absenteeism in the final year of compulsory schooling have yet to be determined. However, it is clear that there are some important short-term sequelae. Firstly, absentees are much less likely to remain on the school into the sixth form. This is scarcely surprising in that the young people have already shown their disenchantment with schooling through their high rate of unjustified absence in the fifth form. Nevertheless, the effect of their dropping out of school at age 16 years is that they are much less likely to go on to acquire further examination successes and so progress to higher education. Of course, they could still do that by leaving school to go on to colleges of further education but in fact very few did so, and the proportion was substantially less than among good attenders. It could be that some of these absentees may regain an interest in education when older, and re-entry would still be possible at a later stage. However, at least in the short-term it seems that absenteeism in the fifth year is usually associated with a cessation of education in the formal sense.

Secondly, not only are absentees less likely to stay on at school into the sixth form, but also they are more likely to leave school at the first possible opportunity before taking national examinations. Once again the main consequence is that the absentees leave school without formal educational qualifications. Several questions follow from this finding. Thus, one may ask whether the absentees stood any chance of passing examinations; perhaps the non-attendance was simply a reflection of the children's recognition that they lacked the necessary cognitive skills to cope with academic work. This seems most implausible in that the absentees were only slightly (and non-significantly) less intelligent than the regular attenders. It may be that earlier absenteeism (or other factors) had meant that the young people were ill-prepared for national examinations but the results do not support the notion that they lacked the necessary intellectual abilities. Or, one may ask whether the correlation represents causation. Did absenteeism *cause* dropout from school before the examinations and did dropout *cause* a lack of educational qualifications? The latter question is easier to answer in that, in a sense, dropout must have been causal. The young people failed to pass examinations, just because they were not present in school to sit the examinations. Moreover, the evidence on the intellectual qualities of the absentees, noted above, suggests that if they had applied themselves and if they had sat the examinations, it is likely that at least some of the absentees would have achieved some passes.

The first question whether absenteeism 'caused' dropout is less susceptible to an unambiguous answer, but is also less meaningful. The findings certainly showed that the association between absenteeism and dropout was not explicable in terms of the background characteristics such as IQ, social class, and ethnicity on which we had information. On the other hand it does not seem sensible to suppose that absenteeism 'caused' dropout in any real sense. After all, both absenteeism and dropout are forms of non-attendance at school. Rather, we may suppose that the factors which led to absenteeism also predisposed to dropout. In addition, possibly, the 'habit' of not going to school in the fifth form may well have made it more likely that the adolescent would decide to legalize his non-attendance by leaving school at the first available opportunity.

A further issue is whether Easter leaving affects employment opportunities. Of course, in this connection, we only have information on what happens during the first year after leaving school and it may be that things change later. However, so far as that first year is concerned, it seems that Easter leaving was associated with some adverse effects on employment (although it is also shortened the period needed to obtain the first job). In part, Easter leaving seemed important in its own right but in greater part it was important because it led to a lack of educational qualifications which in turn had work consequences. The young people who lacked examination successes were most likely to be in less skilled work, had an increased risk of unemployment at one year, and had a markedly reduced chance of being in a job which involved further training. In the long-term, all of these may add up to jobs with little possibility of advancement. But, a follow-up in later adulthood is needed to determine how far this is in fact the case.

Once again it is necessary to ask whether the lack of educational qualifications was causal. Perhaps, it was just that less able youngsters got less skilled work and that the achievement or non-achievement of exam successes was of no direct importance (i.e. low IQ led to *both* less skilled work and a lower level of scholastic attainment). The findings suggested that this was indeed part of the explanation, but only part. For any given level of intelligence, the possession of educational qualifications did make a difference in increasing the likelihood of obtaining skilled work involving further training.

The third major finding on the short-term work sequelae of absenteeism was that, even within the group of young people who stayed throughout the summer term of the fifth year and therefore were able to sit exams, poor attenders were likely to achieve a lower level of scholastic attainment. Because this association was maintained even when IQ, social class, and other background variables had been taken statistically into account, we may infer that it is likely that in part the association represents a causal effect. That is, absentees probably did less well in national examinations partly because they were often away from school and so missed much of the relevant teaching. It is never possible to be certain of causal attributions from correlational data, but it seems very reasonable to suppose that this was an important element in what occurred. This inference is strengthened, perhaps, by the observation that absenteeism was most strongly associated with low examination success among the less able children who may find it more difficult to learn independently from books and hence may be more reliant on direct teaching in the classroom. As already indicated, the lack of educational qualifications in turn has important implications for employment.

The fourth area of results concerns the possibility that absenteeism predisposes to work failure for reasons other than lack of educational qualifications. Thus, it has been suggested that truancy represents a form a maladjustment which is likely to lead to work difficulties in much the same way that it leads to absenteeism (Tyerman, 1974). We found little support for this view. In particular, the results showed no associations between fifth year absenteeism and job skill level, job satisfaction, number of jobs, dismissal from jobs, or further training, once examination achievements has been taken into account. In other words, absenteeism had important consequences for first year employment just because of its connection with low scholastic achievement but (with the possible exception of unemployment) we could detect no influences which operated through other mechanisms.

This finding is important in terms of its demonstration that many young people with very poor attendance records in their last year at secondary school nevertheless not only quickly found work but successfully held that job for at least a year. Absenteeism in the fifth year need not necessarily lead on to work failure. However, before it is assumed that truancy therefore does not matter, three serious caveats must be noted; (a) absenteeism *did* have adverse consequences through its effect on scholastic achievement; (b) the findings apply only to the first year of employment and the later job record may be different; and (c) the results concern absenteeism as evident only in the *final* year of compulsory schooling. Of course, some of these fifth year absentees will also have truanted throughout their schooling, but many will not have done so. All studies have shown that there is a massive increase in absenteeism during the last few years of secondary school and it is very likely that the outlook for these final year truants may be substantially better than that for young people whose truancy has been a persistent feature throughout their schooling. Certainly this is the implication of the findings of Farrington, described in Chapter 3, and of Robins and Ratcliff, described in Chapter 4.

A further area of interest in the study was the extent to which school influences extended into the field of employment. Earlier research (Rutter *et al.*, 1979) had shown important school effects on children's behaviour and attainments while at school. Did experiences at school also influence young people's work performance during the first year after leaving school? The answer to that question has implications for our concepts of development and of how experiences influence development. The findings showed that there *were* school effects on employment in so far as schooling influenced attendance, school dropout, examination success, and continuation of schooling into the sixth year. But there were no consistent school effects on employment which did not operate through these mechanisms. The findings are consistent with a view of development which supposes that environmental experiences may exert a very important influence, but also that very few experiences have long-term effects which are independent of intervening circumstances (Rutter, 1975, 1979). In other words, schooling does have effects on employment because its immediate results set in motion a train of events which has persistent sequelae. Thus, school influences on children's attendance, behaviour and attainments may have long-term consequences, *not* because they permanently change children's mode of functioning, but rather because the immediate effects (in terms of school dropout or educational qualifications) either open up or close down further opportunities.

The final conclusion concerns the assessment of employment. It is clear, both from our own study and from other work (e.g. Cherry, 1976), that the different indices of work do not necessarily intercorrelate very highly. There was a tendency for job skill level to be associated with measures of work satisfaction, of frequency of job changing and of unemployment, but most of the associations were only of modest strength and to some extent the different aspects of employment had different predictors. We may add that a longer-term follow-up study is needed to determine the extent to which these work indices in the first year of employment are predictive of later work performance and attainments.

ACKNOWLEDGEMENTS

This study was financed by a grant from the Department of Education and Science and the paper was written while M.R. was a Fellow at the Center for Advanced Study in the Behavioral Sciences, supported by grants from the Foundation for Child Development, the Grant Foundation, the Spencer Foundation and the National Science Foundation (BNS 782 4671).

REFERENCES

Aitken, M. (1978). 'The analysis of unbalanced cross-classifications. *J. Royal Statistical Society Series A.*', **141**, 195–211.

Bachman, J. B., Green, S., and Wirtanen, I. D. (1971). *Youth in Transition Vol. III. Dropping Out — Problem or Symptom.* Ann Arbor, Institute for Social Research, Michigan.

Bienstock, H. (1967). 'Realities of the job market for the high school dropout'. In Schreiber, D. (Ed.), *Profile of the School Dropout.* Random House, New York, pp. 101–124.

Bishop, Y. M., Fienberg, S. E., and Holland, P. W. (1975). *Discrete Multivariate Analysis: Theory and Practice.* M.I.T. Press.

Cherry, N. (1976). 'Persistent job changing — Is it a problem?', *J. Occup. Psychol.*, **49**, 203–221.

Coombs, J., and Cooley, W. N. (1968). 'Dropouts: In high school and after school', *Amer. Educ. J.*, **5**, 343–363.

Cox, A., Rutter, M., Yule, B., and Quinton, D. (1977). 'Bias resulting from missing information: some epidemiological findings', *Brit. J. Prev. Soc. Med.*, **31**, 131–136.

Department of Education and Science (1978). *Truancy and Behavioural Problems in Some Urban Schools.* HMSO, London.

Hathaway, S. R., Reynolds, P. C., and Monachesi, E. D. (1969). 'Followup of the later careers and lives of 1,000 boys who dropped out of high school', *J. Cons. Clin. Psychol.*, **33**, 370–380.

Inner London Education Authority (1976). Attendance at Secondary Schools on ILEA on 23 April 1975 R. S., ILEA, London, 656–676.

Millham, S., Bullock, R., and Hasie, K. 61978). 'Juvenile unemployment: A concept due for recycling?', *J. Adolesc.*, **1**, 11–24.

Rutter, M. (1975). *Helping Troubled Children.* Penguin, Harmondsworth, Middlesex.

Rutter, M. (1979). *Changing Youth in a Changing Society: Patterns of Adolescent Development and Disorder.* Nuffield Provincial Hospitals Trust, London.

Rutter, M., Yule, B., Quinton, D., Rowlands, O., Yule, W., and Berger, M. (1975). 'Attainment and adjustment in two geographical areas', *Brit. J. Psychiat.*, **126**, 520–533.

Rutter, M., Maughan, B., Mortimore, P., Ouston, J., and Smith, A. (1979). *Fifteen Thousand Hours: Secondary Schools and Their Effects on Children.* Open Books, London.

Schrieber, D. (Ed.) (1967). *Profile of the School Dropout.* Random House, New York.

Swanstrom, T. E. (1967). 'Out-of-school youth'. In Schrieber, D., *op cit.*, pp. 85–100.

Tyerman, M. 61974). Who are the truants? In Turner, B. (Ed.), *Truancy.* Ward Lock Educational. pp. 9–19.

Note 1

When referring to schools in the United Kingdom dropout means leaving school at the earliest legal time; when referring to the United States it means leaving school before grade 12.

Index